INTERNATIONAL THEOLOGICAL COMMISSION

TEXTS AND DOCUMENTS, 1969–1985

INTERNATIONAL THEOLOGICAL COMMISSION

TEXTS AND DOCUMENTS
1969–1985

With a Foreword by Joseph Cardinal Ratzinger

Edited by Reverend Michael Sharkey

IGNATIUS PRESS   SAN FRANCISCO

Cover by Riz Boncan Marsella

© 1989 Ignatius Press, San Francisco
All rights reserved
ISBN 0-89870-227-5
Library of Congress catalogue number 88-83749
Printed in the United States of America

CONTENTS

FOREWORD

The idea of founding an international theological commission was suggested in various quarters at the first of the postconciliar Synods of Bishops, which met in 1967. Close cooperation between pastors and theologians had been one of the characteristic marks of the Second Vatican Council. The desire expressed at the Synod was to give that cooperation an institutional form, and thus some continuing existence even when the great moment of the Council itself had passed. Also uppermost in the minds of the bishops who proposed the commission was the thought that a rapprochement of scholarly reflection and pastoral responsibility was not the least urgent need of a period when intellectual problems were becoming ever more complex, and scholarship was leaving its impress on the lives of men in modern society, whether at a sophisticated or a simple level. Pope Paul VI at once took up the idea, so that as early as autumn 1969 the Commission's members were getting together for the first time. It consisted of thirty theologians, selected on the basis of advice from episcopal conferences in different parts of the world. In this way, the Commission would not just represent different theological disciplines, diverse language groups with their attendant cultural specificities and varying approaches to theological method. In addition, this procedure would also entail collaboration between the universal primate and the world episcopate as well as a *commercium* between pastors and teachers. For, although admittedly an individual theologian could only represent his own scholarly competence, yet he would be aware that he brought with him the confidence of his own bishop and that his labors were serving the bonds that should hold between bishops and theologians. The term of appointment was five years, after which time the Commission would be reconstituted by the same process. Thus it was hoped that a balance could be struck between continuity and renewal. The Commission is not an organ of the Curia but an autonomous body. However, it is linked with the Church's organizational leadership in that the Prefect of the Congregation for the Doctrine of the Faith is its president.

Once a year, generally in autumn, the thirty professorial members assemble for a week-long session, prepared for during the year by correspondence or more limited workshops of small groups. By and large, the Commission chooses its own themes, but if the higher levels of the Church's leadership wish to propose a topic for discussion, the Commission takes this into account as it plans its program. In this way, it has made a notable contribution to the various Synods of Bishops, as well as to such curial organisms as the Commission for Justice and Peace or the Pontifical Council for Culture. Out of some fifteen years of this common work an impressive number of documents has emerged, but until now these have only been accessible in widely scattered sources and so have lacked that appreciation of their cumulative value that they deserve. In these circumstances, it is hardly surprising that one constantly hears the criticism that the Commission is not active enough and has nothing to offer the wider life of the Church. However, anybody who has expectations that the Commission might represent a kind of permanent "his Majesty's opposition" to the Church's Magisterium, offering a running commentary of speculative objections against Rome for the benefit of the multitude, is going to be disappointed by a revelation of the serenity and objectivity of the Commission's labors. On the other hand, anybody who is looking for world-shaking scholarly discoveries has misunderstood the whole point and nature of a commission. Thirty very different voices have to be brought to speak in harmony: the scholarly pursuits of individuals are not the object of the exercise. The special contribution of the Commission is to gain a hearing for the common voice of theology amid all the diversities that exist. For notwithstanding the legitimate pluralism of theological cultures in the Church, the unity of theology must remain and empower theologians to offer some common account of their subject. In these pages, therefore, one will not find the exciting theses of innovative individuals. If there is excitement here, it lies in the discovery that even in our contemporary situation it is possible to say something together despite all our differences and so to take part together in a further exploration of the one Faith of the Church. All the texts that follow are the fruit of a long and often difficult dialogue. In that dialogue not only have various disciplines, methods, and ways of thought found a common path. Over and above that, the wider dialogue of theologians with the bishops, as well as between bishops and the Petrine office in the Church, has found a voice. It is precisely for this reason that the Theological Commission represents an authentic continuation of the great experience of the Council and a clarification of its true bearing.

On this account I wish to express my heartfelt thanks to the editor who has assembled the published texts of the Theological Commission from the last fifteen years and laid them before the English-speaking public. He has rendered accessible a portion of postconciliar theological history whose significance is as yet far from fully evaluated. I hope that this book will find a wide readership and so serve the creative development of theology in the original spirit of the Second Vatican Council.

Rome, October 16, 1985   *Joseph Cardinal Ratzinger*

PRELIMINARY NOTE

The present volume gathers all the documents published by the International Theological Commission during the first fifteen years of its existence (1969–1985).

As one will note, the breadth of thought of these documents varies greatly. One may say the same for their literary genre, which extends from relatively brief theses or propositions, some of which include introductions or comments, to more elaborate reports or declarations.

As regards their juridical statute, these documents obtain from the Commission, after two initial votes which permit the introduction of modifications, an approval that may assume two forms (cf. Definitive Statutes, article 12):

1. The formal approval ("in specific form"), conceded by absolute majority on the part of the members of the Commission present at the plenary session, concerns the entire text, including the ideas, the wording, the presentation.
2. The general approval ("in generic form") implies only that the Commission accepts the principal ideas of the text, the rest remains the responsibility of its author or authors. In the present volume the type of approval that this document has obtained is clearly indicated. In the majority of cases, nevertheless, the approval is "in specific form".

Gathered in an appendix are some elements of information on the Commission, that is, both provisory and definitive statutes, and a list of its members. There are also indicies to the present documents.

For the history of the institution and the works of the Commission, the interested reader will find important elements in the following publications of its General Secretary, Monsignor Philippe Delhaye: Preface to the volume of M. Gilbert, J. L'Hour, and J. Scharbert, *Morale et Ancien Testament* (Louvain-la-Neuve, Collection "Lex Spiritus Vitae" n. 1, 1976), 1–7; "Memoirs of the First Five Years of the International Theological Commission", in *L'Osservatore Romano* (July 1, 1976), p. 1; "Paul VI et la Commission Théologique Internationale", in *Revue Théologique de Louvain* 9 (1978): 417–23; Presentation of the volume of the Commission: *Problèmes théologiques du mariage chrétien* (Louvain-la-Neuve, Collection "Lex Spiritus Vitae" no. 4, 1979), 13–21; "L'après Vatican II et la constitution de la Commission Théologique Internationale", in *Revue Théologique de Louvain* 16 (1985): 288–315. See also

G. Caprille, *Il Sinodo dei Vescovi* (1967), Edition "La Civiltà Cattolica" (Rome, 1968), Analytical Index under II/2/B, 5, p. 665. A brief account of the annual activities of the Commission can be found in the volumes of the collection *L'Attività* Acta Apostolicae Sedis (Rome, Libreria Editrice Vaticana).

1

REFLECTIONS ON OBJECTIVES AND METHODS

FINAL COMMUNIQUE ON THE FIRST SESSION OF THE
INTERNATIONAL THEOLOGICAL COMMISSION

The first session of the International Theological Commission was held at
Rome, at the *Domus Mariae,* October 6 to 8, 1969, with His Eminence
Cardinal Seper presiding. Of the Commission's thirty members, twenty-nine
were present. The object of this first session was to permit the members to
meet each other and make initial contacts, to form a more exact concept of the
nature and objectives of the Commission, to express their opinions on the
most urgent questions to be dealt with, to specify working procedures, and to
form subcommissions for study of these questions.

The statutes of the Commission, created this year by Pope Paul VI, at the
request of the Synod of Bishops in 1967, specify that it is at the service of the
Holy See, and especially of the Congregation for the Doctrine of the Faith,
with regard to doctrinal questions of great importance. The Commission is
not a part of the foresaid Congregation but rather is governed by its own
particular norms. Nonetheless, its president is the Cardinal Prefect of the
Congregation. The results of its work are transmitted directly to the Holy
Father before being communicated to the Congregation.

The Commission does not deal with specific doctrinal problems, such as
the examination of a book or an article, but studies the most fundamental
doctrinal problems that are crucial in the life of the Church today.

The psychological climate at the session was excellent. In the three days
during which they were together, the theologians had the opportunity of
exchanging ideas with the greatest liberty, and they did so indeed. The same
climate of liberty and fraternal confidence prevailed during the study session.

Some time before the session the theologians had received a volume
containing a report by Father Rahner on the principal questions that, in his
opinion, should be dealt with by the Commission, a report by Monsignor
Philips on the spirit and the method of organization of the work, and the
opinion of each of the members on problems to be dealt with and methods of
work to be employed.

In the study sessions the discussion centered especially on the problem of

1

theological pluralism and on the Magisterium and the practical exercise of its power in the present circumstances.

Exhaustive discussions were not planned. It was, rather, a question of becoming aware of the scope of the problems. In raising these questions, the theologians sought better to understand the present crisis in the Church. Of course, all admitted that there exists a pluralism that is legitimate and necessary, even in regard to doctrine.

The divergence of their opinions became evident on the subject of the extension of this legitimate pluralism. It seemed that certain points should be discussed more deeply in order to safeguard the unity of the Faith and of the Church.

The Commission sought to establish the manner in which men today really receive the interventions of the Magisterium. It was observed that the present situation renders the task of the Magisterium more difficult, but that it also requires of theologians a keener sense of their responsibility.

They saw the importance of a sound notion of the nature and the value of religious knowledge—as well as of all knowledge—and its authenticity, as much for the question of pluralism as for that of the Magisterium.

It is evident that these problems need to be seriously studied and that this should be done with the most absolute fidelity to the Church and complete understanding of the needs of our era.

The methodological norms to be applied in the future work of the Commission were worked out chiefly from the experience of the Second Vatican Council, and they are sufficiently flexible to permit any modifications that may be necessary as the work proceeds.

At present, from among the subjects that the Commission offered to study, the four following questions have been chosen:

1. the unity of the Faith
2. the priesthood
3. the theology of hope: the Christian Faith and the future of humanity
4. the criteria for Christian moral conscience

Four subcommissions were formed to study these themes. It is up to each group to decide precisely on its particular theme.

Other themes will be dealt with later.

2

THE PRIESTLY MINISTRY

This study on the priestly ministry was prepared by a subcommission of the International Theological Commission. The subcommission, named for this purpose, was composed of Fr. Hans Urs von Balthasar, Msgr. Carlo Colombo, Fr. Gonzalez De Cardedal, Fr. M.-J. Le Guillou (President), Fr. Lescrauwaet (Secretary), and Msgr. J. Medina-Estevez.

After a general discussion during the plenary session of the International Theological Commission (October 5–7, 1970), this study was approved by the Commission as a "working document", i.e., "in forma generica", to be transmitted to the Synod of Bishops. This general approval obviously does not engage the authority of the Commission members for all the affirmations or all the details of the report.

INTRODUCTION

Among the many problems raised by the crisis of the priesthood that is shaking the Church, we have decided to consider the following points, which, leaving aside the sociological analysis, are essentially of a *theological* nature:

   I. the condition of the priest in the world of today
  II. the theological roots of the crisis of priestly identity
 III. the Church, the priestly people of God
 IV. the Christological foundation of the priestly ministry
  V. the apostolate and the priestly ministry
 VI. the priestly ministry as eschatological service
 VII. the insertion of the priestly ministry in the world of today
VIII. the spirituality of the priest

We conclude with a few rapid remarks toward a solution of the crisis.

Today many priests experience a grave feeling of unrest and insecurity. With some, the unrest is so great that it leads to a systematic critique not only

Translated by James Dupuis, S.J.

of the sociological status of the priest in the world of today but also of the very concept of the priestly ministry.

This crisis of *identity in the priest* is the result of a number of causes, of which it is difficult to get a coherent view. Most often attention is given only to fragmentary considerations mostly concerned with the *sociological approach to the problem*. The interest goes primarily to "changes in mentality": a new style of relationship between priests and laity; a new attitude of Christians more open toward the values of the profane world, etc. At a more doctrinal level, it has been pointed out that a "shift of emphasis" has taken place regarding the common priesthood and the ministerial priesthood, a shift that is supposed to have taken place at the Second Vatican Council. This change is understood to have perturbed the idea that the Catholic priests have had of themselves for many centuries. It is frequently added that this traditional idea, so characterized by the politico-ecclesiological circumstances that favored its development, is not well founded in the New Testament doctrine, a situation that calls for a thorough theological reappraisal of the theological doctrine of the ministries going far beyond the timid reevaluations inscribed in the Conciliar Documents.

There is surely some truth in these affirmations, and that is why we begin this report with a rapid sociological survey; but we hold that the study of the *theological reasons properly so-called* of the crisis of priestly identity is much more decisive and much more instructive. It will form the object of Section II.

I. THE CONDITION OF THE PRIEST IN THE WORLD OF TODAY

The world is in a process of deep mutation, and this situation is not without affecting the Church deeply.

Vatican II has already noted that in our times the role of the priest has become "more and more difficult",[1] on account of the profound and rapid changes that affect his human and pastoral situation.[2] But after the Council, this situation has been considerably aggravated. Thus one can justly speak of a "crisis of the priesthood". This crisis is widespread today in all parts of the world, even if the reasons for it are different and its intensity and range vary greatly.

---

[1] *PO*, 1.

[2] *PO*, 22. For the redaction and the evolution of this text, cf. *Schema Decreti de ministerio et vita presbyterorum*, textus emendatus et relationes (Rome, November 1965), 22 A, and *Schema Decreti de presbyterorum ministerio et vita*, textus recognitus et modi a patribus conciliaribus propositi (Rome, December 1965), modus 5.

A. *Symptoms of the Present Crisis*

In the course of the last five years, the chief symptoms of the crisis are the following:

1. Numerous Defections from the Priestly Ministry

In a few years the number of priests discontinuing their priestly ministry has increased so much that bishops, priests, and public opinion have been alerted. The numbers of defections that are being mentioned seem exaggerated, but in reality it is difficult to evaluate them. One thing is certain: the central service of ecclesiastical statistics at the Vatican has noted a rapid increase in the requests for dispensation from the exercise of the priestly ministry. From 640 in 1964, they have jumped to 2,263 in 1968. The number of priests who have abandoned the ministry without a request for dispensation has not been published except in very few dioceses, but it is surely not negligible.[3]

The literature concerning the crisis of the priesthood has attempted to classify in categories the different types of priests who abandoned the ministry.

[3] *Central Service of Ecclesiastical Statistics at the Vatican* (published by *Central d'information de presse*, Brussels, March 9, 1970).

DIOCESAN PRIESTS

Year	Requests for dispensation	Dispensation granted
1962–63	91	—
1964	371	200
1965	579	374
1966	730	649
1967	771	709
1968	1026	1017

RELIGIOUS PRIESTS

Year	Requests for dispensation	Dispensation granted
1962–63	76	—
1964	269	115
1965	549	247
1966	688	605
1967	988	669
1968	1237	1067

United States: The National Association for Pastoral Renewal has sought information in 110 dioceses (out of 152) and 25 religious congregations (out of 160): Losses: 1966: 228 priests; 1967: 480 priests; 1968 (first eight months): 463 priests.

Italy (*Confidential Note 6*, Brussels, *Pro Mundi Vita*, March 1969): Losses: diocesan priests, 1964–68: about 800; religious priests, 1964–68: at least 600.

England (*The Times*, August 17, 1968): Losses in 1967: more than 100 priests.

The first group consists of those who have never had a vocation or who were never suited to the priesthood; their ordination was simply a mistake. Such cases have always existed, but now these men can leave the ministry more easily than before.

The second group consists of priests unable to bear the internal tensions of the Church. They find themselves torn between structures that they consider outdated and their desire to commit themselves to the world, to insert themselves in the process of its development, to participate in its style of life, and to found a family.

The third group is made up of priests who are discouraged, who feel they have become strangers to the modern world. Their anxiety to find ways of communicating with this world and words to come in contact with it, the apparent sterility of the work they have been doing so far, the hardships of a solitary life combined with material difficulties, including perhaps actual want due to lack of *remuneration,* have led them to discouragement.

The fourth group consists of priests who have not been able to resist the difficulties arising from their concept of life and the doubts that have assailed them. Some among them have lost the Faith, at least in an established Church; others, desirous to be sincere, have solved for themselves, by the abandonment of the ministry, the incompatibility that they think exists between their functions and their personal opinions.

The question of compulsory celibacy has made the problems proper to each of these groups more acute.

The defections have touched all ages; they are, however, more frequent among young priests and among those between thirty-five and forty-five years of age. They affect priests in all different functions but seem mostly to affect those engaged in scientific work.[4]

2. Fall in the Number of Vocations

Statistics pertaining to seminarians who are preparing for the priesthood are more exact. Their number is decreasing almost everywhere, and this is a source of general concern. The ecclesiastical statistics of the Vatican indicate that between 1966 and 1968 the number of seminarians has fallen from 166,000 to 147,000. In the major seminaries of France, Germany, Spain,

---

Holland (Pastoral Institute of the Dutch Ecclesiastical Province, Rotterdam): Losses: 1965: 30 priests, diocesan and religious; 1966: 60 priests, diocesan and religious; 1967: 145 priests, diocesan and religious; 1968: 198 priests, diocesan and religious.

[4] For other classifications, cf. S. Burgalassi, *C'è un domani per il prete?* (Rome: Mondadori, 1968), W. Quant, *The Priests Who Go* (London, 1969).

Austria, Belgium, Canada, and Brazil, the fall is about 40 percent. In England the percentage seems to be less. In Holland, on the other hand, it seems to be more. The enrollment in the major seminaries of Ireland has reportedly clearly diminished. The graph of those to be ordained falls much in the same proportions as that of those in the major seminaries.[5]

Publications dealing with the fall of vocations attribute it to the following causes:

a. Confrontation of youth with a world filled with doubt, often critical of the Christian Faith. The minds of these youth are penetrated with ideas of secularization and the claims of positive sciences and technology.
b. Disregard of youth for the past as also for the present order of society. This opposition to the structures of a world that offers to them no prospect for the future is extended to the Church. In their eyes, the Church too in many respects forms part of present-day society, and its structures appear to them a hindrance to their development.
c. Polarization of the aspirations of young people by the world problems of today: peace, just distribution of goods, racial equality, etc. The priesthood does not appear to make a contribution toward the solution of these basic problems.
d. The unattractiveness for youth of the image of the priest, who appears insufficiently adapted to modern life, lacking in freedom, without prospect for the future. The obligation of priestly celibacy, moreover, appears to them as contrary to the rights of men and to the respect that is due to the concrete reality of this world.[6]

3. Conflicts between Bishops and Priests

In different countries some priests have assembled in action groups with the purpose of imposing a reform on the Church and of leading it to change its attitude toward the world. They aim at making pressure on the hierarchical authority. They are not afraid to provoke, though they reject the label of contestation as too negative and claim the title of solidary priests.

These groups differ from one country to another. Their motives for action

[5] Cf. Commission épiscopale du clergé et des séminaires du Canada; report of December 1968, Quebec; Commission Episcopal de Seminarios en España, *Confidential Note* 7, Brussels, *Pro Mundi Vita*, May 1969; Amtliche Zentralstelle für kirchliche Statistik des katholischen Deutschlands, Cologne, May 1969; Katholiek Sociaal-kerkelijk Instituut, Den Haag 1968; some private letters of the vocation board director in London, of the director of "The National Conference of Diocesan Vocation Directors" in Ohio, and of the major seminary in Malta.

[6] Cf. the review *Vocation*, January 1968, pp. 3–122.

originate, in general, from considerations of a pastoral nature. Nevertheless, in certain countries, political aims come into play. In others, the purpose is to obtain a new state of life for priests. All desire that priests and laity be able to make their voice effectively heard. Their preference is for a type of priest fully integrated in the life of society and for a Church playing an important role in social action.

Some of these groups include members of the laity. Others maintain relations with priests who have had to leave the ministry because they married. National groups have more and more effective contacts between themselves.

The activity of these groups brings the crisis to a high degree of tension, which can be very enlightening.[7]

B. *Changes in Mentality and Sociological Foundations of the Crisis*

1. General View

The recent and deep reforms in the life of the Church, the fundamental change in its relations with the world, have partly brought about the crisis that today affects the priesthood. These reforms have been either realized or ratified—as reforming tendencies already active in the Church—by Vatican II. This evolution is reflected in the decree on the ministry and the life of the priests.[8] The image of the priest has been considerably changed by it. The period of unrest that the application of the conciliar decisions and their further evolution brings about should not be astonishing.

The truth is that the crisis of the priesthood reveals above all the crisis that the Church itself is undergoing. If the actual problem that marks the priesthood is a crisis of identity, it is in reality an indication of the crisis of identity of the Church in its totality. This crisis of the Church is tied up to the sociocultural transformation that affects Western civilization today. This transformation—rightly characterized as secularization—poses the fundamental question of knowing whether, in certain new perspectives on man and society, any place is left for the Church. Whatever may be the answer that one

[7] Cf. the review: Freier Informationsdienst für priesterliche Solidarität (FIPS), Salzburg; Septuagint van Chur naar Rome (Amersfoort, Holland, 1969); *Une Eglise à libérer pour libérer le monde,* Conférence des délégués des groupes de prêtres à Rome, 1969; *Van Rome naar Utrecht,* Dossier van de internationale priestergroepen (Amersfoort, Holland, 1969); A. Manaranche, "Remous dans le sacerdoce en France", in *Cahiers d'action religieuse et sociale,* n. 487 (January 1969): 1–12.

[8] Cf. R. Wasselynck, *Les prêtres.,* Elaboration du décret de Vatican II, Histoire et genèse des textes conciliaires (Paris, 1968).

can give to this question, a problem remains: How should the Church present itself to men in the future? It goes without saying that these questions are burning problems for those who as priests are closely bound to the Church in their personal life and daily work.

2. Particular Aspects

All the above mentioned factors, which together bring about restlessness, are closely connected among themselves. Let us sketch them, at the risk of oversimplifying.

a. *Change in the classical image of the priest within the Church*

For more than a century and a half the image of the priest had not undergone any change. Since the Council of Trent no doctrinal evolution had touched the status of the priest in the Church. The priest knew what were his place and specific functions in the Christian community. He had the privileged task of administering the sacraments, chiefly the Eucharist and the absolutions of sins; he lived "sacerdotally", with the overtones of cult and the separation that this word evokes in the Old Testament. He knew himself to be responsible for the safeguard of the "true and unchangeable doctrine". He had to explain it very faithfully, somewhat like a Church official, and eventually to defend it in a disciplinary way. Hence it did happen that the priest considered himself as belonging to a special class, superior to that of other Christians. Gathering "his faithful", he guaranteed the permanence of the Church in a world that was regarded above all as a threat.

Vatican II has modified this priestly image in two respects. The Council has dealt with the common priesthood of all the faithful before treating of the ministerial priesthood, and the epithet "ministerial" has been added deliberately.[9] It has, moreover, put in relief the place of the bishop, the center of the particular Church and member of the universal college of bishops. The place of the priest in the Church has thus become less clear.

After Vatican II, the ministry of the priest has become more diversified, and the limits of his work are henceforth less sharply delineated than in the manuals of theology. It does not suffice any more for him just to perform his sacramental functions and all that goes directly with them. The new liturgical rites in the regional language require from him a personal application and a

---

[9] *LG,* 10; *PO,* 2. When in these pages we speak of a change in the classical image of the priest within the Church, what is meant is not a change in the concept of the priesthood as it has been handed down through the centuries but a presentation that differs from that usually adopted in the recent textbooks of theology, though it is deeply traditional.

great suppleness of adaptation. This does not mean that the ministry of the word has yet been very much stressed, but having to take into consideration the frequently changing needs of our contemporaries in the test to which their faith is subjected, this ministry demands from the priest a more profound knowledge and a deeper ability to communicate conviction. The priestly office becomes "presbyteral" in the sense given to this word in the New Testament. The formerly familiar term of "power" is now replaced by that of "charge" and is always explained as "service". It is further required that the priest fulfill his function in dialogue with other Christians, his brethren, and encourage their active participation in the proclamation of the word and the liturgy. Henceforth his place is no longer above that of the simple faithful but in their midst, although with a proper and specific mission. Again, much more than before, he must cooperate with his confreres, the ministry conceived in somewhat an individual fashion having given way to collegial ministry, exercised by the "presbyterium" sharing in the responsibility of the bishop.[10]

This is to say that the concept of a priesthood somewhat static, dominating, and individualistic has been substituted by that of a priesthood that is more dynamic, multiform, conceived as a service, and collegially exercised. This renewal of the concept of the priesthood is still creating today considerable confusion and restlessness in many churches.

b. *The Church and the world*

Vatican II has brought the whole Church to face the world in a positive manner. It has broken ecclesial isolation and has opted for solidarity and communication with the world. It has recognized that the world was created by God in his love, saved by Christ, destined to be perfected in him, and entrusted to men. It has made the Church conscious of its being-in-the-world and of its obligation to be the sign of God's will to reconcile it with himself. Thus the Church wishes to recognize the signs of the times in order to respond to them and to contribute to the progress of the world. Nor is it by indifference to its proper mission but, on the contrary, by a more definite understanding of this specific mission that she has received from Christ that the Church means to be of service to the world, in dialogue and collaboration with it.

For the priest, this change of perspective means that he must learn to honor human values, without losing sight of the fact that he is not of the world. He ought to apply himself to the problems proper to our times and effectively demonstrate the solidarity of the Church with men.[11]

The society of today will not welcome a Truth that does not respond to its

---

[10] *LG,* 28.
[11] *PO,* 3, 4, 17.

noblest aspirations or a Salvation that does not contribute to the relief of its present miseries. Priests, therefore, must cease to remain aloof from this society and on the contrary must understand its aspirations and take part in its searchings. They ought to find the means that will enable them to communicate the Truth and Salvation that the men of today are seeking.

This openness to the world demands, then, from many priests that they reconsider their way of thinking, their language, and their style of life, that they accept the uncertainty of unforeseen situations and associate themselves in the searchings of a fast-changing world.

c. Crisis in the Church

Confronted with a world full of change and of which it is a part, the Church is affected by the crisis. The process of secularization raises the problem of the raison d'être of the Church. This question not only concerns the concrete forms in which she exists at present and which are too little adapted to the temper of the modern world; it concerns even more *its real raison d'être;* in the final analysis, it is the Christian life that is subjected to a radical critique. The depth of the crisis comes from the fact that it touches the very heart of the *Christian Faith.*

Secularization can be characterized as a historicosociocultural process that allows man to give their full significance to the values of the world, its structures, its purposes, and its norms. After having explored the world, man has learned to manipulate it as his property. It is his world. Now he considers himself capable of assuming the entire responsibility for human existence. The time when man, to take his place in the world, was calling directly on God, the Church, or the priest has passed away.

Vatican II has clearly affirmed man's right to autonomy with regard to his secular tasks. "If by the autonomy of earthly realities we understand that created things and societies have their own laws and values, which man must gradually come to know, use, and organize, then it is altogether right to demand that autonomy; it is not only requested by men of our day; it is also in accordance with the will of the Creator" (*GS*, 36). The Church must therefore respect this autonomy in her pastoral work when she addresses herself to men in her cult and in her preaching.

On account of this situation, relatively new, many priests, when they find themselves restricted to tasks that are specifically ecclesiastical, suffer from a feeling of frustration. They experience difficulties in presenting that which is explicitly spiritual or religious in a manner that answers the questions and meets the needs of their contemporaries. They belittle the importance of liturgy and of the specifically pastoral service of their ministry to modern society.

The transformation of society finally has made many priests conscious of their role as adult men, responsible and free. Hence some ecclesial structures appear to them obsolete and unadapted to the modern world. They do not wish to be considered as "sons of the bishop", much less as functionaries of an institution. They demand that their ministry be exercised in coresponsibility in virtue of the trust the Church has put in them. Some seek to gain recognition as full citizens and aspire to a respected status in professional life that would make them financially independent. They wish they were able to exercise their role as priests freely at the same time as a profession in the world, to be married and to share as all other men in social life.

This process of secularization of the Church creates many problems for the Faith. If the life of faith of a good number of the faithful is affected with uncertainty, this is even more so with those who have dedicated themselves totally to its service. The suffering that the crisis of faith has brought about today touches profoundly the heart of the priest. The progress of positive sciences and technology creates an unfavorable climate for religious reflection. Current philosophical ideas, which are widely diffused, make the convictions and traditional religious practices appear foreign to actual life. De-Christianization, scepticism, the change in the pace of life, the vast and rapid development in communications, leisure, traveling, all tend to make the exercise of the priestly ministry more complex.

This explains that often the priest has the impression of living in a social milieu that takes him less and less seriously in what is most personal to him and represents his own deepest commitments. He has not been prepared by his formation in the seminary for this situation, and an updating that would keep pace with the ever-accelerated evolution is unfortunately not possible.[12]

---

[12] Cf. M. Bellet, *La peur ou la foi, Une analyse du prêtre* (Paris, 1967); J. M. Hennaux, "La peur ou la foi, l'analyse du malaise sacerdotal selon M. Bellet", *Nouvelle revue théologique* 91 (1969): 136–48; J. J. Blomious, *Priesthood in Crisis* (Milwaukee, 1969); A. Görres, "Psychologische Bemerkungen zur Krise eines Berufstandes", in *Weltpriester nach dem Konzil*, edited by Fr. Henrich (Munich, 1969), pp. 119–42; N. Greinacher, "Solidarisierung der Priester—mit wem?" in *Weltpriester nach dem Konzil*, op. cit., pp. 97–120; W. Kasper, "Krise und Wagnis des Glaubens im Leben des Priesters", *Geist und Leben* 42 (1969): 244–50; F. Louvel, *Pour moi, vivre c'est le Christ.* 350; *prêtres parlent du Christ,* special number of *La Vie spirituelle* (July 1964); D. P. O'Neill, *The Priest in Crisis: A study in Role and Change* (Dayton, 1968); K. Rahner, "Der Glaube des Priesters heute"; *Geist und Leben* 40 (1967): 269–85; Secrétariat Général de l'Episcopat Français; *Documents sur le sacerdoce* (Paris, 1969).

II. THE THEOLOGICAL ROOTS OF THE CRISIS
OF PRIESTLY IDENTITY

In order to put in bold relief the *properly theological* roots of this identity crisis of the priest, we may say, at the risk of simplifying and schematizing the arguments, that this crisis is due to a resurgence of the most fundamental problems raised by the Reformation and to the long cultural evolution that led in our own days to the creation of a secularized world.

A. *Resurgence of the Most Fundamental*
Problems Raised by the Reformation

For a large part the crisis has resulted from the rebirth, at the heart of the Catholic Church, of the problems posed by the Reformation. These problems were themselves only the consequence of grave deficiencies in the theology of the priestly ministry and in its concrete exercise during many centuries.

These problems were not, moreover, tackled at their roots by the Council of Trent. They were adjourned and underestimated rather than truly overcome and solved. The Council in fact was content with proclaiming strongly the existence of the sacrament of Order as ordained to the celebration of the Eucharist; it did not take up the problem of the significance of the priestly ministry in its theological and spiritual depth.

The perspective of the apostolate, in the full sense of the word, is not found in Luther's teaching.[13] This being said, we may sum up the main points of the critique of the Reformer as follows:

1. The New Testament applies the word priest (*hiereus*) and its derivatives only to Christ and the assembly of the baptized.
2. Under the New Covenant there is properly speaking only one Priest

---

[13] We borrow our formulations from an excellent specialist on Luther, Fr. Daniel Oliver, in his book *Les deux visages du prêtre* (Paris, 1971). Besides the books and reports quoted, we have benefited for the elaboration of this document from the following (mainly unpublished) studies: P. Toinet, *La condition sacerdotale dans le monde de ce temps*; P. Grelot, "Reflexions sur la structure ministérielle de l'Eglise d'après Saint Paul" (published in *Istina* [1970]: 389–424); P. Grelot, *Paul et les Douze*; E. Cothenet, Conclusion of his thesis *Le prophétisme dans le Nouveau Testament*; A. Feuillet, *La doctrine des évangiles synoptiques sur L'Eglise et les problèmes de l'heure présente*; Gonzalez de Cardedal, *Le célibat*; J. Lécuyer, *Problèmes actuels du sacerdoce*. Essai de synthèse de la réunion des experts faite sur l'initiative de la Congrégation sur le Clergé (November 18–20, 1968); H. R. Gagnebet, *Les problèmes actuels du sacerdoce*. Relation sur les travaux des experts (November 18–20, 1968).

whose priesthood is invisible, "before God". Christ the Priest has direct access to God; he offers himself to God without intermediary. He intercedes for his brethren and teaches them the mystery of salvation.

3. As members of the Body of Christ, all the baptized are priests in this fashion (in the invisibility of the Faith) and all in the same way: *consacerdotes ei sumus* (*Christian Liberty*).

4. The "priests" (of the Roman clergy) are not less priests than other Christians, but every faithful is as much priest as they are. From the point of view of the priesthood, in the Church, all have the same rights and the same spiritual powers. No one is in need of any other man to enter into relation with God for salvation, to receive his gifts, or to offer him worship in spirit and in truth. God himself has no need of any ministerial priesthood distinct from the common priesthood in order to transmit the grace of salvation.

5. The distinction between priest and laity cannot claim divine institution. It arises from ambition and from an exercise of authority in a worldly spirit. The true authority conferred by the word of God in view of the ministry is that of "stewards", of "servants". It cannot interfere in the domain of the liberty of each faithful.

6. Participation in the priesthood of Christ is conferred by baptism. Holy Orders is not a sacrament. "The Church of Christ does not know of it. It has been invented by the Church of the Pope" (*Capt. Babyl.*).

7. All that is valid in the notion of the ministerial *priesthood* is included in the notion of *ministry*. The ministry, according to the New Testament, consists in nourishing and in sustaining the Faith by the word and the sacraments of the word. In this perspective the apostolic succession is presented as a faithful (and pure) proclamation of the Gospel. The ministry does not confer any other supplementary power. It results only from the need that the Church feels for *organizing* itself for the service of God. This is why a Church deprived of bishops and of priests can always provide for this service by confiding to one of its members, priest among priests, equal among equals, the task of the ministry.

The intellectual tool due to which the ministerial priesthood came to be questioned was the Lutheran theology of salvation, which defined the conditions and manner of salvation from the point of view of *existence, that is to say from the spiritual act by which each one decides his destiny.* The event of the word taking possession of each person defines for him a situation "before God" in which he is left face to face "with his Savior".

Wishing to clarify what appeared to him to be the decisive moment in the economy of salvation (that is to say, when redemption becomes effective for a given individual), Luther ended up by making *existence,* understood as stated above, the only criterion for a proper evaluation of everything that he found in the Church of his time:

1. All that which is of decisive importance in leading to existential *conversion* is necessary, for example, the preacher. Luther includes these necessary elements under the category—existential and not "ontological"—"interior", "invisible", "before God", *coram Deo.*
2. All that existentially is not decisive is "contingent" ("exterior"): cult, disciplinary details. This can be changed and eventually suppressed.
3. All that turns man away from his existential responsibility (for example, the doctrine of "merit" through works, which turns away the attention from the *personal* act) or tries to substitute itself for Christ in one way or another (priest, pope) or to restrict the liberty that faith in Jesus Christ gives to every Christian is heretical, impious, and null and void.

The "revolution" brought about in the domain of the priestly ministry is linked in Luther, to his giving up of the "ontological" perspective of salvation (in the sense implied by the dogma of Chalcedon) in favor of a perspective that is purely "existential" and individually "existential". There is no place for an ecclesial mediation to have access to the Father, for a communitarian mediation restoring for man the bonds broken by sin; no place for a priestly mediation (subordinate to the one Mediator) inserting each person in the universal people, within the hierarchical unity of the trinitarian life assuming the life of mankind. In other words, this questioning of the priestly ministry is tied up with a *new view of the Church.*

This *"existential" climate*—in the above sense—has spread so largely after the sixteenth century that it has become one of the components of *modern culture.*

The very great development of historical sciences, in particular as regards early Christianity, and of biblical and patristic sciences has also brought about the diffusion, rethinking, and in-depth study of the questions posed by the Reformation concerning the structures of the Church and the priesthood.

Thus in the Protestant history of the Church early Christianity, which was evangelical and apostolic, has come to be opposed to the Church of the Fathers, considered as the germ of later Catholicism. In his *Essence of Christianity* Harnack is one of the last protagonists of this trend.

This fundamental opposition is at the heart of the modernist crisis. Thus Alfred Loisy in his refutation of some of the position taken up by the great protestant historian, in his book *The Gospel and the Church,* still remains a prisoner of some of the presuppositions on which the typically protestant history of the Church was built. According to him a cleavage separates apostolic Catholicism—in the sense that it was the work of the apostles themselves starting with St. Paul—and Jesus. This is the position that the post-Bultmannian school itself, in particular Conzelmann, attempts to maintain even in our day (for him Luke would be primarily responsible for *Frühkatholizismus*). But the Scandinavian exegetical Protestant school, led by Anton Fridrichsen, has well shown that the opposition between a *Frühkatholizismus* and Jesus is a fictitious construction, the fruit of an a priori doctrinal position belied by the facts and texts. Whatever that may be, even if it is becoming more and more clear that the Church of the Fathers, at least in its broad outlines, has succeeded with relative homogeneity the Church that developed and took shape in the New Testament, some fundamental questions remain under acute discussion. Let us cite only one major example, concerning the problem of the priesthood. It has been remarked, for example, that the New Testament hardly speaks of a ministerial "priesthood" but of a people, a "kingdom of priests"; that it attaches importance to the specific ministries, which are "services" by which the salvation brought by Christ is made available to the faithful. It becomes quite natural, then, to ask if the evolution that has taken place in the direction of the priesthood, from almost the beginning of the life of the Church, is not a perversion of the Christian mystery, and if it must not be explained by the influence of the Old Testament on the Christian community and, later, after Constantine, by the transfer of the prerogatives of the pagan priesthood to Christian ministers; or again, if ordination is not just one among the lawful forms of accession to the ministry, not necessarily the only form possible.[14]

B. *A Long Cultural Evolution*

As the remarks of the foregoing paragraphs give us to understand, the problems concerning the priestly ministry today are not only the simple resurgence of the problems posed by the Reformation; they have been enlarged and aggravated by a long *cultural evolution* that, however, is not without connection with the Reformation itself.

Briefly, let us say that the present *uneasiness* results basically from the confrontation in our culture between two views of the world. The one agrees with Catholic Tradition and presupposes a world as created, as a reality wherein one discovers the gift of God, as a sign of his presence, as a witness of his action and the link between God and man. The other proceeds from a radical "secularization" of existence in the world—this is a philosophical

---

[14] It could be shown that throughout the history of the Church a crisis of the priestly ministry has always coincided with a crisis of the Church. With regard to the developments in the history of the Church viewed from a Protestant standpoint, the bibliography is extensive. Let us refer here only to the book of Louis Bouyer, *L'Eglise de Dieu, Corps du Christ* (Paris, 1970).

position that has nothing in common with secularization understood as a legitimate autonomy of earthly things (GS, 36)—and is expressed and enlarged in the dialetics of some modern philosophies of history, idealist as well as materialist, which leave no room for a Transcendence operating in the world. These philosophies in fact present the development of the Spirit or of Man or of the World as a kind of self-creation. They regard the personalities who set this historical process in motion as privileged "moments" in the evolution of the Spirit, or as enlightened guides of a collectivity in "revolutionary travail".[15]

As the witness and sacramental agent of the eschatological kingdom, and as the instrument of our Lord Jesus Christ for the work of eternity in time, the priest cannot pretend to meet the requests of the "anthropogenesis" or of the "noogenesis" of modern philosophies of history.

Many of the actual priestly problems thus arise from the fact that the priests do not gauge sufficiently to what degree the phenomenon of "secularization", understood in the radical sense we have spoken of, is a constituent element of our Western culture and, in a certain measure, of a sizable part of the civilization of the world. A world closed on itself, which refuses every dependence on its principle and end, a world that finds itself within the narrow boundaries of its own self-reinterpretation, a world that has no other values except those created by its own efforts, has no place for the priest.

This means that a human world that discovers itself as autonomous, without realizing its need to search for meaning, and in complete self-reliance, makes it impossible for the priest to find his identity. For the priestly ministry as understood by the Catholic Church implies a sacramental or "mysteric" concept of the Church, a definite anthropological and ontological conception (in particular, as we have said above, a created world as the sign of God).

Our analysis leads us therefore to distinguish clearly (1) secularization understood in its most radical sense of a world closed on itself and (2) secularization understood in the sense of a legitimate autonomy of earthly things (GS, 36). Only this distinction can enable us to avoid some of the confusions and equivocations that are the source of many grave misunderstandings.

Perhaps it would be better to use the word "secularism" to designate the

---

[15] For a thorough analysis of the crisis. cf. P. Toinet, op. cit.

The questions would have to be asked why Kant, Fichte, Schelling, and especially Schleiermacher and Hegel claimed the patronage of Luther and why Hegel thought that by undermining the hierarchical structure of the Church, Luther had brought about the true freedom and autonomy of the Spirit—which unfolds as universal in itself and by itself—and thus had contributed to the evolution of the divine in man (cf. Hegel, *Philosophie der Rechts— Vorrede*, ed. Laffon [Leipzig, 1930], F.W., vol. 6, p. 16; cf. *Geschichte des Philosophie*, ed. Michelet [Berlin, 1844], W.W. pt. 15, pp. 217ff.; 230ff.).

A similar view is found in Marx, "Annales Franco-Allemandes", in *Oeuvres Philosophiques* (Molitor-Costes, March 1844), vol. 1: 97–98.

first process, but it does not depend on us only whether or not this distinction in terminology is always observed.[16]

The more we are bound by our Faith to denounce a secularism that tends to make a closed-up world an idol, the more we have the duty in the name of our Faith to recognize the benefits of a sane view of secularity as we have affirmed above after *Gaudium et Spes.* This view corresponds in truth to certain fundamental demands of the Gospel, as for instance the demand that the whole life of man be an act of worship. It requires from us a more refined understanding of the proper nature of Christian worship, conceived as cult of the *Faith,* assuming the entire existence and bringing to its term the offering of life in the community celebration of the Lord's Pasch in the Eucharist.

C. Conclusion

From the reflections made above, it appears clearly that, in view of its depth and gravity, the crisis of the priesthood in which we find ourselves offers the Church an exceptional opportunity. It is for the Church a grace if it knows how to receive it. Henceforth, the Church is bound to give an answer, *through a radical deepening, both theological and spiritual,* to the questions that were not answered at the Reformation. She is led to examine whether the priestly ministry had not been unduly overlaid with alien elements from which it must be freed; thus, she must show with greater relief what is its *specific character,* according to the will of Jesus Christ and the word of God revealed to us.

Thus, we are led to study the Church as a priestly people, then the priesthood of Christ and the possibility of basing on it the priestly ministry.

Note on the Sacred
by Louis Bouyer

It has become fashionable to react against "religion" in the name of "faith" and to oppose the "sacred" to the "secular" in which true Christianity, it is said, ought to manifest itself. These attitudes imply, besides a lack of perception for what is unique in Christian spirituality, a number of confusions and ambiguities.

---

[16] Secularization, in the radical sense, excludes every idea of a Church with a hierarchical structure. Let us quote but one text: "Secular faith and hierarchical authority exclude each other. Consequently, the Church of the future must differ from what it has been in the past" (J. Sperna Weiland, *La nouvelle théologie* [Desclée de Brouwer, 1969]).

To go to the root of the problem, it would be necessary to elucidate perfectly the relation between the notions of faith and religion, of sacred and profane. We limit ourselves to transcribing a note written by L. Bouyer.

It is not possible to dispel them in a short note. Let us mention that some non-Catholic theologians (mostly Anglican) have contributed much to this, in particular, Archbishop Michael Ramsey (*Sacred and Secular; God, Christ and the World*) and Professor J. Macquarrie (*God and Secularity*).

The notion and the reality of the "sacred" would have to be studied first, not by abstract speculations and a priori definitions, but according to a deep phenomenological study based on a truly scientific comparative history of religions. One should have recourse here in particular to the works of R. Otto, G. Van der Leeuw, and Mircea Eliade. We have tried to give an outline of the results of such a study, in particular in our work *Rite and Man*.

The first remark to be made is this: "sacred" is whatever appears in this world, and especially in the life of man, as a sign that reveals the existence, the presence, and the action of God. To look, then, for a Christianity in which the sacred would be altogether overcome and abolished would amount to advocating a Christianity where God would no longer and could no longer be named, or even be alluded to. To reject the sacred leads therefore, wittingly or unwittingly, to what goes by the name of "death of God" but should be called simply the oblivion of God.

Depth psychology, however, seems to show (this is, in particular, one of the most positive contributions made by the school of Jung) that this oblivion is never more than an appearance. The removal of the "sacred" from the sphere of consciousness brings about, as all other repressions, a monstrous proliferation of it in the subconscious. For not having been accepted by human consciousness as the friend par excellence, it becomes its enemy, an enemy on whom one can turn one's back but from whom one cannot escape.

What is in fact rightly but obscurely felt today by Christians who wish to reject the "sacred" are the paradoxical tension and opposition between the "sacred" and human life that are found in human religions besides Judaism and Christianity. The sphere of God and of the divine action seems, at least at first sight, foreign or even hostile to the sphere of man and of his actions.

In all these religions, the "sacred" is separated from man's daily life and from the world in which he lives; nevertheless, it claims for the Divinity the right to be the master of life and of the whole world. By paying his due to the Divinity at certain moments and in certain places through rites and formulas, man hopes then to acquire, in exchange for the tithe he has paid to the "sacred", the right and the assurance of remaining the master of his own life and of the world in all other spheres. In his search for controlling and humanizing the whole world, modern man thus tends to evacuate the sacred. . . .

The attitude of Judaism, and of Christianity after it, is exactly the reverse. This is why at first sight Christianity may seem to stand for a world fully "secularized" (this is the appealing but too simple idea of Harvey Cox, especially in his *Secular City*). In fact, Judaism and Christianity (and, we may say, all the major religions, though less radically and less effectively) aim at abolishing the distinction, and a fortiori the tension, between the sacred and the secular. But their intention is not to reduce everything to the secular but rather to consider everything as sacred. The sacred, however, is not understood as an affirmation of God that extinguishes man; the formula of St. Irenaeus must rather be applied to it: *Gloria Dei homo vivens . . . ,* though what he adds immediately should not be forgotten: the only true life for man is to "know" God.

In Judaism, the sacred stands, in fact, for the sacredness of a God who is not foreign to man but is his Creator. It is revealed in a historical process; historical events take on the precise meaning of signifying God's reentry into the history of man estranged from him: God reveals himself as Savior and Reconciler.

Nevertheless, revelation makes use of the signs of natural sacrality, or better, of the sacrality that persists in a fallen world. This cannot be separated from the sacred as transfigured by the personal intervention of God in human existence as Creator and Savior.

Thus God makes use of the sacrificial rite, in its most elementary and most radical form: the sacred meal (where in an exchange with God man becomes conscious of receiving his life from him). But of the Paschal meal, which originally was a simple seasonal ritual symbolic of the yearly rebirth of vegetation, he makes the Jewish Pasch, a ritual that symbolizes an ever-renewed Covenant, a perduring memorial of the intervention of God who has saved his people from destruction. . . . At the Last Supper, which marks the end of what may be called the prophetic experience, Christ revealed the meaning of his Cross, which fulfilled all the sacrifices of Israel and solved the "natural" mystery of life and death. He also left to those who were his the memorial that would enable them forever to commune in his unique sacrifice.

But the eucharistic Communion in the sacrifice of Jesus (summit of sacredness in Christianity) does not initiate into a sacred reality separated from life and opposed to it. On the contrary, it establishes a relation between the real (and not merely ritual) sacrifice of the death of Jesus on the Cross, which unveils the meaning of his entire life, and our life, which must constantly be renewed through assimilation to his. Christian sacredness does not therefore constitute a world beside the world, a life separated from life; rather, it establishes communication, in a way that faith alone can perceive, between the life of Christ, who through his Resurrection has entered the new world, and our own life, transfigured by his and reshaped after his image, while we await in this world the judgment of the Cross and the final transformation of the parousia.

In this perspective, Christ assumes and radically transforms the priestly function and quality, which make of the priest "the man of the sacred". But in this unique and entirely new priesthood, every man who becomes a Christian through baptism and faith is called to participate. Yet, the sacrament of Order is that which is explicitly destined to extend to all men the unique priesthood of Christ and to every life his unique sacrifice; for it consecrates those whom he sends and makes them, especially in the announcement of his word and the celebration of its sacramental signs, the "ministers", that is to say, the instruments of communication to all of the priesthood of Christ. Thus, always and everywhere, the new sacredness of the reconciliation of all men with God proceeds entirely from Christ alone: where and only where a representative of Christ the Head speaks and acts in his name, the Body of those who are reconciled is constituted and grows.

III. THE CHURCH, THE PRIESTLY PEOPLE OF GOD

By his whole life, his teaching, his Cross, and his Resurrection, which communicates the gift of the Spirit, Christ, the one and eternal Priest, has brought to existence a Church, all the members of which constitute a priestly people, the sacrament of salvation for the world.

In the unity of a diversified body, the entire Church is associated with the priesthood of Christ, its Head. All the members have free access to God (Rom 5:2; Eph 2:18) in the freedom of the word (2 Cor 3:12; Eph 3:12; Heb 4:16; 10:19). In brief, all are priests.

The priestly office of the people of God, fundamentally united to the priestly sacrifice of Jesus (Rev 1:5; cf. 5:9ff. and 7:13ff.) is not only rooted in Christ but also exercised in him and through him: "*Through* him (who has sanctified the people by his own blood: Heb 13:12) let us continually offer up a sacrifice of praise to God, that is, the fruit of lips that acknowledge his name" (Heb 13:15).

This priestly office comprises in the first place the offering of praise (Heb 13:15; cf. 10:22), which invites us, according to the apostle, to say "Amen" to the work of God and of Christ (2 Cor 1:20) and to ratify, by a confession of faith, a *homologia,* the celebration of the Eucharist (cf. Heb 13:15; 1 Pet 2:9, where the expression "to declare the wonderful deeds of God" refers to the praise of God in the liturgy—cf. LXX, Ps 9:15; 70:15; 72:28; etc.). It implies in the second place the "spiritual sacrifice" of Romans 12:1–2, which consists in witnessing, by the exercise of charity (Heb 10:24; 13:16; James 1:26–27; 2:22ff.), to a new spiritual life. Finally, it can be expressed by the witness of martyrdom, the supreme form of a spiritual priesthood (Phil 1:19–30; 1 Pet 2:20ff.; Rev 1:6; 5:9–10; 6:11; 7:13–14).[17]

---

[17] Cf. H. Schlier, "Grundelemente des priesterliches Amtes im Neuen Testament", *Theologie und Philosophie* (1969): 168–71; cf. also the articles mentioned in the following note.

In a similar manner, the first letter of Peter teaches that the Church is a priestly community. The correct translation of 1 Peter 2:9—according to the most recent studies—is probably the following: "You are a chosen nation, a *royal household* [*basileion*], a priestly community [*hierateuma*], a holy nation, a people acquired by God."[18]

Since the Greek translators have coined this word *hierateuma*, a collective term, on the pattern of the nouns ending with *euma,* which denote a gathering of men fulfilling a function, it is clear that the entire Church performs a priestly function in the midst of the nations.

This collective worship of the people of God is a *spiritual* one. This means that it is celebrated in the most fundamental of all realities, the spirit of God, who gives to different members their place in the body by conferring on them different "ministries", some spontaneous and temporary, others publicly recognized by authority, and still others of a special importance and proceeding from the apostles.

This is why the collective spiritual priesthood is always exercised according to a certain *order,* as is well shown in the eucharistic celebration, which has always been, according to Scripture and Tradition, an essentially collective act. Nothing, moreover, conforms more to the biblical concept, which shows always the people of God as a hierarchical people. Without this organic unity it would not be the messianic flock governed and protected by the good *shepherds* foretold by the prophets.

The communitarian perspective of Exodus 19:5–6 was, moreover, by no means opposed to the recognition of the levitical institution. As found in 1 Peter 1:9, it is clearly not opposed either to the institution of a pastoral ministry. The same first letter of Peter speaks of the pastoral ministry (1 Pet 5:2–5) and of the priestly character of the community.

This collective priesthood penetrates and underlies the life of the faithful in order that it be entirely permeated and transformed by the eucharistic blessing and the love of God. Likewise the infinitely diversified initiatives that permit each one to witness, by his words and his whole life, to the

---

[18] On this theme see, among others: John Hall Elliot, *The Elect and the Holy; An Exegetical Examination of 1 Peter 2, 4–10 and the Phrase "Basileion hierateuma",* Supplements to Novum Testamentum XII (Leyden: B. J. Brill, 1966); J. Coppens, "Le sacerdoce royal des fidèles: un commentaire de 1 Petri 2, 4–10", in *Au service de la parole de Dieu. Mélanges en l'honneur de Mgr Charue* (1969): 61–75 (this article contains a very complete bibliography); E. Cothenet, "Nation élue, résidence royale, communauté sacerdotale. . . . Le sacerdoce des fidèles d'après la Petri", *Esprit et vie* 11 (March 1969): 169–73. According to J. H. Elliot, against the background of LXX *basileion* cannot be a predicate expressing the dignity of the *hierateuma.* Therefore, it is not correct to translate, as is usually done, by "royal priesthood". *Basileion* is a neuter noun opposed to *hierateuma* (parallel to *oikos pneumatikos,* spiritual temple); it means royal residence, palace.

special priestly grace given to all, ought to be coordinated around those who, after the apostles, are the heads of the Christian community. It is always as members of one and the same Body—in which intrinsic unity in the Spirit and in love cannot be separated from union with the apostles and their successors—that Christians appear to the world, even when they seem to act individually.

Just as it is impossible to think of a body without internal order between its organs (the more a body is developed, the more it is organized), so too it is impossible to think of the Church, the priestly Body, without its own proper order, that is to say, without a hierarchical structure.

IV. THE CHRISTOLOGICAL FOUNDATION OF THE PRIESTLY MINISTRY

The priestly ministry can only have for its foundation the priesthood of Christ. In the New Covenant there is no other priesthood except that of Christ, which fulfills all the ancient priesthoods by surpassing them.

It is therefore necessary that we analyze first of all, in the economy of salvation, the evolution of the notion and reality of the priesthood.

A. *The Fulfillment and the Surpassing of the Ancient Priesthoods*

The cult of the tabernacle, later of the temple, expressed the perpetual consecration of Israel to the living God who saved it, adopted it as his child through the renewal of the Covenant with Abraham on Sinai. In it, the faith of Israel in the word of God is condensed, the ritual—like the Pasch itself—being the perpetual memorial of the Covenant sealed on the holy mountain at the Exodus from Egypt.

The setting apart of priests allows the cult of the people of God to find a social and visible expression. Its purpose was to assure for Israel the realization of a cult worthy of God, in which the conversion of heart—obedience to the word of God and observance of his law, which covers all the aspects of life—is the fundamental reality. The cultic mediation of priests and the spiritual relations between the community and its God were mutually conditioned.

It would, however, be a mistake to restrict the study to the levitical priesthood alone in order to determine the exact meaning of the priesthood in Israel, because the very idea of the priesthood, from Judges to the New Testament, underwent a serious transformation.

1. Moses

In the history of Israel, the figure of Moses stands out with a brightness that will only be surpassed at the other pole of the revelation by the Messiah. In his own person, he assumed a diversity of mediations that later were divided among different persons, kings, priests, prophets. By his prophetic mission, Moses was in fact the mediator of the word of God. The charism of his particular vocation made him the leader of his people. By reason of this charism he exercised the priestly office in the name of all the people (Ex 24:6–8).

2. The Royal Priesthood

The priesthood of the heads of families, of clans, of tribes, preceded in Israel the priesthood of the tribe of Levi. It developed into a royal priesthood at the time of institution of the monarchy of David, the depositary of the divine promises (cf. 2 Sam 7:8–16). Even if this aspect was somewhat overshadowed later, the image of the *king-priest,* appearing before Yahweh on behalf of Israel (1 Kings 8:14–66; 2 Kings 23:1–3) and before the people as the representative of Yahweh (Ps 2:6–9) keeps a certain importance in the history of revelation (2 Sam 7:8–16; cf. mostly Ps 110:4: "You are a priest for ever after the order of Melchizedek").

3. The Levitical Priesthood

In virtue of a divine choice and of a particular vocation, the levitical priesthood exercised a mediation between God and the people in the service of the cult and of the law. In the liturgies of Israel, it recalled to the people the great deeds done by Yahweh in the history of salvation, announced his requirements, and brought down his benedictions (Nb 6:24–27). It presented to God the praise and supplication of the community and of individuals.[19]

4. Priesthood and Prophetism

The limits of the levitical priesthood were clearly brought to the fore by the experience that Israel made of the deep reality of sin, destroyer of the Covenant.

[19] See article "Mediator" in *Dictionary of Biblical Theology* (London, 1970), col. 303; *Vocabulaire de théologie biblique,* 2nd ed. (Paris, 1970), col. 726.

There resulted an acute consciousness of the need for an *eschatological redemption* and a true change in the idea of the priesthood.

In the prophetic utterances, the perfect cult, capable of assuring fully the glory of God and salvation of men, found itself, little by little, relegated to "the last times". It would not be simply the expression of grace within men's hearts; it would always necessitate a renewed priesthood (Jer 31:14; Ezek 40–48; Is 25:6; Malachi 3:1–4).

Jewish spirituality, being more and more assured that the time of final restoration was still a long way off, concentrated on all that concerned the expiation of sins: importance of the feast of forgiveness (Lev 16:23, 26–32); multiplication of potential liturgies, long traditional but now understood in relation to the spirituality of the prophets (cf. Joel 2:12–17); search for spiritual purity (cf. Ps 51).

But, while the priests were called to "carry the burden of the sins of the people" (Nb 17:27; 18:7), it became clearer and clearer that the exercise of this priestly mediation demanded far more than a simple ritualistic consecration (cf. Lev 22:1–9); it demanded a radical transformation of hearts.

The case of the high priest is particularly significant; he carried on his pectoral twelve stones with the names of the twelve sons of Israel (Ex 28:27–28), showing thus that he took on himself the interests of the whole nation. But his own sins weakened the efficacy of his priestly mediation. Thus, in the ritual of the Day of Expiation (*Yom Kippur*), he had to offer sacrifice for his own sins and for those of other priests before celebrating the expiatory rite for the sins of Israel (Lev 16:11–19).

Israel thus came to wait unconditionally for the *eschatological* event by which God would bring about, by pure grace, that which men were unable to accomplish.

The prophets were the great proponents of this profound evolution in the idea of priesthood. On the foundation of the experiences of Jeremiah and Ezekiel, who considered themselves as carrying the sins of the people and expiating for them, there slowly emerges the image of an eschatological Savior, the Servant of Yahweh.

5. The Servant of Yahweh

At the heart of a world, where sin is a universal reality, the Servant is the only just one, the Innocent One, who takes on himself the sins of all to obtain their justification (Is 53:11). His vocation is "to be wounded for our transgressions, bruised for our iniquities" (Is 53:5). Struck by God, he shares in the lot of those who for their conduct are subject to the judgment of God. He identifies himself with them, as it were, in order to "bear their grief and to carry their sorrows" (Is 53:4).

This was the result of a mysterious design of God, humanly incomprehensible (Is 53:10) but fully accepted by the Servant who gave himself up to death (Is 53:12). This act of obedience, at the end of which he was "stricken for our transgressions" (Is 53:8), has sacrificial value. The Servant "offered his soul [that is, his living person] in expiation" (Is 53:10).

This prophetic figure is unintelligible without the retransposition of the ritualistic and liturgical data that were brought about by the prophetic experience; this is shown by the use the prophets make of liturgical terminology. The Servant obtains from God that which the expiatory victims, offered in the temple by the Israelite clergy, were incapable of achieving: "He bore the sins of many and made intercession for the transgressors" (Is 53:12).

The design of God begins to unfold itself: God's intention is that through the offering of sacrifice, the heart of man be totally given to him. The sacrifice that God expects from his people is the *full man*, the life of man thus becoming in breadth and depth a liturgy.

This is very expressly the fundamental affirmation of the Epistle to the Hebrews: "Consequently, when Christ came into the world, he said: 'Sacrifices and offerings you have not desired, but you have prepared a body for me; in burnt offerings and sin offerings you have taken no pleasure.' Then I said: 'Lo, I have come to do your will, O God', as it is written of me in the roll of the book" (Heb 10:5–7, where reference is made to Ps 40:7–9, underlying the spiritual character of the sacrifice). It is in the line of the fulfillment and surpassing of all the ancient sacrifices that the priesthood of Christ is found: "By a single offering he has perfected for all times those he has sanctified" (Heb 10:14).[20]

B. *The Priesthood of Christ*

We distinguish the study of other writings of the New Testament from that of the Epistle to the Hebrews because the latter alone speaks explicitly and formally of the priesthood of Christ.

1. Other Writings of the New Testament

a. *The reality of the priesthood of Christ*

The priesthood of Christ is affirmed in the New Testament, where, in a more or less *typological* way, the sacrifice of Christ on the Cross is considered as a

[20] See especially the book of P. Grelot, *Le ministère de la nouvelle alliance* (Paris: Cerf, 1967).

self-oblation. Let us cite, for example, the formula of the First Epistle to the Corinthians: "Christ, our Paschal Lamb, has been sacrificed" (1 Cor 5:7), the reference to the blood of Christ (Mk 14:24; Rom 3:5; 5:9; Eph 1:7; 2:3), the expressions where occurs the *"hyper hêmôn"*, "for us" (Jn 6:51; 10:11, 15; Lk 22:19; Mk 10:45), the Johannine expression: "Behold the Lamb of God who takes away the sins of the world" (Jn 1:29; cf. 1:36; 19:36). The typology of the Paschal Lamb is found again in Revelation: "You were slain and by your blood did ransom men for God from every tribe and tongue and people and nation, and have made them a kingdom of priests, to our God, and they shall reign on earth" (Rev 5:9–10), and in the First Epistle of Peter (1 Pet 1:18). Jesus, the just one, is presented in 1 John 2:2 as the expiatory victim (*hilasmos*) for the whole world, that is, as a sacrifice for sin, as is suggested by Ezek 44:27 (cf. Ezek 45:1; Nb 5:8; 2 Macc 3:33). The sacrifice of Christ consists in the offering that he made of himself: Jesus Christ "gave himself for our sins" (Gal 1:4; cf. Gal 2:20; Eph 2:25; 1 Tim 2:6; Titus 2:14). This self-oblation is especially well illustrated by the image of Good Shepherd, which prolongs that of that Servant of Yahweh (Jn 10:11; 17:19). The love of Christ living himself for his Church is once more expressed through the image of sacrifice in Ephesians 5:25, and its content is exactly defined by the following text: "Walk in love as Christ loved us and gave himself up for us, a fragrant offering and sacrifice to God" (Eph 5:2).[21]

In all these texts, if the word "priest" is not directly used, it is to avoid equivocation, for it could be misleading by recalling the levitical priesthood. Jesus, however, is undoubtedly the Priest who offers himself as a Victim for sin.

The words by which in the Gospel Jesus defines his mission as "suffering Servant" on whom the Spirit rested confirm this certainty by their deep priestly overtones.

According to the testimony of the Synoptic Tradition and of St. John, Jesus has conceived his ministry along the line of the prophecies of the Servant of Yahweh (Is 53 in particular). As such, he is the Priest and Victim of the sacrifice that reconciles sinful humanity with God (cf., for instance, Mk 10:45 and parallel texts, where four allusions to Is 53:10–12 are found).[22]

At the Last Supper, Christ explicitly spoke of himself as the Servant who establishes the New Covenant and institutes the new people of God. In sprinkling the people with the blood of the victims, Moses, the mediator of the Sinai Covenant, had said: "Behold the blood of the Covenant, which the Lord has made with you in accordance with all these words" (Ex 24:8). Jesus, comparing his gesture to that of Moses, said: "This is

[21] We borrow here the remarks made by H. Schlier, op. cit., 161ff.
[22] On the theme of the suffering Servant, cf. A. Feuillet, "Les trois prophéties de la Passion et de la Résurrection des évangiles synoptiques", *Revue Thomiste* (1967): 534–60; (1968): 41–74.

my blood, the blood of the Covenant, which is to be poured out for many" (Mk 14:24).

The sacrificial act, supreme token of love, embraces thus the whole of the life of Jesus and expresses the perfect gift that he made of himself to *God*, for the sake of *all*, in order that his Father may make the whole of mankind share in his Spirit of Love. Thus man's life becomes in its entirety an act of worship and offering to God.

Further, in John 17, Christ is presented as the High Priest; the structure of the priestly prayer seems clearly to follow that of the Feast of Pardon (*Yom Kippur*), in which the high priest, pronouncing the name of God, prayed for himself, for the priests, and for all the people.[23]

The same perspective of the Feast of *Yom Kippur* is probably found again in Revelation 1:10, where Christ appears clothed in a sacerdotal robe.[24]

The conclusion of Luke (Lk 24:51)—the relations of which to John are becoming more and more evident—also shows us Christ as the High Priest blessing his people (cf. Sir 50).

Finally, Christ may have presented himself implicitly as Priest if it is true that he applied to himself with predilection Psalm 110, in which the Messiah is both King and Priest, according to the order of Melchizedek.

As all the teaching of Jesus culminates in the announcement of his death and Resurrection, prefigured also by his powerful works (miracles, exorcisms, and healings), it can be said that his entire *eschatological ministry, exercised in the Spirit, was priestly*. Was Jesus not the one whom the Father had *consecrated and sent into the world* (Jn 10:36) and who had received from him the *command to lay down his life* (Jn 10:17–18)?

Thus there appear a continuity and mutual relationship between the messianic mission of Jesus (cf. Lk 4:16–30; 7:18–29) and his sacrifice. The sacrifice consecrates his mission, by defining it as that of the Servant of Yahweh, while the mission to announce the Gospel and to show the signs of the Kingdom is perfected in the sacrifice. The Good News announced by Jesus is in fact the New Covenant of reconciliation of all men by the blood of Christ, their unity with God and between themselves restored through the Cross of Christ (Eph 2:11–22). It is indeed in the New Covenant instituted and sealed by the blood of Jesus that God's choice of the messianic people finds its consecration.

The different aspects of the eschatological ministry of Christ are united in the image of the Good Shepherd (Christ shows how truly God is the Shep-

---

[23] This point, already hinted at by M. J. Colson, is justified in a long study by M. A. Feuillet (unpublished).

[24] W. Stote, "A Note on the Word '*kuriakê*' in Apoc. 1, 10", *New Testament Studies* (1965/1966): 70–75. Christ is seen as the High Priest entering the Holy of Holies for *Yom Kippur*.

herd of his people), or, to use another but similar image, the Servant of Yahweh: everything in his mission is ruled by his pastoral love, which leads to the familiarity of a living communion (Jn 10:4–16).

The gift of his life that the Good Shepherd makes constitutes the summit of his prophetic work: it is the supreme testimony to the truth (Jn 18:37), which sums up and guarantees all his teachings.

The sacrifice shows the supreme authority of him who freely gives his life (Jn 10:17) and who has the power to give it and to take it up again (Jn 10:18): he is the King, as he calls himself before Pilate (Jn 18:36–37).

Finally, in delivering himself to death, the Good Shepherd fulfills the worship "in spirit and in truth" (Jn 4:23), which the whole of the Old Testament had announced and longed for: was not his sacrifice a free and total obedience to the will of the Father (Jn 10:18)?

The priesthood of Christ, then, is truly founded on his mission as the well-beloved Son.

b. *Christ associated his apostles to his priestly and eschatological ministry*

The way of acting of the Jesus of the Gospel allows us to affirm, moreover, that he made *the Twelve,* whom he had *set apart* to be with him in a special manner, *share in his eschatological ministry.*

As the Servant of Yahweh, the Shepherd of the eschatological people, he willed to associate the group of the apostles to his eschatological ministry and made them shepherds of his eschatological flock.

This association of the Twelve in the ministry of Christ will be the object of the next chapter.

2. Epistle to the Hebrews

The Epistle to the Hebrews alone speaks explicitly of the priesthood of Christ. It therefore deserves special study.[25]

Taken in itself, the Epistle to the Hebrews, according to which, in opposition to the levitical priesthood, the priesthood of Christ is eternal, final, unchangeable (*aparabaton,* Heb 7:24), hardly provides an explicit foundation for the possibility of a ministerial priesthood. However, it permits

---

[25] Cf. C. Spicq, *Epître aux Hébreux* II (Paris, 1953): 119–39; H. Bouesse, *Le sacerdoce chrétien* (1957): 71–104.

us to make three kinds of considerations that are not without interest for our purpose.[26]

a. *Christ realizes in himself the synthesis of the different aspects of the Old Testament priesthood*

1. The priesthood of Christ and the levitical priesthood. In the Epistle to the Hebrews the external properties of the priesthood of Christ are characterized with reference to the purpose, function, and different offices of the levitical priesthood in the temple: intercession for men before God, offering of the gifts and the sacrifices for their sins (Heb 5:1; 8:3), call and installation by God himself (Heb 5:4), solidarity with the ignorant and the wavered who ought to be taught and guided (Heb 5:2), feast of expiation (Heb 9:7), and the rite of expiatory blood (Heb 9:7, 12ff., 19–22).

The levitical priesthood was thus an image prefiguring the priesthood of Christ. However, between the "shadow" or type (Heb 9:9; 8:5; cf. 9:23) and the reality, namely, the fullness of Christ, there is, as it were, an *infinite distance* (*maior dissimilitudo*): the ancient priesthood did not in fact realize its proper aim (and consequently not its concept either), since true reconciliation of the sinner with God (Heb 7:11) remained unaccomplished; Jesus, too, "if he were on earth, would not be a priest at all" (Heb 8:4).

In other words, when the reality of the *eschatological* priesthood and sacrifice has become present (Heb 9:26; 9:27; it is through this priest and his eschatological ministry that God has spoken "in these last days": Heb 1:1) and the *eschatological Covenant* is constituted (Heb 8:8; 10:16ff.; cf. Jer 31:31ff.), the typological image fades away.

The appeal to Melchizedek, king of justice and peace, without genealogy, only serves to prove the inadequacy of the levitical priesthood in relation to the priesthood of Christ.

But, as was to be expected after our study of the Old and New Testaments,

---

[26] In the description of the "priestly" work of Christ there is a basic imagery that makes it difficult to decide to what element the concept of "priesthood" precisely applies. It is impossible to determine the *"analogatum princeps"* of the priesthood. This fact is not sufficiently taken into account in the theology of the priesthood of Christ and of the hierarchical priesthood. It would enable us to see how the supreme and unique "priesthood" of Christ, which can only be defined by approximations, can be shared in through various legitimate forms of participation: the common priesthood of all the faithful based on baptism, and the ministerial priesthood based on ordination.

These forms of participation do not clash; each in its place is necessary and refers to the other; each finds legitimately its source in the supreme priesthood of Christ. For the priesthood of Christ as "archetype" in the letter to the Hebrews, cf. P. Idiart.

other themes—wider than those of the levitical priesthood—are assumed into the priestly perspective of the Epistle to the Hebrews.

2. Priesthood of Christ and the shepherding of the flock. With Melchizedek, and above all, through the constant reference to Psalm 110,[27] the theme of the king, connected besides with that of the shepherd (the king being the guide of his people), appears side by side with that of the priest. Like Moses and David, shepherds of the people of God,[28] Jesus is called "the great shepherd of the sheep" (Heb 13:20), in the sacrificial context of the "blood of the eternal Covenant". Thus, there exists a theology of the King-Shepherd, which runs without a break from the Old Testament,[29] to the parable of the Shepherd (Mt 18:12–14; Lk 15:5–7), where God himself through Jesus goes in search of the lost sheep, and finally to John 10:11–18, where the theme of the Shepherd laying down his life for his flock and that of the priest (in the sense of Heb 9:12–26; 10:10, 12) merge together in the Servant of Yahweh.

The title of the "great Shepherd of the sheep" thus becomes equivalent to the title of the "High Priest". This underlines the role of head and guide assumed by the Son of God in his priesthood. As pastor, and thanks to the offering of his blood, Christ marches at the head of the human community with which he has identified himself. Here is a Pastor, who, on behalf of men, his brothers, whom he embraces in his merciful goodness (Heb 2:17; 5:1), now faces the Father, for them and in their name (Heb 5:7–10). The priesthood of Christ thus combines, under the title of Pastor, the qualities of priest and king (cf. the comparisons with Moses and Joshua).

3. Sacrifice of Christ and sacrificial immolation. The idea of self-immolation finds a third root in the Epistle to the Hebrews. Chapter 11, in which the prefigurations of the Faith all positively point to Jesus, who is the *"archêgos kai teleiôtês"* of the Faith (Heb 12:2), often shows us some of the representative persons in a sacrificial attitude. Abraham[30] immolates his son, the pledge of the divine promise (Heb 11:17 and James 2:21; with the same motivation as Rom 4:17ff.).

---

[27] Heb 5:6; 6:20; 7:11, 17. According to Heb 1–3 the kingship of Christ consists in the fact that he is superior to the angels and to Moses.

[28] According to late Judaism Moses and David are the shepherds of the flock of God. Cf. O. Michel, *Der Brief an die Hebräer,* 6th ed. (1966), p. 536.

[29] Jer 2:8; 10:21; 23:1–3 (the bad shepherds); 3:15; 23:4–6 (the promise of the good shepherd: the "seed" = the Messiah); Ezek 34; Zech 11:4–7. Ezekiel (God as Shepherd seeks and nurses the lost sheep) is the literary source of the parable of Mt 18:12–14 and Lk 15:4–7, and finally of Jn 10:11–18; here the theme of the shepherd giving his life for his sheep merges with that of the priest in Hebrews.

[30] In the case of Abel (11:4), faith and martyrdom are united only at the end of the verse. Their union is not immediately intended, as in Mt 23:35, where Abel is mentioned first among the innocent martyrs.

Moses is at once the one who bears the insult of Christ and who institutes the rite of the Paschal Lamb and the sprinkling of its blood; therefore, there are here at once an existential assimilation to Jesus and the institution of a "priestly" cult. The last series of witnesses of the Faith extend from judges and kings to prophets and martyrs. The sufferings borne in view of eschatological salvation (of a "better resurrection": Heb 11:35b) are sharply illustrated. These heroes of a faith that implies suffering prefigured the death and the Resurrection of Christ. They must "wait for him" (Heb 11:13–16, 39ff.), but, with his coming, they will enter into the "city prepared by God". The relationship here is much less one of disjunction (as was the case with the levitical priesthood) than of fulfillment; the threshold is being crossed. Did not Jesus himself interpret his destiny in solidarity with that of the just and the suffering prophets (Mk 6:4; Mt 23:37; Lk 13:32ff.)? And did not the image of the Servant of Yahweh, the *Ebed Yahweh*, dominate the entire New Testament interpretation of the life of Jesus?[31]

Finally, the themes of Melchizedek, of the King-Shepherd, of some of the great believers and sufferers, and above all, of the Servant of Yahweh who sums them all up, determine more profoundly the priesthood of Christ than does the levitical priesthood.[32]

The priesthood of Christ is therefore undeniably presented with royal and prophetic characteristics. Jesus is truly the King-Priest, justifying men and bringing them the peace of God, from now onward "seated at the right hand of the majesty on high" (Heb 1:3; cf. 1:5–13). He is the Priest-Prophet (cf. the mention of the Servant of Yahweh). Furthermore, does not the prologue (Heb 1:1–2) present the Son of God as exercising in its fullness the ministry of the word that had been exercised by the prophets?

This priesthood expressed itself in the sacrifice that he made of himself, in obedience to his Father (Heb 5:7–10), "being made perfect" (Heb 5:9) by the Resurrection and Ascension and able to save "those who draw near to God through him" (Heb 7:25).

---

[31] The Servant is a "paradigmatic condensation of the image of the prophet, which during the seventh century became more and more that of a suffering mediator": G. Von Rad, *Theologie des Alten Testaments* II, p. 271; *Old Testament Theology* II (London, 1966), pp. 250ff.

[32] The idea of the victorious "forerunner" (Heb 6:20) to whom we look while running our own race expresses solidarity, as is well observed by W. Vischer: "No one wins the victory alone—this is the exciting experience of a relay race [*Staffellauf*]—; all win together and share in the same victory, when the last runner reaches the mark" (*Das Christuzeugnis des Alten Testaments* I, [1946], p. 303). According to Hebrews, the people of God, following in the footsteps of Jesus, is in the process of entering the heavenly temple (10:19ff.; 20:22ff.).

b. *The priestly dignity of Christ, by his abasement and radical obedience, qualifies him to assume and bring to perfection all the priestly attitudes of the Old Testament, leading them to the eschatological fullness of his role as Mediator*

The incomparable character of the priesthood of Christ, the basis of its eschatological position and efficacy, rests, according to the Epistle to the Hebrews, on the dignity of the Son of God, who contains fully in himself and transforms the multiple offices and ministerial functions of the Old Testament.

This dignity raises Christ above the "ministering spirits sent forth to serve" (Heb 1:14),[33] above "Moses, the faithful servant" (Heb 3:5),[34] above the priests chosen and installed in their office (Heb 5:1ff.);[35] it gives him a unique ministry (*leitourgia:* Heb 8:6). His position as Savior of the world does not, however, dispense him from having to be *installed* in his ministry (Heb 5:5; 7:11, 15), in an initial act of obedience that far exceeds that of other men charged with an office (Heb 10:5ff.); it also imposes on him a more radical experience of obedience (Heb 5:7–9) and effects in him the identification of an active sacrificial act (*prospherein:* Heb 9:25) with a total spiritual and physical immolation (*prosenechteis:* Heb 9:28). This obedience of the Son of God embraces both the ministerial priesthood and the existential attitudes of the other Old Testament offices, while surpassing them all, since his sacrificial obedience was exercised in virtue of an "eternal Spirit" (Heb 9:14) and of an "indestructible life" (Heb 7:16). These expressions seem to indicate how his obedience leads him irrevocably to agony and death. "This Spirit, therefore, is not something in Jesus' possession, but it is a Power that sustains his office and his sacrifice."[36] The dignity of the Son, which raises Jesus above all the priests

---

[33] *Leitourgika pneumata eis diakonian apostellomena:* 1:14.

[34] *Moyses. . . . Pistos. . . . Hôs therapôn:* 3:5.

[35] The ministerial character of the levitic priesthood is manifested by the priest's "installment" in the various cultic functions (5:1ff.) that "must" (*opheilei:* 5:3) be performed. The priest is *Kath' hēmeran leitourgōn:* 10:11.

[36] O. Michel, loc. cit., pp. 272, 314. The "dynamics" (7:15) that presides over the fate and death of Jesus "is a power that sustains Christ, not a characteristic inherent in his destiny": ibid., p. 273. Saint Paul expresses this by saying that Jesus is in full possession of the Spirit only after his Resurrection (2 Cor 3:17; Rom 1:1–5; 1 Cor 15:45; 5:17; Rom 8:9–11 to be compared with 1 Pet 3:18; 1 Tim 3:16). In the synoptics the investiture with the Spirit in baptism follows primarily the Old Testament scheme: Jesus speaks and acts *under* the impulse of the divine Spirit resting on him (Is 61:1 = Lk 1:18ff.); he possesses the Spirit and has him at his disposal only after his exaltation (Acts 2:33). John underlines that the Spirit "rests" upon Jesus (1:33) "in fullness" (3:34), but only after his glorification can Jesus breathe the Spirit (20:22), and only then will he be attested and justified by him. (Cf. R. Koch, *Geist und Messias* [1950]: 71–127. Luke extends the gift of the Spirit to the Incarnation itself, but the idea remains the same, for the Spirit has the active role in the Incarnation while the Son *allows* himself to become incarnate. This inversion in the soteriological functions of the Son and of the Spirit in relation to the immanent Trinity is fundamental as regards the priesthood of Christ and the ecclesial priesthood derived from it.)

of the Old Testament, immerses him more deeply than anyone else in the execution of his unique office, the ministerial character of which[37] is all the more clearly manifested as its discharge is more demanding: the "abasement" (Heb 2:9) of obedience that the only Son has to "learn" (Heb 5:7ff.) has no parallel in any purely human ministry.[38] Its dignity is equal to the holiness and absolute purity of the Son (Heb 7:26); it predestines him at once to be the definitive Priest (*ephapax*) *by a total ministerial obedience to the Spirit* and to be the definitive Victim which carries all sins (Heb 9:28). But the Son, in his priestly action, does not wish to show his own dignity. He is only the guarantee (*engyos*: Heb 7:22) of the "oath" of God who, by the death and Resurrection (Heb 13:20) of the Son, manifests himself as Truth and Fidelity.

In other words, the "priestly" work of Christ takes up and recapitulates in its unique structure all religious attitudes, personal and sociological; far from denying them or regarding them as extinct, it reaffirms them more forcefully.[39]

c. *The preceding considerations lead to the following conclusion: if the Epistle to the Hebrews does not permit one to deduce a New Testament ministerial priesthood from the priesthood of Christ, it permits one, however, to foresee its theological possibility*

The diverse "soteriological" functions of the Old Testament were not simply liquidated by Christ; they were rather taken up and perfected from within by his eminent dignity, which made possible an abasement (and thereby a ministry) without parallel.

The radical novelty of a priesthood founded on the divine Sonship appears everywhere, while at the same time the continuity with the traditions of Israel is made manifest.

[37] In his study *Das Wirken des Heiligen Geistes in den Gläubigen* (quoted after *Gott alles in allem*, Gesammelte Aufsätze [Mainz, 1961]: 86–112), H. Volk shows that in the consecration of Christ, which makes him the eschatological High Priest, there is besides the element of love and surrender a ministerial and juridical element. "When Christ receives the *gratia Capitis*, his consecration to the ministry includes a juridical element; his power as Savior could not be adequately defined without this. Grace itself includes elements of office and of law [p. 91]. In theology, these are true aspects of grace. They come from above. In the sacred subject (*sacer*), the Spirit brings about a right; this is why ecclesiastical law has a pneumatic element attached to it [p. 95]." We are here at the Christological source wherefrom the *"ius sanctum"* can originate in the Church; it necessarily supposes a juridical power capable of controlling and of safeguarding this right, that is, an actual and efficacious ministry.

[38] The adversative *kaiper* (Heb 5:8) does not only indicate the contrast between "Son of God" and "obedience"; it also points to an existential tension: the Lord must "learn" to obey.

[39] The convergence of the three functions already initiated in the Old Testament (Moses is guide, prophet, mediator, suffering, etc.) is fully realized in the transcendent function of Christ; after him it will become impossible to distinguish adequately the various functions. For a critique of the doctrine of the "three offices", cf. W. Pannenberg, *Jesus God and Man* (London, 1968), pp. 212ff.; Otto Semmelroth, *Das Geistliche Amt* (Mainz, 1958), pp. 108ff.

The entire people of God will have to follow the example of Christ (Heb 12:2ff.).[40] But, if the role of the great representatives of the Old Covenant has been taken so seriously, one can at least expect to see new ministries spring up (Heb 13:17) in the midst of the new pilgrim people. The doctrine of the Epistle to the Hebrews, then, is not at all opposed to the existence of a priestly ministry in the Christian community, if it is attested to by the rest of the Gospel.

C. Conclusion

Christ alone realized the perfect sacrifice in the offering he made of himself to the will of his Father. Thanks to this, he is the "mediator of the New Covenant" (Heb 9:15).

This priesthood based on the transcendence of his divine Sonship assumes the qualities of king and prophet. The priesthood of the New Covenant carries with it, then, in the amplitude of its mediation, the various other mediations that we have found in the history of Israel, notably those of the prophets and guides of the people. "It is necessary always to keep in view all these mediations in order to have an exact idea of the priesthood of Christ as found in the New Testament."

This priesthood is a ministry, a "service". It is the service of him who accomplishes the work of salvation willed by the Father by giving his life for men in a sacrifice of expiation. This is the service of the "Servant of Yahweh", of the Shepherd who gathers and builds up the community by making it heed the call of God and bringing to it his truth and his light.

This priestly ministry of Christ is rarely defined in priestly terms. But it is not words that count, but *the reality.* To go by words alone—leaving aside the explicit but late witness of the Epistle to the Hebrews—one could cast doubt on the priestly character of the eschatological ministry of Jesus. This leads to an important consequence: there is no reason to be astonished if the apostolic ministry is not explicitly presented in the New Testament in priestly terminology.

In this eschatological ministry of an entirely new kind, since it does not come from man but from God, Christ associated some of his disciples in a special manner, in order that they may represent him at the head of the community and, as it were, facing it. This is what we shall now study.

---

[40] According to Hebrews the people of God is still on its way to the Sabbath, which only Jesus has reached fully. This is why the New Covenant retains a character of *"nomos"* (7:12), of *"taxis",* of "legislation" (8:6). The great exhortations show that the salvation of the individual is not fixed, and that consequently the economy of faith, distinct from the Old "Law", continues under other forms in the New.

V. THE APOSTOLATE AND THE PRIESTLY MINISTRY

A. *The Mission of the Twelve*

We shall study successively the mission of the Twelve, the organization of the apostolic mission, the priestly terminology, communion, and service.

1. The Existence of the Group of Twelve

From the first decade, the group of Twelve, with Peter, far from being a collection of individuals was a group recognized as such. *The oldest confession of the Faith, that of the Palestinian Church* (1 Cor 15:15), gives a unique place to Peter and the group of Twelve (the Twelve are distinct from the "apostles" in the broad sense of the word: 1 Cor 15:7). Furthermore, *the most ancient stratum of the Synoptic Tradition* agrees with what is indicated in 1 Corinthians 15:15 and uses the phrase "the Twelve".

The Twelve who wielded authority in the Palestinian community were a group of privileged disciples chosen by Jesus and constituted by him *from the time of his earthly ministry*. The existence of this group before the Passion is *confirmed* by the reference to Judas as "one of the Twelve" (Mk 14:10, 20; Mt 26:14, 17; Lk 22:47; Jn 6:71).[41]

2. The Group of Twelve Is an Eschatological Institution

The phrase "he made the Twelve" (see Douay-Rheims, Mk 3:13–19) shows that the group was an *institution*. The verb "to make", used with names of persons or of a group of persons as direct object, refers to an Old Testament usage related to the institution of priests (1 Kings 13:33; 2 Chron 2:18). It is also said of God: "He made Moses and Aaron" (1 Sam 12:6). See also the New Testament formulas (Heb 3:2; Acts 2:36). Thus the group was *set*

---

[41] This question is treated in several excellent exegetical studies: H. Schlier, op. cit., 161–80; *Schreiben der deutschen Bischöfe über das priesterliche Amt, Eine biblisch-dogmatische Handreichung,* Sonderdruck herausgegeben vom Sekretariat der Deutschen Bischofskonferenz (Trier: Paulinus-Verlag, 1969); J. Coppens, "Le sacerdoce chrétien", *Nouvelle revue théologique* (1969): 225–45, 337–51 (published in book form under the title *Le sacerdoce Chrétien; Ses origines et son développement* [Leyde, 1970]; contains an up-to-date bibliography); J. Giblet, "Les Douze, histoire et théologie", in *Le prêtre; foi et contestation* (Gembloux: Duculot and Paris: P. Lethielleux, 1970), pp. 44–77; J. Colson, *Ministre de Jésus-Christ, ou le sacerdoce de L'Evangile* (Paris, 1961).

apart to play a role in the realization of the new world inaugurated by Jesus.

The institutional structure is again underlined by the saying "to be with Jesus". The primitive formula "he made the Twelve to be with him" (Mk 3:13, 16) signifies that the Twelve are *a creation of Jesus endowed with special powers.* They share his condition, and they are intimately associated with his person and his activity.

Furthermore, according to Matthew 19:28 and Luke 22:28–30, Jesus, head of the Kingdom that he had inaugurated, Son of Man raising up the new Israel foretold by the prophets, associates the group of the Twelve in his rule of the people of God.

At the decisive moment of the institution of the Eucharist, which reveals the meaning of his death, Jesus takes as his witnesses the Twelve in order to signify the role they would have to play one day in the New Covenant.

The Twelve, therefore, belong to the heart of the work of Jesus; instituted with a view to rule the new Israel, they were by that very fact charged with a *mission of an eschatological nature.*

3. The Apostles

Acts shows the direct relationship between the post-Resurrection exercise of the apostolate and its institution by Jesus, as well as the conferring of the Spirit as gift of the Savior (Acts 1:8; 4:29; 10:42). According to Luke, the Twelve are the *witnesses* (1:8; 10:34–43) not only of Christ risen and ascended into heaven but also of Christ who shared in our history (cf. Acts 1:21, 22). Their witnessing appears as a charge, an office (*episkopê:* 1:20), the *ministry of apostolate* (*diakonia apostolês:* 1:25). This is a function given by God in view of the salvation of the people of Israel and of the Gentiles.

After Mark (6:7) Luke reserves the title "apostle" to the Twelve (6:13; 9:10; 17:5; 22:14; 24:10). This title refers essentially to a *mandate* and to *authority:* "He who hears you hears me; and he who rejects you rejects me; and he who rejects me rejects him who sent me" (Lk 10:16). Thus the Church has more and more clearly understood that the ministry and the power of Jesus had been communicated to what represents the apostolate in a preeminent way, that is, to the *institution of the Twelve,* to the apostolic college centered around Peter.[42]

---

[42] The question may be asked whether Jesus used the term apostolos, or rather its aramaic equivalent. J. Dupont, in his study "Le nom d'apôtre a-t-il été donné aux Douze par Jésus?" *Orient Chrétien* (1965): 44ff., concludes negatively.

4. The Priestly Consecration

The Gospel of John reveals the meaning of the formula of institution of Mark 3:13–19. In the priestly prayer Christ is presented as the High Priest. As at the feast of the great Pardon (*Yom Kippur*) the high priest pronounced the name of God and prayed for himself, for the priests, and for the people, Christ revealed the name of God and prayed for himself, for the apostles, and for all the people. He prayed for the apostles that they might be *consecrated* in the truth (Jn 17:17).

"Father, consecrate them in the truth: your word is truth" (Jn 17:17). This is truly the formula of a sacerdotal institution (cf. Ex 29:1: "You will consecrate them to serve me in the priesthood"). The apostles were consecrated *in truth*; in relation to this consecration, that of Aaron and of his sons was only a shadow, as the law of Moses was itself only a shadow of the truth of the *Logos* (Jn 17:17 to be related to Jn 1:17). They were consecrated to preserve the word, that is, to gather men together by the Word that is Christ, in order that they might believe in him, and to raise up in the world "worshippers in spirit and in truth" (Jn 4:23–24).[43]

Thus, after the image of him whom the Father had consecrated and sent into the world (Jn 10:36), the apostles are consecrated and sent into the world (Jn 17:18; 20:21). It is for this that they share in the eschatological judicial power of Jesus, the Son of Man (Jn 20:22–23).

Like Jesus, the Servant-Shepherd, they are the servant-shepherds of the eschatological flock (cf. Jn 13:12–20; 21:15–17); they share in his eschatological service and are on this account made to share in the eschatological suffering of Christ and in his death. (In the Synoptic Gospels and in John the calls to the *apostolê* and the *apostolic mandate* are bound to the fact of following Christ and of being associated with the mystery of his suffering: Mk 8:34; 9:35ff.; 10:35ff.; Jn 13:1ff., 36ff.; 21:15ff.; Rev 1:24; 9:16; 21:9.)

5. The Apostolate and the Priestly Ministry

Therefore it is not surprising that in the apostolate of the Twelve there clearly appear the characteristics of the priestly ministry of the Savior.

---

[43] This point, already hinted at by M. J. Colson, is made clearly by a study of A. Feuillet, *Le sacerdoce chez Saint Jean* (unpublished). We may also mention the remark made by A. Feuillet: "Conscious as they are of having been chosen by Jesus for a sacred function, the apostles, in the Acts, are anxious to know whom Jesus has chosen to replace Judas in his office. By drawing lots in order to know this, they follow a custom that was commonly followed in the temple for the assignment of the various liturgical functions (Lk 1:9)" (*La doctrine des évangiles synoptiques sur l'Eglise*) (unpublished).

a. The first task is to announce the Gospel of the Kingdom. The apostles chose the service of the word in preference to the exercise of all other ministry (Acts 6:2–4).
b. The apostles are the *"episkopoi"*, the pastors of the flock (Acts 5:1–11; 8:14–17; 20:17–35).
c. Alongside the service of the word there is that of prayer (Acts 6:4). The liturgical and cultic function is little emphasized. There are, however, some indications: the apostles have the mission and power to baptize (Mt 28:19) and to remit sins (Mt 16:19; 18:18; Jn 20:20–23; Lk 24:47), the obligation and the right to celebrate the Lord's Supper (1 Cor 11:24–25; Lk 22:19); they are invited to anoint the sick (Mk 6:12); and they have authority over evil spirits (Mk 6:7).

6. Paul and the Apostolate of the Twelve

The vocation of Paul confirms the above. He never considered his ministry as different from that of the "apostles before him" (Gal 1:17). He is the ambassador of Christ, and as such is endowed with full *exousia*. He understands his mission as a delegation of the powers of Christ (cf. Gal 1:15; 2:8; 1 Cor 1:1; 15:10). Paul owed to God his vocation and his powers and called himself the messenger, the delegate, the ambassador, the plenipotentiary of Christ (2 Th 3:6; 1 Cor 1:10, 17; 2 Cor 5:20; 10:8; 13:3). As we will see later on, he often described his apostolate in formulas with priestly overtones.[44]

His constant, almost obsessive, preoccupation was to establish his right to the apostolate on a vision and mandate of the Lord; this shows that the apostolic Church, before which he had to explain his right, knew and admitted no other apostolate than that which derives from the express will of Jesus and is totally dependent on him.

The ministry of the Twelve, as that of Paul, was established by the call of Christ and by a mission from Christ in the power of the Spirit. It was not at all *founded* on charisms, though it *abounded* in them. *It was founded on a mandate of Christ.* It was a sending out (*apostolê*), a service (*diakonia*), a function (*oikonomia*), a public ministerial function (cf. Rom 1:1, 5; 10:15–17; 1 Cor 1:1, 17; 2:4ff., 10ff.; 9:16; 12:28; 2 Cor 3:6; 4:7ff.; 5:18ff.; 13:10; Gal 1:12ff.; Eph 3:2ff.; 4:11; Col 1:25).

This ministry consists in the proclamation and the presentation of Christ who died and rose for the world, in the actualization of the offering of Christ through the apostolic preaching of the Gospel by which is brought about the

[44] Cf. on this topic the study of P. Grelot. *Pierre et les Douze* (unpublished); E. Cothenet, *Les prophètes du Nouveau Testament* (unpublished).

building up of the Church. It is through this that Christ makes his sacrifice present.

Christ works through Paul in order to obtain the obedience of the gentiles (Rom 16:15, 18). The apostle was the ambassador of Christ (2 Cor 5:20); he preached Christ (1 Cor 15:12; 2 Cor 1:19; 4:5; Phil 1:17–18; Col 1:28; Gal 1:16) and him crucified (1 Cor 1:23; Gal 3:1). In the proclamation of the apostolic Gospel, Christ crucified made himself and his sacrifice present, as he made himself present in the announcement of his death through the eucharistic celebration (1 Cor 11:26). In his envoy Christ is present (Mt 10:40; Lk 10:16; Jn 13:20) and fulfills his office of reconciliation (2 Cor 5:18–20).

The apostolic service is therefore *priestly* in the sense that through the Gospel announcement, Christ makes himself present in his sacrifice. It draws the apostle into the suffering and death of Christ and makes him share in his Passion. Through this *eschatological* suffering the advent of the eschatological time is brought about (2 Cor 6:12; 1 Cor 10:10; Rom 10:14–17; 13:11).[45]

7. The Meaning of the Apostolate of the Twelve

The *exousia* of Jesus is prolonged and perpetuated in the community of believers only through the *apostolate* in the strict sense, that is, by the ministry of the Twelve.

Since the *exousia* of Christ is eschatological and priestly, the apostolate of the Twelve—and of Paul—is equally so because it is a participation in it.

The apostolic function that rested on the express will of Christ, on a *mandate* and on the charismatic gift of the Spirit, has therefore for its fundamental role to call men to become the priestly people whom Christ presents to his Father. Its priestly value comes from this: that it is the *efficacious sign,* willed by Christ, that the priestly people is not constituted by giving to itself the word that summons and sanctifies but receives it from God as a grace.

B. *The Organization of the Apostolic Mission*

The participation in the priestly apostolate of the Twelve through the different ministries instituted and sanctified by the apostolic Church, which was interpreting the will of the Savior, appears less clearly than the facts

---

[45] On this question, cf. H. Schlier, op. cit., 164–68.

that we have analyzed above. The reason is that a long period of maturation was necessary for the Church to determine its ministries.[46]

The fundamental task of bearing witness to the farthermost extremities of
the world (Acts 1:7–8) and to rule the community of believers had been
entrusted to the Twelve. But the Twelve by themselves could not spread this
message throughout the world. They were assisted by other missionaries, but
always with reference to the Twelve and to their witness. This is the sense in
which one can speak of succession, or better, of association with their task.
This view is confirmed by the apostolic writings such as the letter of Barnabas
(8:3) and Justin (1 Apol. 31; 39; 40; 42; 43; 5; 50; 53), who declare that each
Christian has been put in direct contact with the witnessing of the Twelve.

The apostles, chosen and instituted by Christ, chose collaborators (*episkopoi*,
presbyters, deacons), who derive their mission from the Spirit (Acts 20:28).
These ministers were like the apostles themselves workers of the Gospel (1 Cor
3:3–4, to be compared with 2 Tim 2:15), soldiers of the good fight (cf. 2 Cor
10:3, to be compared with 2 Tim 2:3), fellow workers (1 Th 3:2; 2 Cor 8:3) in
the militia of Christ (Phil 2:25). They are often referred to with the metaphor
of the pastor (Acts 20:28; Eph 4:11; 1 Pet 5:2).

The Acts and the Epistles of St. Paul offer us material to reconstruct the
outlines of the constitution of the hierarchy: institution of the "seven" at
Jerusalem (Acts 6:1–6), of presbyters (Acts 11:30; 14:23; 15:2–6; 20:17; 21:18;
22:23) whom we find at Jerusalem, Lystra, Iconium, Antioch of Pisidia and
Miletus and to whom the pastoral Epistles (1 Tim 4:14; 5:17; Titus 1:5), the
First Letter of Peter (1 Pet 5:1), and the Letters of John (2 Jn 1; 3 Jn 1) make
allusion.

1. Charismatic or Institutional Structure?

Basing themselves on the studies of Käsemann, some Catholic writers distinguish two types of structures in the Church, the "charismatic structure",
distinctively Pauline, and the structure of the Palestinian communities (with
the presbyterate and the imposition of hands for the conferring of the power
of Order).

"In Corinth there were neither *episkopoi* nor presbyters, nor ordinations,
but, apart from the authority of the apostle, only a spontaneous manifestation
of charisms. Despite this, according to the testimony of Paul himself, the
Church at Corinth was a community provided with everything that was

[46] For this topic we refer to the study of P. Grelot, "Reflexions sur la structure ministerielle
de l'Eglise selon Saint Paul" (chap. 2, n. 1) and to that of E. Cothenet, mentioned here above
in n. 44. See also J. Colson. *Ministre de Jésus-Christ, ou le sacerdoce de l'Evangile* (Beauchesne,
1961).

necessary, equipped with the preaching of the word, baptism, the celebration of the Lord's Supper, and other ministries."[47]

This position, based on the thesis of the Bultmannian school, according to which the Christian community would have been governed by charismatics, that is, by prophets who transmitted, expounded, and put together the prophetic and apocalyptic logia of the Lord (as, for instance, Mt 11:21–24; 25:1–13; Lk 6:22–23; 19:42–44; 23:28–31), the institution of *episkopoi* and deacons being a later innovation, cannot stand up to a critical analysis. But it obliges us to show more clearly the place of the Spirit in the primitive Church.

2. The Apostles as Prophets of the New Covenant

Prophetism in the New Testament is strictly *connected* with the apostolate, or, to be more exact, the apostolate has a *prophetic* character. According to the first Gospel, Jesus stands at the beginning of a new prophetism: "Behold I am sending you prophets and wise men and scribes" (Mt 23:34; cf. also the logia with an archaic terminology where the ambassadors of Jesus are presented as "prophets and righteous men": Mt 10:41; cf. 13:17). Superior to their predecessors of the Old Covenant because they receive the revelation of the mysteries of the Kingdom (Mat. 13:11 and parallel texts; 16:17; cf. 11:25ff.), the disciples whom Jesus chose and established as *the Twelve* with his full authority (Mk 3:14 and par.) are his envoys, just as the prophets were those of Yahweh.

The Acts, moreover, attribute a very important place to the intervention of the Holy Spirit in the early Church. The text of Joel announcing the outpouring of the Spirit in prophecy (quoted in Acts 2:17–21) is considered as a program for the future. This Spirit enables the Twelve to exercise their role of witness: "We are witnesses of these things, we and the Holy Spirit" (Acts 5:32).

The strict connection between apostolate and prophecy is also well known as far as Paul is concerned. He received his mission by a revelation (Gal 1:15), and he considered his mission in the same terms as Jeremiah and the suffering Servant. Moreover, the charism of the apostolate implies in a sense all other gifts (cf. 1 Cor 12:28; Eph 4:11).

Finally, the expression "apostles and prophets" (Eph 2:20) probably denotes the apostles, inasmuch as they were revealers of the mysterious plan of God. It refers to the unique and incommunicable function of the apostles as founding witnesses from whom is necessarily derived the knowledge of Christ. By using the image of the foundations, this text alludes to the investiture of

---

[47] H. Küng, *Die Kirche* (Freiburg, 1967), p. 520; cf. *The Church* (London, 1967), p. 442.

Cephas and is strongly rooted in the long Tradition that regards the community of salvation as the temple of God or the heavenly Jerusalem. This thought is very near to that of the major Epistles. One cannot, therefore, on the basis of Ephesians 2:20, oppose the charismatic view of the Church, which would be that of Paul to the institutional view, which from Jerusalem would have spread to Asia Minor under the influence of the pastoral Epistles, and later of St. Ignatius of Antioch.[48]

3. Apostles, Prophets, and Teachers

Along with the Twelve and Paul joined to them as the one born out of time (1 Cor 15:8), the "apostles and teachers" played an important role in the life of the early community. The prophets mentioned in 1 Corinthians 12:28 are not just any kind of inspired persons of Corinth; they are "prophets" of the early community. In the triad "apostles, prophets, teachers", the theological value of the verb used (*etheto*), the importance given to the triple classification (*prôton, deuteron, triton*), and the awkwardness of the insertion in the development of the sentence show that Paul is using here a traditional list and refers to the *fundamental structures of the Church.* To the Corinthians, tempted to build a community according to their own liking, Paul emphatically recalls that the word of God did not originate from among them but from Jerusalem (1 Cor 14:36) and that it is necessary to hold to the *kerygma* as unanimously proclaimed and taught in the Church.

The early list—"first apostles, second prophets, third teachers"—is to be compared to the logia in which Christ announced the sending of "prophets and righteous men", or of "prophets, wise men, and scribes". The terminology was not fixed at the first attempt, but the essential notions were there: the mission depending on Christ, the interior assistance of the Holy Spirit, the duty of proclaiming the message to Jews and gentiles, and afterward to give a more methodical instruction to the converts.

The Acts give some indications as regards the activity of these "prophets" (cf. *Barnabas* and also the *Seven,* and above all *Stephen* and *Philip*). There is no incompatibility between the charism of prophecy and the institutional organization of the Church: the apostles and the elders of Jerusalem sent, in fact, *Judas* and *Silas,* who were prophets (Acts 15:32), to Antioch to explain to the converted gentiles the decree that proclaimed their liberty in relation to the law. At Antioch, moreover, prophets and teachers jointly directed the community (Acts 13:1).[49]

---

[48] Cf. R. Bultmann, H. F. Von Campenhausen, E. Kasemann, E. Schweitzer, H. Küng. For this entire question we follow the remarks made by E. Cothenet in the study mentioned in n. 44.

[49] Here also we follow the argumentation of E. Cothenet.

4. Structuring of the Communities

At the very moment when the Holy Spirit raised up new initiatives and vocations necessary for the life of the early Church, as the Acts and the First Epistle to the Corinthians testify, there took place a first structuring of the communities, in Palestine with the college of the elders and at Philippi with the *episkopoi* and the deacons.

Paul never thought he was organizing the communities on any other model than that of the Churches in Judaea, even though he proclaimed liberty with regard to the law. He was constantly concerned with the cohesion between the communities that he founded among the gentiles and the mother Church of Jerusalem. He refers to the traditions of this Church in order to correct the abuses at Corinth or to reestablish the purity of doctrine (1 Cor 11:16–23; 15:1, 11; 1 Th 2:14).

Furthermore, when, at Ephesus, Paul wrote his Letter to the Corinthians, the reason why he addressed it to "all the saints" is that the heads of the community were with him (16:15–18). The request "to be subject to such men" (16:16) recalls 1 Thessalonians 5:12ff. The existence of charisms, therefore, does not in any way exclude the function of the local heads of the community.

There are even many indications that there were presidents appointed (1 Th 5:12) in the community of Corinth. This appears in particular in the discussions at the beginning of the letter on the importance given to Apollo, who is put on the same footing as Paul and Cephas (1:12; 3:4–5) and who receives like Paul the title of "God's fellow worker" (3:9), of "steward of the mysteries of God" (4:1). It is true that Apollo was not at Corinth when Paul wrote his letter, but he is due to go there without delay (16:12), and nothing allows us to think that in his absence there was no "pastor" in that town.

The comparison between the Church of Corinth and the Church at Philippi, the Church so dear to Paul, is also very enlightening. We read in the address of the Letter to the Philippians, the doctrinal affinities of which with the major Epistles (Rom; 1 Cor; 2 Cor; Gal) is being more and more stressed by exegetes today: "Paul and Timothy, servants of Jesus Christ, to all the saints in Christ Jesus who are at Philippi, together with their *episkopoi* and *deacons*" (Phil 1:1). Paul, therefore, did not rely simply on the blossoming of charisms for keeping the communities in the right faith and in the fervor of charity. This witness permits us to connect the prescriptions given in the pastoral letters with the activity of the apostle—whatever opinion one may have as regards the redaction of these Epistles. And it is impossible to reject as a nonhistorical interpolation of Luke the indication given in Acts 14:23 according to which Paul from his very first journey established presbyters in each Church.

The comparison between the different lists of charisms shows that besides the three titles of apostles, prophets, teachers, which were well rooted in the oldest organization of the Church (cf. Acts 13:1), there is no other fixed terminology. The situation was fluid in this period when so many young communities were born.

5. Apostolic Tradition

The role of the ministers appointed by the apostles to be their collaborators is defined in the first place by the proclamation of the Gospel (*euaggelizesthai, kêrussein, didaskein, lalein, parakalein, paraggelein:* cf. 2 Tim 1:8, 13; 2:2; 4:2, 5; 1 Tim 4:11, 13; 6:20). But it includes also the direction of liturgical service (1 Tim 3:9; 4:13) and the activity of guiding the community (1 Tim 3:15; 5:17–19; cf. 1 Pet and the pastoral Letters).

These ministries (presbyteroi *or episkopoi*) were linked to the apostles, and, as the pastoral Epistles show, they were *founded* on the apostolic Tradition and governed by it (1 Tim 3:7, 15; 4:6, 11–16; 6:17; 2 Tim 1:13ff.; 2:2, 7; 3:11–14; Titus 1:5). 1 Corinthians 4:17 already makes this apostolic dependence explicit.

The pastors who were responsible for the Churches never exercised their function except to assure the faithfulness of their communities to their initial *apostolic* structure.

Hardly forty years after the First Letter to the Corinthians, Clement of Rome writes to them another famous letter in which he affirms, as an uncontested and well-known truth, that, from the time of the apostles, there have always been pastors officially established in the Churches and especially at Corinth. In this connection he recalls that Apollo was one of these men to whom obedience was due, a man tested and appointed by the apostles (47:4), as were the *episkopoi* (42:4) and their successors (44:2). Clement does not only speak of authority and obedience. He refers to the role of *episkopoi*, priests, and deacons in the liturgy, in the offering of gifts and the priestly service (41:2; 43:2–6; 44:4).

The patristic Tradition remained unanimous on these points. In the Letters of Ignatius of Antioch, there is no place for a community without an established hierarchy; there is no Eucharist without the presidency of the bishop or his delegate. St. Irenaeus, in the struggle he was engaged in against the gnostic heresy, insists above all on the teaching function of the bishops, who have received the "sure charism of the truth" (*Adv. Haer.,* IV, 26, 2). Hippolyte of Rome presents the bishops as the successors of the apostles in the triple function of teacher, priest, and pastor; the presbyters were their collaborators.

Such is the unanimous conviction of the Catholic writers of the patristic period. Such is also the teaching that appears in the ancient liturgical texts.[50]

While leaving place for an important evolution in the ministries, one cannot therefore oppose a "charismatic constitution" of the Pauline Churches to the "episcopal-presbyteral constitution". For, in the mind of the Christians of the early Church, there was no opposition between the freedom of the Spirit in the outpouring of his gifts (1 Cor 12:11) and the existence of a fundamental structure in the Church (1 Cor 12:18).

Besides, very soon a liturgical action came to express both the continuity with the unique fact of the Incarnation and the movement coming from the Spirit; it is the imposition of hands. This gesture has its roots in Jewish customs and, before that, in the example of Moses, who laid hands on Joshua to communicate to him the Spirit of wisdom (Dt 34:9). The prophecy mentioned in this context (1 Tim 1:18) signifies the liturgical words that communicated the Spirit.

Thus, it is an undue projection of our modern problems that induces some to discover in the Church, at the end of the first century and the beginning of the second, a struggle between the charismatics and the institutional ministry. The "men of the Spirit" are the bishops, like Ignatius of Antioch, the "theophorous" (Ad Eph., 9, 2), like Polycarp of Smyrna, the "apostolic and prophetic teacher", as the author of his Martyrdom calls him (XVI, 2). In the Didache we see the transition from one stage to the other without any appearance of conflict on this point. Polemics, on the contrary, are vigorously carried on against the innovators.

---

[50] See the report of J. Lécuyer (unpublished). The problem of the succession of bishops at Alexandria in the first centuries cannot be treated here. Cf. on this point J. Lécuyer, "Le problème des consécrations épiscopales dans L'Eglise d' Alexandrie" Bulletin de littérature ecclésiastique (1964): 241–57. It has been maintained that the patriarch of Alexandria did not receive the episcopal consecration through the laying on of hands by the bishops, but was enthroned and perhaps consecrated by the presbyters of the city. Cf. W. Telfer, "Episcopal Succession in Egypt", The Journal of Ecclesiastical History 3 (1952): 1–13. This opinion is refuted by E. W. Kemp, "Bishops and Presbyters at Alexandria", Journal of Ecclesiastical History 6 (1955): 125–42. In the last years, however, various Catholic studies on the ministry have taken for granted the affirmations of W. Telfer. Cf. Fr. Van Beeck, "Towards an Ecumenical Understanding of the Sacraments", Journal of Ecumenical Studies 3 (1966): 83, n. 45 ("Telfer concludes his careful historical analysis as follows . . . "); H. J. McSorley, "Protestant Eucharistic Reality and Lack of Orders", The Ecumenist, July 5, 1967, p. 69; D. J. O'Hanlon, "A New Approach to the Validity of Church Orders", in Reconsiderations, Roman Catholic, Presbyterian and Reformed Theological Conversations 1966–1967 (New York, 1967), p. 148, and p. 155, n. 26. (The author goes even beyond Telfer, for he extends the case to "a number of churches in the first centuries", p. 148.)

J. Lécuyer has shown in his article published in Bulletin de littérature ecclésiastique that none of the arguments brought forth stands the test of serious scrutiny.

C. *Priest or Servant?*

Two further important questions arise from the New Testament.

Why does the New Testament not use a priestly terminology to define the functions of the ministers of the Church?

Why and how was the priestly terminology reintroduced to designate the ministers of the Church? What is the meaning of this fact?

1. Priestly Ministry and Priestly Terminology

The word *archhiereus* in the Epistle to the Hebrews is applied to Christ only. Further, the word *hierateuma* is given to the people of God only in 1 Peter 1:9, and the word *hiereus* is found only in Revelation (1:15, etc.). The verb *hierourgein* is indeed used by Paul, but it can be said that in general the ministries examined in the preceding pages are not described in priestly terms.

The absence of a specifically priestly terminology in the beginning of the Church is easily explained. The term *hiereus* in fact designated, on the one hand, the priests of the Old Law and, on the other, the ministers of pagan cults. Borrowing from Jewish terminology would have been all the more ambiguous as the faithful of the Judaeo-Christian churches continued for some time to frequent the temple of Jerusalem. The Epistle to the Hebrews and later the Letter of Barnabas are the first documents that treat *explicitly* of the Jewish temple. Neither did the early Church use the terms current in profane circles to designate its own hierarchy, *archê, telos, timê,* because it was conscious of the specific character of its own institutions.

a. *The specific character of Christian terminology*

Christ never gave to himself the title "high priest"; he designated himself as the *Servant* and the *Pastor* who gives his life for his sheep. He was thus able to show his priestly ministry in its specific character without connecting it to Jewish images that could have contaminated its meaning.

It was therefore inconceivable that the apostles could have designated themselves by any other title than *servant,* all the more so since Christ, "who came not to be served but to serve and to give his life for the multitude", had frequently insisted on the necessity that they should be, like him, servants.

This term is thus the best indication of the Christological foundation of the Christian ministry.

To take only two striking examples, Peter and Paul conceived their ministry in terms of servant.

Peter and the Servant: Peter had been confronted with the mystery of the

Servant (Mt 16:23), and he had denied it. To be made by Christ the head of the Church, Peter needed to discover through tears the mystery of his Lord who became Servant.

Like Christ, Peter became par excellence the pastor of the flock. He found himself conformed to Christ the suffering Servant who gave his life for his sheep, and he imitated his master even unto death (Jn 21:15–20).

He exhorted the presbyters who exercised pastoral care (1 Pet 5:2–5) to be models for their flocks (cf. Jn 21:15; the formula "not as domineering . . . but being examples" recalls also the washing of the feet: Jn 19:13–14).

The only title of glory for the apostle, then, was to be pastor and servant after the image of the Servant.[51]

Paul and the suffering Servant: The numerous references in the Epistles or the Acts to Isaiah 42:53 allow us to affirm that Paul used to apply these prophecies to himself. When he spoke of his own mission he recalled what Isaiah had said of the mission of the Servant. The references to Isaiah in Galatians 1:15–16 have often been highlighted by exegetes; likewise, the allusions to Isaiah in Acts (13:47; 18:9–10; 21:11, 36; 22:22; 26:16–18) are well known. They show clearly that the mission of the apostle to the gentiles is described with traits borrowed from the suffering Servant and from Christ of the Gospels. In brief, the Acts of the Apostles and the Pauline Epistles concur in showing that the mission of the apostle to the gentiles fulfilled the prophecies of the Servant, in imitation of the life and suffering of Christ.

The mystery of this likeness of Paul to the suffering Servant appears clearly in the crucifying paradox of his apostolic life, as summarized in the beautiful expression "we carry this treasure, [the apostolate and the glory of the New Testament] in earthen vessels" (2 Cor 4:7). Paul bore in himself the poverty of the agonies of Christ (Col 1:24) and his death, to give life to those to whom he preached the word. Death is Paul's participation in the mystery of the Servant; it is his humble condition as apostle (1 Cor 2:3–5; 2 Cor 4:7); it is the oppositions, the misunderstandings that he encountered, the suffering for the salvation of others (1 Cor 15:31), leading up to the desire to be poured out as a libation on the sacrifice of the Faith of the believers (Phil 2:17). Life is the glory of the word of God transforming souls and making their lives fruitful.

In short, in the numerous trials of his apostolate (poverty, persecution, manifold privations: 2 Cor 3:7–9), Paul experienced the sharing in the Passion of Christ, conformity to his death (Phil 3:10; Gal 2:19; 2 Tim 2:9–11), in order that the Spirit might enter into the hearts of the gentiles. The ministry of the Spirit that he exercised is the reflection of the life of Jesus on a body that is undergoing the death of Jesus (2 Cor 3:1–11). The Second Epistle to the

---

[51] On this theme, cf. M. J. Le Guillou, "Pierre et le Serviteur", in "La participation dans l'Eglise", in *Problems actuels du catholicisme français*, C.C.I.F. (Paris: Desclée de Brouwer, 1969) 148–55.

Corinthians, like an apostolic charter, sums up the entire apostolic paradox (2 Cor 5:20–6:10).

The fundamental law of the apostolic life is, therefore, the manifestation of the power of the Lord in the weakness of the apostle (2 Cor 12:9). It reproduces in the apostle's life the spiritual pattern of the life of Christ.

In such a perspective it is clear that the priestly terminology as such could not be in the foreground. But this does not mean that it is totally absent.[52]

b. Indications of a priestly terminology

The term "service" is the one usually used for the apostolic activity, but it can also include all activities in the Church. That is why, in order to determine what exactly the apostolic service was—an eschatological service of the people of God—it is good to specify that it is not any kind of service. It was a service for God (2 Cor 6:4; 1 Th 3:2), for Christ (2 Cor 11:23; Col 1:7), for the Gospel (Eph 2:7; Col 1:23; 1 Th 3:2), for the New Covenant (2 Cor 3:6), for believers and their salvation (1 Cor 3:5), a service in the Lord (Eph 6:21; 2 Cor 4:17).

The "pastoral" and "servant" terminology, no doubt, implicitly supposes a priestly perspective, specified by the unique character of the mystery of Christ.

But many indications show, particularly in Paul, a specific consciousness of priesthood. Paul understood his apostolate as a priestly work, and he used priestly terminology (Rom 15:15–16, to be compared with Sir 50). In this perspective the loss of his own life was for him a sacrifice (Phil 2:17). Further, Paul, in his apostolic work, relentlessly tried to bring about the sacrificial reconciliation of the world with God (2 Cor 5:20); this terminology is typically priestly. He explained his personal mission as the prolongation of that of Christ, that is, a true reconciliation of the world with God (2 Cor 5:18). He qualified it as "ministry of reconciliation", diakonia tês katallagês (2 Cor 5:18), which he exercised as a plenipotentiary of Christ (2 Cor 5:20). One could also mention the terminology of blessing. Paul will come "in the fullness of the blessing of Christ" (Rom 15:29). And we have seen above that his entire ministry made present the sacrifice of Christ.[53]

Here we may add, as has already been remarked above, that in the New

---

[52] On this topic, cf. L. Cerfaux, "Saint Paul et le Serviteur de Dieu d'Isaïe", in Recueil Lucien Cerfaux, vol. 2: 439–54. See Acts 13:17 with the quotation from Is 49:6; 18:9–10, with an implicit quotation of Is 41:9–10; 21:11, with an allusion to Christ the suffering Servant; 21:36 and 22:22, with an allusion to Is 53:7; 26:16–18, with an allusion to Is 42:7–16. This view has been developed by H. Denis and A. Feuillet.

[53] Cf. H. Schlier, op. cit.; J. Coppens. op. cit., 236–37. See also Cl. Wiener, "Hierourgein (Rom 15:16)", in Studiorum Paulinorum Congressus Internationalis Catholicus, 1961 (Analecta Biblica, 17–18 [Rome, 1963], vol. 2: 399–404). See also A. M. Denis, "La fonction apostolique et la liturgie nouvelle", Revue des sciences philosophiques et théologiques 52 (1958): 401–36, 617–56.

Testament the ministry of the *presbyteros* or of the *episkopos* is not a priestly ministry because it makes present the sacrifice of Christ in the eucharistic celebration. It is priestly in the sense that *in his entire activity* the *presbyteros* or the *episkopos* makes present the priestly service of Christ, his offering, his being "for us", in the word, in sufferings, in patience, in short, in his whole life.

2. Terminology Priestly or Ministerial

The ministries studied above are only in rare occasions described in expressly priestly terms. From this it has often been concluded that the "sacerdotalization" or the "resacralization" of the ministry is explained by the influence of the Old Testament on the Christian community, and later, after Constantine, by the transfer of the prerogatives of the pagan priesthood to the Christian ministers.

One fact is certain: though the New Testament and the greater part of the first Christian writings avoid not only the terms that designated the priests of the Old Testament but also all connection or comparison with them, little by little Christian writers have taken up these very terms and made comparisons.

In all likelihood, priestly terminology occurred in a *typological* perspective, which brings out more clearly the distance that separates the image from the reality. Does not St. John already have a doctrine of Christ the High Priest and of the apostles as consecrated, even though the terms "high priest" and "priest" are not used? Is not the opposition between the shadow and the reality (Moses and Christ) already present in his teaching? Along with him, Paul, in his Second Epistle to the Corinthians, opposes the ministry of Moses to that of the Spirit (2 Cor 3:7–10).

In the comparisons that were made, the essential fact remained. Any continuity between the institutions of the Old and the New Testament is always very firmly excluded: the ministry of the New Testament is derived not from Aaron or from Moses but from the apostles and from Christ himself. The priestly ministry in the first Christian generations, free from a possible contamination through Jewish ideas, affirms its distinctive character in relation to the Old Testament.

However, this approach, basically quite legitimate, is not without danger, if the specific nature of the priesthood of Christ should be obscured.

It has, in fact, happened that the influence of the Old Testament on the Christian concept of ministry made itself felt to the point of lessening its evangelical character. The Fathers of the period of the martyrs invoked the institutions and legal dispositions of the Old Testament as a support either for the order established in the Church or for the rules of morality laid down for the clergy, or for the obedience due to the hierarchical ministries. Thus, the reference to the Old Testament has contributed to fix the priestly and cultic terminology of Christianity and to give a certain prestige to the clergy and even to a particular clerical state. This moralizing tendency went on increasing, especially in the West, after the invasion of the fifth century.[54]

Moreover, the tendency to find the origin of Christian institutions in the Old Testament has affected the concept of priesthood itself. St. Jerome opened the way, and St. Isidore passed on to the Middle Ages the idea that the different orders (from bishop to porter) had their type and origin in the Mosaic cultic service. There is no doubt that such considerations emphasized the cultic character of the priestly ministry. This evolution was, moreover, in keeping with the sacral view of society as it developed in the Middle Ages and in which there persisted the influence of a supratemporal and sacralizing essentialism, with its lack of perceptiveness for human initiative and history. This sacralization undoubtedly brought about, at least partly, the explosion of the Reformation.[55]

D. *Service and Communion*

The remarks that we have made show how necessary it is to be deeply aware of the *radical newness* of the priesthood of Christ, expressed in his demeanor of Son of Man, who came as Servant of God, to give his life for men (Mk 10:45; Mt 20:18).

This is as necessary for a deep understanding of the meaning of Christian life itself as it is for the rediscovery of the priestly ministry in its theological dimension. For Vatican II has defined the work of the Church and the priestly ministry as "service".

The whole life of the Church, through the sacraments, particularly the Eucharist, is in fact a communion in the mystery of the Servant, obedient to his Father who has *consecrated and sent him* into the world (Jn 10:36) *to give his life* for this world (Jn 10:17–18).

All Christians, therefore, Pope, bishops, priests, and faithful, share in the same mystery of obedience to the Father in the Spirit. All live together, according to each one's condition, the same mystery of obedience, so that their mutual relations are defined by a common spiritual structure of obedience. Each shows to the other the mystery of obedience in the Spirit that he is called to live.

It is this common obedience to the Spirit and in the Spirit that makes the entire life of the Church a "communion", a worship "in spirit and in truth", a worship of faith that embraces the life of the world to offer it in thanksgiving to the Father in the fire of the Spirit.

[54] On this topic, cf. Y. Congar, "Two Factors in the Sacralization of Western Society During the Middle Ages", *Concilium* n. 47 (1969): 28–33.

[55] Cf. op. cit., 54–55ff.

Pastors and faithful, "who are all called to holiness and have all equally received the Faith that leads them in the justice of God" (cf. 2 Pet 1:1) (*LG*, 32), are united with one another in the fraternal ties of communion and service.

This is, and we repeat it once more, that the ministerial priesthood is never separated from the Church: it exists *within* the assembly, *under* the sacraments; it is *open* to the light of God in Christ, in order that the whole community may become conformed to the image of God.

Thus, the people cannot exercise their ministry without priestly minister, but, similarly, the latter—bishop or priest—cannot fulfill his priestly office without the people, for he exists only in the priestly community. "No Church without bishop and no bishop without Church", said St. Cyprian later.[56]

VI. THE PRIESTLY MINISTRY AS ESCHATOLOGICAL SERVICE

The present crisis and the data of Scripture and Tradition oblige us to insist on some *theological* points.

A. *The Radical Newness of the Priestly Ministry*

The priesthood of Christ brought about in human history an *absolute break* while *fulfilling the promises in an unforeseen manner.* It ushered in the eschatological era with a *radical newness.*

Because he was the Son of God, Christ, by a free act of love—an act made once for all, though it comprised several moments: the Cross and Resurrection, the gift of the Spirit, the mission confided to the apostles for all times— redeemed mankind and founded his Church, giving it, along with grace and eternal life, its essential structures and its means of grace.

The apostolic ministry was marked so deeply by this action of Christ that, breaking away from the ancient ministries, it appeared as the *ministry of a radical newness, the ministry of the Spirit* (2 Cor 3:4–12).

Therefore, there can exist in the Church no priestly ministry that would not go back to this initial act of foundation. This is the meaning of what we call apostolic succession. It means that the priestly ministry had its origin in the will of God, historically expressed in Jesus Christ, through the sacramental sign of the imposition of hands. It is a form of existence of the active,

---

[56] This idea is always stressed in the Eastern tradition, especially among the Orthodox.

efficacious, and eternal presence of the risen Christ to his Church: "And lo, I am with you always, to the close of the age" (Mt 28:20).[57]

This is to say that the fundamental structure of the priestly ministry depends entirely on the mystery of Christ, the Word of God unveiling the fullness of his meaning and efficacy in his death and Resurrection.

As eschatological service destined to lead men to call upon the name of Christ (Rom 15:20), the priestly ministry cannot be reduced to some sort of sociological function within the Church; as such, it cannot either be considered as a spiritualized or mortalized version of an ancient religious structure or, on the contrary, as the sacralization of pagan and worldly structures. It is *theologically* founded on the singular eschatological ministry of Christ. We may say that it is the service of the active and properly eschatological power of the Word of God, Jesus Christ who died and rose again; its visible signs are the announcement of the Gospel and the sacramental actions.

It has become a necessity for the Church of today to put in full relief the absolutely unique and properly eschatological structure of the priestly ministry. For this ministry is no more protected by the sociological structures of a Christian society; its authority, respect for which has often been guided by sociological habits, is now questioned. It is, therefore, of the utmost importance that the authority of this ministry be given its true meaning, which has nothing to do with power understood in the sense of the world. Just as Christ was given the power to represent his Father only by being humble and self-dispossessed (cf. Jn 5:19ff., 22), so too the priestly ministry has only the power of representing Christ in the measure in which it shares in the mystery of Christ humbling and emptying himself. As the New Testament underlines, participation in the eschatological ministry of Christ supposes a radically new concept of authority, namely, that of the Servant (Mk 10:42–45), which includes the participation in the eschatological sufferings of Christ. Only a ministry exercised in the spirit of the Servant will recover its credibility; it is the weakness of the minister that reveals the power of the Spirit (cf. 2 Cor 12:10).

The image of the Shepherd, which shows the continuity between the ministerial character of the priesthood of Christ and the ministry derived from it, underlines also this perspective. For, from a Christological viewpoint, the "Shepherd" is one who has received from God the "mandate" and the "power" (Jn 10:18) to give his life for his sheep.

This identification of office and love in the unique priesthood of Christ can only be shared by those who are pastors after him under a double condition: on the one hand, there are the office and an objective power based on an objective *"configuratio Christo Sacerdoti"*; on the other hand, there is the command (accompanied by a promise: Jn 20:18ff.) demanding an assimilation

---

[57] J. Mouroux has shown this very well in "Reflexions sur l'intercommunion", *Vers l'unité chrétienne* (Feb.–Mar. 1970): 20–22.

as complete as possible to the attitude of Christ who gave his life out of love.

The image of the shepherd places the priest on the side of Christ, face to face with the community. We should add that this relationship to the community is realized within the Church, since by baptism the priest is a member of it. This fact is important, for it shows that the role of the representative of Christ vis-à-vis the people can only be instituted and assumed by *an act of Christ* (through means of the hierarchy) and that the people by themselves have no right to set apart one of their members and to attribute to him the role of the representative of Christ.

B. *The Christian Community Is Inconceivable without the Eschatological Ministry on Which It Is Founded*

The preceding remark shows that no Christian community can exist without a common consciousness in which the faithful, as a community, recognize that they are summoned, called, gathered by the Word of God—Christ who died and rose again—and thanks to which they attain to a knowledge of their salvation.

In other words, the Christian community exists and becomes aware of itself only by its *encounter* with the priestly ministry, through which is manifested the gracious divine initiative that brings it into being—just as a person exists truly only by being called and suscitated by someone who comes to him and whom he recognizes. A child will never know his name if he is not called.

Let us make this point more precise. The ecclesial community in which the Christian comes to existence is constituted as such *in its unity* by the Word of God.

The fact that it is through the eschatological service of Jesus Christ that God manifests to the Church the divine vocation that constitutes it is not called in question by any Christian. But the question remains: How does this divine call manifest itself to the ecclesial community after the death of Christ?

If it were to come to the faithful on an individual basis, men would be tied down to the particular way in which they experience the divine call. This would lead to an insurmountable solipsism.

A properly *institutional* encounter is necessary, given the fact that the gift of God to man is inseparable from, and comes together with, his insertion into the community.

The objection, according to which the Spirit acting in each one's conscience, by revealing to him the meaning of Scripture, creates the Christian community and reveals to it the transcendence of the divine call, does not hold, for *the action of the Spirit must be received and signified in a communitarian manner. It must, therefore, take place not merely at the level of each individual but also at the level of the community itself.* This is why it manifests itself in a living person, or in an organic group of persons who become, as it were, the *symbols* of the community.

The faithful, then, know themselves to be a community called by the Word of God, thanks to the minister, insofar as he, being eschatologically consecrated by divine action, signifies in himself what, in the mystery of his salvific action, God wills to signify efficaciously in him. The minister, moreover, can only play this role inasmuch as he himself is called by the Word and inasmuch as he is united to the universal Church.

It is, moreover, thanks to the minister that the faithful come to the knowledge of their salvation, in their response to the divine initiative, for the unity of the vision of faith must be expressed, and can only be expressed, through a consciousness. The minister thus becomes for the faithful the symbol of the insertion of the vision of faith in the unity of Tradition. He takes the faithful and the community beyond themselves, to the bishop, and through him, to the episcopal college with the Pope at its head, that is, to the universality of the Church in the world. The historic succession signifies the universality of the Church in time and its reference to the event of the Cross and the Resurrection on which it is founded.[58]

Let us add one more remark: we have insisted above on the obedient submission of Christ to the Spirit during his earthly life, and we have noted that the Spirit is the will of the Father in some way objectified as a "rule" of action. Because of this submission of Christ to the Spirit, we must affirm that the submission of the earthly Church to Christ implies that it accepts the Spirit as its "rule", without, however, identifying him too easily and subjectively with its own divine "mentality". The apostolic ministry is there as a necessary guarantee, though its role differs vastly from that of the "law" in the Old Testament, since the obedience of the New Law is spiritual.

C. *Bishops and Priests*

The priestly ministry in its fullness, as Vatican II has well shown, is the episcopal ministry in which the apostolic ministry is actualized for the Church today.

In view of the multiplicity of their tasks and of the magnitude of the salvific mission, the bishops have chosen collaborators and have entrusted to them various ministries. Among these, the priests are most closely associated

---

[58] We have borrowed and summarized (and partly modified) the views expressed by R. Didier, "Le sacerdoce et l'existence historique des communions chrétiennes", in *Essais de théologie sacramentaire*, Faculté de théologie de Lyon, Profac., pp. 19–26.

with the ministry of the bishops (celebration of the Eucharist, remission of sins, proclamation of the word of God).

1. Priestly Consecration

From the beginning, priests have been ordained for their function, not by a simple designation or election but by a rite of imposition of hands. This rite repeats on a lower tone the solemn rite of episcopal ordination, thus indicating the *substantial identity of powers and of grace* and, at the same time, the mission and the subordinate function that determine the exercise of those powers. This is why priests are called, according to an old formula of the sacramental rite of ordination, *"secundi meriti sacerdotes"*, *"secundi praedicatores"*.[59]

The substantial identity of the rite and the unity between the various offices of the apostolic ministry in which priests are called to collaborate shows for certain that, as the bishops in their episcopal consecration receive the *"munus sanctificandi"* and the *"munus docendi et regendi"*, so too *the priests in their ordination receive, along with the "munus sanctificandi", a participation in the "munus docendi et regendi"* that will be exercised in communion with and under the direction of the episcopal college, represented most often by the Ordinary.[60]

---

[59] Cf. *LG*, 28, with the witnesses quoted in the text. It is not possible to define the priesthood of the New Testament without reference to the episcopate, for the episcopate continues the apostolic mission and powers by which the Church is established *"per singula loca"*. The whole history of the Church witnesses to this fact. It is attested in particular by the liturgical texts of the rites of ordination, starting with the "apostolic Tradition". This sacramental rite has been accepted everywhere in the East and has also been recognized as valid by the Roman Church. For the relationship between episcopate and presbyterate according to the various rites of ordination, cf. B. Botte, "Holy Orders in the Ordination Prayers", in *The Sacrament of Orders* (London, 1962), pp. 5–23.

[60] The Second Vatican Council has clearly affirmed that all the episcopal powers, not only the power over the sacraments (*munus sanctificandi*) but also the teaching (*munus docendi*) and pastoral (*munus regendi*) office, are based on the sacrament. This teaching can be applied to the ordination to the presbyterate as follows: the ordination does not merely confer on the priest the sacramental powers; it also gives an ontological foundation for the teaching and pastoral office, which he is called to exercise as collaborator of the episcopal college.

This doctrine is based on the substantial identity of the apostolic ministry possessed in its fullness by the bishops and shared in a lesser degree by the priests; the same substantial identity is found in the rites of ordination. There remain, nonetheless, differences. Priests do not have the fullness of the apostolic powers; therefore, they do not have the fullness of gifts that the entire Tradition attributes only to the bishops: only the bishops are the authentic doctors of the Faith and have the function of guiding the faithful with true governing authority.

The descent of the Holy Spirit in the priestly consecration is, therefore, the source of the mission and powers of the priest, as it is also the source of interior grace, the principle of a deep transformation. It establishes those who receive it in a definitive state, as almost all the liturgies testify, concluding as they do the rite of ordination by a gesture or a proclamation, the intention of which is to affirm that a new state has been definitely entered into through a signing or anointing that is an indelible mark. This sets those ordained apart (the liturgies use the verb *aphorizô* of Acts 13:2) and lays hold of their entire person to consecrate them for their mission.[61]

By this consecration—which is an unction of the Spirit, a participation in the unction of Christ (cf. Lk 4:18)—priests are configured to Christ the Priest, in order that they may be able to act in the name and person of Christ the Head (*PO, 2*).

By reason of this consecration, priests cooperate in building up the Church as the Body of Christ and the sacrament of salvation, by exercising in their degree the mission confided by Jesus to his apostles and continued by the episcopal college. They exercise this mission by announcing the Gospel with authority according to the teaching of the Magisterium, by administering the gifts of grace according to the Tradition and lawful discipline of the Church, by educating the faithful and the community to understand and to fulfill their Christian vocation in order that they may be witnesses to Christ and saviors of their brethren. They are consecrated for all these duties by their ordination. Their assignment to particular tasks, always in communion with their legitimate pastors, depends on various circumstances—the needs or demands of the moment, personal aptitudes and qualities, pastoral customs—but no priest can ever cease to be called to announce Jesus Christ and administer the gifts of

---

Furthermore, priests can exercise their teaching and pastoral function only in accordance with the doctrine and the discipline established authoritatively by the successors of the apostles, more directly in dependence on the bishop, who represents the episcopal college in a particular place.

To say that all the priestly actions of the priest (the teaching and pastoral action as well as the strictly sacramental actions) have their ontological foundation in the sacrament helps to clarify the distinction between the common priesthood of all and the ministerial priesthood; the specific function of the ministerial priesthood in the building up of the Church also appears more clearly. There will result among the Christian people a deeper appreciation of the ministerial priesthood and among priests a deeper realization of the meaning of their life, not without repercussion on their pastoral action. The various pastoral functions assigned to the permanent diaconate should be based in a similar way on the sacrament.

Since the exercise of the "ministries" conferred through ordination as participations in the power of the bishops can be determined by the supreme authority (Pope and episcopal college), a teaching and pastoral function similar to that of priests can be attributed to the diaconate with a proportionate ontological foundation.

[61] Cf. M. Martimort (unpublished).

grace in collaboration with the apostolic mission of the episcopate. This is his first vocation, his proper vocation in the Church.[62]

Called by a sacramental consecration to be the collaborators of the episcopate, the priests, therefore, share in the responsibility of the successors of the apostles; likewise they share, according to their own degree, in their gifts and are ordained to carry out their service by a personal activity. Thus, their function is not limited to executing and interpreting the apostolic mission; it implies also giving help and advice in the search for the most opportune means to be adopted in order that the saving word of God may spread among men and save them. The role of the juridical forms that govern the collaboration of priests in the episcopal ministry is to ensure in a way adapted to the times the spiritual unity required for the exercise of the mission as a visible sign of interior charity and the orderly utilization of all the gifts and energies in serenity and peace, so that the world may believe in Christ the Savior (Jn 17:21–23).[63]

2. Variations in the Organization of Offices

The amplitude of the tasks included in the apostolic mission and the necessity of adaptation to different spiritual and historical conditions of various peoples

---

[62] The tasks inherent in the ministerial priesthood by virtue of its participation in the apostolic succession of the episcopal college constitute an organic unity and are universal. This being said, it must be admitted that their exercise has taken different modalities in the history of the Christian community and in the case of individual priests. We indicate the factors that have come into play to bring about these variations.

It is not difficult, in fact, to show that the differences in the exercise of the priestly ministry, at least for long periods, are due to different pastoral situations. Where the Faith is widely spread and is handed down to a large extent in the home and through the social environment, the stress is on the ministry of the sacraments, which either follows or prepares the pastoral ministry. Where, on the contrary, the Faith is lacking or threatened, the ministry of the education of the Faith prevails. These facts can be explained without having recourse to an influence of the Old Testament concept of the priesthood; such an influence is not proved (cf. Arnold, *Il ministero della fede*, chap. 1).

[63] Priests have in a subordinate manner and by participation coresponsibility with the college of bishops in their apostolic mission; this is based on their ordination to the presbyterate and the gifts that it confers. Once the principle of coresponsibility is understood, it becomes evident that priests must be made to cooperate in a responsible and effective manner in the apostolic mission. To this end, appropriate and juridical forms (the pastoral counsels) must be set up, in which their experience and personal charisms will be made use of. It must also be noted that the liturgical formularies for the ordination of priests (*Traditio Apostolica*) insist on a certain *"spiritum gratiae et consilii, presbyteris ut adiuvet"* conferred on them, that is, a grace of collaboration with the college of priests, which includes a "spirit of counsel" or of supernatural prudence in pastoral work.

and places have already in the past led the local Churches and the universal Church—in accordance with the Tradition of the primitive Church—to adopt different organizations of offices and sacred ministries. This diversity is possible on the condition that it safeguards the norm according to which only the bishops possess the fullness of the apostolic ministry, while the exercise of the lower ministries is subordinated to the supreme authority of the Church.

This authority has been handed down from Jesus Christ through the apostles, and it lasts to this day in the Church. The supreme authority, to which primarily belongs the duty of making the Church the "universal sacrament of salvation", that is, the Pope and the Episcopal college united to him, can therefore, even today, organize the ministries of the Church in new ways, on the condition that the distinction between the episcopate and the presbyterate be safeguarded as regards the fullness of the apostolic powers and that the distinction between bishops, priests, and others be safeguarded with regard to the strictly sacramental powers reserved to priests by the unanimous and universal Tradition of the Church.[64]

Let us finally recall that the priest exercises *ex officio*, that is, "publicly", a certain number of tasks that *all* Christians can perform but also others that all *cannot* do. For the priestly ministry is constituted by a special participation in the priesthood of Christ, by virtue of which the priest represents Christ at the head of the community and, as it were, facing it (celebration of the Eucharist, forgiveness of sins, announcing the word officially—publicly, authentically).

D. *A Problem Arising from a Theological Evolution*

One cannot deny that the theological teaching of the Church concerning the priestly ministry has evolved. It would be better, however, to speak of an

---

[64] Two things are affirmed in this paragraph:

a. In the history of the Church the ministries, at least in their lower degrees, are organized in different ways, and the distribution of sacred functions between episcopate and presbyterate varies, though the distinction between the fullness of the priesthood or the apostolic ministry that belongs to the bishops and the subordinate priesthood of the priests is always maintained.

b. The Church still possesses today the same power that it has had in the past, after the death of the apostles. Even today, therefore, it can change and give different forms to the articulation of the priestly ministries and to the participation in the apostolic mission. While doing so, it must, however, maintain the distinction between the fullness of the priesthood and the subordinate priesthood and between the priesthood proper and the inferior ministries, which can have priestly tasks and gifts without having the power to celebrate the Eucharist.

Pius XII has made use of this principle to determine what is the matter and form of the Sacrament of Order (cf. *Sacramentum Ordinis*, Nov. 30, 1947, n. 3).

evolution of *theology* on some particular points than of an evolution of the Faith as it is manifested in liturgical rites, in the life of the ecclesial community, or in the official pronouncements of the Magisterium.

It is true, for example, that Western theology, after the twelfth century, has insisted much more on the "powers" conferred, and especially on the power to consecrate the Eucharist, than on the sacramental grace received; hence the tendency has arisen to attach less importance to the imposition of hands than to the handing over of the symbols of office (*traditio instrumentorum*).

Similarly, and again because of the stress put on the eucharistic Consecration, less importance came to be given to the episcopal consecration by theologians in the West. In the overall concept of the sacrament of Order, the "priestly" power to consecrate the body of Christ has eclipsed the other powers of the Magisterium and pastoral government. This tendency shows itself clearly in the Council of Trent itself.

In the same line, there has also been a tendency to separate the "priesthood" from the care of souls: in the Middle Ages, clerics were the depositaries of culture and received in society a place of honor with considerable material advantages. Many oratories and private churches were erected and were entrusted to the priests, who had no other duties than to look after the cult. Many benefices were founded without *cura animarum*. Priests were ordained for a benefice and not for the needs of the people. Thus, little by little, the awareness of the bond between the presbyterate and the "service" of the people of God was lost; most priests no longer had any duty but to celebrate Masses, without the obligation to preach or instruct the people. As the benefice was no longer strictly connected with the pastoral duty, bishops themselves lost the sense of the duty to "reside" among their flock.

One understands then why the reformers of the sixteenth century reacted so strongly against the priesthood and even against the Mass and insisted on the service of preaching the word of God. One understands also why the Council of Trent, reacting against their excesses, proclaimed so strongly the existence of the sacrament of Order as ordained to the celebration of the Eucharist; at the same time, however, it repressed certain abuses, especially concerning residence and preaching. But, its primary aim being to reply to the "innovators", it did not wish to abolish the order and discipline established in the Middle Ages.

In a less polemic atmosphere, the Second Vatican Council was able to complete the declarations of the Council of Trent and to restore a more harmonious balance between the different aspects of the ministry. Its teaching is well known and does not need to be exposed here.[65]

---

[65] We follow here the summary made by J. Lecuyer in his (unpublished) report. For the position of Trent and Vatican II, cf. the summary of Mgr. Jedin (unpublished).

This evolution raises the question: What is, in the overall concept of the priesthood, the essential element?

Among the sacred functions, the decree *Presbyterorum Ordinis* gives the first place to preaching, while the Council of Trent made the offering of the sacrifice of the Mass the first and most important function of the priest.

What are we to conclude?

From this apparent opposition, some draw extremely radical conclusions: the priestly ministry, of which the primary function is the service of the word, understood in opposition to the cultic and sacramental aspect, ought to be desacralized and declericalized.

Others, on the contrary, basing themselves on the decrees *Sacrosanctum Concilium*, 20, and *Presbyterorum Ordinis*, 5, underline that the Eucharist is presented as the end toward which the entire sacred ministry is ordained and the source of its fecundity. They conclude that the eucharistic celebration is the most essential and the most excellent function of the priest, preaching being his primary function only by a priority of time.[66]

It is clear that the priest cannot be defined solely by his liturgical powers, chief of which is the eucharistic Consecration, as a study of the formularies of ordination shows; but neither can he be understood without them: the priest is the man who can make evangelization reach its goal, that is, baptism and the Eucharist; he is the man who, associated with his bishop or sent by him, can put the seal of unity on the local community: "One bread, one chalice, one Lord". He is the minister of Christ who pardons and heals. If he was not involved in the apostolic and pastoral responsibility of his bishop, he would run the risk of returning to a Judaic concept of the priesthood. On the other hand, if he did not exercise his sacramental power, he would lose the very sense of his priesthood and would no longer be able to present to men the authentic mystery of Christ—a mystery accomplished once and for all but efficaciously renewed throughout the time of the Church. The priest lives in his person the wonderful paradox of the economy of salvation: he must achieve unity in his own life to help others to discover the same unity.[67]

---

[66] Cf. the article by D. F. Haarsma, "A Few Pastoral-Theological Theses Concerning the Priest", in *The Priest in a Secularized World,* Conferences of the Third International Congress at Lucerne (Sept. 18–22, 1967) (Maastricht, 1968), p. 81. "The assertion that the cultic-sacramental function of the priest is neither the unique, primary, nor exclusive role of an ecclesiastical office should assist the desacralization and declergification of this office. . . . That it is not the first or primary function is clear from the pertinent passages of the New Testament about the apostolic office, and is confirmed by Vatican II. Both give the first place to the proclamation of the word." P. Gagnebet insists on his part that the eucharistic celebration is the primary function (annex document).

[67] We borrow the formulations of M. Martimort (unpublished).

The dilemma, word or Eucharist, must therefore be overcome. It can be overcome by defining, as we have done, the priestly ministry as *the service of the active, properly eschatological power of the Word of God—Jesus Christ who died and rose again*—of which the visible signs are the announcement of the Gospel message and the sacramental actions.

The word, in fact, ought not to be understood merely as intelligible content of a message; taken in the fullness of its mystery, it includes the sacrifice of Christ, his death, and his Resurrection. It is the creative force of salvation, and we have seen that the New Testament teaches that the exercise of the apostolic ministry makes present the priestly service of Christ, his offering, his being "for us", in the word, the signs, and the entire existence of the minister.

When we speak of preaching the word, we must, therefore, never forget that it includes the sacrifice of Christ, which it makes present, and that by itself it calls for the Eucharist.

The priest is, in the service of the people of God, the herald of the word of God up to the highest degree of intensity, which it reaches in the sacramental order, especially in the Eucharist.

But it took the Church a long period of reflection before the Eucharist came to be seen as the innermost and most objective presence of the sacrifice of Christ and the ultimate constitutive element in the building up of the Church.[68]

The ministerial priesthood is thus defined by the specific nature of the sacrifice of Christ, made present efficaciously and with perfect unity in the efficacious announcement of the Gospel message and in the eucharistic celebration. Hence it is also defined by the glory of God, since it is in the sacrifice of the Cross that the Father is glorified by the Son; it is also defined by the blessing, since it is by the crucified Word that we are introduced into the divine blessing (Eph 1).

Perhaps we can conclude these remarks by emphasizing that the priestly ministry implies a definite concept of the Church. The crisis of the priesthood, moreover, makes this clear, for the crisis of the priestly identity is at the same time a crisis of the identity of the Church.

---

[68] K. Rahner rightly defines the priesthood as follows: "We may say, perhaps riskily because briefly, that the priest is he who, related to an at least potential community, preaches the word of God by mandate of the Church as a whole and therefore officially, and in such a way that he is entrusted with the highest levels of sacramental intensity of this word. In very simple words, he has the mission to preach the Gospel in the name of the Church. He does this at the highest level at which this word can operate in the anamnesis of Christ's death and Resurrection through the celebration of the Eucharist" ("What Is the Theological Starting Point for a Definition of the Priestly Ministry?" *Concilium,* n. 43 [1969]: 46).

For the Catholic Church, *an ecclesiology of communion* cannot be separated from *an ecclesiology of institution*—institution being not understood as merely juridical but as giving structure, as vital and spiritual.[69]

E. *An Analysis of the Conditions Necessary in Order That a Priestly Ministry Exercised Today Can, with Certainty, Declare Itself to Be in Continuity with the Apostolic Succession*

The *Documents on the Priesthood* issued by the General Secretariat of the French episcopate contain the following remarks:

> Some ask questions concerning the absolute necessity of a sacrament received in the historical succession of the apostles, for the valid exercise of the hierarchical ministry at the service of the community. They do so because they are sensitive to the Protestant doctrine of ministry (non-sacramental) or to new findings in exegesis and the history of early Christianity that show no clear distinction or determination of the various functions in the hierarchical service of the community.
>
> In the same line the question is raised as to what is necessary for declaring with certainty that a ministry exercised in the Church today is in continuity with the apostolic succession, and hence is legitimate, authentic, and validly conferred by the choice of the Holy Spirit. Could he not proceed by directly conferring a charismatic gift? Has he not often done so in the history of the Church, starting with Paul himself? In such cases, would not the hierarchy have to ratify—and not necessarily to confer by a liturgical act of consecration—the ministry confided by God for the service of the community?

Let us try to answer these questions by examining the relationship between *the Spirit and the institution.*

The presupposition, implicit or explicit, of most of these questions is that there is opposition between the charismatic and the institutional structures of the Church, an opposition that, as we have seen, cannot be accepted. Furthermore, the case of Paul cannot be invoked to defend the thesis of a charismatic intervention, because Paul's situation in relation to Peter and the Twelve does not have any parallel in subsequent history. His prophetic apostolate is part of the prophetic action that is at the origin of the Church; it belongs properly to the apostolic times and is formally distinct from the "spiritual gifts" that the Spirit gives to whom he wills.

Often the charismatic aspect of the ministries exercised in Christian com-

---

[69] We borrow a formulation of J. Mouroux in his article "Reflexions sur l'intercommunion", 22.

munities is alleged as a reason for demanding their recognition. But the reference to the Spirit does not suffice where there is no formal reference to the Christological institution.

With regard to the ministry in the apostolic succession and its relationship to ministries foreign to it, the fundamental question is not whether in such or such a case there is apostolic succession—each case must be studied by itself—but whether the apostolic succession itself is essential for the authenticity of the life of the Church.

The fundamental argument for affirming its essential character is as follows: the continuous action of the Holy Spirit and the singular fact of the Incarnation are bound together by the fact that the Paraclete is the supreme gift that the glorified Christ gives to those who were with him "from the beginning" (Jn 15:26–27) and who fulfill a ministry in his Church (Eph 4:8–12). The mission of the Spirit applies the work of Christ to men of all times; *it does not substitute for his intervention.*[70]

The insistence on the necessity of "being integrated" in the apostolic succession in order to have a valid ministry that is from Christ is bound up, according to the whole Catholic Tradition, with the impossibility of conceiving in this world a "Church of Christ" that would not go back to the Incarnation and to the historical activity of Christ. The apostolic continuity exists at one and the same time in the word and the sacraments and in the pastoral mission to which these are connected.

This is not to say that those who do not have the ministry as we have described it are necessarily deprived of the benefits that derive from the mystery of Christ through apostolic succession. But all the gifts of the Holy Spirit that they can have are connected with the divine word and the sacramental signs entrusted to the pastoral charge, which goes back to the apostles. The gifts that they have already received truly postulate their entry into the community of Christ as established by him, as is seen, for instance, in the case of the baptism of Cornelius and Paul.

The authenticity of the Faith they already have in the historical Christ—in what he has done and decided once for all—and of all the saving graces that come to them from the Father through the Spirit, is in proportion with their disposition to receive from the apostolic succession—when the occasion arises for them to come in contact with it again—the consecration that so far they have not received from it. By this, and by this alone, will their ecclesial communities avoid a local and temporal particularism and be integrated into

[70] In the article mentioned above, J. Mouroux asks: "Would it be correct and sufficient to speak here of 'substitution'? Can we attribute to the Holy Spirit a role of innovation and of creation, *independent* of the role of Christ, when we see that Christ has always presented the role of the Holy Spirit as the living prolongation of his own mission?" (n. 13).

the *Catholica* of all places and all times, to become *the* unique society that Christ had founded and that he propagated *as his own* through the mission of *his* apostles. Thus, for these separated brethren, this consecration, far from denying the authenticity of the gifts previously received or transmitted, ought to be recognized as their consecration without which the gifts already received by them would be deprived of the fulfillment for which they were meant from the beginning.

The fundamental principle that ought to orient our judgment is therefore the following: we cannot know the action of the Spirit outside the reference to the Christological institution, that is, independently of the sign that he has given us.

The Church maintains, therefore, that the imposition of hands, legitimate in the present order of the history of salvation, is the only certain sign of apostolic succession that has been given to us and therefore the only guarantee we have of the transmission of the powers of the Magisterium, of the celebration of the Eucharist, and of the pastoral government.

It cannot be admitted, therefore, that in an urgent case the community could recognize that God himself has given to it in one of its members the gift of the ministerial priesthood. To affirm such a recognition, however precarious it might remain pending the recognition by the universal Church speaking in Council, or by its head, the Pope, would be to attribute to the community a power that it does not have. Moreover, in the supposition mentioned above, faith and salvation are rigidly bound up with the sacraments of the Church at the very moment that the charismatic intervention of the Spirit is asserted.

It does not seem that Oriental doctrine of the "economy" offers a ground for recognizing the ministries of the communities that lack the conditions that we have described.[71] For, as understood by the Oriental theologians, the principle of economy: (1) applies only to those who want to be reconciled to the Church and (2) supposes that the Church makes up for an eventual lack of

---

[71] For the principle of "economy", see the article of K. Duchatelet, "La notion d'économie et ses richesses théologiques", *Nouvelle revue théologique* (1970): 291: "The economy is . . . a certain compromise made by lawful pastors, which is justified provided that the integrity of dogmas and canons is safeguarded. It consists in adopting in various matters of doctrine and Christian life broad rather than strict norms, in view of the salvation of men, especially of the faithful. Their salvation makes it necessary or opportune to adopt such broad norms in order to avoid scandal, to strengthen the faith of those who are weak, to help the heretics who repent, or to counteract their assaults. Thus, the economy can be viewed as prolonging· the salvific intention of God in the Incarnation: this intention has been made manifest in the Savior; it has been followed by the apostles and applied by the Church through the centuries."

the true Faith in those who have conferred or received the sacrament, but not for dispensing with the sacramental act itself.

With the problem of recognizing the ministries are bound up (1) the problem of common celebrations of the Eucharist between Catholic ministers and ministers who are not in the apostolic succession as we have presented it and (2) that of the reception by Catholics of the Eucharist or other sacraments celebrated by ministers who do not have this succession.

As to the first point, we think that when Catholic priests participate in such celebrations, in conditions that make ambiguous the fundamental difference between the ministry with which they are invested and that of other celebrants, the sacramental sign is vitiated and consequently becomes doubtful.

Such celebrations run the risk not only of being a scandal for the Catholic faithful and non-Catholics as well but also of creating grave illusions, as if union had already been achieved in its essentials.

As for the second point, we think that the Catholic who receives the sacraments from a minister outside the apostolic succession not only creates ambiguity for others as regards his Catholic Faith, but also puts his own faith in danger.

VII. THE INSERTION OF THE PRIESTLY MINISTRY IN THE WORLD OF TODAY

The different problems arising from the insertion of the priest in the world cannot be correctly approached without a clear knowledge of what may be called the "specific character" of the Church. The reason is that the Catholic priestly ministry is, as we have said, the service of the truly eschatological realities that make up the fundamental nature of the Church.

A. *Salvation*

It is important, therefore, that we briefly clarify in what this specific nature of the Church consists. Let us simply say: the Church is an organic community in which the *salvation of Christ* is at work by the power of the Spirit. This salvation is realized by the discovery that man makes of his true vocation in the light of revelation: Christ as the Son of God, and his Pasch, establishing the New Covenant that will be fulfilled in the parousia. The proclamation of the mystery of salvation is, then, the source of the identity of the Church: Christ is a teacher and a witness, but he is more than that: *he is the Savior.* For mankind destined to death and the other consequences of sin, the Lord is the only possible source of true fullness of life. Without him we are dead, and without knowing him we are in darkness. His word is at once judgment and pardon. It shows us the abyss of our nothingness and leads us to communion with the Father, the Son, and the Holy Spirit in the Church. It reaches its summit in the Eucharist, the celebration of which makes the Church.[72]

This salvation is not without its consequences for the temporal activities and the structures of this world, but it cannot be reduced to them. It surpasses technology and political action, both on the level of the Kingdom to come and on the level of the depth of the human heart. Indeed, full human freedom exists only in the measure in which men are able to enter into the mystery of salvation in Christ. Certainly, the Church sincerely desires to collaborate with all efforts towards humanization, but its most valuable contribution is to *announce, with eschatological effectiveness, Christ as the Savior of the world.*

The priestly ministry is bound to this specific core of the Church's mission. The structure willed by Christ for the Church implies that its sacramental nature can be realized only through the ministry, without which "one cannot speak of Church", according to the trenchant expression of St. Ignatius of Antioch. Whoever would reduce the Church to be just another factor in the development of temporal structures or would think that the Christianity of the future ought to be "anonymous" would make the identity of the Church disappear and the priesthood lose its meaning. Thus, the priestly ministry can justly be called the "sign of catholicity", for it truly assures a necessary form of Christ's presence in the community, and it urges the community to live by the mystery of Christ in its catholicity, as Paul said: it brings to the Church "the fullness of the blessing of Christ" (Rom 15:29).

From this point of view, one understands better the fundamental reason for the permanence of the priestly ministry, not only in the community but also in the person of the minister. As marriage is the image of the indissoluble bond between Christ and his Church, similarly the priesthood is the sacrament of the bond that makes the Lord the Head and the Spouse of the Church. One can surely speak of the priestly "function" of the ministry, but this "function" ought not to be understood as the performance of a chain of isolated actions, more or less impersonal and magical, but rather as a consecration, that is, as the fundamental calling (*Grundberuf*) of a life devoted to the service of the proclamation of the word of salvation and to the celebration of the Christian liturgy. It is in this sense that we can speak of a twofold Christian consecration: the

---

[72] The first redaction contained here a text by Mgr. J. Medina-Estevez showing clearly the specific character of the Church. It is now found in a supplement to this chapter.

baptismal consecration and the ministerial consecration, not in order to oppose the two or to establish any preference between them but to distinguish different and complementary roles.

B. *Priestly Ministry and Human Activities*

The priest remains, assuredly, a man and a Christian. He remains a member of the earthly community, and he retains his place in the people of God in which and for which he is a priest. In a certain sense, the most important thing for him remains his condition as a Christian. Among his activities there are many that pertain to him as a member of the temporal community and others that he shares in common with all Christians. But his ministerial role conditions these activities, for he cannot make abstraction of the "function" that pervades his entire existence. The priestly ministry does not have temporal development for its direct and immediate goal, but its role in the economy of salvation will not fail to exercise an influence on the temporal; the efficacy of this influence cannot always be easily measured because it is exercised at a level that escapes sociological observation. This being said, it must be affirmed that the ministry is not to be understood as a state of "withdrawal" from what is human but rather as a state of the person whose functions condition his entire existence. It must be admitted that the concrete realization of the ministry in its different involvements cannot be subject to simple juridical rules.

A superficial consideration of the above remarks might give the impression that the ministry is an impoverishment, or even a mutilation. In fact, we have here an application of a general law of human existence: every option supposes that one puts aside other possibilities; this does not in any way imply that the value of the other possibilities is minimized. It is not just a question of availability of time but also and primarily of real incompatibilities: an advocate, for example, cannot simultaneously hold the office of judge. Similarly, the priest, as sign of Catholicity and the ministry of unity, whose whole existence must be marked with the eschatological meaning of salvation, will have to consider with the greatest attention how far this or that activity is in fact compatible with his role, even if these activities are really worthwhile or even necessary. He must anchor his vision in the Faith in order to remind himself always that his work is not measurable by earthly standards of success, but that he shares in the mystery of the self-emptying of Christ and that the fruits of his work remain the secret of the Father.

C. *Criteria of Judgment*

These views enable us to sort out certain criteria that are helpful in reaching a practical judgment in the difficult task of finding the right equilibrium between the ministerial and nonministerial activities of the priest.

1. *The safeguard of the real possibility of exercising the ministry is a fundamental principle in the choice of other activities and the judgment that bears on them.* It is necessary to consider not only personal desires, however legitimate, but also and above all the needs of the Christian community and of those who have not yet received the Gospel message. If this principle is set aside in practice, one is exposed, by the very nature of things, to losing the sense of personal consecration, in view of which one has been called to the priestly ministry. The concrete circumstances of one's milieu will always have a great importance in the application of this principle, but the priesthood can never become for the priest a side occupation (*Nebenberuf*). In spite of all difficulties, he must render *his* service of unity in Christ and in the Church.

2. *The priest, inasmuch as he is the minister of Christ and the Church, must always act as the sign and instrument of unity.* In the face of opposition that originates from sin and disregard of the Gospel, it is his duty to speak with firmness in the name of the word, but he cannot confine himself only to the exposure of injustice. His ministry obliges him to make an incessantly renewed effort to lead men to unity in Christ. This means that he cannot allow himself to be carried away by an avenging anger; he must overcome it by a charity that feels the double suffering of witnessing the anguish of the oppressed and the rejection of the Gospel by the powerful. This suffering is a typical manifestation of the heart of Christ reflected in the heart of the pastor.

3. *Certain activities* presuppose a *technical* judgment that sometimes is open to divergent evaluations. With regard to these, the Church is not competent to judge, except in cases where the means employed are in contradiction with the Gospel and human dignity is flouted. A certain coherence may sometimes seem to exist between such or such option and the plan of salvation in its temporal repercussions; but, since this coherence does not constitute the only possible way of handing in the Gospel message, the attitude of the Church cannot be an official commitment, as it is a question of contingent and provisional viewpoints. Even in this case, the personal option of the priest ought to be marked by a discretion and a moderation demanded by the specific role that he has in the ecclesial mission.

4. *Political activity* poses even more delicate and often extremely intricate problems. In this field conflicts are most often the rule, even among Christians. As regards the means employed, it is painful to observe how difficult it is at times to combine political success with evangelical sincerity. One should not conclude from this that political activity is forbidden to the Christian; in fact,

it is recommended and even necessary. But, if one keeps in mind the role of the priest as we have described it above, it seems that his normal attitude in the field of political options should be not to compromise himself by political militancy but to announce with full freedom and independence the demands of the Gospel, as regards both means and goals. Since no political action can be considered as definitively free from sin or as the perfect translation of the Gospel, the priest, *"witness of what is yet to be"*, must keep his distance. His activity in the political field will, paradoxically enough, increase in efficacy if he is able to renounce seeking immediate results. The attitude of the priest should remind Christians that the Gospel cannot be reduced to politics and that no political action, even if it answers real needs, can replace the contemplation of the mystery of Christ and its celebration in the liturgy of the Church.

Perhaps we can summarize all these criteria by saying that, in all his activities, the priest ought to maintain an *"eschatological reserve"* (*eschatologische Vorbehaltung*). This, moreover, is in perfect agreement with what we have said about the priestly ministry as an *eschatological service*.

It remains for us now to consider the question of celibacy in its broad outlines.

D. *Celibacy*

1. Present Position of the Problem

a. Celibacy today is subjected to a radical questioning. Questions are raised as to its meaning and, above all, as to the necessity of the connection that in fact exists in the Western Church between celibacy and the apostolic ministry. Basically, however, the problem is connected with a number of much deeper questions: the very meaning of the ministry, the relation of Christian values to the present world, the action and the task of the Church when it is faced with other ways of interpreting the meaning of man.[73]

b. The present situation is made up of different factors: the lawful necessity of rethinking Christian realities in a totally new cultural setup; the existence and large-scale acceptance of certain postulates of non-Christian origin that make some of the practical demands of Christianity inconceivable and even more unrealizable; the necessity, strongly felt by the Church, of verifying its message not only on the level of transhistoric hope but also on the level of its historic efficiency.

---

[73] For the question of celibacy, see the long analysis by O. Gonzalez de Cardedal (unpublished). A select bibliography is appended to this chapter.

c. The new historical phenomenon, which we are witnessing today, can be characterized as "transculturalization". From unconscious patterns and some collective a priori conceptions on which was based the interpretation of life and death, the world is passing to new patterns of thinking, from a spiritualistic European outlook to a universal scientific-technical approach. In the latter, celibacy is one of the values or forms of Christian existence that are being questioned inasmuch as they are signs of the hope and the explicit affirmation of transcendent and unverifiable values that man receives through grace and cannot acquire through his own effort. The concrete reasons that have led to the generalized crisis as regards the connection between celibacy and priesthood, and finally to the crisis of celibacy itself, are of various kinds and origin. They are the following: a loss of the sense of celibacy at the sociological level, a new way of perceiving the relations between transcendent values and their service to the world, a transition from a sacred interpretation to a secular interpretation of reality, a theological revaluation of marriage and the rejection of non-Christian motivations of celibacy, a positive approach to human sexuality and the insistence on the need of interpersonal relationships for full human maturity, an awareness of the demands of full solidarity from which celibacy seems to be a withdrawal, the question of the forms of pastoral service existing in the Church today, a comparison with the ways in which the ministry is exercised in other Christian confessions and with the ministry in the Oriental Catholic Church, the practical difficulties arising from the solitude that celibacy imposes on the priest in a world where man is lost in the mass and finds intimacy only in the home, the pastoral requirements of evangelization, and the lack of celibate priests in some continents.

d. Any definitive attitude with regard to the problem of celibacy implies a threefold preliminary process: a way of understanding the values and central exigencies of the Gospel; a way of evaluating the actual situation of culture and of human evolution in a religious perspective; a manner of conceiving the task of the Church in this world, emphasizing one or other aspects of the Gospel, witnessing to one or other value, and correcting one or other emphasis of the Church's past history.

2. The Christian Meaning of Celibacy

a. Celibacy is first of all a valid form of human existence. It is the result of a person being drawn to and fascinated by a certain value or order of values. This attraction is such that in all freedom he feels himself obliged to renounce other positive values for which he has no time left, and to which he could not devote himself with the generosity and full commitment that they deserve.

b. Christian celibacy "for the love of Christ and the Gospel" shares in common with other forms of celibacy the same selfless dedication to a historic task, the commitment to a certain value, the service of a reality perceived as claiming total attention and leaving no place psychologically for the absolutely gratuitous love and service that a wife and children have a right to expect.

He who, as a Christian, opts for celibacy makes no theoretical judgment of value: "This is more perfect than that", or, "This is holy while that is profane"; he humbly follows Christ who calls him. For the Christian, everything can be perfect and everything can be sanctified. Celibacy is a grace and a charism. It is the expression of a response to a call from God drawing a person to "the following" of Christ for the service of the Kingdom. It gives witness to an obedience that needs to be incessantly and faithfully renewed (cf. Mt 19: 10–12: "Not all can understand this language, but only those to whom it is given. . . . Let anyone accept this who can").

c. By a celibate life, the Christian witnesses to Christ as the absolute value, as the supreme truth, capable of giving inspiration to his whole life. Through this exclusive consecration he publicly affirms that Christ is in his person the value, supreme and necessary for all, that cannot be conquered by force or violence but is received as a gift and a grace. By celibacy the believer testifies that man's vocation does not coincide with his earthly vocation, much less with sexual fulfillment, and that present values are sound only in the measure of their openness and positive reference to him who is their Source: God revealed in Christ.

d. This celibate life in Christ needs to draw ever new vigor from its source: the love of God and zeal for the Kingdom. Celibacy only reveals its meaning and has its value as a witnessing, when it appears as the concrete manifestation of a transfiguration, effected by the love of God and the service of men, of all the affective powers and thereby of the whole human being. Naturally, it has to express itself in a universal and open love that broadens life, establishes wider contacts with all, makes for total self-gift at the service of the whole world.

3. Celibacy and the Apostolic Ministry

a. The historical connection between celibacy and the apostolic ministry is not a necessary one. The ministry is possible without celibacy, just as celibacy is possible without the ministry. The union or dissociation introduced by ecclesiastical Tradition between these two realities is not motivated by a dogmatic necessity but suggested by a practical pastoral judgment.

b. Some of the arguments invoked in the course of history for the law of celibacy were dependent on philosophical visions of the world, political situations, and ecclesiastical interests, which had little to do with the Gospel. In some cases they were even objectively false.

c. Celibacy has been maintained and will be maintained in the Church as the expression of a deep Christian conviction, prior to any conceptualization such as: "Not to marry, out of love for Christ, in order to be totally at the service of the word that must be announced and of the men who are waiting for it: this is better."

d. The successors of the apostles are right when they favor this form of Christian existence witnessed to and recommended by the writings of the New Testament, as the most perfect and best adapted form of the apostolic ministry. They cannot but encourage it.

e. The early Church, by including the life and writings of Paul in the canon (Acts and Epistles), inclines us to think that it saw in him the exemplary type of apostle. To be a priest of the New Covenant is to be a minister of the Gospel, and, in the light of the concrete life of Paul, the Church understood what is the supreme, exemplary, and normative form for carrying out the apostolate as witness to a personal love of the Lord Jesus and to a total involvement in the proclamation of the Gospel and in the daily solicitude for the Churches. The hierarchy and the people of God in general rightly considered that the faithful who have received the gifts of virginity, along with other charisms, are the most fit disciples to be charged with the ministry of reconciliation. The apostolic life of Paul, celibate and absolutely free in all the hazards of the announcing of the Gospel, will always be the exemplary form of the apostolate and consequently the ideal form for every ministry in the Church.

f. The minister who, by concretely living his celibacy in love, joy, and hope, explicitly and actually refers his life to Christ, gives credibility to the Gospel, which he announces as a total and definitive value, a value of grace that transcends time. His life authenticates with a seal his announcement of the word of God.

g. When the hierarchy links virginity and ministry, it does not alter the nature of the charism but rather emphasizes its communitarian reference and intent, as belongs essentially to every charism. The fact that the Church requires a charismatic gift in those who exercise the ministry witnesses to the transforming power of the sacrament (word and Spirit), which confers the ministry and animates the apostle throughout his life. A radical separation between charism and law ignores the specific character that the Church derives from the Incarnation. By the Incarnation God submits himself to place and time; he receives the human nature from Mary; he depends on a few apostles and on a Church as the witnesses of his life and his words.

h. Apostolic celibacy does not imply a division of reality into profane and sacred; it presupposes the sanctity of Christian marriage as a permanent condition of its own sign value as indicating that there exists an even greater value. In its turn, virginity recognizes the sacramental dimension of marriage, that is, its causality in the order of grace, which is not due to the mere dynamism of the love of the spouses but to the explicit reference to Christ who made the love of one for the other the channel and the cause of his grace.

i. Celibacy does not imply a lack of esteem for temporal values. As every man who believes in God, the Christian always is a sign of transcendence. These signs do not ignore the values of the present world, nor do they make little of them, but they refer the realities of this world to a personal God, the Origin and end of all things. It is only in its reference to God that this world finds its meaning and fulfillment. The Church can and ought to present such signs of transcendence and of grace through the official witnesses of its message.

j. The celibate minister of the Gospel, by his word and life, is an invitation to break through the narrow boundaries of a world that reduces man to one dimension and limits his horizon to his own self. He shows man the possibility of opening himself to realities that set him free from his own fulfillment by means of a self-renouncing love and of a totally gratuitous service of the neighbor. On the one hand, celibacy possesses the efficacy of the Faith, which renounces justification by works because it (celibacy) is a gift of God and expects from him the grace of fidelity. On the other hand, it shows the effectiveness of the word of Jesus who is above all an offer of love, as well as the power of his death, which, despite its apparent insignificance, gives to the world its ultimate meaning. It is in fundamental harmony with the eschatological character of the ministry.

4. Perspectives for the Future

a. To say that a life of a disciple of Christ lived in poverty, virginity, joy, and the service of the neighbor ought to be considered by the hierarchy as best suited for receiving the apostolic ministry is not equivalent to saying that the hierarchy ought to require this always and from all possible candidates in the same measure. If those who live in virginity witness to certain aspects and values of the Gospel that they preach, those who live in marriage, if they are called to the ministry, can witness to other values of the same Gospel.

b. The hierarchy, which is responsible for the permanent, efficacious, and universal proclamation of the Gospel as the word of life and sacramental fount of grace, can choose for the exercise of the apostolic ministry either those who have been called and already live by the charism of virginity or those who, in marriage, by an experience of many years, have acquired human and professional maturity, happy family relationships, and above all an apostolic worth in the sense indicated in the pastoral Epistles.

c. If this double kind of ministry is allowed, he who is celibate will be the public, permanent, and ecclesial sign of the Gospel as a value that is eschatological, total, and irreplaceable. He bears this testimony not only in his personal name but also in the name of the believing community. The authenticity of this testimony demands a definitive commitment. Consequently, if, for a personal reason, celibacy becomes impossible for him, he ought to discontinue the exercise of his ministry; he does not have the possibility of exercising it in marriage, as the universal Tradition of the Church bears out.

d. The supreme law is "that the Gospel be announced". The concrete criteria for determining the forms of the ministry at a particular moment in the life of the Church or in a given country are dictated by that law. The criteria for a decision will be the following: the missionary proclamation of the Gospel must be assured in the most qualified and efficacious manner, provision must be made for the further maturing of the Christian life in those who are already baptized, and the concrete embodiment of the demands of the Gospel must become a living witness for all men.

e. The problems of obligatory celibacy arise within a very complex ecclesial context, which must be taken into account in order to overcome all clericalism and to promote the apostolic vocation of the laity. It is urgent to create much more diversified structures of the Church's pastoral action as regards both its ministries and its members, if the Church is to be faithful to its missionary and apostolic vocation. The Church must recognize the importance of the diversity of the charisms that manifest themselves in it and establish a structure of pastoral service that will ensure the mobility and availability that it needs in order to be present with its signs of grace in a pluralistic world.

f. It is not by reducing its evangelical demands that celibacy will be seen as a sign but rather by increasing them, that is, by placing it in the context of a true apostolic life (*apostolica vivendi forma*), fully determined by service, poverty, joy, availability, hope, and love. Only in this way will the inevitable ambiguity of every sign that implies some renunciation be overcome. Given the present sociological context, a life of celibacy cannot, as a rule, be lived without a minimum of community life. Groups of priests or of priests and laymen together will constitute the milieu most conducive to it.

g. The situation in which the Church is living today shows that the celibate apostle is totally available for the service of the Gospel in all its exigencies; he is the type most in accord with the demands implied in the New Testament. Combining word and action, he is the supreme sign of the presence of God and at the same time a living "contestation" of a world that is closed in on itself and thus is condemned to a spiritual asphyxiation: though called to the fullness of the Infinite, it has opted for the finite as its all-sufficient end. This is why celibacy, like the Gospel, the Faith, and the Church, will always remain a scandal and a stumbling block for those who do not live the obedience in spirit to the mystery of Christ. The Church cannot acclimatize itself to the world, and even less can it hope that the world will be in agreement with its signs, its life, and its actions.

Supplement on the Specific Character of the Church
by Mgr. Medina-Estevez

A careful study of the writings of the New Testament allows us to affirm for certain that the Gospel of Christ and the way in which it has been understood by the first Christian generations has in view not merely a new relationship of individuals with the Father outside all social and institutional structure but a New Covenant with the new people of God, which is the Body of Christ.

This is perfectly coherent with the mystery of the incarnate Word. Though the relationship between the two natures of Christ, on the one hand, and the two elements, interior and visible, of the Church, on the other hand, is not strictly parallel, the analogy is nevertheless valid: in both cases a true union exists between the two elements. The human nature of Christ is the instrument of the Divinity; in a similar fashion the visible elements in the community of the New Covenant, mostly those that belong to the sacramental economy, are at once the expression of the invisible realities and the channel through which men are inserted into the community.

The Christian consciousness must always be aware of the possibility of Christological deviations and of their implications for Ecclesiology. St. Ignatius, the martyr, saw a close relationship between the docetist tendencies of his time and the denial of the Eucharist. St. Irenaeus also traced the gnostic refusal of an ecclesial structure to a mistaken pneumatology. In our own days, the ecumenical movement has led to a deeper awareness of the need for visible structures that is inherent in the nature of the Church, despite the deep divergences that still exist as regards the role and the modalities of these visible structures.

From the viewpoint of the Catholic Faith, it must be affirmed that there exists a necessary relationship between interior communion and visible communion. Better still, there exists between the two a certain unity, so that neither can be perfect without the other. What is more, visible communion is the sacramental means leading to interior communion and effecting it. This is the reflection of the mystery of Christ on the nature of the Church.

It must be admitted that the interior elements are superior to the structures in dignity and in reality, to use the terms of St. Augustine, and there is room for structures only in the present condition of the pilgrim Church. Nevertheless, before the parousia the structures are so necessary that St. Ignatius, bishop, could rightly say that outside the ministry of bishops, priests, and deacons, "there is no Church".

Two aspects can be distinguished in the action of Christ the Lord in his Church: through communion with him, Christ brings the Church to unity by grace in the Holy Spirit; also by the power of the Spirit, Christ continues to exercise his role as Head of the Church.

There is of course no separation or division between these two aspects. Here as everywhere in the mystery of salvation there is interdependence. The growth of communion in a certain diversity is, no doubt, the fruit of the Holy Spirit, but this growth cannot overlook the sacramental structures of the Church and lay the stress only on its charismatic riches. Neither can the exercise of the role of Christ as Head through the hierarchical ministries exhaust the ecclesial reality; it must be attentive to the action of the Spirit "who breathes where he wills". It is certain, however, that, human limitations notwithstanding, the discernment of charisms belongs in the last resort to the ministry of the hierarchy.

The eucharistic celebration is the privileged place where the mystery of the Church in itself and in its relations to the world can best be discovered.

The Eucharist is celebrated in the context of the proclamation of the word of God by which the work of the Father and his saving design are revealed to us. Christ is the cornerstone of this saving design, which is brought to perfection through the mission of the Holy Spirit.

The Christian community is gathered to listen to the wonderful deeds of God and to be inserted into Christ in order to perform its highest task of praise. But the power of the word and of the Holy Spirit who renews the face of the earth reaches its climax in the Real Presense of Christ in answer to the prayer of his Church always awaiting his coming. This most efficacious word can only be authentically pronounced by the ministers of the Church, who, humbly but also with power, make Christ the Lord actually and visibly present. Thus, through Christ, with him and in him, the Church is able to do what it could never do with its own human strength.

This is the identity of the Church: it is the gathering up of those who, by grace and through faith, have received the explicit knowledge of the plan of the Father who has sent his Son into the world to give it life in the Spirit and who brings this plan to its realization by their sacramental Communion in the Body of Christ.

In this perspective, it is clear that the Church cannot exist without the proclamation of the word and the celebration of the Eucharist, for these two elements, which converge in the liturgy, constitute its specific nature.

It is clear that the Christian life cannot be reduced to some devices conducive to human coexistence. Christian morality is a way of life regulated by the light, which the First and the Second Coming of Christ project on human existence. To live as a Christian is to live in the Spirit by ceaselessly confronting one's actions with the Gospel, in the expectation of the Kingdom. This is why Christianity cannot be reduced to an "orthopraxy"; the foundation of "orthopraxy" is orthodoxy.

Without entering into the different meanings given to the term "world", we may say that the Church lives in the world and directs it to its goal.

To say that the Church directs the world to its goal does not only mean that the world is destined to be absorbed in the Kingdom; it also means that the word of God has the power to raise men to an image more deeply conformed to the humanity of the Son, that is, enjoying more justice, greater freedom, in one phrase, a fuller life. Thus, the Church is at once inserted in the world and foreign to it. It is associated with it but also transcends it. The Christian community as such is not identical with the world. Individual Christians and the Church must, no doubt, contribute to temporal development, but their specific service is the explicit witness of the Faith. To obscure this witness is to fail in the mission that Christ has entrusted to the Church and for which he has given it his Spirit.

Christ is the Head of the entire creation, and the Eucharist celebrates liturgically the recapitulation of all things in him. This is why in its liturgy the Church is "recentered" on Christ and strengthened in its mission of service to the world. For the Christian these two aspects are inseparable.

SELECT BIBLIOGRAPHY ON CELIBACY

I. Recent Documents of the Magisterium

Dutch Episcopate. *Official Communication to the Press.* January 19, 1970.

Dutch Pastoral Council. *Recommendations on the Ministry and Celibacy.* January 6, 1970.

French Episcopate. *Documents sur le sacerdoce.* Paris, 1969.

German Episcopate. *Official Declaration.* February 19, 1970.

German Episcopate. *Schreiben der deutschen Bischöfe über das priesterliche Amt. Fulda and Trier:* Paulinus-Verlag, 1969.

John XXIII. Cf. G. Caprile, "Jean XXIII et le célibat". In *Le Concile Vatican II*, vol. 5. Rome, 1969, p. 708.

Paul VI. *Addresses to the Faithful Assembled in St. Peter's Square.*

Paul VI. *Allocution to the Consilium of the General Secretariat of the Synod.* May 15, 1970. AAS 62 (1970): 443–46.

Paul VI. *Letter to Cardinal Alfrink.* December 24, 1970.

Paul VI. Letter to the Cardinal Secretary of State. Published in *L'Osservatore Romano.* February 4, 1970.

Paul VI. *Sacerdotalis Coelibatus.* AAS 59 (1967): 657–97.

Paul VI. Sunday Homily. February 1, 1970. Published in *L'Osservatore Romano.* February 2, 1970.

Suenens, Cardinal. *Declaration devant la télévision française.* Published in *Informations Catholiques Internationales,* n. 360 (May 15, 1970): 20–22.

Suenens, Cardinal. Interview with H. Fesquet. *Le Monde,* May 12, 1970.

Suenens, Cardinal. Interview with H. Fesquet. *Le Monde,* 1970; cf. *Le Monde,* May 23, 1970.

Vatican Council II. *Optatam Totius,* 10.

Vatican Council II. *Perfectae Caritatis,* 12.

Vatican Council II. *Presbyterorum Ordinis,* 16.

II. *Bibliographical References*

G. Da Vigolo. "Elenco delle publicazioni recenti sul celibato e sulla castità perfetta 1950–1962". *Rivista d'Ascetica e Mistica* 8 (1963): 95–99, 210–12.

Ephemerides Theologicae Lovanienses 40 (1964). Elenchus Bibliographicus, 153–56.

O. Gonzalez de Cardedal. "Crisis de seminarios o crisis de sacerdotes?" *Meditación de una España postconciliar.* Madrid, 1967, 117–43.

Lexikon für Theologie und Kirche, vol. 5. 1213–19 ("Jungfräulichkeit").

"Zur Auseinandersetzung über die Zölibatsfrage". *Herder Korrespondenz* 24 (1970): 128–39.

III. *Some Fundamental Studies*

A. Antweiller. *A propos du célibat du prêtre.* Paris, 1969.

J. P. Audet. *Structures of Christian Priesthood.* London, 1967.

L. Beirnaert. "Célibat sacerdotal et sexualité". *Études* (March 1964), 367–74.

J. Blinzler. "Eisin eunocoi. Zur Auslegung von Mt 19, 12". *Zeitschrift für neuestamentliche Wissenschaft* 48 (1957): 254–70.

F. Böckle. *Der Zölibat, Erfahrungen-Meinungen-Vorschläge.* Mainz, 1968.

R. Bunnik. *Priests for Tomorrow.* New York, 1969.

Le Célibat du prêtre, un problème d'Eglise. L'enquête officielle de l'Eglise des Pays-Bas. Paris, 1969.

Centre Catholique des Médecins Français. *Célibat et sexualité.* Paris, 1970.

G. Denzler. "Priesterehe und Priesterzölibat in historischer Sicht". In *Existenzprobleme des Priesters,* 13–52.

B. Gardet. "Le célibat sacerdotal met en question notre culture". *Supplement à la vie spirituelle* 78 (1966): 435ff.

I. F. Görres. "Priestertum der Frau". In *Be-denkliches.* Donauwörth, 1966.

F. Henrich. *Existenzprobleme des Priesters.* Munich, 1969.

L. Hödl. "Die Lex Continentiae. Eine problemgeschichtliche Studie". *Zeitschrift für Katholische Theologie* 83 (1961): 325–44.

F. Klostermann. *Priester für morgen.* Innsbruck-Vienna-Munich, 1970.

K. Mörsdorf-L. M. Weber. "Zölibat". In *Lexikon für Theologie und Kirche* 10: 1395–1401.

M. Oraison. *Le célibat. Aspect négatif, réalités positives.* Paris, 1966.

K. Rahner. "Der Zölibat des Weltpriesters im gegenwärtigen Gespräch". *Geist und Leben* 40 (1967): 122–38 and 41 (1968): 285–304; summarized in *Servants of the Lord.* London, 1967, 149–72.

J. Ratzinger. "Zur Frage nach dem Sinn des priesterlichen Dienstes". *Geist und Leben* 41 (1968): 347–77.

L. Rinser. *Priester und Frau.* Würzburg, 1968.

E. Schillebeeckx. *Autour du célibat du prêtre. Étude critique.* Paris, 1967.

H. Vorgrimler. *Das Priestertum. Quaestiones Disputatae.* Fribourg, 1970.

F. Wulf. "Der christologische Aspekt des priesterlichen Zölibats". *Geist und Leben* 41 (1968): 107–22.

F. Wulf. "Die heutige Zölibatskrise und ihre Bewältigung". *Geist und Leben* 42 (1969): 137–45.

F. Wulf. "Zur Anthropologie von Zölibat und Jungfräulichkeit". *Geist und Leben* 36 (1963): 352–60.

F. Wulf. "Zur Theologie der christlichen Ehelosigkeit und Jungfräulichkeit". *Geist und Leben* 36 (1963): 341–51.

VIII. THE SPIRITUALITY OF THE PRIEST

A. *Principles*

Is there any special spirituality of the priest? A positive answer to this question supposes an objective unity in his office, capable of producing a unity of consciousness. The center of this unity will be the delegation by Christ of his priestly character in a derived ministerial form. This continuity is visible, above all, in the image of the pastor: Christ applied it to himself (for the sacrifice of his life: Jn 10); the apostolic age followed suit (1 Pet 2:25; 5:4; Heb 13:20; Rev 7:17; cf. Mt 25:32; 26:31). But Jesus applied it equally to Peter (Jn 20:15–17), and the New Testament commonly uses it—above all in the First Epistle of Peter—for the activities of the apostles and their collaborators and substitutes (Acts 20:28; Eph 4:11; 1 Pet 5:2; cf. Mt 9:36 and parallel texts). The First Epistle of Peter on the one hand joins together Christ and the office of bishop by calling Christ "the great pastor and *episkopos* of your souls" (2:25) and, on the other hand, the office of Peter and that of the presbyters who succeeded him; Peter calls himself "copresbyter" and teaches the leaders of the Churches to pasture their flock in a Christian manner; they await together the return and the judgment of their "chief Shepherd" (5:3ff.).

From a Christological point of view, the "pastor" is he who has received from God the "mandate" and the "power" (Jn 10:18) to give his life for his sheep. As we have already said, this identity of office and love in the supreme and unique priesthood of Christ can only be shared by succeeding pastors on a twofold condition: on the one hand, there are an office and objective power based on an objective *"configuratio Christo Sacerdoti"*; on the other hand, an order (accompanied by a promise: Jn 20:18), requiring as close an assimilation as possible to Christ's attitude in giving his life out of love. All priestly spirituality is governed by this postulate inherent in the ministry and made possible by the grace of the Lord. It is a special spirituality because the pastor, in the exercise of his office, is placed on the side of Christ himself, radically distinct from his flock, though definitely united and associated with them. He shares in the "expropriation" of the Son of God, which gives him his being-for-others. By expanding this fundamental idea, we can discover the elements of a priestly spirituality.

1. Jesus offers his own life, including the Eucharist and the Cross, in order to reveal to men the efficacy of the Father's love and pastoral solicitude. His doctrine is that of the Father (Jn 7:16; 12:49; 14:14); his works are wrought by the Father (Jn 10:32, 37); in his Passion the Father glorifies his own name (Jn 12:28). In the Son the most complete commitment to men coincides with the most complete surrender to the Father, so that under both aspects he may be

the Father's perfect revelation. The more the Son surrenders himself, the more the Father can make himself known *to him* and *by* him *to the world.* Following this trinitarian and Christological law, the priest will have indissolubly to unite his "own sanctification" (Jn 17:18, meaning the consecration of his existence through prayer and through a habitual availability to the will of God) and his application to the pastoral charge given him by God. He must hand on a doctrine that is not his own, which, consequently, cannot be a scientific theology learned from outside but must be an experimental knowledge (not necessarily mystical) of the divine, such as a sincere abandonment to God provides in prayer and self-denial. This alone can nourish and enlighten souls in search of the supernatural. The priestly office implies in itself a spiritual element, but it also requires that the minister "rekindle the gift of God" (2 Tim 1:6).

The total availability of the priest toward God includes an availability, in principle no less spontaneous, toward the Church, at the service of which he has dedicated himself. His obedience to the bishop is the concrete expression of his unreserved self-gift to the incarnate Word. He can and ought to place at the service of his ministry all his forces of mind and imagination, his creative and inventive power, but he cannot claim any strict *right* to a particular apostolic method, to a particular field of action, or to work among a particular group of men. He should not evaluate his efforts in terms of concrete results; success is not, as Martin Buber well said, one of the names of God. Outward failure and the humiliation that often accompanies it can be, on the contrary, the condition for bearing more essential fruits of divine grace; as we have seen, a sharing in the priestly ministry of Christ always implies a sharing in his eschatological suffering.

2. Christ "offered himself once for all to take away the sins of many" (Heb 9:28) and by his identification with sinners became the brother of all to present himself in communion with them before the Father (Heb 2:10ff.). For us, henceforth, every man is a "brother for whom Christ died" (Rom 14:16; 1 Cor 8:11). After the example of the Good Shepherd, the solicitude of the ministry will demand from the minister a similar kind of life for the service of the souls entrusted to him. Paul's life sets here the example; his doctrine formulates it. The Church has already been "acquired" by the blood of Christ (Acts 20:28), but the service to which the minister is pledged and which can go even to the shedding of blood remains nonetheless efficacious and necessary for the communities (Phil 2:17ff.), thanks to the union of the passion of the apostolic servants with Christ's own Passion (Col 1:24ff.). Evidently this pledge takes first of all the form of active work continued as long as possible, but constantly accompanied by "the sufferings of the death of Jesus" (2 Cor 4:10); this is the condition whereby the "life of Jesus" is manifested in apostolic labors. And, as Christ united to his flock leads it to the Father,

so also his minister, in fraternal solidarity with his sheep, will lead them to the Lord.

3. In the fulfillment of his mandate Jesus came in contact with all strata of society: simple and learned, men and women, honored and slandered, laity and priests. He spoke to crowds, to small groups, and very often to individuals. He adapted himself to their spiritual capacity, to the religious categories of their times. Paul also became "all things to all men for the sake of the Gospel" (1 Cor 9:22ff.). The ministries of the Church ought, today as ever, to seek men where they are, sociologically and intellectually, and approach them with an attitude and language that they can understand. This does not exclude specialized tasks, but every specialization must maintain a Christian openness toward the integral human reality.[74] As Christ is always the representative of the Father before all, the priest ought always to represent the one Church of Christ. And, as Christ is the representative of the whole of mankind before the Father and its intercessor (Rom 8:34; Heb 7:25; Jn 17; 1 Jn 2:1ff.), so the priest ought to represent before the Father his flock, in what makes it one as Church—Body of Christ, by an "incessant" ministerial prayer (Phil 1:3). The "divine office", whatever may be its prescribed form, is an integral part of the priestly ministry; it belongs intrinsically to the apostolic labors. Work and prayer support each other and tend to an ever deeper mutual compenetration.

4. Christ is "Priest" in virtue of the identity—realized in him alone—between offerer and offered; he is thus in an eschatological state of givenness. He is the Father's definitive gift to the world: an eternal Eucharist containing his death and Resurrection (Rev 13:8). It is necessary that the minister-pastor not only conduct the eucharistic mystery in the midst of his community but also be himself conformed to it as much as possible, since his ministry is derived from a eucharistic priesthood. Because Jesus is wholly pure, "his whole body is food and his whole blood is drink, for each of his works is holy and each of his words is true. . . . In the second place after his flesh, Peter and Paul and all the apostles are food; in the third place their disciples".[75] Furthermore, it befits a pastoral spirituality that the minister of sacramental absolution included in his gesture his own conformity to him who on the Cross has merited for us a full absolution; by his entire life he ought to express the "ministry of reconciliation" that is "confided" to him (2 Cor 5:18).

Just as the actualization of the Paschal and eucharistic mystery is essentially the work of the Holy Spirit, so the life of the minister cannot be transformed into an efficacious gift except by the work of the same Spirit. The criterion in the last analysis is not of a psychological order; the decisive radiance does not

---

[74] Consequently, priests *"numquam alicui ideologiae vel factioni humanae inserviunt"* (PO, 6; end of the text).

[75] Origen, *In Lev. hom.,* 7, 5; *GCS,* VI (Baehrens), p. 387.

depend on natural gifts or purely fraternal "virtues" but on the truly Christo-logical humility that allows the priest at all times to be permeated by the action of the divine Spirit. By this (unconscious) transparency he will be able to give concrete shape to the ever present and actual blessing of God on his people and to turn into a living reality the unified act of praise that rises from the people toward God.

B. *Consequences*

From the above there follow some consequences with regard to (1) the motives for the priestly vocations, (2) the life-style of the priest, and (3) his formation.

1. The *motives* that impel young people to choose the priestly ministry will be more authentic and more efficacious as they come closer to the Christologi-cal synthesis that is the source of every office in the Church. This synthesis transcends the dilemma: either turning toward God or toward the world, because consecration to God and *his* work (with the segregation that it implies) is essentially made for the sake of humanity. In this indivisible choice, the priest obeys Christ who calls him to himself and sends him out to men; by this, moreover, he only explicitates in his own life the twofold movement proper to the whole Church.[76] Neither of the two sides can prevail over the other, because God himself is *Non-Aliud*; nothing is "opposed" to him, and he is both transcendent and immanent to the world. A serious reflection on "the principle and end of all things" (Dz, 1785) and the adoration of the primordial mystery are nonetheless incumbent on all Christians and on all men. Indeed, they must be the foundation of all pastoral care. In one way or another, the man who brings effective help to the world always comes from God. The psychological point of insertion may well be human misery, physical or spiritual; but the more one reflects on the cause of this misery, the more one finds that social and political involvement, however deep, does not go to the root of the evil. The *"cura corporum"*, as a means to lead to the *"cura animarum"*, is not only justified; it is also necessary (Lk 10:25ff.; Mt 25:35ff., 42ff.; 1 Jn 3:17; James 2:1ff.). But no change of social and economic structures will automatically suppress spiritual misery. True help comes from God's commit-ment to man in Christ. To make this commitment visible and efficacious is the decisive motive for a priestly vocation. God has given up for us what is most precious to him; his Son has given himself, emptied himself fully to become this gift of the Father and to put himself at the service of mankind. He arouses

---

[76] P. Colin, "Le prêtre; un homme 'mis à part' mais non 'séparé' ", in *Vatican II; Les prêtres,* Unam Sanctam, 68, 1968, pp. 261–74.

in Christian youth the generosity to "leave everything" in order to follow him — in the pastoral solicitude of the Father and the Son.

2. The *life-style* of the priest varies according to cultural and social conditions.[77] The tendency to form a separate "caste" ought ceaselessly to be resisted and new forms of communion with men ought to be invented. Various specializations can open the way for efficacious action; in order to establish contact, taking up a secular work (priest-workers) can be a useful, even necessary way. Where religious teaching is suppressed in schools, the teaching of other subjects can be the last opportunity to speak about religion to the young. In persecuted countries the priest will have to cloak his identity even more. Will priests live and act in groups or alone? Theologically speaking, this is a secondary question, but in practice it is important. Both solutions are possible, but a minimum of contact with the community will be required. The ways of contacting men will always be for the priest means that he uses according to his mission and his aim. As priest, even in a case of extreme specialization, he will always represent the whole reality (God in Christ and in the Church), and he will have to act as the center of a crystallizing process, not for his own sake but effacing himself before Christ. He will not bind the laity to his person or to his organizations but will arouse in them their own charisms and initiatives for the formation of Christian centers of union. Even the liturgical assembly of the community gathered together to hear the word and to celebrate the Eucharist, where the priest represents Christ before the people and the people before Christ, will only attain to its full meaning and identity if the priest knows how to efface himself.

3. The fundamental rule for the *formation* of the priest[78] requires that an existential experience of the living God and an involvement in men's lives and their sufferings grow simultaneously and by reciprocal interaction. On the one hand, it is necessary to learn to pray and to live in constant union with God if, later, a simple sermon and much more the example of life are to bear fruit; on the other hand, an apostolic orientation must be explicitly given from the beginning, though this does not imply that everything one learns must have immediate application. The tension between these two things can only be sustained by a living theology that never loses sight of the unity of biblical revelation and remains capable of approaching the details in the light of the broad synthesis. It ought to safeguard the connection between theology and anthropology, to show along which way the man of today can find access to the Christian mystery. But it must not slur over any of the essential mysteries but rather must maintain a just proportion between them.

---

[77] *Prêtres d'hier et d'aujourd'hui,* Unam Sanctam, 28, 1954.

[78] E. Marcus, "L'initiation au ministère. Condition d'exercice de cette fonction ecclésiale", in *Vatican II; Les prêtres,* Unam Sanctam, 68, 1968, pp. 345–71.

A living theology opens the doors in two directions: toward prayer and meditation, and toward action and achievements in the midst of the world of today.

CONCLUSION

The limits of this study are too evident to need stressing: there could be no question of writing a complete treatise on the priesthood, but simply of sorting some important guidelines.

Considering that the questioning of the ministerial priesthood reflects above all a *theological and spiritual* crisis, we have tried to clarify the biblical and traditional foundations of the priestly ministry.

We have strongly insisted on the Christological and apostolic foundation of the priestly ministry and thereby on the aspect of eschatological service. In the light of this fundamental vision we have examined the question of the insertion of the priesthood in the world of today and of a priestly spirituality.

We think, in fact, that a better understanding of the *specific nature* of the priestly ministry will provide an answer to the questions that are asked today, with a clearer perception of what is absolutely essential and what is only relative.

As we said at the beginning of this report, the solution of the crisis can only come from a theological and spiritual deepening.

PROPOSITIONS

1. *In the Church every hierarchical ministry goes back to the institution of the apostles. This ministry, willed by Christ, is essential to the Church, for through it the saving act of the Lord becomes sacramentally and historically present to all generations.*

2. *In the New Covenant there is no other priesthood than that of Christ. This priesthood fulfills and supersedes all the old priesthoods. In the Church all the faithful are called to share in it. The hierarchical ministry, however, is necessary for the building up of the Body of Christ in which this vocation is realized.*

3. *Christ alone performed the perfect sacrifice by the offering made of himself to the will of the Father. The episcopal and presbyteral ministry, therefore, is priestly inasmuch as it makes the ministry of Christ present in the effective proclaiming of the Gospel message, in bringing together and leading the Christian community, in the remission of sins, and in the celebration of the Eucharist by which in a special manner the one sacrifice of Christ is actualized.*

4. *Thus the Christian who is called to the priestly ministry receives by his ordination not a merely external function but a new sharing in the priesthood of Christ, by virtue of which he represents Christ at the head of the community and, as it were, facing the community. The ministry is therefore a specific way of exercising the Christian service in the Church. This specific character is seen especially in the priest's role of presiding at the Eucharist, a role that is necessary for the full realization of the Christian worship. The preaching of the word and the pastoral office are ordered toward the Eucharist, which consecrates the Christian's entire life in the world.*

5. *Though one must acknowledge a certain development in the structures of the early Church, one cannot maintain that some Churches—the Pauline ones—had a purely charismatic constitution, in contrast with the ministerial constitution of other Churches. For the primitive Church there is no opposition but rather complementarity between the freedom of the Spirit in dispensing his gifts and the existence of a ministerial structure.*

6. *The ministry of the New Covenant has a collegial dimension that is realized analogically at different levels: the bishops around the Pope in the universal Church, and the priests around their bishop in the local Church.*

Rome, October 10, 1970

3

THEOLOGICAL PLURALISM

The text of the propositions approved by the plenary meeting held on October 10 and 11, 1972. After the votes on each proposition and on the elucidations examined and received by the subcommission, the whole text was unanimously approved by all members present.

THE DIMENSIONS OF THE PROBLEM

1. Unity and plurality in the expression of the Faith have their ultimate basis in the very mystery of Christ that, while being at the same time a mystery of universal fulfillment and reconciliation (Eph 2:11–22), goes beyond the possibilities of expression of any given age and thus eludes exhaustive systematization (Eph 3:8–10).

2. The unity-duality of the Old Testament and the New, as the fundamental historical expression of the Christian Faith, provides a concrete point of departure for the unity-plurality of this same Faith.

3. The dynamism of Christian faith, and its missionary character, requires an account of it in rational terms; faith is not a philosophy, but it does give a direction to man's thinking.

4. The truth of the Faith is bound up with its onward movement through history, from Abraham on to Christ, and from Christ to the parousia. Consequently, orthodoxy is not consent to a system but a sharing in the onward movement of the Faith and so, in the Church's own selfhood that subsists, identical, through all time, and the true subject of the Credo.

5. The fact that the truth of the Faith is lived in an onward movement involves its relation to the praxis and to the history of this Faith. Since Christian faith is founded on the incarnate Word, its historical and practical character distinguishes it in its essence from a form of historicity in which man alone would be the creator of his own direction.

6. The Church is the comprehensive subject giving unity both to New Testament theologies and to dogmas as they arise throughout history. It is

Reprinted from *The Tablet*, Jul. 7, 1973.

founded on confession of faith in Jesus Christ dead and risen, which she proclaims and celebrates in the power of the Spirit.

7. The criterion that makes it possible to distinguish between true and false pluralism is the Faith of the Church expressed in the organic whole of her normative pronouncements: the fundamental criterion is Scripture as it relates to the confession of the believing and praying Church. Among dogmatic formulas, those of the earlier Councils have priority. The formulas that express a reflection of Christian thought are subordinate to those that express the facts of the Faith themselves.

8. Even if the present situation of the Church encourages pluralism, plurality discovers its limits in the fact that faith creates the communion of men in the truth, which has been made accessible in Christ. This makes inadmissible every conception of faith that would reduce it to a purely pragmatic cooperation, lacking any sense of community in the truth. This truth is not linked to any theological systematization, but it is expressed in the normative proclamations of the Faith. Faced with doctrinal statements that are gravely ambiguous, even perhaps incompatible with the Faith of the Church, the Church has the capacity to discern error and the duty to dispel it, even resorting to the formal rejection of heresy as the final remedy for safeguarding the Faith of the people of God.

9. Because the Christian Faith is universal and missionary, the events and words revealed by God must be each time rethought, reformulated, and lived anew within each human culture, if we wish them to inspire the prayer, the worship, and the daily life of the people of God. Thus, the Gospel of Christ leads each culture toward its fullness and at the same time submits it to a creative criticism. Local Churches that, under the guidance of their shepherds, apply themselves to this difficult task of incarnating the Christian Faith must always maintain continuity and communion with the universal Church of the past and of the present. Thanks to their efforts they contribute as much to the deepening of the Christian life as to the progress of theological reflection in the universal Church, and guide the human race in all its diversity toward that unity wished by God.

PERMANENT NATURE OF DOCTRINAL FORMULATIONS

10. Dogmatic formulations must be considered as responses to precise questions, and it is in this sense that they remain always true. Their permanent interest depends on the lasting relevance of the questions with which they are concerned; at the same time it must not be forgotten that the successive questions that Christians ask themselves about the understanding of the divine word as well

as already discovered solutions grow out of one another, so that today's answers always presuppose in some way those of yesterday, although they cannot be reduced to them.

11. Dogmatic definitions ordinarily use a common language; while they may make use of apparently philosophical terminology, they do not thereby bind the Church to a particular philosophy but have in mind only the underlying realities of universal human experience, which the terms in question have enabled them to distinguish.

12. These definitions must never be considered apart from the particularly authentic expression of the divine word in the sacred Scriptures or separated from the entire Gospel message to each age. They also provide, for that message, norms for an ever more suitable interpretation of revelation. Yet this revelation remains always the same, not only in its substance but also in its fundamental statements.

PLURALISM AND UNITY IN MORALS

13. Pluralism in morals appears first of all in the application of general principles to concrete circumstances, and it is accentuated when contacts occur between cultures that were ignorant of one another or as a result of rapid changes in society.

A fundamental unity is manifested, however, in a common esteem for human dignity, carrying with it imperatives for the conduct of human life.

The conscience of every man expresses a certain number of fundamental demands (Rom 2:14), which have been recognized in our times by public expressions of the essential human rights.

14. The unity of Christian morality is based on unchanging principles, contained in the Scriptures, clarified by Tradition, presented to each generation by the Magisterium. Let us recall the principal emphases: the precepts and example of the Son of God revealing the heart of his Father; conformity to his death and his Resurrection; life in the Spirit in the bosom of the Church, in faith, hope, and charity, so that we may be renewed according to the image of God.

15. The necessary unity of faith and communion does not hinder a diversity of vocations and of personal preferences in the manner of coming to terms with the mystery of Christ and of life.

Christian liberty (Gal 5:13), far from implying a limitless pluralism, demands a struggle toward totally objective truth no less than patience with less robust consciences.

Respect for the autonomy of human values and legitimate responsibilities in this area carries with it the possibility of a variety of analyses and options on temporal matters for Christians. This variety is compatible with total obedience and love.

4

CATHOLIC TEACHING
ON APOSTOLIC SUCCESSION

This study sets out to throw light on the concept of apostolic succession, on the one hand, because a clear presentation of the Catholic doctrine would seem to be useful to the Catholic Church as a whole, and, on the other hand, because it is demanded by ecumenical dialogue. For some time now ecumenical dialogue has been going on in various parts of the world, and it has a promising future provided the Catholics taking part in it remain faithful to their Catholic identity. So we propose to present the Catholic teaching on apostolic succession in order to strengthen our brothers in the Faith and to contribute to the mature development of ecumenical dialogue.

We begin by listing some of the difficulties that are frequently encountered:

1. What can be deduced, scientifically, from the witness of the New Testament? How can one show the continuity between the New Testament and the Church's Tradition?
2. What is the place of the imposition of hands in apostolic succession?
3. Is there not a tendency in some quarters to reduce apostolic succession to the apostolicity that is common to the whole Church, or, conversely, to reduce the apostolicity of the Church to apostolic succession?
4. How can one evaluate the ministry of other churches and Christian communities in relation to apostolic succession?

Behind all these questions lies the problem of the relationship between Scripture, Tradition, and the dogmatic pronouncements of the Church.

The dominant note in our thinking is provided by the vision of the Church as willed by the Father, emerging from Christ's Paschal mystery, animated by the Holy Spirit, and organically structured. We hope to set the specific and essential function of apostolic succession in the context of the whole Church, which confesses its apostolic Faith and bears witness to its Lord.

We rely upon Scripture, which has for us a twofold value as a historical record and an inspired document. Insofar as it is a historical record, Scripture

Reprinted from *The Tablet*, Jul. 27, Aug. 3, and Aug. 10, 1974. This document was approved by the Commission *"in forma specifica"*.

recounts the most important events in the mission of Jesus and the life of the Church of the first century; insofar as it is an inspired document, it bears witness to certain facts and at the same time interprets them and reveals their inner significance and dynamic coherence. As an expression of the thought of God in the words of men, Scripture has a normative value for the thinking of Christ's Church in every age.

But any interpretation of Scripture that regards it as inspired and therefore normative for all ages is necessarily an interpretation that takes place within the Church's Tradition, which recognizes Scripture as inspired and normative. The recognition of the normative character of Scripture fundamentally implies a recognition of that Tradition within which Scripture itself was formed and came to be considered and accepted as inspired. The normative status of Scripture and its relationship to Tradition go hand in hand. The result is that any theological considerations about Scripture are at the same time ecclesial considerations.

This, then, is the methodological starting point of the document: any attempt to reconstitute the past by selecting isolated phrases from the New Testament Tradition and separating them from the way they were received in the living Tradition of the Church is contradictory.

The theological approach that sees Scripture as an indivisible whole and that links it with the life and thought of the early community that acknowledges and "recognizes" it as Scripture certainly does not mean that properly historical judgments are eliminated in advance by an ecclesiological a priori, which would make impossible an interpretation in conformity with the demands of historical method.

The method adopted here enables one to grasp the limitations of pure historicism: it admits that the purely historical analysis of a book in isolation from its effects and influence cannot show with certainty that the way Faith actually developed in history was the only possible way. But these limits to historical proof, which one cannot doubt, do not destroy the value and weight of historical knowledge. On the contrary, the fact that the early Church accepted Scripture as constitutive is something to be constantly meditated upon: that is, we have to think out again and again the relationship, the differences, and the unity between the different elements.

That also means that one cannot dissolve Scripture into a series of unrelated sketches, each one of which would be an attempt to express a life-style founded on Jesus of Nazareth, but rather that one must understand it as the expression of a historical unfolding path that reveals the unity and the catholicity of the Church. There are three broad stages along this path: the time before Easter, the apostolic period, and the subapostolic period, and each period has its own specific value; it is significant that what the dogmatic constitution "On Divine Revelation", *Dei Verbum* (18) calls "*viri apostolici"* should be responsible for some of the New Testament writings.

This helps one to see clearly how the community of Jesus Christ solved the problem of remaining apostolic even though it had become subapostolic. This explains why the subapostolic part of the New Testament has a normative character for the Church at a later period, for it must build on the apostles, who themselves have Christ as their foundation. In the subapostolic writings, Scripture itself bears witness to Tradition and gives evidence of the Magisterium in that it recalls the teaching of the apostles (see Acts 2:42; 2 Pet 1:20). This Magisterium really begins to develop in the second century, at the time when the idea of apostolic succession is made fully explicit.

Scripture and Tradition taken together, pondered upon and authentically interpreted by the Magisterium, faithfully transmit to us the teaching of Christ our Lord and Savior and determine the doctrine that it is the Church's mission to proclaim to all peoples and to apply to each generation until the end of the world. It is in this theological perspective—fully in accord with the doctrine of Vatican II—that we have written this document on apostolic succession and evaluated the ministries that exist in churches and communities not yet in full communion with the Catholic Church.

I. THE APOSTOLICITY OF THE CHURCH AND THE COMMON PRIESTHOOD

1. The creeds confess their Faith in the apostolicity of the Church. That means not simply that the Church continues to hold the apostolic Faith but that it is determined to live according to the norm of the primitive Church, which derived from the first witnesses of Christ and was guided by the Holy Spirit, who was given to the Church by Christ after his Resurrection. The Epistles and the Acts of the Apostles show how effective was this presence of the Spirit in the whole Church, and that he not only ensured its diffusion but also and more importantly the transformation of hearts: the Spirit assimilates them to Christ and his feelings. Stephen, the first martyr, repeats the words of forgiveness of his dying Lord; Peter and John are beaten and rejoice that they should be found worthy to suffer with him; Paul bears in his body the marks of Christ (Gal 6:17), wants to be conformed to the death of Christ (Phil 3:10), to know nothing save the crucified One (1 Cor 1:23; 2:2), and he considers his whole life as an assimilation to the expiating sacrifice of the Cross (Phil 2:17; Col 1:24).

2. This assimilation to the "thoughts" of Christ and above all to his sacrificial death for the world gives ultimate meaning to the lives of those who want to lead a Christian, spiritual, and apostolic life.

That is why the early Church adapted the priestly vocabulary of the Old Testament to Christ, the Paschal Lamb of the New Covenant (1 Cor 5:7), and then to Christians whose lives are defined in relation to the Paschal mystery of Christ. Converted by the preaching of the Gospel, they are convinced that they are living out a holy and royal priesthood that is a spiritual transposition of the priesthood of the Old Testament (1 Pet 2:5–9; see Ex 19:6; Is 61:6) and that was made possible by the sacrificial offering of him who recapitulates in himself all the sacrifices of the Old Law and opens the way for the complete and eschatological sacrifice of the Church (see St. Augustine, *De Civitate Dei*, X, vi).

Christians as living stones in the new building that is the Church founded on Christ offer to God worship in the Spirit who has made them new; their cult is both *personal,* since they have to "present their bodies as a living sacrifice, holy and acceptable to God" (Rom 12:1; see 1 Pet 2:5), and *communal,* since together they make up the "spiritual house", the "royal priesthood" and "holy nation" (1 Pet 2:9), whose purpose is to offer "spiritual sacrifices that Jesus Christ has made acceptable to God" (1 Pet 2:8).

This priesthood has a moral dimension—since it must be exercised every day and in ordinary situations—and an eschatological dimension, since it is in eternity to come that Christ has promised to make of us "a line of kings, priests to serve his God and Father" (Rev 1:6; see 5:10; 20:6); but it has also a cultural dimension, since the Eucharist by which they live is compared by St. Paul to the sacrifices of the Old Law and even—though only to make a sharp contrast —to pagan sacrifices (1 Cor 10:16–21).

3. Now Christ instituted a ministry for the establishment, animation, and maintenance of this priesthood of Christians. This ministry was to be the sign and the instrument by which he would communicate to his people in the course of history the fruits of his life, death, and Resurrection. The first foundations of this ministry were laid when he called the Twelve, who at the same time represent the new Israel as a whole and, after Easter, will be the privileged eyewitnesses sent out to proclaim the Gospel of salvation and the leaders of the new people, "fellow workers with God for the building of his temple" (see 1 Cor 3:9). This ministry has an essential function to fulfill toward each generation of Christians. It must therefore be transmitted from the apostles by an unbroken line of succession. If one can say that the Church as a whole is established upon the foundation of the apostles (Eph 2:20; Rev 21:14), one has to add that this apostolicity, which is common to the whole Church, is linked with the ministerial apostolic succession, and that this is an inalienable ecclesial structure at the service of all Christians.

II. THE ORIGINALITY OF THE APOSTOLIC FOUNDATION
OF THE CHURCH

The apostolic foundation has this special characteristic: it is both historical and spiritual.

It is historical in the sense that it comes into being through an act of Christ during his earthly existence: the call of the Twelve at the start of his public ministry, their commission to represent the new Israel and to be involved ever more closely with his Paschal journey, which is consummated in the Cross and Resurrection (Mk 1:17; 3:14; Lk 22:28; Jn 15:16). Far from destroying the pre-Easter structure, the Resurrection confirms it. In a special manner Christ makes the Twelve the witnesses of his Resurrection, and they head the list that he had ordered before his death: the earliest confession of Faith in the Risen One includes Peter and the Twelve as the privileged witnesses of his Resurrection (1 Cor).

Those who had been associated with Jesus from the beginning of his ministry to the eve of his Paschal death are able to bear public witness to the fact that it is the *same Jesus* who is risen (Jn 15:27). After Judas' defection and even before Pentecost, the first concern of the Eleven is to replace him in their apostolic ministry with one of the disciples who had been with Jesus since his baptism, so that with them he could be a witness of his Resurrection (Acts 1:17–22). Moreover Paul, who was called to the apostolate by the risen Lord himself and thus became part of the Church's foundation, is aware of the need to be in communion with the Twelve.

This foundation is not only historical; it is also spiritual. Christ's passover, anticipated at the Last Supper, establishes the New Covenant and thus embraces the whole of human history. The mission and task of preaching the Gospel, governing, reconciling, and sanctifying that are entrusted to the first witnesses cannot be restricted to their lifetime. As far as the Eucharist is concerned, Tradition—whose broad lines are already laid down from the first century (see Lk and Jn)—declares that the apostles' participation in the Last Supper conferred on them the power to preside at the eucharistic celebration.

Thus the apostolic ministry is an eschatological institution. Its spiritual origins appear in Christ's prayer, inspired by the Holy Spirit, in which he discerns, as in all the great moments of his life, the will of the Father (Lk 6:12). The spiritual participation of the apostles in the mystery of Christ is completed fully by the gift of the Holy Spirit after Easter (Jn 20:22; Lk 24:44–49). The Spirit brings to their minds all that Jesus had said (Jn 14:26) and leads them to a fuller understanding of his mystery (Jn 16:13–15).

The kerygma, if it is to be properly understood, must not be separated or treated in abstraction from the Faith to which the Twelve and Paul came by their conversion to the Lord Jesus or from the witness to him manifested in their lives.

III. THE APOSTLES AND APOSTOLIC SUCCESSION IN HISTORY

The documents of the New Testament show that in the early days of the Church and in the lifetime of the apostles there was diversity in the way communities were organized, but also that there was, in the period immediately following, a tendency to assert and strengthen the ministry of teaching and leadership.

Those who directed communities in the lifetime of the apostles or after their death have different names in the New Testament texts: the *presbyteroi-episkopoi* are described as *poimenes, hegoumenoi, proistamenoi, kyberneseis.* In comparison with the rest of the Church, the feature of the *presbyteroi-episkopoi* is their apostolic ministry of teaching and governing. Whatever the method by which they are chosen, whether through the authority of the Twelve or Paul or some link with them, they share in the authority of the apostles who were instituted by Christ and who maintain for all time their unique character.

In the course of time this ministry underwent a development. This development happened by internal necessity. It was encouraged by external factors, and above all by the need to maintain unity in communities and to defend them against errors. When communities were deprived of the actual presence of apostles and yet still wanted to refer to the authority, there had to be some way of continuing to exercise adequately the functions that the apostles had exercised in and in relation to them.

Already in the New Testament texts there are echoes of the transition from the apostolic period to the subapostolic age, and one begins to see signs of the development that in the second century led to the stabilization and general recognition of the episcopal ministry. The stages of this development can be glimpsed in the last writings of the Pauline Tradition and in other texts linked with the authority of the apostles.

The significance of the apostles at the time of the foundation of the earliest Christian communities was held to be essential for the structure of the Church and local communities in the thinking of the subapostolic period. The principle of the apostolicity of the Church elaborated in this reflection led to the recognition of the ministry of teaching and governing as an institution derived from Christ by and through the mediation of the apostles. The Church lived in the certain conviction that Jesus, before he left this world, sent the Twelve on a universal mission and promised that he would be with them at all times until the end of the world (Mt 28:18–20).

The time of the Church, which is the time of this universal mission, is therefore contained within the presence of Christ, which is the same in the apostolic period and later and which takes the form of a single apostolic ministry.

As one can see from the New Testament writings, conflicts could not always be avoided between individuals and communities and the authority of the ministry. Paul, on the one hand, strove to understand the Gospel with and in the community and so to work out with them norms for Christian life, but, on the other hand, he appealed to his apostolic authority whenever it was a matter of the truth of the Gospel (see Gal) or unyielding principles of Christian life (see 1 Cor 7 and so on).

Likewise, the ministry of governing should never be separated from the community in such a way as to place itself above it: its role is one of service in and for the community. But when the New Testament communities accept apostolic government, whether from the apostles themselves or their successors, then they obey and relate the authority of the ministry to that of Christ himself.

The absence of documents makes it difficult to say precisely how these transitions came about. By the end of the first century the situation was that the apostles or their closest helpers or eventually their successors directed the local colleges of *episkopoi* and *presbyteroi*. By the beginning of the second century the figure of a single bishop who is the head of the communities appears very clearly in the letters of St. Ignatius of Antioch, who further claims that this institution is established "unto the ends of the earth" (*Ad Eph.*, 3, 2).

During the second century and after the Letter of Clement this institution is explicitly acknowledged to carry with it the apostolic succession. Ordination with imposition of hands, already witnessed to in the pastoral Epistles, appears in the process of clarification to be an important step in preserving the apostolic Tradition and guaranteeing succession in the ministry. The documents of the third century (Tradition of Hippolytus) show that this conviction was arrived at peacefully and was considered to be a necessary institution.

Clement and Irenaeus develop a doctrine on pastoral government and on the word in which they derive the idea of apostolic succession from the unity of the word, the unity of the mission, and the unity of the ministry of the Church; thus apostolic succession became the permanent ground from which the Catholic Church understood its own nature.

IV. THE SPIRITUAL ASPECT OF APOSTOLIC SUCCESSION

If after this historic survey we try to understand the spiritual dimensions of apostolic succession, we will have to stress first of all that the ordained ministry, although it represents the Gospel with authority and is essentially a service toward the whole Church, nevertheless demands that the minister should make Christ present in his humility (2 Cor 4:5) and make present Christ crucified (see Gal 2:19ff.; 16:14; 1 Cor 4:9ff.).

The Church that it serves is informed and moved by the Spirit, and "Church" here means the Church as a whole and in its members, for everyone who is baptized is "taught by the Spirit" (1 Th 4:9; see Heb 8:11; Jer 31:33ff.; 1 Jn 2:20; Jn 6:45). The role of the priestly ministry is therefore to bring to mind authoritatively what is already embryonically included in baptismal Faith but can never be fully realized here below. Likewise the believer should nourish his Faith and his Christian life through the sacramental mediation of the divine life. The norm of Faith—which is formally known as the *regula fidei*—becomes immanent in Christian life thanks to the Spirit while it remains *transcendent* in relation to men, since it can never be purely an individual matter but is rather by its very nature ecclesial and catholic.

Thus in the rule of Faith the immediacy of the divine Spirit in each individual is necessarily linked to the communitarian form of this Faith. Paul's statement is still valid; "No one can say 'Jesus is the Lord' except in the Holy Spirit" (1 Cor 2:3): without the conversion that the Spirit is always ready to grant to human hearts, no one can recognize Jesus as the Son of God, and only those who know him as the Son will know the one whom Jesus calls "Father" (see Jn 14:7; 8:19, and so on). Since, therefore, it is the Spirit who brings us knowledge of the Father through Jesus, Christian Faith is trinitarian: its pneumatic or spiritual *form* necessarily implies the *content* that is realized sacramentally in baptism in the name of Father, Son, and Holy Spirit.

The *regula fidei*, that is, the sort of baptismal catechesis in which the trinitarian content of Faith is developed, constitutes in its form and content the permanent basis for the apostolicity and catholicity of the Church. It realises *apostolicity* because it binds those who preach the Faith to the christopneumatological norm: they do not speak in their own name but bear witness to what they have heard (see Jn 7:18; 16:13ff.).

Jesus Christ shows that he is the Son in that he proclaims that he comes from the Father. The Spirit shows that he is the Spirit of the Father and the Son, because he does not devise something of his own but reveals and recalls what comes from the Son (Jn 16:13). This prolongation of the work of Christ and of his Spirit gives apostolic succession its distinctive character and makes the Church's Magisterium distinct from both the teaching authority of scholars and the rule of authoritarian power.

If the teaching authority were to fall into the hands of professors, Faith would depend upon the lights of individuals and would be thereby exposed to influence from the *Zeitgeist,* the spirit of the age. And where Faith depends upon the despotic power of certain individuals or groups, who themselves would decide what the norm was, then truth is replaced by arbitrary power. The true Magisterium, on the contrary, is bound by the word of the Lord and thus ushers those who listen to it into the realm of liberty.

Nothing in the Church can forego this need to refer to the apostles. Pastors and their flocks cannot avoid it; statements of Faith and moral precepts must be measured by it. The ordained ministry is bound to this apostolic mediation in a double way, since on the one hand it must submit to the norm of Christian origins and on the other hand it has the duty of learning from the community of believers, who themselves have the duty to instruct it.

We draw two conclusions from what has just been said:

1. No preacher of the Gospel has the right to proclaim the Gospel according to personal theories he may happen to have. He proclaims the Faith of the apostolic Church and not his own personality or his own religious experience.

This implies that we must add a third element to those we have already mentioned as belonging to the rule of Faith—form and content: the rule of Faith presupposes a *witness who has been entrusted with a mission,* who does not authorize him to speak, and that no individual community can authorize him to speak; and this comes about in virtue of the transcendence of the word. Authorization can only be given sacramentally through those who have already received the mission. It is true that the Spirit can freely arouse in the Church various charisms of evangelization and service and inspire all Christians to bear witness to their Faith, but these activities should be exercised with reference to the three elements mentioned in the *regula fidei* (see *LG,* 12).

2. This mission (trinitarian in its basis) enters into the rule of Faith and implies a reference to the catholicity of Faith, which is at once a consequence of apostolicity and a condition of its permanence. For no individual and no community by itself has this power to send on a mission. It is only in relation with the whole—*kath'holon,* catholicity in time and in space—that permanence in mission can be guaranteed. In this way catholicity explains why the believer, as a member of the Church, is introduced into an immediate participation in the trinitarian life through the mediation not only of the God-Man but of the Church who is intimately associated with him.

Because of the catholic dimension of its truth and its life, the mediation of the Church has to be achieved in an ordered way, through a ministry that is given to the Church as one of its constitutive elements. This ministry does not have as its only point of reference a historical period that is now no more (and that is represented by a series of documents); given this reference back, it must be endowed with the power of representing in itself its Source, the living Christ, through an officially authorized proclamation of the Gospel and by authoritative celebration of sacramental acts, above all the Eucharist.

V. APOSTOLIC SUCCESSION AND ITS TRANSMISSION

Just as the divine Word made Flesh is itself both proclamation and the communicating principle of the divine life into which it brings us, so the ministry of the word in its fullness and the sacraments of Faith, especially the Eucharist, are the means by which Christ continues to be for mankind the ever-present event of salvation. Pastoral authority is simply the responsibility that the apostolic ministry has for the unity of the Church and its development, while the word is the source of salvation and the sacraments are both the manifestation and the *locus* of its realization.

Thus apostolic succession is that aspect of the nature and life of the Church that shows the dependence of our present-day community on Christ through those whom he has sent. The apostolic ministry is, therefore, the sacrament of the effective presence of Christ and of his Spirit in the midst of the people of God, and this view in no way underestimates the immediate influence of Christ and his Spirit on each believer.

The charism of apostolic succession is received in the visible community of the Church. It presupposes that someone who is to enter the ministry has the Faith of the Church. The gift of ministry is granted in an act that is the visible and effacious symbol of the gift of the Spirit, and this act has as its instrument one or several of those ministers who have themselves entered the apostolic succession.

Thus the transmission of the apostolic ministry is achieved through ordination, including a rite with a visible sign and the invocation of God (*epiklesis*) to grant to the ordinand the gift of his Holy Spirit and the powers that are needed for the accomplishment of his task. This visible sign, from the New Testament onward, is the imposition of hands (see *LG,* 21). The rite of ordination expresses the truth that what happens to the ordinand does not come from human origin and that the Church cannot do what it likes with the gift of the Spirit.

The Church is fully aware that its nature is bound up with apostolicity and that the ministry handed on by ordination establishes the one who has been ordained in the apostolic confession of the truth of the Father. The Church, therefore, has judged that ordination, given and received in the understanding she herself has of it, is necessary to apostolic succession in the strict sense of the word.

The apostolic succession of the ministry concerns the whole Church, but it is not something that derives from the Church taken as a whole but rather from Christ to the apostles and from the apostles to all bishops to the end of time.

VI. TOWARD AN EVALUATION OF NON–CATHOLIC MINISTRIES

The preceding sketch of the Catholic understanding of apostolic succession now enables us to give in broad outline an evaluation of non-Catholic ministries. In this context it is indispensable to keep firmly in mind the differences that have existed in the origins and in the subsequent development of these churches and communities, as also their own self-understanding.

1. In spite of a difference in their appreciation of the office of Peter, the Catholic Church, the Orthodox church, and the other churches that have retained the reality of apostolic succession are at one in sharing a basic understanding of the sacramentality of the Church, which developed from the New Testament and through the Fathers, notably through Irenaeus. These churches hold that the sacramental entry into the ministry comes about through the imposition of hands with the invocation of the Holy Spirit, and that this is the indispensable form for the transmission of the apostolic succession, which alone enables the Church to remain constant in its doctrine and communion. It is this unanimity concerning the unbroken coherence of Scripture, Tradition, and sacrament that explains why communion between these churches and the Catholic Church has never completely ceased and could today be revived.

2. Fruitful dialogues have taken place with Anglican communions, which have retained the imposition of hands, the interpretation of which has varied. We cannot here anticipate the eventual results of this dialogue, which has as its object to inquire how far factors constitutive of unity are included in the maintenance of the imposition of hands and accompanying prayers.

3. The communities that emerged from the sixteenth-century Reformation differ among themselves to such an extent that a description of their relationship to the Catholic Church has to take account of the many individual cases. However, some general lines are beginning to emerge. In general it was a feature of the Reformation to deny the link between Scripture and Tradition and to advocate the view that Scripture alone was normative. Even if later on some sort of place for Tradition is recognized, it is never given the same position and dignity as in the ancient Church. But since the sacrament of orders is the indispensable sacramental expression of communion in the

Tradition, the proclamation of *sola scriptura* led inevitably to an obscuring of the older idea of the Church and its priesthood.

Thus through the centuries, the imposition of hands either by men already ordained or by others was often in practice abandoned. Where it did take place, it did not have the same meaning as in the Church of Tradition. This divergence in the mode of entry into the ministry and its interpretation is only the most noteworthy symptom of the different understandings of Church and Tradition. There have already been a number of promising contacts that have sought to reestablish links with the Tradition, although the break has so far not been successfully overcome.

In such circumstances, intercommunion remains impossible for the time being, because sacramental continuity in apostolic succession from the beginning is an indispensable element of ecclesial communion for both the Catholic Church and the Orthodox churches.

To say this is not to say that the ecclesial and spiritual qualities of the Protestant ministers and communities are thereby negligible. Their ministers have edified and nourished their communities. By baptism, by the study and the preaching of the word, by their prayer together and celebration of the Last Supper, and by their zeal they have guided men toward faith in the Lord and thus helped them to find the way of salvation. There are thus in such communities elements that certainly belong to the apostolicity of the unique Church of Christ.

5A

NINE THESES IN CHRISTIAN ETHICS

by Hans Urs von Balthasar

AN APPRAISAL OF CHRISTIAN ETHICS

The subcommittee for ethics[1] of the International Theological Commission (ITC) has carried on its research in a number of different directions: the use of Holy Scripture in Christian ethics; the teaching of the Magisterium (this point will be studied in a broader context in 1975); the criteria for the *actus honestus;* the meaning of Christian ethics; the use of the human sciences. With regard to this last point, several valuable studies were gathered together by the Secretariat and published in *Studia Moralia* of the Alphonsian Academy in 1974.[2] The research material on Holy Scripture is very extensive. Several of these papers as well as the studies on the criteria for the *actus honestus* will be published in the near future.

The study of "the fundamental principles and meaning of Christian ethics" is an undertaking so vast as to discourage anyone from attempting it: one would indeed expose oneself to the risk of merely repeating cliches. However, Father Hans Urs von Balthasar has successfully treated this theme in a masterful way, displaying the profundity, openness, and genius for synthesis that characterize his other works. For this reason the members of the ITC, while they approved his text *in forma generica,* did not want simply to publish it in a collective report and so leave it anonymous.[3]

Reprinted from the *Homiletic & Pastoral Review,* Feb. 1976. This document was approved by the Commission *"in forma generica".*

[1] During the first quinquennium the following theologians belonged to this subcommittee: Fr. Lonergan, S.J.; Fr. Feuillet, P.S.S.; Mgr. Oleynik; Fr. Vagaggini; Fr. Schürmann; Bishop Delhaye. The last three members were reappointed in 1975, and Frs. Ernst, Hamel, S.J., Inlender, and Mahoney, S.J., have joined them.

[2] A considerable number of the papers on the subject of human sciences and Christian ethics, which experts put at the disposal of the ITC, have been published in *Studia Moralia,* vol. 12 (Rome: Academia Alphonsiana, 1974).

[3] This text, therefore, is semiofficial. The official texts (two declarations and five theses) were submitted to the Secretary of State for approval in January 1975.

CHRIST DOES GOD'S WILL

The nine theses of Fr. Urs von Balthasar's paper attempt to state what is specific in *Christian* ethics, namely, how it springs forth from the Person of Christ, who is the perfect revelation of the love of God that extends to all men, who is the concrete and universal norm of all moral activity.

The life of Christ is at once celebration and action. It celebrates God's salvific work, which was prepared for in the nonbiblical religions and ethical systems, which was concretized in the promise and the Law of the Covenant, which was accomplished in the crucifixion and Resurrection of Christ and in the communication of the Holy Spirit. This life of Jesus actualizes the love of the Father for the world, for it fully accomplishes God's will and makes us children of God. In this way Christ, the prototype of perfect obedience to the Father, and the Holy Spirit who is given to believers, transform our sinful liberty. The example of Christ and the grace of the Spirit enable us to develop in the Church a moral, personal, and social activity that seeks the perfection of charity and is inclined to compassion.

The witness of unity given by Christians goes beyond mere fraternity between human beings—the reciprocity prescribed by the Golden Rule. It is the fruit of the Spirit of God and expresses among men the mystery of "poverty", which characterizes the interpersonal exchange in the divine life. This unity finds its finest expression in the eucharistic assembly, where Christians celebrate the word that constitutes their community, and where they share in the Body of Christ, the only Son of God and the universal brother of all men.

Contrary to what one might expect, such an analysis of Christian ethics does not simply disregard or discard pre-Christian or "post-Christian" ethical thought. Rather, it emphasizes those values in it that can be used and those that should be rejected.

Mgr. Philippe Delhaye
Secretary General of the ITC
Chairman of the Subcommittee
for Ethics

PRELIMINARY OBSERVATIONS

The Christian who lives by faith has the right to base his moral activity on his faith. Since the content of his Faith, namely, Jesus Christ, who revealed to us God's trinitarian love, assumed not only the form and the guilt of the first

Adam but also the limitations, anxieties, and decisions of his existence, there is no danger that the Christian will fail to find the first Adam in the Second Adam and along with him his own moral dilemma. Even Jesus had to choose between his Father and his family: "My child, why have you done this to us?" (Lk 2:48). Thus the Christian will make the basic decisions of his life from Christ's perspective, that is, from his Faith. One cannot properly designate an ethics, which proceeds from the fullness of revelation and then works back to the defective preparatory stages, as a "descending" ethics (in contrast to a so-called ascending ethics, which proceeds from anthropological data as its primary foundation).

HE LIVED HIS OBEDIENCE

Nor should one qualify this ethics as nonhistorical just because it gives priority to the New Testament over the Old. One must remember that the road is determined and illumined by the destination—a point that applies even to this unique road of salvation, which attains its goal only in the dialectic between discontinuity and superabundance (stressed by Paul), and inner fulfillment (stressed by Matthew and James). It is undoubtedly correct to say that from the historical and chronological point of view Theses 5 and 6 should have come before the Christological theses, and that Theses 7 and 9 should have preceded all of them. However, it is a fact that the Christian lives in the specifically "eschatological age". He must constantly strive to overcome in himself those tendencies that belong to the preparatory stages so that he can pass on to what belongs to the final stage of human existence. Rather than excluding, this includes the fact that Christ too lived his obedience to the Father not only in a prophetic, as it were, immediate vision of him, but also by keeping the Old Law and by believing in the promise. The Christian follows him in that too.

Our theses are given only in outline form, and many essential points have been omitted. For instance, the text speaks of the Church only indirectly. Nothing is said about the sacraments or about their relationship to the authority of the Church. Nothing is said about various opinions of far-reaching consequences that confront the Church today and that she must face eventually. We only wanted to consider Christian ethics as it comes forth from and depends on the mystery of Christ, which is the center of the history of salvation as well as of the history of man.

I. THE FULFILLMENT OF MORAL LIFE IN CHRIST

1. *Christ as the Concrete Norm*

THESIS 1:

Christian ethics must be elaborated in such a way that its starting point is Jesus Christ, since he, as the Son of the Father, fulfilled the complete will of the Father (= everything that must be done) in this world. He did this "for us" so that we might gain our freedom from him, the concrete and plenary norm of all moral action, to accomplish God's will and to live up to our vocation to be free children of the Father.

1. Jesus Christ is the concrete categorical imperative, in the sense that he is not only a formal, universal norm of moral life, which can be applied to everyone, but also a concrete and personal norm. By virtue of his suffering for us and the eucharistic giving up of his life for us as well as his handing it on to us (*per ipsum et cum ipso*), he has given us the interior strength to do the will of the Father *with him* (*cum ipso*).

Thus his imperative is based on the "indicative" (cf. Rom 6:7ff.; 2 Cor 5:15). The will of the Father, however, is twofold: (1) to love his children in him and with him (1 Jn 5:1f.) and (2) adoration in spirit and in truth (Jn 4:23). Christ's life is at the same time action *and* cult. This unity is the perfect norm for the Christian. It is only with an attitude of deep respect (Phil 7:12) that we can cooperate in the saving work of God. His absolute love infinitely surpasses us, being more unlike our love than like it (*in maiori dissimilitudine*). Liturgy therefore cannot be separated from moral life.

2. The Christian imperative places us beyond the question of autonomy vs. heteronomy:

a. Because the Son of God, begotten by the Father, is "another" (*heretos*) but not something other than (*heteron*) the Father. As God he is autonomously equal to the Father (his Person coincides with his procession and thus with his mission). On the other hand, as man he possesses in himself the divine will and his own affirmation of it as the very foundation of his existence (Heb 10:5f.; Phil 2:6f.) and as the inner source of his personal activity (Jn 4:34ff.). This also holds true for those cases in which he wishes to experience in suffering the resistance of sinners to God.

Strength Comes from Eucharist

At this point please note: When the divinity of Christ is not acknowledged, he appears necessarily only as a human model, and so Christian ethics once again becomes *heteronomous* on the supposition that the Christ-norm is considered simply binding on my moral activity. Or, it becomes *autonomous* when his example is still interpreted as the perfect way for the human moral subject to determine himself.

b. As created beings we remain *"heteron"*, but we are also given the capacity to unfold our personal and free activity by virtue of God's strength (the "drink" becomes in us a "spring" or "well" [Jn 4:13ff.; 7:38]). This strength comes to us from the Eucharist of his Son through our being reborn with him from the Father and through the gift of their Spirit. Since God in bestowing his grace works gratuitously, and since we likewise should act gratuitously when we love (Mt 10:8; Lk 14:12–14), the "great reward in heaven" (Lk 6:23) can therefore be nothing else but Love itself. Thus in God's eternal plan (Eph 1:10) the last end coincides with the first movement of our freedom (*interior intimo meo*; cf. Rom 8:15ff., 26ff.).

By virtue of the reality of our divine filiation all truly Christian actions are performed in freedom. To be more precise: for Christ the total burden of the saving task laid upon him (*dei*)—which will take him to Calvary—flows forth from his privilege of revealing in full liberty the saving will of God. For us sinners, however, the freedom of the children of God often becomes a heavy cross both with regard to our personal decisions and in the framework of community life. Even if it is true that the purpose of the rules of the Church is to free the believer from the alienation of sin and to lead him to his true identity and freedom, they may and indeed often must seem to be harsh and legalistic to the imperfect believer, just as the will of the Father appeared harsh to Christ hanging on the Cross.

2. The Universality of the Concrete Norm

THESIS 2

The norm of the concrete existence of Christ is both personal and universal, because in him the Father's love for the world is realized in a comprehensive and unsurpassable way. This norm, therefore, embraces all men in their different ethical situations and unites all persons (with their uniqueness and freedom) in his Person. As the Holy Spirit of freedom it also hovers over all men in order to bring them to the kingdom of the Father.

1. The concrete existence of Christ—his life, suffering, death, and bodily Resurrection—takes up in itself, supplants, and abrogates all other ethical systems. In the last analysis, a Christian has to give an account of his moral life only to this norm, which proposes the prototype (Jesus) of perfect obedience to God the Father. Christ abolishes in his own being the difference that separates those "who are subject to the law" (Jews) from those "without the law" (gentiles) (1 Cor 9:20ff.), slaves from their masters, men from women (Gal 3:28), etc. In Christ all have received the same freedom of the children of God and strive for the same goal. The "new" Commandment of Jesus (Jn 13:34) as realized in Christ is more than the principal command of the Old Law (Dt 6:4ff.). It is also more than just the sum of the Commandments of the Decalogue and their particular applications. The perfect fulfillment of the will of the Father in the Person of Christ is an eschatological, unsurpassable synthesis. Hence it is itself an a priori, universal norm.

2. Since Christ is the incarnate Word and the Son of God, he abolishes in himself the separating duality of the Old Testament Covenant. More even than a mediator (who intervenes between opposed groups), he is a personified encounter, and for this reason he is a "unifier": "an intermediary implies more than one; but God is one" (Gal 3:20). The Church of Christ is nothing else but the plenitude of this one Person. She is his "Body" to which he gives life (Eph 1:22f.). She is his "Bride" insofar as he forms "one Flesh" (Eph 5:29) or "one Spirit" (1 Cor 6:17) with her. Even as "the people of God" she is no longer many, but "you are all one in Christ Jesus" (Gal 3:28). To the extent that Jesus' work of salvation was accomplished "for all", life in his community is at the same time both personalizing and socializing.

3. That our destiny was already determined by Jesus' death on the Cross ("one has died for all; therefore all have died . . . that those who live might live no longer for themselves", 2 Cor 5:14–15), that we have been inserted "into Christ", does not constitute our alienation. Rather, it constitutes our being "transplanted" out of the "darkness" of our sinful and alienated being into the truth and freedom of divine sonship. It is for this that God created us (Eph 1:4ff.). By the power of the Cross we have been given the Holy Spirit of Christ and of the Father (Rom 8:9–11). In that Spirit the Person of Christ and his work are made present in all ages and are also at work in us. The same Spirit also makes us continuously present to Christ.

This mutual inclusion has a markedly ecclesial dimension for the believer. For, love for one another, which is the object of the new command that Jesus gave us to fulfill, is poured out into the hearts of the faithful (Rom 5:5) antecedently in a more profound way through the outpouring of the Holy Spirit of the Father and of the Son as the divine "We". On the personal level of the Church, actual membership in "one Body" includes the conferring of a personal consciousness of one another among the members. The moral task of the Christian is to accomplish this in a vigorous way. In this way the Church is open to the world, just as Christ is open to the Father and his all-embracing Kingdom (1 Cor 15:24), and both "mediate" only in immediacy. Such personal immediacy characterizes, therefore, all Church structures and activities—even to the most particular ones.

3. The Christian Meaning of the Golden Rule

THESIS 3

On Jesus' lips and in the context of the Sermon on the Mount, the "Golden Rule" (Mt 7:12; Lk 6:31) can be described as the sum total of the law and the prophets only because it firmly roots in Christ all that Christians mean to each other and give to each other. This rule, therefore, goes beyond mere human fraternity and includes the interpersonal exchange of the divine life.

1. The "Golden Rule" occurs in Matthew—and even more directly in Luke—in the context of the Beatitudes, of a forsaking of claims of distributive justice, of the love of one's enemies, of the demand to be "perfect" and "merciful" as the heavenly Father is. For this reason, gifts received from the Father are precisely what a Christian may expect from his neighbor and what he should give to his neighbor. This confirms once again that both the "law" and universal "brotherly love" have their "end" (Rom 10:4) in Christ.

2. The "law" itself was not just an expression of brotherly love. Rather, it revealed the faithfulness of God our Savior, who wanted to enter into a Covenant with his people (cf. Thesis 6). The prophets, however, spoke of a fulfillment of the law that would not be possible until God should abolish all heteronomy and place the law of his Spirit in the hearts of men (Jer 31:33; Ezek 36:26f.).

3. From the Christian point of view no social ethics or ethics of the person can abstract from the fact that God is addressing himself to us. In order to be morally correct, dialogue between men presupposes, as the very condition of its possibility, a dialogue between God and man, whether human beings are explicitly aware of it or not. Man's new relationship with God, however, has a direct relationship to the dialogue between Jew and gentile, master and servant, man and woman, parents and children, rich and poor, etc. But this dialogue must now be conducted on a new level.

Thus Christian ethics takes on the form of the Cross: though both vertical and horizontal, this "form" can never be isolated from its concrete content, that is, from Jesus who was crucified and lifted up between God and men.

He makes himself present as the only norm in every situation. "All things are lawful for me" (1 Cor 6:12; cf. Rom 14–15), if I only remember that I owe my liberty to my belonging to Christ (1 Cor 6:19; cf. 3:21–23).

4. *Sin*

THESIS 4

Only where God in his love has gone to the very end does human guilt appear as sin, and the attitude behind it as proceeding from a spirit positively hostile to God himself.

1. The unique and concrete character of the personal moral norm (= Jesus) implies, whether one admits it or not, that all moral guilt refers to Christ, is accountable to him, and was carried by him on the Cross. The nearness of the morally functioning Christian to the source of divine holiness, which vivifies him because he is a member of Christ, turns guilt with regard to a mere "law" (according to the Jewish view) or with regard to a mere "idea" (according to the Greek view) into sin. The holiness of the Holy Spirit in Christ-and-Church convinces the world of its sinfulness (Jn 16:8–11)—a world to which we also belong ("if we say we have not sinned, we make him a liar", 1 Jn 1:10).

2. The presence in the world of God's absolute love increases man's guilt so that it becomes a demonic No, more negative than man realizes; indeed, it tries to lure him into the anti-Christian camp (cf. what the book of Revelation says about the beast, what St. Paul says about the powers of this world; cf. also 1 Jn). The individual, as a part of the battle of Christ-and-Church against these powers, must also fight with the "armor of God" (Eph 6:11). The work of the devil shows itself above all in a proud gnosis without love, which pretends to be coextensive with the agape that is submissive to God, but actually "puffs up" (1 Cor 8:1). Because this gnosis does not want to acknowledge the concrete personal norm (Jesus), it depicts sin as mere guilt—as a transgression of a law or as opposition to an idea—and it will try to exculpate the guilt by appeals to psychology, sociology, etc.

3. The full impact of anti-Christian sin strikes the very center of the personal norm: it pierces the heart of the Crucified, who concretely represents in this world the trinitarian love of God. That Jesus on the Cross took upon himself our sins remains a mystery of Faith—one that cannot be shown by philosophy to be "necessary" or "impossible". Hence judgment over sin is

reserved to the crucified Son of Man, to whom "all judgment" has been given (Jn 5:22). "Do not judge" (Mt 7:1).

II. THE OLD TESTAMENT ELEMENTS OF THE FUTURE SYNTHESIS

5. *The Promise (Abraham)*

THESIS 5

The moral subject (Abraham) is constituted by God's call and by obedience to this call (Heb 11:8).

1. After Abraham had made his act of obedience, the deeper meaning of his call as an unforseeable, universal promise becomes clear (for "all peoples" but brought together in one individual: "semini tuo", Gal 3:16). The name of the obedient one is the same as the name of his mission (Gen 17:1–8); since the promise and its fulfillment stem from God, Abraham is given a supernatural fertility.

2. Obedience is faith in God and thereby a valid response (Gen 15:6), which takes possession not only of the mind but also of the body (Gen 17:13). Obedience, therefore, requires that one must be prepared to return the freely given gift (Gen 22).

3. Abraham lives in a spirit of obedience, which, in view of the unreachable stars above, waits for the promise.

Concerning 1: All biblical ethics is based on the call of a personal God and on man's answer to it in faith. God shows himself in his call as the One who is faithful, truthful, just, merciful, etc. From the name of God the name of the one who answers (i.e., his unique personality) is derived and fixed. The divine call sets the human subject apart for the encounter with God (Abraham must leave his tribe and land). By answering the call ("Here I am", Gen 22:1) he receives his mission, which then becomes for him an obligatory norm of behavior. In his dialogues with God Abraham becomes, as a result of his mission, the founder of a community. In the perspective of the Bible all relations within this community depend on the vertical relationship of the founder or mediator with God, or on God's intervention, which establishes the community (Ex 22:20; 23:9; Dt 5:14ff.; 15:12–18; 16:11ff.; 27:17ff.). This divine intervention is the grace that God offers and over which man has no power but which is the norm of all his actions (cf. the parable of the Unforgiving Debtor in Mt 18:21ff.). In the Old Testament the actual open-endedness of Abraham's blessing is gradually and more clearly understood as having a messianic fulfillment. Thus the "opening up" to "the Gentiles" (Gal 3:14) is effected in the gathering together of Jesus' followers and the bestowing on them of the Holy Spirit (through faith in him).

Concerning 2: The moral subject is affected in all his dimensions by the "Covenant" (Gen 15:18ff.), which is based on God's call and man's response: it concerns the challenge of faith and also his body and possessions ("my Covenant shall be in your flesh an everlasting Covenant", Gen 17:13). In order that Isaac, who was conceived and born by God's power, might be protected against all subsequent human self-will, Abraham is ordered to give him back to God. If the faith of the childless Abraham was already faith in God, "who gives life to the dead and calls into existence the things that do not exist" (Rom 4:17), then the faith of the father, who returns the son God promised to him, is indeed a firm faith in the resurrection. "He considered that God was able to raise men even from the dead" (Heb 11:19).

Concerning 3: Abraham's life (and with it the period of the whole Old Covenant, including the period of the law) can only be a clinging to God in faith, without the possibility of changing God's promise into his fulfillment. The people of the Old Testament could only "look forward" (Heb 11:10) in a type of "seeking" (ibid., 14) that cannot be more than a "having seen it and greeted it from afar" and a recognition of the fact that they remain "strangers and exiles" in this world (ibid., 13–14). Precisely because the Fathers of old were not able to attain the goal—but still persevered—were they worthy of praise (Heb 11:39). This point is important for what follows.

6. The Law

THESIS 6

The law proclaimed at Sinai goes beyond the promise made to Abraham to the extent that it explicitly reveals—even if provisionally from outside and from above—the mind of God. The purpose of this new revelation is to make possible a more intense response from those living under the Covenant: "I am holy; therefore you also must be holy." This "must", which has its foundation in God's innermost being, is directed at man's inner attitude. That man can respond to this "must" follows from the absolute truthfulness of God, who offers man the Covenant (Rom 7:12). However, this truthfulness of God does not yet find its counterpart in a similar absolute truthfulness of man. Such truthfulness resides only in the promise made to Abraham, which is later repeated in a new and more precise way in the sayings of the prophets.

Law Is Perfected in Christ

1. The law is given in addition to the promise and does not abrogate the promise (Rom 7; Gal 3). For this reason it is intended to be only a more precise determination of a faith that waits. From different directions it throws light on the conduct of the man who is "just in the eyes of God". Of course, this conduct agrees with the fundamental structures of man's existence (natural law) because God the author of grace is also the Creator. However, the motive of this correct conduct is not man but the more profound revelation of God's holiness as found in his fidelity to his Covenant. Hence, there is no question here of an imitation of God's essence in the Greek sense, but of a response to his conduct as manifested in his "mighty deeds" toward Israel. But since the one perfect response (Jesus) remains the object of the promise, the law retains its dialectical character in the way St. Paul understands it: in itself good, it still increases transgressions. To that extent it is both a positive and a negative "taskmaster" that eventually leads to Christ.

2. Looked at from God's point of view, the "must" of the law is an offer to live a holy life before God in the security of the Covenant. Yet this gracious offer is only the first act of God's saving activity that will be perfected only in Christ. For the time being this activity reveals not only the positive attitude of man but also his (negative) incapacity to respond fully—a perfect response remaining as before the object of the promise. The discrepancy between man's response as demanded by the law and the insufficiency of his actual response is felt by man to be unbearable. One can sustain it only with the patience that faith and hope give. In two ways man seeks to get around this problem:

a. He tries to make the law (Torah) an absolute that takes the place of the living God. By trying to fulfill literally the letter of the law, the Pharisee thinks that he can give a perfect response (something that is actually impossible). Many different ethical systems have been derived from this attitude, which makes an abstract and formal "must" the fundamental norm. For example, one may point to neo-Kantian ethics, which postulates a realm of "absolute values", to structuralistic and to phenomenological ethics (Scheler). All of these systems tend to establish the human subject as his own legislator, as an idealized, autonomous subject who imposes limitations on himself in order to reach perfection. The germs of these types of ethical systems lie in the ethical formalism of Kant.

b. A second way to overcome this tension is to consider the law a foreign element and then replace it with promise and hope. It is argued that a law that is imposed from outside and declares us guilty in our hearts (e.g., Kafka) cannot proceed from a faithful and merciful God but only from a tyrannical demiurge (this point of view explains E. Bloch's alliance with gnosticism;

compare also Freud's superego). As an illusion of former generations this "demiurge" must be overcome by hope in the future—a hope that proceeds from man's own autonomous resources.

c. Both escapes come together in dialectical materialism, which identifies the law with the dialectical movement of history and in this way eliminates the law. Marx knows that it is not the negative abolition of the law (namely, communism) that will bring about the desired reconciliation, but only a positive humanism that allows the law to be absorbed into the spontaneity of freedom. We are dealing here with an atheistic counterpart to Jeremiah 31 and Ezekiel 34. Corresponding to the provisional character of Old Testament ethics, transcendental reconciliation in the Old Testament (as in its modern imitations) remains primarily a political "liberation". Its subject is primarily the people as a whole and not the person whose unique worth comes to light only in Christ.

3. When Christian faith in the fulfilled promise of Christ dies out, it is not the extrabiblical ethical systems that dominate the history of mankind; rather, it is the Old Testament forms, which are related to the Christian ones. Because an awareness of the fulfillment brought by Christ lingers on, Old Testament ethics returns as a most grotesque absolutism: absolute law and absolute prophecy.

III. FRAGMENTS OF EXTRABIBLICAL ETHICS

7. *Conscience*

THESIS 7

1. *Extrabiblical man is awakened to theoretico-practical self-awareness as the result of a free, loving call from his fellowmen. When answering this call he experiences (in his "cogito ergo sum") both the intelligibility of reality as such (as true and good), which reveals itself and thereby constitutes man in freedom, and the fact that his freedom is marked by a relationship to other human beings.*

2. *Man's entire being has a natural inclination ("necessitate naturalis inclinationis", De Veritate, q. 22, 5) to the transcendental good. This inclination to the known good takes the form of first moral principles (synderesis or basic conscience). There also exist tendencies to the good in the sensible part of man's being since the whole is permeated by his spirit.*

Neither the self-discovery involved in the first insight, nor the strong attraction of particular temporal goods, nor the fact that sin often obscures man's awareness that the good is a gift—none of these can destroy the innate orientation of man to the good. Thus St. Paul could say that the pagans are judged "by Jesus Christ according to my Gospel" (Rom 2:16).

3. Abstract formulas that state man's inclination to the good as the result of natural law"—for example, the statement that human fellowship is a "categorical imperative"—have been derived from this basic conscience and actually refer back to it.

Concerning 1: In the act of being called or loved by his fellowman, man awakens in his "*cogito ergo sum*" to an awareness of the identity between intelligibility and reality. He also experiences this identity, which is a created reality, as not absolute, simply because it appears to him as a gift. In this transcendental disclosure of reality three things are given simultaneously:

a. Man is confronted with the absolute identity of spirit and being, and thus with a most perfect self-possession in full freedom. This Absolute lets things share in itself (we call this Absolute God, "*qui interius docet inquantum huiusmodi lumen animae infundit*", St. Thomas, *De Anima,* 5 ad 6).

b. When man is awakened to God who gives himself, he becomes aware of the difference between absolute freedom and given freedom. In seeing this difference he becomes aware of the invitation to respond in freedom to this absolute gift.

c. At first there is not sharp distinction between the call from the Absolute and that coming from one's fellowmen. Experience will show that the other is "merely" one who has also been awakened. However, this experience shows that the original unity of both invitations (i.e., from men and God) cannot be dissolved.

Concerning 2:   Just as, in the original identity of being and intelligibility (as true, good, and beautiful), freedom as autonomy and grace as gift (*"diffusivum sui"*) are together, so also in the created being freedom and inclination toward the good are inseparable. The active drawing power of the absolute good confers on the act of the free response an element of "passivity" that does not violate its freedom (*S. Th.,* I, q. 80, a. 2; q. 105, a. 4; *De Veritate,* 25, 1; 22, 13, 4).

Moral Task: To Be Ethical

This tendency to let oneself be determined and conducted by what is good in itself is present in man's entire being. Of course, if one abstracts from man's totality, then it is clear that man's sensible nature by itself cannot attain a knowledge of the absolute good but must stop at the level of particular goods. Man's true moral task is to render his entire bodily and spiritual life ethical (*ethizesthai*). The result of this process is called "virtue". This is also necessary because the call of his fellowmen obliges him to let his freedom be determined by other free, bodily persons. It also obliges him to determine the freedom of others. This must take place under the influence of the good, but each time it requires the intellectual illumination of the matter that mediates the process.

The Good Cannot Be Forgotten

The insight into the good itself, once attained in the *"cogito ergo sum"* (in other words, the transparency of the *"imago Dei"*, which enables man to see its source in God), does not remain actualized. Nevertheless, it perdures in the memory *"tamquam nota artificis operi suo impressa"* (Descartes, *Med.,* III, Adam-Tannery, VII, 51). Since this insight has codetermined the first awakening of the mind, it cannot be totally forgotten, even when one turns away—either consciously or habitually—from the light of the good in order to pursue particular goods that are either pleasurable or useful. Moreover, the insight is at least a transcendental preknowledge of revelation; it constitutes, as it were, the *place* from which the "positive" revelation of the Old and New Testaments has always been addressed to all men. However, when this revelation proceeds from concrete historical events, then we should not forget that the call of our fellowmen (which is both transcendental and dialectical) is just as original as the call of the good itself (*bonum in communi*).

Only the *Magister Interior* can measure the intensity and clarity that such a "positive" revelation might have outside of the Old and New Testaments. But according to St. Paul, the *Magister Interior* judges the hearts even of the pagans according to the norm, which is now sufficiently explicit, of God's gift of himself in Jesus Christ.

Concerning 3: The original radiancy of the good as grace and love expects a free answer of loving gratitude. When this light of the good itself has grown dim, a warning sign appears. Its purpose is not to take the place of one's better self or to represent it, but only to call it back into mind. Insofar as the warning sign concerns the main situations of an incarnate and socially constituted mind, it reveals itself as the "natural law". This natural law should not be divinized; rather, it must retain its essentially relative character of referring to the good. In this way natural law will not become stifled but will be able to point to the liveliness and self-giving nature of the good. Kant's categorical imperative has not escaped the danger of unbending harshness, for his formalism made him place abstract "duty" over against the natural "inclination" of the sensible part of our being. What true ethics should do, however, is to give to the person's inclination to the

Absolute Good priority and dominion over contrary particular inclinations. Thus the inclinations man fully accepts and makes his own in view of the absolute norm coincide with surrendering himself to the divine good and with giving himself to his fellowmen.

8. *Prebiblical Natural Order*

THESIS 8

Wherever a self-revelation of the sovereignly free and personal God is absent, man tries to find the bearings for his moral life in the order of the world around him. Since man owes his existence to a multiplicity of cosmic laws, it is quite natural that he both fuse and confuse his origin from God with his origin from nature. However, such a theocosmological ethics disintegrates wherever biblical revelation comes in contact with a particular culture.

1. Prebiblical ethics, which finds its norms in nature, can ask about the good that is proper to human nature (*bonum honestum*) by setting up an analogy with the good that is proper to infrahuman existing things. This human good, however, will be contained within the limits of the surrounding natural order. Insofar as this natural order has an absolute (i.e., divine) aspect, it opens up a certain area for orderly moral behavior; but insofar as it contains a this-worldly, finite aspect, it does not allow man's personal freedom to reach its full perfection. The result is that the goals of human activity remain partly political (within a micropolis or a macropolis), partly individualistic, and partly intellectualistic, since pure knowledge of the constant laws of the universe appears to be the most noble thing man can strive for.

2. When biblical revelation enters on the scene, the supremely free God, who is radically different from created nature, invites man to share in a type of freedom that is not modeled on anything found in infrahuman nature. But wherever man refuses to acknowledge, in a Christian way, that this freedom is really a gift from God, logically he can locate the source of his freedom only in himself and so understand moral behavior as a type of legislation for himself. In its first stages this may take the form of a return to the prebiblical mythical understanding of the universe (cf. Spinoza, Goethe, Hegel), but later even this will be abandoned (cf. Feuerbach, Nietzsche).

3. Once this development has begun, it is irreversible. It is true that there exists a tendency (cf. above, 6, 3) to reduce Christian ethics to what was, in the Old Testament, a stage of preparation. Yet we can also notice a certain influence of the light of Christianity on non-Christian religious and ethical thought (e.g., the Christian influence on Indian social thinking: Tagore,

Gandhi). Besides an explicitly dogmatic knowledge of God there is also an existential knowledge; this reminds us of the warning "do not judge".

9. Post-Christian Anthropological Ethics

THESIS 9

A possible basis for a post- but non-Christian ethics can now be sought only in a dialogue relationship with other men (e.g., I—thou; I—we). Since gratitude to God for one's life, expressed in divine worship, is now no longer the permanent, fundamental act of the free human person, mutual gratitude between human subjects can have no more than secondary, purely relative value. The limitations placed on one another by free persons who experience their own unlimited transcendence appear to be imposed on them from outside. A synthesis between the fulfillment of the individual and that of the community is not possible.

1. In a post-Christian age, what remains of the "nature" or "structure" of human existence is the reciprocity of two finite freedoms. Only by means of a call from another person do both of them become aware of themselves and of their ability to respond and to call others. In this way it seems that the "Golden Rule" is attained once again. However, since the one who is addressed by another does not simply receive his freedom from that other (if he did, he would necessarily be "heteronomous"), and since God's call—which is the real foundation of both freedoms—is excluded, the mutual self-surrender of both persons remains limited and calculating. Intersubjectivity will either be understood as a secondary and basically unintelligible quality of the subject, or the two human subjects remain monads with no influence on one another.

2. The so-called human sciences can contribute valuable knowledge about particular aspects of the phenomenon of man, but they cannot offer a solution to this fundamental problem of interhuman relations.

3. The anthropological problem reaches its climax at the point where the death of the individual person renders the synthesis between his personal perfection and his social integration simply impossible. The meaningful elements in both of these aspects remain disconnected. Therefore, they even make the development of an obvious this-worldly ethics impossible. However, in face of the meaninglessness of death—and thus of his life, which is always moving toward death—man can refuse to acknowledge any ethical norms.

Personal and social fulfillment are harmonized only in the Resurrection of Christ, who is the guarantee not only for the fulfillment of the individual but also for the Church community and through her for the whole world so that God, without eliminating the reality of the world, can be "all in all".

5B

THE QUESTION OF THE OBLIGATORY CHARACTER OF THE VALUE JUDGMENTS AND MORAL DIRECTIVES OF THE NEW TESTAMENT

by H. Schürmann

I. THE PROBLEM

No. 1.   Vatican II affirmed, "The treasures of the Bible are to be opened up more lavishly, so that richer fare may be provided for the faithful at the table of God's word" (*SC*, 51, see also *DV*, 22). Consequently, it was the wish of the Council that, in their homilies, priests use the Sacred Scriptures to elucidate "the mysteries of the faith and the guiding principles of the Christian life" (*SC*, 52; *DV*, 24). However, one difficulty appeared: does one not find, here and there, in the Old Testament (cf. *DV*, 15), and even in the New Testament, moral judgments conditioned and determined by the era in which these books were written? Does this authorize us to assert, as a general rule, as one so often hears today, that the obligatory character of all the value judgments and directives in the Scriptures should be questioned because they are all conditioned by the times? Or at least should one admit that the moral teachings regarding certain questions cannot claim a permanent value precisely because of their dependence on one epoch? Is human reason then to be the final criterion for evaluating biblical value judgments and directives? Can the value judgments and the directives of Holy Scripture not assert, in and of themselves, any permanent value, or at least a normative value? Are Christians of other eras obliged to consider them only as paradigms or models of conduct?

No. 2.   Although the books of the Old Testament, "written under divine inspiration, remain permanently valuable" (*DV*, 14; cf. Rom 15:4) and God in his wisdom has willed that "the New Covenant be hidden in the Old and that the Old be explained by the New" (Aug. Quaest. in Hept., 2, 73, *PL* 34, 623), in the pages that follow we will not limit our examination to the writings of the New Testament. In effect, "the books of the Old Testament with all their

This document was approved by the Commission "*in forma generica*".

parts, caught up into the proclamation of the gospel, acquire and show forth their full meaning in the new Testament" (*DV*, 16). Consequently, the question of the obligatory character of biblical value judgments and directives must be addressed especially with regard to the writings of the New Testament.

The issue of knowing what is the nature of the obligation attached to the New Testament value judgments and prescriptions is an hermeneutic matter in moral theology. It includes, however, an exigetic question regarding the type and degree of obligation that these New Testament assessments and directives claim for themselves. We are especially committed to studying this problem with regard to the Pauline value judgments and directives, because this moral problematic is reflected in a special way in the *Corpus Paulinum*. Moreover, in spite of a surprising diversity (for example in the writings of Paul, John, Matthew, James, etc.) the New Testament writings present a remarkable convergence in the domain of morality.

No. 3.   In the case of value judgments and directives in matters of morality, the New Testament writings can claim a particular value, given that the moral judgment of the Church from her beginnings is crystalized in them. As "nascent Church" she is indeed already present at the sources of revelation and she is marked in an exceptional manner by the Spirit of the Glorified Lord. Consequently the deeds and words of Jesus, as final criterion of moral obligation, may be seen revealed in a particularly valid manner in the value judgments and directives set out in the Spirit and with authority by the apostle, as by the other Spiritual writers of the Church from the beginning and in the *paradosis* and the *parathêkê* of the first Christian communities as proximate norms of action.

The nature and the modality of the obligatory character—doubtless analogical—of these two criteria on which the moral prescriptions of the New Testament are based (compare 1 Cor 7:10–25 and 7:12–40), like the various value judgments and directives based on these two criteria (that is to say the various moral prescriptions and exhortations), will be briefly set forth in concise theses in the following propositions. However it should be noted that New Testament proofs cannot be given here except in an allusive and succinct manner and that a certain oversimplification in the classification is inevitable.

II. THE CONDUCT AND THE WORDS OF JESUS AS THE ULTIMATE CRITERION IN MATTERS OF MORAL JUDGMENT.

No. 4.   For the authors of the New Testament, the words and deeds of Jesus are held to be the normative criterion for judgment and as the supreme moral norm, as the "law of Christ" (*ennomos*) "written" in the hearts of the faithful (Gal 6:2; cf. 1 Cor 9:21). Moreover, for the New Testament writers, Jesus' directives, given during the prepaschal period, have a decisive and obligatory value in the context of imitation of the example given by the earthly Jesus and even more so by the pre-existent Son of God.

THESIS I

The conduct of Jesus is the example and the criterion of a love which serves and gives of itself

No. 5.   Already, in the synoptics, the "coming" of Jesus, his life, and his actions are understood as a service (Lk 22:27) which attains its ultimate accomplishment in death (Mk 10:25). At the pre-Pauline and Pauline stage this love is depicted in terms of *kenosis* as a love which is fulfilled in the Incarnation and in the Son's death on the Cross (Phil 2:6f.; 2 Cor 8:9). According to the *Johannine* perspective, this love attains its "fulfillment" (Jn 19:28–30) in the "descent" of the Son of Man by his Incarnation and death (Jn 6:41f., 48–51, etc.) in his purifying gift of himself on the Cross (Jn 13:1–11); thus Jesus' love is depicted as his "life work" (Jn 17:4; cf. 4:34). In conclusion then, the conduct of Jesus is distinguished as the love that serves and gives itself up "for us" and renders visible the love of God (Rom 5:8; 8:31; Jn 3:16; 1 Jn 4:9). The moral behavior of the faithful is fundamentally summed up in the acceptance and the imitation of this divine love; it is life with Christ and in Christ.

a. In the New Testament writings—especially in those of Paul and John—*the obligation of love* draws its motivation and, at the same time, its own peculiar characteristic, that radicalism of going beyond its own limits, and perhaps also a *special content,* from the way in which the Son empties himself (Paul), or, in other words, "descends" (John). This love, which gives itself up to human existence and to death, represents and brings to light the love of God. This trait is even more characteristic of New Testament morality than its eschatological orientation.

b. The *"Sequela Jesu"* and imitation of him, the *association* with the Incarnate and crucified Son, and the life of the baptized in Christ, also determine in a specific manner the concrete moral attitude of the believer toward the world.

THESIS II

The word of Jesus is the ultimate moral norm

No. 6.   The words of the Lord explain the attitude of love shown by Jesus, he who came and who was crucified. They must be interpreted in light of his own person. Thus, seen in the light of the pascal mystery and "remembered" in the Spirit (Jn 14:26), these words constitute the ultimate norm for the moral conduct of believers (cf. 1 Cor 7:10–25).

a. Certain of Jesus' words, even in their literary style, do not present themselves, strictly speaking, as laws; they must be understood as *models of conduct* and should be considered as paradigms.

b. For Paul the words of the Lord have a definitive and permanent obligatory force. However in two passages where he expressly quotes the directives of Jesus (cf. Lk 17:7b and par.; Mk 10:11 and par.), he can counsel to observe them in their deepest intention and as closely as possible in situations that have become different or more difficult (1 Cor 9:14, 7:12–16). Thus he departs from the legalist interpretation, in the manner of late Judaism.

III. THE JUDGMENTS AND DIRECTIVES OF THE APOSTLES AND PRIMITIVE CHRISTIANITY ARE ENDOWED WITH OBLIGATORY FORCE

No. 7.   The obligatory character of these directives recorded in the New Testament have several foundations: the attitudes and the utterances of Jesus, the conduct and the teaching of the apostles and of the other spiritual writers of early Christianity, the way of life and the traditions of the primitive communities inasmuch as the nascent Church was still marked in a special manner by the Spirit of the Risen Lord. In this context it must not be forgotten that the Spirit of truth, especially with regard to moral conscience, "will guide you into all the truth" (Jn 16:13).

No. 8.   It will also be observed that about the various value judgments and directives of primitive Christianity, considered either in their form or for their content, the claim of an obligatory authority was very different according to the case, and that these directives, in widely varied areas, were marked by a practical-pastoral finality.

THESIS III

Certain value judgments and certain directives are permanent by reason of their theological and eschatological foundations

No. 9.   In the writings of the New Testament the principal parenetic interest, and, in consequence, the importance as related to the intensity and the frequency of affirmations, is directed toward the value judgments and the directives (essentially formal ones) which require, as a response to the love of God in Christ, total abandonment, in love, to Christ, actually to the Father, and a conduct in keeping with the reality of eschatalogical time, that is to say, with the salvific action of Christ as well as the state of the baptized.

No. 10.   To these value judgments and directives, so defined, inasmuch as they are unconditionally founded on the eschatalogical reality of salvation and motivated by the Gospel, one should attribute a character of permanent obligation.

a. The main commandment of the New Testament writings is made up of a call to the total gift of self in Christ to the Father. As a precept "going to the extreme" it possesses the form of absolute obligation.

b. A value of unconditional obligation is also claimed on the basis of the number of eschatalogical opinions and imperatives in the New Testament writings which, for the most part, remain on the level of formal morality. These call the believer, on one hand, to conduct himself in faith and love, in line with reality and the situation, in view of the eschatalogical coming of salvation, to place himself in the redemptive work of Christ, that is to say, in the state of the baptized. On the other hand, they warn that he must let himself be conditioned in hope by the nearness of the reign of God, that is to say the parousia, in continual vigilance and readiness.

THESIS IV

Particular value judgments and directives imply a diversity of obligations

No. 11.   Beside the value judgments and directives already mentioned, the New Testament writings also enunciate value judgments and directives having a bearing on particular spheres of existence, that is to say, on specific conduct and, although in different manners, also have a permanent obligatory force.

a. One frequently encounters—and in a particularly accentuated manner in the New Testament writings—directives and obligations relating to *fraternal love* and *love of one's neighbor* which often refer to the conduct of the Son of God (e.g., Phil 2:6f.; 2 Cor 8:2–9) alluding to the words of the Lord. These demands, inasmuch as they remain general, take on an unconditional value as "the law of Christ" (Gal 6:2) and as "new commandment" (Jn 13:14; 15:12; 1 Jn 2:7f.). In them the law of the Old Testament is "accomplished" (Gal 5:14; cf. Rom 13:8f.; also Mt 7:12; 22:40), that is to say, they are concentrated in the commandment of love and finalized by it. However where the commandment of love is "incarnated" in these special concrete directives, one must verify if, and in what manner, judgments conditioned by the epoch and the particular historical circumstances color the fundamental requirement to the point where, in different circumstances, one would require only an application that was analogous, similar, modified, or motivated by the same intention.

b. Next to the commandment of love—but very often in the context of the requirement of love—the New Testament writings present other value judgments and moral directives which relate to particular spheres of existence. The "accomplishment" of the law by love (Gal 5:14; cf. Rom 13:8f.) places itself on the level of intentionality. But love does not deprive other virtues or ways of behaving of their own consistency. It expresses itself through different ways of acting and virtues not fully identified with itself. One sees, for example (1 Cor 13:4–7; Rom 12:9f.), the moral teachings of the pastoral letters and the Epistle of James, especially the lists of virtues and vices and the domestic depictions of the New Testament writings.

aa. One must not forget that a large part of these particular value judgments and special directives present a very marked spiritual character and thus determine in that perspective the life of the community. The exhortations to joy (Phil 3:1; 12:15), to prayer without ceasing (cf. 1 Th 5:17), to "divine folly" as opposed to the wisdom of the world (1 Cor 3:18f.), to indifference (1 Cor 7:29f.) are certainly permanent Christian precepts which go to the limit, which result in the "fruits of the Spirit" (cf. Gal 5:22). Others are "counsels" (1 Cor 7:17–27f.). A number of these spiritual directives are formulated in very concrete terms and cannot be followed today, as they stand, in the context of contemporary community relations (see only 1 Cor 11:5–14; Col 3:16; Eph 5:19). They retain, however, something of their original normative authority and demand to be "carried out" in a modified or analogous manner.

bb. As for particular value judgments and norms of moral conduct—in a special concrete sense—one would establish their obligatory moral character by considering in what way they are motivated by the fundamental theological-eschatalogical requirements or by the universal moral obligatory force or what *Sitz im Leben* they have in the communities. For example, this holds for the baptismal exhortations (cf. Eph 4:17–21), where the catechumens are confronted with the principal pagan vices such as impurity (1 Th 4:9f.) and dishonesty (1 Th 4:6). Such demands, just as the warning against idolatry (Gal 6:20f.), are strongly thrown into relief by their own nature.

One cannot, however, ignore the fact that, in the case of several concrete moral value judgments referring to particular spheres of life, value judgments and real judgments conditioned by the epoch can condition morality and put it into perspective. If, for example, the writers of the New Testament considered woman as subordinate to man (cf. 1 Cor 11:2–16; 14:33–36f.)—which is understandable for the epoch—it seems to us that on this question, the Holy Spirit has led contemporary Christianity, together with the modern world, to a greater intelligence about the moral requirements of the person. Even if one cannot indicate more than this one example in the writings of the New Testament, this should suffice to show that with regard to value judgments and directives about particular precepts therein, the question of hermeneutic interpretation cannot be sidestepped.

CONCLUSION

No. 12.   The majority of New Testament value judgments and directives call the believer to concrete forms of behavior toward the Father as he reveals himself in Christ and thus open out on a theological-eschatological horizon. This holds particularly true for the requirements laid down by Christ (I), but also for most of the apostolic directives (III, 3): the demands and the admonitions of this type would bind without condition and transcend the historic diversities. Even the value judgments and directives concerning particular areas of life participate to a great extent in this perspective; at least when they postulate in the most general manner the love of one's neighbor as perceived in its connection with love of God and of Christ (III, 4a). Furthermore, the vast domain of the "spiritual" exhortations of the New Testament (III, 4, b, aa) is imbued with this theological-eschatalogical horizon and is defined by it. It is only in the domain—the relatively narrow one—of concrete and particular directives and operative norms (III, 3, b, bb) that the moral judgments and the exhortations of the New Testament should be rethought.

Our exposition thus in no way encourages the opinion according to which all the value judgments and directives of the New Testament would be conditioned by time. This "relativization" does not hold even in a general manner for the particular judgments which, in the great majority can in no way be understood hermeneutically as pure "models" or as "paradigms" of behavior. Only a small portion of them can be considered as being subject to conditions of time and situation. But even so there are some. This means that in the face of these value judgments and directives, human experience, the judgment of reason and also the theological-moral hermeneutic have a role to play.

If this hermeneutic takes the moral force of the Scripture seriously, it cannot proceed either in a simply "biblicist" manner or according to a purely rationalist perspective in the search for criteria for a moral theology, for example, in the establishment of the moral character of acts. It would obtain positive results only in a spirit of "encounter", that is to say, in the ever renewed confrontation of today's critical consciousness with the moral givens of the Scripture. It is only in listening to the word of God—*Verbum Dei audiens* (cf. *DV*, 1)—that one can, without danger, interpret the signs of the times. This work of discernment should be done within the community of the people of God, in the unity of the *sensus fidelium* and of the Magisterium with the aid of theology.

6

THESES ON THE RELATIONSHIP BETWEEN THE ECCLESIASTICAL MAGISTERIUM AND THEOLOGY

INTRODUCTION

"The relations between the Magisterium and theology not only . . . are of the greatest importance but must also be considered to be of very great contemporary interest today."[1] The following pages are an attempt to clarify the relationship between "the mandate given to the ecclesiastical Magisterium to protect divine revelation and the task given to theologians to investigate and explain the doctrine of the Faith".[2]

THESIS 1

By "ecclesiastical Magisterium" is meant the task of teaching that by Christ's institution is proper to the College of Bishops or to individual bishops linked in hierarchical communion with the Supreme Pontiff. By "theologians" are meant those members of the Church who by their studies and life in the community of the Church's Faith are qualified to pursue, in the scientific manner proper to theology, a deeper understanding of the Word of God and also to teach that Word by virtue of a canonical mission. When the New Testament and the subsequent Tradition discussed the Magisterium of pastors, theologians, or teachers and the relationship between them, they spoke analogously, in terms of both similarity and dissimilarity; along with continuity, there are rather profound modifications. The concrete forms in which they have been related to one another and coordinated have been rather varied in the course of time.

This document was approved by the Commission *"in forma specifica"*.
[1] Pope Paul VI, "Address to the International Congress on Theology of Vatican II", Oct. 1, 1966, *AAS* 58 (1966): 890.
[2] Ibid.

I. ELEMENTS COMMON TO THE MAGISTERIUM AND TO THEOLOGIANS IN THE EXERCISE OF THEIR TASKS

THESIS 2

The element common to the tasks of both the Magisterium and theologians, though it is realized in analogous and distinct fashions, is "to preserve the sacred deposit of revelation, to examine it more deeply, to explain, teach, and defend it",[3] for the service of the People of God and for the whole world's salvation. Above all, this service must defend the certainty of faith; this is a work done differently by the Magisterium and by the ministry of theologians, but it is neither necessary nor possible to establish a hard-and-fast separation between them.

THESIS 3

In this common service of the truth, the Magisterium and theologians are both bound by certain obligations:

1. They are bound by the Word of God. For "the Magisterium is not above the Word of God but serves it, teaching only what has been handed down, as . . . it listens to this, guards it scrupulously, and expounds it faithfully; and it draws from this one deposit of faith all that it proposes as being divinely revealed."[4] For its part, "sacred theology relies on the written Word of God along with sacred Tradition as on a permanent foundation, and by this Word it is most firmly strengthened and constantly rejuvenated as it searches out, under the light of faith, all the truth stored up in the mystery of Christ."[5]

2. They are both bound by the *"sensus fidei"* (supernatural appreciation of the Faith) of the Church of this and previous times. For the Word of God pervades all time in a living manner through the supernatural appreciation of the Faith (*communi sensu fidei*) of the whole People of God, in which "the whole body of the faithful, anointed by the Holy One, cannot err in believing",[6] if "in maintaining, practicing, and confessing the Faith that has been handed down, there is a harmony between the bishops and the faithful".[7]

3. Both are bound by the documents of the Tradition in which the common Faith of the People of God has been set forth. Although the Magiste-

---

[3] Ibid., 891.
[4] *DV,* 10.
[5] Ibid., 24.
[6] *LG,* 12.
[7] *DV,* 10.

rium and the theologians have different tasks with regard to these documents, neither of them can neglect these traces of the Faith left in the history of salvation of God's People.

4. In exercising their tasks, both are bound by pastoral and missionary concern for the world. Although the Magisterium of the Supreme Pontiff and of the bishops is specifically called "pastoral", the scientific character of their work does not free theologians from pastoral and missionary responsibility, especially given the publicity that modern communications media so quickly give to even scientific matters. Besides, theology, as a vital function in and for the People of God, must have a pastoral and missionary intent and effect.

THESIS 4

Common to both, although also different in each, is the manner, at once collegial and personal, in which the task of both the Magisterium and the theologians is carried out. If the charism of infallibility is promised to "the whole body of the faithful",[8] to the College of Bishops in communion with the Successor of Peter, and to the Supreme Pontiff himself, the head of that College,[9] then it should be put into practice in a coresponsible, cooperative, and collegial association of the members of the Magisterium and of individual theologians. And this joint effort should also be realized as much among the members of the Magisterium as among the members of the theological enterprise, and also between the Magisterium on the one hand and the theologians on the other. It should also preserve the personal and indispensable responsibility of individual theologians, without which the science of Faith would make no progress.

II. DIFFERENCES BETWEEN THE
MAGISTERIUM AND THEOLOGIANS

THESIS 5

Something must first be said about the difference in the functions proper to the Magisterium and to theologians.

1. It is the Magisterium's task authoritatively to defend the Catholic integrity and unity of faith and morals. From this follow specific functions; and,

[8] *LG,* 12.
[9] Ibid., 25.

although at first glance they seem particularly to be of a rather negative character, they are, rather, a positive ministry for the life of the Church. These are: "The task of authoritatively interpreting the Word of God, written and handed down",[10] the censuring of opinions that endanger the faith and morals proper to the Church, the proposing of truths that are of particular contemporary relevance. Although it is not the work of the Magisterium to propose theological syntheses, still, because of its concern for unity, it must consider individual truths in the light of the whole, since integrating a particular truth into the whole belongs to the very nature of truth.

2. The theologians' function in some way mediates between the Magisterium and the People of God. For "theology has a twofold relation with the Magisterium of the Church and with the universal community of Christians. In the first place, it occupies a sort of midway position between the Faith of the Church and its Magisterium."[11] On the one hand, "in each of the great sociocultural regions, . . . theological reflection must submit to a new examination, guided by the Tradition of the universal Church, the facts and words revealed by God, contained in the Scriptures, and explained by the Fathers of the Church and by the Magisterium".[12] For "recent research and discoveries in the sciences, in history and philosophy, bring up new questions that . . . require new investigations by theologians".[13] In this way, theology "is to lend its aid to make the Magisterium in its turn the enduring light and norm of the Church".[14]

On the other hand, by their work of interpretation, teaching, and translation into contemporary modes of thought, theologians insert the teaching and warnings of the Magisterium into a wider, synthetic context and thus contribute to a better knowledge on the part of the People of God. In this way, "they lend their aid to the task of spreading, clarifying, confirming, and defending the truth that the Magisterium authoritatively propounds".[15]

THESIS 6

The Magisterium and the theologians also differ in the quality of the authority with which they carry out their tasks.

1. The Magisterium derives its authority from sacramental ordination,

---

[10] *DV,* 10.
[11] Pope Paul VI, loc. cit., 892.
[12] *AG,* 22.
[13] *GS,* 62.
[14] Pope Paul VI, loc. cit., 892.
[15] Ibid., 891.

which "along with the task of sanctifying confers also the tasks of teaching and ruling".[16] This "formal authority", as it is called, is at once charismatic and juridical, and it founds the right and the duty of the Magisterium insofar as it is a share in the authority of Christ. Care should be taken that personal authority and the authority that derives from the very matter being proposed also be brought to bear when this ministerial authority is being put into effect.

2. Theologians derive their specifically theological authority from their scientific qualifications; but these cannot be separated from the proper character of this discipline as the science of faith, which cannot be carried through without a living experience and practice of the Faith. For this reason, the authority that belongs to theology in the Church is not merely profane and scientific but is a genuinely ecclesial authority, inserted into the order of authorities that derive from the Word of God and are confirmed by canonical mission.

THESIS 7

There is also a certain difference in the way in which the Magisterium and the theologians are connected with the Church. It is obvious that both the Magisterium and the theologians work in and for the Church, but still there is a difference in this ecclesial reference.

1. The Magisterium is an official ecclesial task conferred by the sacrament of Orders. Therefore, as an institutional element of the Church, it can only exist in the Church, so that the individual members of the Magisterium use their authority and sacred power to build up their flocks in truth and holiness.[17] This responsibility applies not only to the particular Churches under their charge, but "as members of the episcopal College, ... each of them must by Christ's institution and command show a care for the universal Church, which ... would be a great benefit for the universal Church".[18]

2. Even when it is not exercised in virtue of an explicit "canonical mission", theology can only be done in a living communion with the Faith of the Church. For this reason, all the baptized, insofar as they both really live the life of the Church and enjoy scientific competence, can carry out the task of the theologian, a task that derives its own force from the life of the Holy Spirit in the Church, which is communicated by the sacraments, the preaching of the Word of God, and the communion of love.

[16] *LG,* 21.
[17] Ibid., 27.
[18] Ibid., 23.

THESIS 8

The difference between the Magisterium and the theologians takes on a special character when one considers the freedom proper to them and the critical function that follows from it with regard to the faithful, to the world, and even to one another.

1. By its nature and institution, the Magisterium is clearly free in carrying out its task. This freedom carries with it a great responsibility. For that reason, it is often difficult, although necessary, to use it in such a way that it not appear to theologians and to others of the faithful to be arbitrary or excessive. There are some theologians who prize scientific theology too highly, not taking enough account of the fact that respect for the Magisterium is one of the specific elements of the science of theology. Besides, contemporary democratic sentiments often give rise to a movement of solidarity against what the Magisterium does in carrying out its task of protecting the teaching of faith and morals from any harm. Still, it is necessary, though not easy, to find always a mode of procedure that is both free and forceful yet not arbitrary or destructive of communion in the Church.

2. To the freedom of the Magisterium there corresponds in its own way the freedom that derives from the true scientific responsibility of theologians. It is not an unlimited freedom, for, besides being bound to the truth, it is also true of theology that "in the use of any freedom, the moral principle of personal and social responsibility must be observed".[19] But the theologians' task of interpreting the documents of the past and present Magisterium, of putting them in the context of the whole of revealed truth, and of finding a better understanding of them by the use of hermeneutics brings with it a somewhat critical function that obviously should be exercised positively rather than destructively.

THESIS 9

The exercise of their tasks by the Magisterium and theologians often gives rise to a certain tension. But this is not surprising, nor should one expect that such tension will ever be fully resolved here on earth. On the contrary, wherever there is genuine life, tension also exists. Such tension need not be interpreted as hostility or real opposition, but can be seen as a vital force and an incentive to a common carrying out of the respective tasks by way of dialogue.

[19] *DH*, 7.

III. A METHOD FOR PROMOTING TODAY THE RELATIONSHIP BETWEEN THEOLOGIANS AND THE MAGISTERIUM

THESIS 10

The basis and condition for the possibility of this dialogue between theologians and the Magisterium are community in the Faith of the Church and service in building up the Church. They embrace the diverse functions of the Magisterium and theologians. On the one hand, this unity in the communication and participation in the truth is a habitual association that is antecedent to every concrete dialogue; on the other, it is itself strengthened and enlivened by the various relations dialogue entails. Thus dialogue provides excellent reciprocal assistance: the Magisterium can gain a greater understanding as it defends and preaches the truth of faith and morals, and the theological understanding of faith and morals gains in certainty from corroboration by the Magisterium.

THESIS 11

The dialogue between the Magisterium and theologians is limited only by the truth of faith, which must be served and explained. For this reason, the whole vast field of truth lies open to such dialogue. But this truth is not something uncertain and utterly unknown, always having to be sought; it has been revealed and handed on to the Church to be faithfully kept. Therefore, the dialogue reaches its limits when the limits of the Faith are reached.

This goal of the dialogue, the service of the truth, is often endangered. The following types of behavior especially limit the possibility of dialogue: wherever the dialogue becomes an "instrument" for gaining some end "politically", that is, by applying pressure and ultimately abstracting from the question of truth, the effort is bound to fail; if a person "unilaterally" claims the whole field of the dialogue, he violates the rules of discussion; the dialogue between the Magisterium and theologians is especially violated if the level of argument and discussion is prematurely abandoned and means of coercion, threat, and sanction are immediately brought to bear; the same thing holds when the discussion between theologians and the Magisterium is carried out by means of publicity, whether within or outside the Church, which is not sufficiently expert in the matter, and thus "pressures" from without have a great deal of influence, e.g., the mass media.

Before opening an official examination of a theologian's writings, the competent authority should exhaust all the ordinary possibilities of reaching agreement through dialogue on a doubtful opinion (e.g., personal conversation or inquiries and replies in correspondence). If by these forms of dialogue no real consensus can be reached, the Magisterium should employ a full and flexible stock of responses, beginning with various forms of warning, "verbal sanctions", etc. In a very serious case, the Magisterium—after consulting theologians of various schools and having exhausted the means of dialogue—for its part must necessarily clarify the compromised truth and safeguard the faith of the believers.

According to the classical rules, the fact of one's professing "heresy" can only be definitively established if the accused theologian has demonstrated "obstinacy", that is, if he closes himself off from all discussion meant to clarify an opinion contrary to the Faith and, in effect, refuses the dialogue. The fact of heresy can be established only after all the rules of the hermeneutics of dogmas and all the theological qualifications have been applied. In this way, even in decisions that cannot be avoided, the true "ethos" of the dialogue procedure can be preserved.

June 6, 1976

A COMMENTARY ON THE THESES OF THE INTERNATIONAL
THEOLOGICAL COMMISSION ON THE RELATIONSHIP BETWEEN
THE ECCLESIASTICAL MAGISTERIUM AND THEOLOGY

Introduction

The theme that the International Theological Commission discussed in its October 1975 meeting is the same topic that Pope Paul VI spoke about in his address to the International Congress on the Theology of the Second Vatican Council, October 1, 1966. It seems only fitting, then, to refer to some of the views he expressed then.

In particular, it should be noted that the relationship between the ecclesiastical Magisterium and theology is a close one. By way of introduction, this relationship might perhaps be explained as follows: it is the task of the whole Church and therefore of those organs especially delegated for it to proclaim to men the Word that it has heard. Two tasks, then, have to be carried out simultaneously: hearing the Word of God and proclaiming it by a witness of both word and life. This latter must be undertaken by the common witness of all the faithful, but in a special way by the witness of those equipped for this either by official ministry or by scientific qualifications. This indivisible unity of hearing and teaching has a different nuance in the two different ways in which the task of teaching is carried out, ministerially or scientifically. One could perhaps say that the theologians' primary task is the hearing of the Word of God—in a qualified, scientific way, of course—while the task of the ecclesiastical Magisterium is more that of proclaiming the Word of God it has heard, but with the help of theological experts.

THESIS 1

Two questions are considered in this thesis. First it is necessary to discuss what is meant by the terms "ecclesiastical Magisterium" and "theologians". Both of them in fact can be understood to have a teaching office, for the task of teaching belongs both to bishops and to theologians, although in different ways. At the same time, it should be noted that discussion of the ecclesiastical Magisterium and of teachers has not been carried on in univocal terms in every age of the Church. Analogy applies here, both with regard to the understanding of the two realities and with regard to the concrete way in which they are exercised. For example, in some earlier times more than in later ones, the office of bishop and the exercise of theology were undertaken by the same person. Later, the ecclesiastical Magisterium and scientific theology were linked rather by way of cooperation.

Part I considers elements that are common to the ecclesiastical Magisterium and to theologians as they carry out their tasks. For it is very important, while noting the diversity of the two tasks, not to forget that they must cooperate with one another as they fulfill their ecclesiastical functions.

THESIS 2

In fact, true theology, understood in the Catholic sense, is no less a task to be undertaken within the Church than is the ecclesiastical Magisterium. Each task must safeguard the certainty of faith, whether by a deeper understanding and scientific defense of the Faith or by authoritatively proclaiming it and defending it against adversaries.

THESIS 3

Certain common obligations bind both the Magisterium and the theologians. It is true that the authority that each enjoys differs from that of the other, but in both the Magisterium and the theologians' task there is a genuine authority. For this reason, each must be aware that this authority is not absolute but has to be exercised in the form of service, the service of the Word of God. This hearing, or "obedience of faith" (Rom 1:5; 16:26), accomplished by theologians by means of their scientific investigations, serves that better hearing that theologians offer to bishops, and this cooperation with them serves the proclamation of the Word of God that bishops undertake.

In carrying out this common task, both theologians and the Magisterium draw what the Word of God has communicated to the Church from the common Faith (*E communi sensu fidelium*) of the community in the past and in the present. For what belongs to the common patrimony of the Church's Faith becomes manifest in the Faith of the universal Church in its varied dimensions, the whole Church of today and the whole Church of past ages.

In the course of time, the Church has left records in which the Faith by which the Church lived in past ages may be discerned. The investigations of theologians and the witness of the ecclesiastical Magisterium are both bound to these, i.e., documents of various kinds that have come down to us, for they are the documents of the believing Church itself in its passage through history.

Theological investigations and the exercise of the Magisterium's task are not undertaken purely for academic reasons or simply for the sake of polemical controversy. The reason why the truth of faith is investigated, why it is kept intact, why it is proclaimed as the Gospel, is pastoral and missionary. Men must be brought to live by faith. The pastoral character of the ecclesiastical Magisterium is more apparent than that of the theologians. But the theologians themselves cannot undertake their task without some pastoral reference, and the care of souls is even an internal element of the theological enterprise itself. This pastoral character affects theology both negatively and positively. Negatively, it means that the theological effort must be careful that the faith of believers not suffer harm because difficult explanations and disputed questions reported in the public communications media are heard and seen by people who are unduly disturbed by such publications. Positively, it means that the theological effort is used in proclamation and preaching and in religious education. The theological effort, scientific as it is, not only cannot be kept behind closed doors but also, by its very purpose as a ministry in the service of the preaching of the Word of God, affects the life of the ecclesiastical and human community.

THESIS 4

This thesis draws attention to the collegial or communitarian nature of both the Magisterium's task and the theologians' enterprise. Although each of them can and must be carried out through the personal work of an individual bishop or theologian, still the pertinent charism given to each member of the magisterial and theological communities is given because of their link with the College or the ecclesiastical community. This communion and collegiality must be respected in the carrying out of the office or of the scientific work. Special care should be taken for fostering community between the magisterial College and the community of those who devote themselves to the theological enterprise.

The Second Vatican Council made a special point of recalling the collegiality of the episcopal College, so that individual bishops neither should nor can perform their tasks without reference to the College. On the other hand, neither can theologians perform their work if they do not pay attention to the work and opinions of their colleagues, and this not merely because of the demands of scientific method but also because of the needs of a living community that is both intellectual and charismatic.

Part II: The common elements that link the task of the ecclesiastical Magisterium and the ministry of theologians do not eliminate the difference between them. They differ especially on four points: the function proper to each, the quality of authority proper to each, the different way in which each is linked with the Church, and the proper and specific freedom each enjoys.

THESIS 5

The Magisterium exercises the role of defending the integrity and unity of faith and morals. This cannot be done merely by decree but only according to the measure of the truth proposed in the exercise of the role. For this reason, it needs the help and cooperation of the science of the theologians who in fact attempt scientifically to uncover the truth of God's Word hidden in the words of men. The task of defending the integrity and unity of the Faith at first glance appears rather negative or restrictive. In fact, however, it is carried out in a positive way for the life of the Church, i.e., by the authoritative interpretation of the Word of God, which includes at once the exclusion of opinions contrary to faith and, much more, an introduction into a deeper understanding of the Faith.

The remarks in Thesis 5, 2, about the somewhat mediatorial function of theologians between the Magisterium and the People of God, must not be understood exclusively. Still, it is a matter of great importance. For the things that the ecclesiastical Magisterium proclaims as matters of faith or as ecclesiastical doctrines must be communicated with the help of theological interpretation and explanation to the People of God living here and now, who do not always correctly understand what the Magisterium has taught in the past or is teaching now. On the other hand, the Magisterium itself needs the cooperation of the theologians in order to discern what is true and what is erroneous in the Faith of the Christian people, for the Faith of the community of the People of God is also a norm for what the Magisterium can proclaim and require all to accept. Since scientific means must be employed in carrying out this task, the ecclesiastical Magisterium needs the serious cooperation of the theologians. And theologians themselves must, therefore, be aware of this ministry.

THESIS 6

While the sources of the authority with which the ecclesiastical Magisterium and the theologians fulfill their roles are distinct, the valid distinction should not lead to a false opposition.

On the one hand, the specific authority of the ecclesiastical Magisterium derives from the sacramental ordination by which its members are brought into the College of Bishops, to which as such belongs the highest pastoral authority in the Church. But it should be noted that this "formal authority" should coincide with a certain personal authority, deriving either from the person's own behavior or from the scientific authority that a theologian acquires for himself by his study and research. These need not be mutually exclusive, as is clear in the case of a man consecrated a bishop and pastor in the Church who has also acquired the other authority for himself in theological study, or of a man consecrated a bishop and teacher who makes use of the help and cooperation of an expert theologian as he carries out his task.

As for the authority of a theologian, it should be noted that this is not only an intellectual authority but also derives from his share in the life of the Church, whose living Faith is investigated and explained by the theological enterprise.

THESIS 7

There is no doubt that in exercising their tasks, both the ecclesiastical Magisterium and theologians are bound to the Church; but the manner in which each is linked to the Church differs.

With regard to the ecclesiastical Magisterium, the link with the Church derives from the fact that it is an office and ministry in and for the Church, which has no meaning outside the Church. And this is particularly true with regard to the office of teaching—Magisterium—and all the more because this Magisterium must be exercised in the manner of a judge who discerns the truth or falsehood of proposed opinions.

Similar comments hold also for theologians, when and to the degree that they carry out their task not only as researchers but also as teachers and do this by canonical mission. But even when the science of theology is pursued, not as an official exercise but as personal research, it remains linked with the Church, for theology, as the science of faith, can only be carried out truly in the living context of the Church's Faith. For the objective Faith (*fides quae*) can only be investigated by those who live in the Church with a living subjective Faith (*fides qua*).

THESIS 8 .

There is a great deal of talk today about the freedom of the science of theology, and this scientific freedom is often presented as incompatible with the restrictions that authority brings to bear. As a result, it is often overlooked that genuine freedom belongs to both the ecclesiastical Magisterium and theological science, and that the freedom proper to the one must be respected by the other.

In discussing freedom, whether in the ecclesiastical Magisterium or in scientific theology, it must not be forgotten that freedom is not license but is linked with a great responsibility that necessarily puts restrictions on it. This remark must not destroy the scientific freedom of theologians, which itself, however, is not unlimited but is bound by the truth that has been proclaimed by the Word of God and guarded by the Magisterium. No doubt it is very difficult to preserve the freedom of both Magisterium and theologians. It is a constant struggle to exercise this freedom without violating its necessary restrictions and to observe and guard the restrictions without destroying the freedom proper to the ministry of the truth.

THESIS 9

This thesis provides the transition to the third part, which discusses a properly understood dialogue between the Magisterium and theology. For from what has been said, it can hardly be doubted that tension will arise. Constant effort is required in order to keep in harmony the common and different elements.

But such tension is always experienced whenever there are diverse elements that must coexist but that are not easily synthesized. Dialogue is a means, if not simply for removing this tension, at least for making it fruitful.

Otto Semmelroth, S.J.

Part III of the theses offers a contribution to prevent the tension between Magisterium and theologians, described in Thesis 9, from harming the common good of the Church. There are many means and instruments available to prevent this, among which dialogue stands out as the chief way and a valid method for setting up a fruitful relationship between theologians and Magisterium.

The notion of dialogue must be properly understood. It is not a vague conversation, indefinite and interminable. Dialogue serves the search for truth. If dialogue even at the highest level serves the true freedom and "initiative" of all participants, it does not take the place of the role of the judges of the Faith, and it must not impede decisions from the Magisterium that are needed to defend the Faith of the Church. Hence, "dialogue" must not be understood in a superficial and popular sense; it must be purified of these implications and be in accord with the Christian Faith.

THESIS 10

Dialogue has certain presuppositions, without which it would not reach the truth. Every dialogue between the Magisterium and theologians presupposes a basic "solidarity" that consists in the common Faith of the Church. This unity respects and retains the diverse functions of the Magisterium and of theology. True dialogue lives in and arises out of this common basis, and it would lack any sense if this profound community in the Faith were absent or were simulated. For this reason, for a dialogue to lead to the truth, it must not be directed only by expertise but above all by sincerity, by courage in stating the truth, and by eagerness to hear the truth. Since this community is often neglected or doubted today, it is necessary to emphasize this "basis", for all dialogue between Magisterium and theologians must be stressed.

The thesis has another point: the proper functions of the Magisterium and of theology must not be confused. If they keep to their own responsibilities, as these are set out at the end of the thesis, they will be an excellent help to one another. This thesis rejects the attempts of those who would more or less like to do away with the task of the Magisterium and assign *exclusive* competency in matters of faith and morals to scientific theology and so to theologians.

THESIS 11

Consequently, the question arises of the limits of the dialogue between Magisterium and theologians. Two points are of major importance: (1) if community in the Faith is preserved, there is no intrinsic limit to the dialogue, although this does not mean an indefinite process in the search for truth; (2) the dialogue method reaches its limits where the truth of faith is harmed.

But there are dangers intrinsic to dialogue that can destroy conversation. The dialogue can easily be damaged, for example, if means of external coercion are employed. While today this is not a grave danger, there is a new situation in the relation between Magisterium and theologians that has not existed in this form until now. At one time the dialogue between Magisterium and theologians on doubtful matters was conducted *directly,* between the competent authority and the individual theologian. Today, in cases of conflict, "publicity" often intervenes between Magisterium and theologians. Thus pressure is applied, tactical moves are considered, etc., in all of which the "atmosphere" of dialogue is lost. The authenticity of the dialogue is thus reduced. Facts of this sort constitute a new situation, which certainly deserves further consideration.

THESIS 12

The theses do not intend to discuss specific questions and especially not juridical questions about the external structure of the dialogue, particularly in cases of conflict. But the thesis does intend to indicate the significance and the "locus" of the dialogue method before a formal doctrinal investigation is undertaken and, insofar as this is possible, even during the *"Ratio agendi",* (title of a document of the Sacred Congregation for the Doctrine of the Faith outlining the steps of a doctrinal investigation).[20] The doctrinal procedure represents the last and decisive step, when all the other forms (see the text) have become vain and useless. The thesis recommends the use of the dialogue method even to the Magisterium in the sense that it make use of a "graduated store" of reactions to doubtful opinions (see the ones proposed in the text). The classical rules of the hermeneutics of dogmas provide good and clear help. But the thesis also clearly recognizes that dialogue comes to an end when the theologian definitely contradicts the truth of faith. In this case, it is the theologian himself who in the last analysis has refused the dialogue.

Karl Lehmann

[20] *Nova agendi ratio in doctrinarum examine,* Sacred Congregation for the Doctrine of the Faith, Jan. 15, 1974, *AAS* 63 (1974): 234–36.

7

HUMAN DEVELOPMENT
AND CHRISTIAN SALVATION

INTRODUCTION

The problem of the relationship between human development and Christian salvation is of considerable significance everywhere. This is especially evident since the Second Vatican Council, where the Church paid uncommon attention to issues of an appropriate world order within the context of Christian responsibility. Within Latin America and elsewhere, it was different types of liberation theology that increasingly won attention. The International Theological Commission, in its annual meeting, October 4 to 9, 1976, occupied itself less with individual treatises and individual tendencies, more with basic issues touching the relationship between human development and Christian salvation.

The pages that follow should be regarded as an imperfect abridgment of the principal results. This final report takes account of the difficulties inherent in the issues studied and the current status of theological discussion and research. The theological tendencies in question are many and varied, subject to enormous changes; there is constant self-correction; they are intimately linked with social and economic conditions and the political situation in the world and in different geographical areas. Nor should we overlook the disputes that such theological treatises have occasioned on many sides, because theology risks being translated into politics and hurting the genuine unity of the Church. Given this state of affairs, the International Theological Commission wants to address itself to the discussion for a specific purpose: to search out the potential and the risk in such tendencies.

Karl Lehmann
Chairman of the Subcommittee

This document was approved by the Commission *"in forma specifica"*.

I. WORLD POVERTY AND INJUSTICE AS SPRINGBOARD
FOR A THEOLOGICAL MOVEMENT

The Second Vatican Council reminded the Church of its ceaseless duty to "scrutinize the signs of the times and to interpret them in the light of the Gospel".[1] A special incentive to carry out this injunction was provided by the documents emanating from the Second General Assembly of the Latin American Episcopal Conference (CELAM) held in 1968 in Medellín, Colombia: the Church hears the outcries of poor peoples and makes itself the interpreter of their oppressive conditions. The Church's worldwide solicitude in response to the challenge hurled by oppression and hunger is shown not only by papal documents—*Mater et Magistra, Pacem in Terris, Populorum Progressio, Octogesima Adveniens*—but also by documents of the Synod of Bishops held in Rome in 1971 (*Justice in the World*) and in 1974. Pope Paul VI once again highlighted the Church's urgent duty in this regard with his apostolic exhortation of December 8, 1975, *Evangelization in Today's World*.[2]

These circumstances must be taken into account if the theological treatises on these issues are to be understood. Although they have a scholarly face, their primary source is not theoretical, scientific effort. They are not presented in the first instance as a "written" theology; they struggle to preserve close contact with the day-to-day existence of overburdened men and women and with the concrete injunction to action that challenges the Church in this factual situation. They intend to give public expression to the cries of our poor, anguished brothers and sisters—specifically, to hunger, disease, unjust profit, exile, oppression. Add to this the inhuman living conditions of all those who own only what they wear, sleep at night in the streets, live and die there, lack basic medical care. For Christians enlightened by the Gospel, these "signs of the times" are an exceptionally sharp stimulus to bend every effort, in the name of Christian faith, to free their brothers and sisters from inhuman living conditions. This attention to the needy and this affinity with all the oppressed are singularly expressed and exemplified by the biblical words "justice", "liberation", "hope", "peace".

This witness to solicitude for the poor, a witness supported by the Gospel of Jesus Christ,[3] is something of a ceaseless spiritual leaven in all the pertinent theological treatises; it obviously inspires their theological reflections and political options. A spiritual experience arouses innate forces whereby the pressures of Christian love are transformed into commands effective for action by means of human reflection and scientific analysis.

---

[1] *GS*, 4.
[2] Cf. nos. 30–38.
[3] Cf. Lk 4:18ff.

Both elements, a basic spiritual experience and theological and scientific reflection, are mutually complementary and consequently fashion a vital unity. But we must be careful not to confound the two elements. No one, therefore, should condemn these various theological systems if he or she is not listening at the same time to the cries of the poor and seeking more acceptable ways to respond. On the other hand, we must ask whether the types of theological reflection currently in vogue are, in their actual methodology, the only way of responding appropriately to yearnings for a more human world of brothers and sisters. The point is, every theology has service for its function, and so must at times undergo needed changes and corrections, if these help it to achieve its primary commission more effectively.

II. A NEW TYPE OF THEOLOGY AND ITS DIFFICULTIES

The theological treatises of which we have spoken stem from conditions in which men are oppressed, are slavishly subject to others in economic, social, and political life and yearn for freedom. This existential human story is not accepted as an unchangeable destiny; it is understood as a "creative" process that looks to a larger freedom in all sectors of life and ultimately to the fashioning of a "new man". To change inhuman conditions is seen as a divine demand, as God's will: Jesus Christ, who by his redemptive action freed men from sin in all its forms, offers a new basis for human brotherhood and sisterhood.

This way of thinking, which is the springboard for the theological treatises of which we are speaking, gives them a special form that is in a sense new. God reveals his mysterious plan in actual events; and the more intimately the Christian enters into concrete situations and the historical progression of events, the more appropriately he responds to God's word. In consequence, the Christian recognizes the profound unity that links the divine history of salvation accomplished through Jesus Christ to efforts undertaken for the welfare and rights of men and women.

Although secular history and salvation history should not be regarded as simply identical, still the relationship between the two is to be conceived in the first instance as a unity. Their distinction may not be extended to a dualism in which history and salvation would be represented as indifferent one to the other. In fact, human activity acquires an entirely new value in history, a theological value, in that it builds up a more human society; for the construction of a just society is, in a sense, the inauguration of God's Kingdom in anticipation.[4] Therefore Christian faith is understood prin-

---

[4] Reference is made at times to GS, 39.

cipally as a historical praxis whereby sociopolitical conditions are changed and renewed.

This way of thinking contains many elements of great value, for it is indeed true that Christians should have a richer understanding of the total unity that their calling to salvation involves.[5] Nor can we doubt that faith, in its scriptural sense, can be fructified and perfected only by deeds. Moreover, the Second Vatican Council reminds us[6] that the Holy Spirit is active in world history; even outside the visible Church the preludes to faith, that is, the truths and rules of right reason about God and the common good, which are a kind of foundation for the Christian religion, are found to some extent.[7]

Nevertheless, in some theological movements these elemental data are interpreted in a one-sided fashion that is open to objection. The unity that links world history and salvation history may not be so conceived that it tends to consolidate the Gospel of Jesus Christ, which as a supernatural mystery is altogether unique and beyond human intelligence,[8] with secular history. Nor can it mean that the boundaries between Church and world are utterly effaced.

In similar vein, the world in its historical existence is indeed the place where God's saving plan is unfolding—but not in such a way that the force and dynamism of God's word consist totally in its function of stimulating social and political change. And so faith's praxis is not reducible to changing the conditions of human society; for besides laying injustice bare, faith's praxis includes such things as conscience formation, change in mental attitude, adoration of the true God and of our Savior Jesus Christ in distinction from all forms of idolatry. Consequently, "faith as praxis" should not be interpreted in such a way that one's involvement in politics embraces and governs all human efforts and actions totally and "radically". Two points call for clarification here:

1. Political controversy, which is customarily linked with confrontation, should not be carried to the point where it obscures or obliterates peace and reconciliation as the objective and fruit of Christian activity, and what takes priority is an increase of antagonism and the onset of violence.

2. It must remain beyond dispute that for the Christian politics is not the final ground that gives ultimate meaning to all of life; it is not an absolute in the Christian eon; and so its nature is to be an instrument, a servant. Overlook this, and human freedom is threatened by movements that promote dictatorial control. Although theology is oriented in part toward praxis, its more prominent function is to seek understanding of God's word; for whatever engages it,

---

[5] Cf. GS, 10, 11, 57, 59, 61; AG, 8; PP, 15–16.
[6] Cf. GS, 22, 26, 38, 41, 57; DH, 12.
[7] Cf. First Vatican Council, dogmatic Constitution Dei Filius (DS, 3005).
[8] Cf. ibid.

theology must be able to distance itself from a concrete situation, which is almost always attended by various pressures and compulsions to action. It is from the principles of Catholic teaching on faith and morals that we can derive the light to make correct judgments about what has to be done to acquire eternal salvation without risk of losing the freedom of God's children. Only in this way is theology tied to truth; only in this way can it preserve the sovereign authority of God's word and the altogether unique character of that word. And so we have to take special care not to fall into a unidimensional vision of Christianity that would adversely affect Christology and ecclesiology, our view of salvation and of Christian existence, even theology's proper function.

Prophetic charges of injustice and urgent appeals to make common cause with the poor have to do with situations that are highly complex in nature, have roots in history, and depend on social and political realities. Even a prophetic judgment on the circumstances of a time calls for assured reasons or criteria. That is why the different theological treatments of liberation must deal simultaneously with theories that come from the social sciences, which study objectively what the "outcry of the people" expresses.

Theology, however, cannot deduce concrete political norms sheerly from theological principles, and so the theologian cannot settle profound sociological issues by theology's specific resources. Theological treatises that strive to build a more human society must take into account the risks that the use of sociological theories involves. In every instance these theories must be tested for their degree of certitude, inasmuch as they are often no more than conjectures and not infrequently harbor explicit or implicit ideological elements that rest on debatable philosophical assumptions or on an erroneous anthropology. This is true, for instance, of significant segments of analyses inspired by Marxism and Leninism. Anyone who employs such theories and analyses should be aware that these do not achieve a greater degree of truth simply because theology introduces them into its expositions. In fact, theology ought to recognize the pluralism that exists in scientific interpretations of society and realize that it cannot be fettered to any concrete sociological analysis.

III. BIBLICAL–THEOLOGICAL FACETS

Since the theological treatises we have been discussing often appeal to Sacred Scripture, we should take care to uncover what the Old and New Testaments have to say about the relationship between salvation and human welfare, between salvation and human rights. Obviously, our reflections here must be incomplete. On the other hand, we must avoid the anachronism that would read contemporary ideas back into the Bible.

Old Testament

To determine the relationship between divine salvation and human development, practically everyone now cites the Exodus story. The reason is, the exodus from Egypt[9] is actually a salvation event of capital importance in the Old Testament: liberation from foreign tyranny and from works forced by public powers. Nevertheless, "liberation" in the Old Testament is not totally situated in the removal from Egypt and the return from exile; for the liberation is oriented to the Covenant worship solemnized on Mount Sinai,[10] and apart from that orientation it loses its specific meaning. The Psalms themselves, when they deal with need and protest, with aid and thanks, reveal forms of prayer that express salvation and "liberation".[11] There distress is identified not only with social affliction but also with hostility, injustice, blameworthy fault, as well as with that to which this leads: the threat that is death and the void death represents. Less significance, therefore, is placed on felt needs in individual instances; more important is the convincing experience that only God can bring deliverance and salvation.

Consequently, one should not speak of Old Testament salvation in its relation to human rights and welfare without simultaneously revealing the complete theological argumentation: it is not man but Yahweh who effects change. Besides, as long as the exodus lasted, in the desert, it was especially for the spiritual liberation and purification of his people that God provided.

A moving instance of an effort inspired by God's revelation to improve conditions of human living is the rebuke to the social order sounded by the prophets, especially in Amos.[12] Later prophets take up and enlarge the theme initiated by Amos, as when they cry "woe" on those who own large estates.[13] In powerful language Hosea censures the absence of human solidarity.[14] Isaiah explicitly includes widows and orphans among those who must be protected.[15] He threatens that the Lord will take away from Jerusalem "the powerful and the strong", that is, the more potent leaders in the society;[16]

---

[9] Cf. Ex 1–24.
[10] Cf. Ex 24.
[11] Cf., e.g., Ps 18.
[12] Amos 2:6f.; 3:10; 5:11; 6:4ff.; 8:4ff.
[13] Cf. Is 5:8f.; Micah 2.
[14] Hos 4:1f.; 6:4, 6; 10:12.
[15] Is 1:17, 23; 10:1f.
[16] Cf. Is 3:1ff.; 1:21ff.; 10:1ff.

he complains about possessions accumulating in the hands of a few[17] or, more broadly, about the oppression of the poor by the rich.[18] But he is clearly far from calling for revolt against the oppressors, even though this theme is discoverable in Old Testament writings.[19] Presentiment of impending disaster keeps a program for a more equitable society from making its appearance.[20] The prophets believe that there are many different ways of succoring society in its needs. But instead of an optimism supposedly supported by a theology of history, they show a large measure of scepticism on man's ability to actually fashion a different world.

Such a change must be preceded by a way of acting that is proper to interior conversion and justice. "Cease to do evil, learn to do good; seek justice, assist the oppressed, defend the fatherless, plead for the widow."[21] It is God who must give men and women the power to bring about a greater degree of justice in the social sphere: in the last analysis Yahweh alone can efficaciously provide for human rights and welfare, especially of the oppressed.[22] God works salvation beyond the good or evil designs of men.

In this connection, the prophets do recognize something akin to the "corrupt system". As they see it, however, we may not reduce everything to the point where evil is only a sign and effect of society's unjust structures or where we could hope to correct abuses simply by abolishing possessions. Over and above this, we must keep in mind the personal element, which determines the process of "liberation" for the Old Testament. This is particularly exemplified and confirmed by the principle of individual responsibility.[23]

Some significant passages of the Old Testament disclose partial visions of a new society, no longer arranged along the lines of pervasive contemporary structures.[24] Many Psalms speak expressly of God as liberator of the oppressed and defender of the poor.[25] While freeing the people of Israel from oppression, God demands of them that they remove all human oppression.[26] God's lordship, once it comes, will eliminate all tyranny of man over man.

In the Old Testament, however, this hope is long not distinguished with sufficient clarity from concrete history and does not bear on realities that transcend that history. Even down to our own time, a fair number of ideolo-

---

[17] Cf. Is 5:8.
[18] Cf. Is 1:21ff.; 3:14f.
[19] Cf. Jg 9:22f.; 1 Kings 12.
[20] Note a beginning in Joel 3:1f.
[21] Is 1:16f.
[22] Cf. Is 1:24ff.; Ex 3:7–9; Ps 103:6; 72:12ff.; Dt 10:17ff.
[23] Cf. Ezek 18; Jer 31:29ff.
[24] Cf., e.g., Is 55:3–5; Ex 34:40–48; Jer 31:31ff.
[25] Cf. Ps 9, 10, 40, 72, 76, 146; Judith 9:11.
[26] Cf. Ex 22:10; Lev 19:13, 18, 33; Dt 10:18; 24:14; Ps 82:2–4.

gies of a "secularized" salvation look for these promises of God to be realized within the limits of history, and simply in consequence of man's activity; but this, we have seen, the Old Testament rejects. Lastly, we should recall that in the apocalyptic passages of the later Old Testament the hope of a life after this life and the theology of history commend in remarkable fashion man's experienced weakness and God's omnipotence.

New Testament

The New Testament takes up significant elements of the Old[27] or presupposes them.[28] As the discourse on the Beatitudes shows strikingly,[29] the Old Testament insistence on conversion and renewal of the human spirit is intensified, and in the New Testament these demands can be quite effectively realized by the power of the Holy Spirit. Still the impression remains—and it has been stated time and again—that the New Testament is not primarily concerned about the social sphere and human togetherness.

Possibly the unique newness of the Christian message initially tempered concern for questions that involved worldly duties. The personal love of the incarnate God for his new people was so transcendently important that questions prompted by temporal existence could not take priority (recall only the expectation of God's Kingdom). With the spotlight on the mystery of our suffering and risen Lord, sheerly human needs could assume less urgency. The political situation of the Roman Empire prevented Christians from turning their minds freely and extensively to the world.

However, this is not the place to explain in detail how Jesus' good news and New Testament ethics imparted many directive norms and patterns of human conduct that were capable of inspiring a "social critique". Enough that we think of the command to love neighbor and enemy,[30] of the exhortatory and threatening words to the wealthy and the glutted,[31] of the obligation to care for the poor and the weak[32] and the admonition to all to help others,[33] of avoiding the temptation to exercise control over others[34]—on the ground that all human beings are brothers and sisters.[35]

---

[27] Cf., e.g., Is 61:1f., as cited in Lk 4:16ff.
[28] Cf. Mk 12:29ff. and Lev 19:18.
[29] Cf. 5:1–7:29, esp. 5:3–12.
[30] Cf. Lk 6:35f.; Mt 25:31–46.
[31] E.g., Lk 6:24ff.; Mt 6:24; 1 Cor 11:20ff.; Lk 12:16ff.; James 2:1ff.; 5:1ff.
[32] Cf. Lk 6:20; 1 Cor 12:22ff.
[33] Mk 10:21; Lk 12:33.
[34] Cf. Mk 10:42–45; Mt 20:25–28; Lk 22:25–27.
[35] Cf. Mt 23:8; 25:41ff.

Moreover, the New Testament discloses in the faithful a disposition to welcome "institutional" forms of Christian charity. Examples are the contributions taken up for Jerusalem[36] and the arrangement for the ministries of "diaconate" and charitable aid.[37] But it is clear that such "institutional" helps, at least in the beginning, were restricted to the ambit of the Christian communities and were quite undeveloped.

The New Testament also attaches great significance to the element of liberation, but we must be uncommonly careful to uncover its genuine sense. St. Paul's words about the new freedom are closely linked to his message on justification, and so liberation as such is not a theme severed from his other themes. The salvific work of Jesus Christ opened even the inner chambers of the human heart, so it is easy to be mistaken about what constitutes true denial of human freedom, true slavery. The announcing of justification shows with consummate clarity that the human person is prey to evil powers.

Authentic, complete liberty is impossible without the primary liberation[38] from death and perishability (*sarx*), from the power of sin and from the law (note also the "elements of the world"). "It is with this freedom that Christ has set us free."[39]

Liberation from these powers, however, brings a fresh freedom, in consequence of which we can, in the spirit of Jesus Christ, be effective in love so as to serve our brothers and sisters.[40] Here surely we have a foreshadowing of what God will himself accomplish as his gift to the just when he judges the whole story of humankind. The justice of God, through the Spirit and by his power, bestows a liberating action that enables us to work what is good, an action that finds its perfection through love.

And so, when the New Testament speaks of "the liberation that brings freedom",[41] the freedom that is grace, moral stimulus, and eschatological promise, these utterances are inserted into the proclamation of justification. Only if they rest on this foundation do they acquire their full force and power. Only if we bring our reflections to these depths can we understand and actualize the stimulus the New Testament offers Christians for liberating activity.

In the light of the New Testament, society is not genuinely changed unless men and women are reconciled with God and with one another. Only if men and women become a new creation by conversion and justice can the style of human living be adequately and steadily improved. Human rights and welfare,

---

[36] Cf. 2 Cor 8:1ff.
[37] Cf. 1 Cor 12:28; 15:15; Rom 12:7; 16:1; Phil 1:1; 1 Tim 3:8, 12.
[38] Cf. Rom 5–7.
[39] Gal 5:1.
[40] Cf. Gal 5:6, 13.
[41] Cf. Gal 5:1.

therefore, human liberation, are not situated in the category of "having" but primarily within the boundaries that comprise "being"—including, of course, the implications that flow therefrom for shaping all the situations of human living.

IV. SYSTEMATIC AND THEOLOGICAL REFLECTIONS

God as Liberator and Man's Liberating Action

It has been noted that not all the Old Testament affirmations on liberation can be extended in every respect to the New Testament situation. The revelation given us in Christ divides the uninterrupted process of salvation history into two periods: promise and fulfillment. But both Testaments are at one in the conviction that God alone, precisely as supreme and utterly free Lord, administers human welfare; only he is properly liberator. This becomes clear, however, only when the needs of men and women are not reduced simply to their economic and material problems, only when we grasp the complete spectrum of their risk-laden, corrupt situation. Still, the unshakable proposition "God alone really frees" should not be interpreted as a kind of myth (as if we were talking about a *Deus ex machina*); such a myth can only increase the indolence, inactivity, and apathy of those in straitened circumstances. Genuine faith does not condone inhuman living conditions, does not countenance them. God does not come to us in the violent hurricane of a revolution, but by his grace he strengthens the mind and heart of man and woman so that they sharpen their conscience and, led by a living faith, build a more just world. To achieve this, however, the *whole* person must be freed from *all* the powers of evil. That is why an effectual change of mind and heart (*metanoia*) and a renewal of love for God and neighbor bring about actual liberation. But full liberation, according to Christian belief, is not accomplished in the course of earthly events, in history. For history leads to a "new earth" and to the "city of God"; consequently, until this fulfillment is realized, every liberating activity has a transitory character—and at the Last Judgment it will have to undergo its own ultimate testing.[42]

The relevance of our reflections, however, should not be restricted to spiritual reformation or incitement to assist individuals; for there is a kind of "injustice that assumes institutional shape", and as long as this obtains, the situation itself calls for a greater degree of justice and demands reforming. Our contemporaries are no longer convinced that social structures have been

---

[42] Cf. Mt 25.

predetermined by nature and therefore are "willed by God" or that they have their origin in anonymous evolutionary laws. Consequently, the Christian must ceaselessly point out that the institutions of society originate also in the conscience of society, and that men and women have a moral responsibility for these institutions.

We may argue how legitimate it is to speak of "institutional sin" or of "sinful structures", since the Bible speaks of sin in the first instance in terms of an explicit, personal decision that stems from human freedom. But it is unquestionable that by the power of sin injury and injustice can penetrate social and political institutions. That is why, as we have pointed out, even situations and structures that are unjust have to be reformed.

Here we have a new consciousness, for in the past these responsibilities could not be perceived as distinctly as they are now. From this perspective justice means a basic reverence for the equal dignity of all men and women; it means that radical human rights develop in gratifying fashion and are protected;[43] it means an assured equity in the distribution of those goods that are especially needful for human living.[44]

Concrete Relationship between Human Development and Divine Salvation

Reflection on the relationship between the salvation that God effects and the liberating action of man reveals the need to determine with greater exactness the relationship between human development and divine salvation, between the building up of the world and eschatological fulfillment. As is clear from the proofs we have adduced, human activity and Christian hope may be neither utterly divorced—on one side the world of earth exclusively, on the other a life to come utterly severed from the world—nor seen in terms of an "evolutionary optimism", as if God's lordship and man's progressive construction of the world were one and the same thing.

Even the pastoral constitution *Gaudium et Spes* makes a distinction between the growth of God's Kingdom and human progress as between the work of divinization and the work of humanization, or as between the order of divine grace and the order of human activity.[45] Indeed it speaks first of the affinity between the two: the service of men and women on earth "makes ready the

---

[43] Cf. *Schema Pontificiae Commissionis a Iustitia et Pace, The Church and Human Rights* (Vatican City, 1975).

[44] Cf. *PP,* 21.

[45] Cf. *GS,* 36, 38, 39, 40, 42, 43, 58; *AA,* 7.

material of heaven's Kingdom".[46] The good fruits of our diligent activity—
cleansed, however, of all sordidness, lit up and transfigured—we shall discover
afresh in the Kingdom of God, so that it is not only love that will remain[47]
but love's labor as well.[48] Eschatological hope, therefore, ought to find its
expression even in the structures of secular life.[49] That is why the Council
speaks not only of this world's passing away but of its transformation as
well.[50] The earthly city and the heavenly city ought to penetrate each other,
under faith's guidance, with due respect for their distinction and their harmonious union.[51] These ideas are summed up in the decree *Apostolicam Actuosi-
tatem* on the apostolate of the laity: "Christ's redemptive work, while of its
nature directed to the salvation of men and women, involves also the renewal
of the whole temporal order. The Church has for mission, therefore, not only
to bring to men and women the message of Christ and his grace but also to
saturate and perfect the temporal sphere with the spirit of the Gospel. . . . The
two spheres [spiritual and temporal], distinct though they are, are so linked in
the single plan of God that he himself purposes in Christ to take up the whole
world again into a new creation, initially here on earth, completely on the
Last Day."[52]

These passages persuade us that the vindication of justice and participation
in the process of transforming the world should be regarded "as a constitutive
element of the preaching of the Gospel".[53] The words "constitutive element" (*ratio constitutiva*) are still the subject of controversy. If we look at
their strict meaning, it seems more accurate to interpret them as meaning an
integral part, not an essential part.[54] Besides, the texts cited from the Second
Vatican Council have commonly been explained as favoring a *harmony*
between eschatological salvation and the human effort to build a better
world. It is useful, therefore, while maintaining unyieldingly the unity that
links the two, to spell out again, with even sharper clarity, the distinction
between them.

The very resistance of earthly situations to positive change for the better,

[46] Cf. *GS*, 38.
[47] Cf. 1 Cor 13:8.
[48] Cf. *GS*, 39.
[49] Cf. *LG*, 35.
[50] Cf. *GS*, 38, 39.
[51] Cf. *LG*, 36.
[52] *AA*, 5; cf. 7 also.
[53] Cf. 1971 Synod of Bishops, *De iustitia in mundo* (Vatican Press, 1971), Introduction, p. 5.
[54] This is the interpretation that was given by the Synod of 1974. [English translator's
note: This footnote, translated here from the French version, does not appear in the Latin
text sent to the members of the International Theological Commission on June 30, 1977, for
final approval.]

the power of sin and some ambiguous effects of human progress[55] teach us to recognize with even greater clarity within the very unity of salvation history an abiding difference between the Kingdom of God and human development, as well as the mystery of the Cross, without which no activity becomes genuinely salvific.[56] But if, while preserving the unity, it is the difference that is highlighted, this does not introduce a so-called dualism. In fact, this more penetrating vision helps us to carry out the task of promoting human welfare and justice with a greater measure of endurance, steadfastness, and confidence; it can also keep us from being thrown into confusion if our efforts prove ineffective.

This unifying connection and this difference in the relationship between human development and Christian salvation in their existential shape indeed demand further serious research, and this surely has a high priority among the tasks of today's theology. But the basic character of that unity cannot be overturned, for it is rooted at reality's very core.

On the one hand, existential history is in a way the locus where the world is so deeply transformed that it reaches as far as the mystery of God, and that is why love and its fruits abide. It is ultimately for this reason that there can be a link between salvation and human welfare, between salvation and human rights. But they are not linked to perfection, because the eschatological fulfillment "takes away" existential history.

On the other hand, the Kingdom of God "directs" history and utterly transcends all the possibilities of earthly fulfillment; it presents itself, therefore, as the action of God. This involves a certain break with that world, no matter what perfection we recognize therein. This discontinuity in our individual stories we experience as death, but the same discontinuity precisely as "transformation" touches the whole of history: it is the world's "destruction".

In our pilgrim state this "dialectic", which finds expression in these two irreducible principles, cannot be dissolved and ought not be removed. In particular, however, the eschatological fulfillment for which we still yearn (the "eschatological reserve") is the reason why the relationship between God's Kingdom and history cannot be described as either a monism or a dualism, and so from the very nature of this relationship we have to hold its definition in abeyance.

In any event, the relationship between the message of eschatological salvation and the shaping of historical time to come cannot be established univocally, by walking a single line, eyes fixed on harmony alone or difference alone. Perhaps this is what the words in Luke mean: "The Kingdom of God is not coming with outward show; nor will they say 'Lo, here it is!' or 'There!' For

---

[55] Cf. *AA,* 7, for greater detail.
[56] Cf. *GS,* 22, 78.

behold, the Kingdom of God is in the midst of you."[57] The *Pastoral Constitution on the Church in the Modern World* suggests another consequence of this basic relationship between history and salvation: "We do not know when the earth and humanity are to be consummated, nor do we know how the universe is to be transformed."[58]

Here surely lies the formal solution to our problem—a solution commended by the principal acts of revelation. In the concrete working out of this relationship, however, we can discover many ways of realizing it, ways that have different, distinct shapes. The correct choice of means appropriate to this solution in various periods of history and, for example, in areas that belong to the First, Second, and Third Worlds will call for different procedures. What is effective in sections of Europe and North American that have a highly developed industrial economy does not have the same significance on continents and in areas of the world where most of the people are hungry. And still, however considerable the differences, we may not infringe on the above-mentioned basic relationship between human development and Christian salvation.

In this matter we have unambiguous criteria at hand. The basic relationship is deranged, for example, if the practice of social and political liberation has such priority that divine worship, prayer, the Eucharist and other sacraments, individual ethics and all questions about the final destiny of man and woman (death and eternal life), and the exhausting struggle within history against the powers of darkness[59] take second place. On the other hand, in situations of poverty and injustice those truths of the Faith must be proclaimed and practiced in such a way as not to corroborate a frequent reproach: the Church disguises human distress, does no more than lull the poor in their very afflictions. Offering authentic relief is something totally different from raising hopes futilely comforting, hopes that only blunt the feeling of anguish.

Relationship between Human Development and Salvation in the Church's Commission

To commend the significance of the Church for the world is also to stress pungently that the community that is Church is always concretely circumstanced and that in these circumstances political options have already been taken. The Church, though a special kind of community, must always remember that its life is ceaselessly lived on a stage where candidates for power

[57] Lk 17:20f.
[58] GS, 39.
[59] Cf. GS, 13b.

compete with one another, where power is exercised in concrete ways, where power is linked to ideologies.

The Church "is not bound exclusively and inseparably to any race or nation, to any one particular way of life, to any customary pattern of living old or new".[60] In virtue of its origin, supernatural character, religious mission, and eschatological hope, it cannot be confounded with any sociopolitical system or linked with it by necessary, unbreakable ties.

If the Church must be careful not to be entrapped by the power seekers, no more ought it surrender to sheer neutrality or unsympathetic detachment and retire to a purely nonpolitical role. It is a fact that in many parts of today's world the Church is so dreadfully restricted that its witness to faith is invited in other forms, forms no less prophetic; primary among these are suffering in the footsteps of our Lord and silence by coercion.

The Church cannot allow itself the cunning stratagems that characterize politics, but it must take care to anticipate the political consequences of its actions and its omissions. It can share in the blame when it does not denounce the situation of the poor and the oppressed, of those who suffer injustice— much more if it covers such a situation over and leaves it unchanged.

And so the Church, on the model of the Old Testament prophets, should sharpen its conscience, so as to lay a critique on the social order under the guidance of faith. A strong kinship with the poor ("poor" in its largest sense, e.g., those who are afflicted by any serious spiritual, psychological, or material wants) and effective assistance to them have been from olden times among the principal functions of the Church and all its members. In our day, however, this task has become the preeminent witness to a living faith; for many outside the church, it is an inestimable criterion of the Church's credibility.

To build up and shape the social and political order is a task committed in a special way to the laity.[61] But the Church as a whole—represented particularly by the ministerial functions of the supreme Pontiff, bishops, priests, and deacons—may not keep silent in conditions where human dignity and elementary human rights are crushed. This granted, the whole Church is under obligation to express its convictions quickly and courageously.

But in many individual circumstances it is possible for Christians to opt freely among different paths that lead to the one same goal.[62] In consequence, Christians cannot utterly avoid controversy on social and political issues. "Where Christians exercise different options and on the face of it are apparently in disagreement, the Church asks that they try to understand one another's positions and reasons with kindliness and appreciation."[63] Without con-

---

[60] GS, 58; cf. LG, 9; GS, 42.
[61] Cf. AA, 7; LG, 31, 37; GS, 43.
[62] Cf., at greater length, GS, 43.
[63] Paul VI, apostolic Letter Octogesima Adveniens, no. 50.

cealing his or her own convictions, each should try by persuasion and encouragement to contribute to the realization of the common objective. Where opinions differ, therefore, Christians may never forget this maxim of Vatican II: "The bonds that unite the faithful are more powerful than anything that divides them."[64]

Nevertheless, the Church's unity is seriously imperiled if the differences that exist between social "classes" are taken up into a systematic "class struggle". Where you have those "class" differences, you can hardly avoid conflict. Christians are recognized in the first instance by the way they try to solve such tensions: they do not persuade the masses to destroy violence by counterviolence; rather, they try to effect change by, e.g., shaping the consciences of men and women, entering into discussion, initiating and supporting nonviolent action.[65] Nor may the Christian bypass the primary end: reconciliation.

We must also guard against the danger that social and political hostilities might supersede all else, so that, e.g., Christians of divergent positions no longer celebrate the Eucharist together or shut one another out of their Eucharist. The point is, political options may not become so contentious as to damage the universality of the Christian message of salvation. This message is to be carried to all, even the rich and the oppressors; for the Church ought not exclude any human person from its love.

The Church should constantly remind men and women that politics does not have a kind of absolute value and should be increasingly concerned to strip politics of such value. An exclusive political option, intolerant of any other option, becomes despotic and subverts the very nature of politics. It is the Church's obligation—a duty it cannot forego—to oppose the dictatorial claims of a state that would maintain that all the dimensions of human living fall under its sole control.

It is true that in such circumstances the Church at times finds it difficult or impossible to manifest its mind in the public forum. Still, it does its duty surpassingly well if, in imitation of its Lord, it responds to such situations by courageous protest, by silent suffering, even by martyrdom in its various shapes. But even in such extreme situations the Christian liberation that leads to freedom cannot be totally fettered. This is our sovereign comfort; here is the high point of our confidence.

---

[64] GS, 92.

[65] Obviously, we cannot give more extended treatment here to additional issues that concern recourse to force and violence.

CONCLUSION

In dealing with these questions, we become strikingly aware of the diverse situations that confront the local Churches within the Church Catholic; and this diversity is a cause for concern. Social, cultural, and political differences can at times weigh upon us with such increasing heaviness that our common unity in faith, the centrality of faith, seems no longer capable of overcoming our tensions and our rendings.

In our [ITC] discussions we too were able to observe with some clarity the varying situations in which different people live. Now, no one in the Church speaks simply for himself or herself, and so all of us should listen to the cries of our brothers and sisters, all those all over the world who are treated with injustice, are oppressed by tribulations, suffer from poverty, are distressed by hunger. Here too we can learn from one another, so as to keep ourselves from repeating afresh the mistaken solutions that have plagued the history of the Church and of human societies (e.g., when politics is divinized).

In this effort it is the Spirit of Christ that links us all. In this connection, the Church's unity and catholicity amid the variety of her peoples and of human cultures are simultaneously a gift to us and a claim on us. What has been laboriously achieved, however, must not be facilely jeopardized. This is particularly the case with all issues touching the relationship between human development and Christian salvation.

8A

PROPOSITIONS ON THE DOCTRINE OF CHRISTIAN MARRIAGE

1. MATRIMONY AS AN INSTITUTION

1.1. *The Human and Divine Views of Matrimony*

The matrimonial pact is founded upon preexistent and permanent structures that constitute the difference between man and woman and is "instituted" by the spouses themselves, even though in its concrete form it is very subject to different historical and cultural changes as well as, in a certain sense, to the particular way in which the marriage is carried out by the spouses. In this, marriage shows itself to be an institution of the Creator himself, both from the point of view of mutual help in conjugal love and fidelity as well as through the rearing of children born in marriage within the heart of the family community.

1.2. *Marriage in Christ*

As is easily shown in the New Testament, Jesus confirmed this institution which existed "from the very beginning", and cured it of its previous defects (Mk 10:2–9, 10–12) by restoring all its dignity and its original requirements. He sanctified this state of life (*GS,* 48, 2) by including it within the mystery of love, which unites him as Redeemer to his Church. This is the reason why the task of regulating Christian marriage (1 Cor 7:10f.) has been entrusted to the Church.

This document was approved by the Commission *"in forma specifica"*.

163

1.3. *The Apostles*

The Epistles of the New Testament say that marriage should be honored in every way (Heb 13:4) and, in response to certain attacks, they present it as a good work of the Creator (1 Tim 4:1–5). Rather they exalt matrimony among the faithful because it is included in the mystery of Covenant and love that unites Christ and the Church (Eph 5:22–23; *GS*, 48, 2).

They ask, therefore, that marriage be contracted "in the Lord" (1 Cor 7:39) and that matrimonial life be lived in accordance with the dignity of a "new creature" (2 Cor 5:17), "in Christ" (Eph 5:21–33), putting Christians on guard against the pagans' habits (1 Cor 6:12–20; cf. 6:9–10). On the basis of a "right deriving from faith" and in their desire to assure its permanence, the Churches of apostolic times formulated certain moral orientations (Col 3:18ff.; Titus 2:3–5; 1 Pet 3:1–7) and juridical dispositions that would help people live matrimony "according to the Faith" in different human situations and conditions.

1.4. *The First Centuries*

During the first centuries of Church history, Christians contracted marriage "like other men" (*Ad Diognetum,* v, 6) with the father of the family presiding, and only with domestic rites and gestures, as, for example, uniting hands. Still they didn't lose sight of the "extraordinary and truly paradoxical laws of their spiritual society" (ibid., v, 4): they eliminated from the home liturgies every trace of pagan cult. They placed special importance on the procreation and education of offspring (ibid., v, 6), they accepted the bishop's vigilance over matrimony (St. Ignatius of Antioch, *Ad Polycarpum,* v. 2), they showed in their matrimony a special submission to God and a relationship with their Faith (Clement of Alexandria, *Stromata,* iv, 20), and sometimes at the marriage rite they enjoyed the celebration of the eucharistic sacrifice and a special blessing (Tertullian, *Ad Uxorem,* ii, 9).

1.5. *The Eastern Traditions*

From very ancient times in the Eastern Churches the shepherds of the Church themselves took an active part in the celebration of marriages in the place of the fathers of the family or even along with them. This change was not the result of a usurpation but was brought about to answer the requests made by the family and with the approval of civil authority.

Because of this evolution, the ceremonies formerly carried out within the family were little by little included within liturgical rites. As time passed the idea took shape that the ministers of the rite of the "mystery" of matrimony were not only the couple alone but also the shepherd of the Church.

1.6. *The Western Traditions*

In the Western Churches the problem of what element constituted marriage from a juridical point of view arose with the encounter between the Christian vision of matrimony and Roman law. This was resolved by considering the consent of the spouses as the only constitutive element. The fact that, up until the time of the Council of Trent, clandestine marriages were considered valid is due to this decision. Still, the blessing of the priest and his presence as witness of the Church, as well as some liturgical rites, had already been encouraged by the Church for a long time. With the decree *Tametsi,* the presence of the pastor and witnesses became the ordinary canonical form of marriage necessary for validity.

1.7. *The New Churches*

According to the desires of Vatican Council II and the new rite for celebrating matrimony, it is to be hoped that new liturgical and juridical norms will be developed, under the guidance of ecclesial authority, among peoples who have recently come to the Gospel, to harmonize the reality of Christian marriage with the authentic values of these peoples' own traditions.

This diversity of norms, due to the plurality of cultures, is compatible with basic unity and therefore does not go beyond the limits of legitimate pluralism.

The Christian and ecclesial character of the union and of the mutual donation of the spouses can, in fact, be expressed in different ways, under the influence of the baptism that they have received and through the presence of witnesses, among whom the "competent priest" occupies the prime post. Today various canonical adaptations of these various elements may seem to be opportune.

1.8. *Canonical Adaptations*

In the reform of canon law there should be a global view of matrimony according to its various personal and social dimensions. The Church must be aware that juridical ordinances must serve to help and develop conditions that are always more attentive to the human values of matrimony. Nevertheless it must not be thought that such adaptations can bear on the total reality of matrimony.

1.9. *Personalistic View of the Institution*

"The beginning, the subject and goal of all social institutions, is and must be the human person, which for its part and by its very nature stands completely in need of social life" (*GS*, 25). As an "intimate partnership of life and conjugal love" (ibid., 48), matrimony is a suitable place and way to improve the welfare of persons in line with their vocation. Therefore marriage can never be thought of as a way of sacrificing persons to some common good extrinsic to themselves, since the common good is the sum of "those conditions of social life that allow people, either as groups or as individuals, to reach their fulfillment more fully and more easily" (ibid., 26).

1.10. *Structure and Not Superstructure*

While marriage is subject to economic realities at its beginning and for its entire duration, it is not a superstructure for private ownership of goods and resources. While, in fact, the concrete ways in which the marriage and the family subsist may be tied to economic conditions, still the definitive union of a man with a woman in a conjugal covenant responds to human nature and the needs that the Creator put in them. This is the reason why matrimony is not only no obstacle to the personal maturation of couples but rather is a great help to them.

2. SACRAMENTALITY OF CHRISTIAN MARRIAGE

2.1. *Real Symbol and Sacramental Sign*

Jesus Christ disclosed in a prophetic way the reality of matrimony as it was intended by God at man's beginnings (cf. Gen 1:27; 2:24; Mk 10:6, 7–8; Mt 19:4, 5) and restored it through his death and Resurrection. For this reason Christian marriage is lived "in the Lord" (1 Cor 7:39) and is also determined by elements of the saving action performed by Christ.

Already in the Old Testament the matrimonial union was a figure of the Covenant between God and the people of Israel (cf. Hos 2; Jer 3:6–13; Ezek 16 and 23; Is 54). In the New Testament, Christian marriage rises to a new dignity as a representation of the mystery that unites Christ and the Church (cf. Eph 5:21–33). Theological interpretation illuminates this analogy more profoundly: the supreme love and gift of the Lord who shed his blood and the faithful and irrevocable attachment of his Spouse the Church become models and examples for Christian matrimony.

This resemblance is a relationship of real sharing in the Covenant of love between Christ and the Church. From its own standpoint, Christian marriage, as a real symbol and sacramental sign, represents the Church of Christ concretely in the world and, especially under its family aspect, it is called rightly the "domestic Church" (*LG,* 11).

2.2. *Sacrament in a Real Sense*

In such a way matrimony takes on the likeness of the mystery of the union between Jesus Christ and his Church. This inclusion of Christian marriage in the economy of salvation is enough to justify the title "sacrament" in a broad sense.

But it is also at once the concrete condensation and the real actualization of this primordial sacrament. It follows from this that Christian marriage is in itself a real and true sign of salvation, which confers the grace of God. For this reason the Catholic Church numbers it among the seven sacraments (cf. *DS,* 1327, 1801).

A unique bond exists between the indissolubility of marriage and its sacramentality, that is, a reciprocal, constitutive relationship. Indissolubility makes one's grasp of the sacramental nature of Christian matrimony easier, and from the theological point of view, its sacramental nature constitutes the final grounds, although not the only grounds, for its indissolubility.

2.3. *Baptism, Real Faith, Intention, Sacramental Marriage*

Just like the other sacraments, matrimony confers grace in the final analysis by virtue of the action performed by Christ and not only through the faith of the one receiving it. That, however, does not mean that grace is conferred in the sacrament of matrimony outside of faith or in the absence of faith. It follows from this—according to classical principles—that faith is presupposed as a "disposing cause" for receiving the fruitful effect of the sacrament. The validity of marriage, however, does not imply that this effect is necessarily fruitful.

The existence today of "baptized nonbelievers" raises a new theological problem and a grave pastoral dilemma, especially when the lack of, or rather the rejection of the Faith, seems clear. The intention of carrying out what Christ and the Church desire is the minimum condition required before consent is considered to be a "real human act" on the sacramental plane. The problem of the intention and that of the personal faith of the contracting parties must not be confused, but they must not be totally separated either.

In the last analysis the real intention is born from and feeds on living faith. Where there is no trace of faith (in the sense of "belief"—being disposed to believe), and no desire for grace or salvation is found, then a real doubt arises as to whether there is the above-mentioned general and truly sacramental intention and whether the contracted marriage is validly contracted or not. As was noted, the personal faith of the contracting parties does not constitute the sacramentality of matrimony, but the absence of personal faith compromises the validity of the sacrament.

This gives rise to new problems for which a satisfactory answer has yet to be found, and it imposes new pastoral responsibilities regarding Christian matrimony. "Priests should first of all strengthen and nourish the faith of those about to be married, for the sacrament of matrimony presupposes and demands faith" (*Ordo Celebrandi Matrimonium, Praenotanda,* 7).

2.4. *Dynamic Interconnection*

For the Church, baptism is the social basis and the sacrament of faith through which believers become members of the Body of Christ. The existence of "baptized nonbelievers" implies problems of great importance in this respect as well. A true response to practical and pastoral problems will not be found in changes that subvert the central core of sacramental doctrine and of matrimonial doctrine, but only with a radical renewal of baptismal spirituality.

We must view and renew baptism in its essential unity and dynamic interconnection with all its elements and dimensions: faith, preparation for the sacrament, the rite, profession of faith, incorporation into Christ and into the Church, moral consequences, active participation in Church life. The intimate connection between baptism, faith, and the Church must be stressed. Only in this way will it be clear that matrimony between the baptized is "in itself" a true sacrament, that is, not by force of some sort of automatic process but through its own internal nature.

3. CREATION AND REDEMPTION

3.1. *Marriage as Willed by God*

Since all things were created in Christ, through Christ and in view of Christ, marriage as a true institution of the Creator becomes a figure of the mystery of union of Christ, the groom, with the Church, the Bride, and, in a certain way, is directed toward this mystery. Marriage celebrated between two baptized persons has been elevated to the dignity of a real sacrament, that is, signifying and participating in the spousal love of Christ and the Church.

3.2. *The Inseparability of Christ's Actions*

Between two baptized persons, marriage as an institution willed by God the Creator cannot be separated from marriage the sacrament, because the sacramental nature of marriage between the baptized is not an accidental element that could be or could just as well not be, but is rather so tied into the essence of it as to be inseparable from it.

3.3. *Every Marriage between Baptized Persons Must Be Sacramental*

Thus between baptized persons no other married state can exist really and truly that differs from that willed by Christ, in which the Christian man and woman, giving and accepting one another freely and with irrevocable personal consent as spouses, are radically removed from the "hardness of heart" of which Christ spoke (cf. Mt 19:8) and, through the sacrament, really and truly included within the mystery of marital union of Christ with his Church, thus being given the real possibility of living in perpetual love. As a consequence the Church cannot in any way recognize that two baptized persons are living in a marital state equal to their dignity and their life as "new creatures in Christ" if they are not united by the sacrament of matrimony.

3.4. *The "Legitimate" Marriage of Non-Christians*

The strength and the greatness of the grace of Christ are extended to all people, even those beyond the Church, because of God's desire to save all men. They shape all human marital love and strengthen created nature as

well as matrimony "as it was in the beginning". Men and women therefore who have not yet heard the Gospel message are united by a human
covenant in a legitimate marriage. This legitimate marriage is not without
authentic goodness and values, which assure its stability. These goods, even
though the spouses are not aware of it, come from God the Creator and are
included, in a certain inchoative way, in the marital love that unites Christ
with his Church.

3.5. *Union of Christians Who Pay No Heed to the Requirements of Their Baptism*

It would thus be contradictory to say that Christians, baptized in the Catholic
Church, might really and truly take a step backward by being content
with a nonsacramental marital state. This would mean that they could be
content with the "shadow" when Christ offers them the "reality" of his
spousal love. Still we cannot exclude cases where the conscience of even
some Christians is deformed by ignorance or invincible error. They come to
believe sincerely that they are able to contract marriage without receiving the
sacrament.

In such a situation, on the one hand, they are unable to contract a valid
sacramental marriage because they lack any faith and lack the intention of
doing what the Church wishes. On the other hand, they still have the natural
right to contract marriage. In such circumstances they are capable of giving
and accepting one another as spouses because they intend to contract an
irrevocable commitment. This mutual and irrevocable self-giving creates a
psychological relationship between them that by its internal structure is
different from a transitory relationship.

Still this relationship, even if it resembles marriage, cannot in any way
be recognized by the Church as a nonsacramental conjugal society. For
the Church, no natural marriage separated from the sacrament exists for
baptized persons, but only natural marriage elevated to the dignity of a
sacrament.

3.6. *Progressive Marriages*

It is therefore wrong and very dangerous to introduce within the Christian
community the practice of permitting the couple to celebrate successively
various wedding ceremonies on different levels, even though they be connected,
or to allow a priest or deacon to assist at or read prayers on the occasion of a
nonsacramental marriage that baptized persons wish to celebrate.

3.7. Civil Marriage

In a pluralistic society, the public authority of the state can impose on the engaged a public ceremony through which they publicly profess their status as spouses. The state can furthermore make laws that regulate in a precise and correct manner the civil effects deriving from marriage, as well as rights and duties regarding the family.

The Catholic faithful ought to be adequately instructed that these official formalities, commonly called civil marriage, do not constitute real matrimony for them, except in cases when—through dispensation from the canonical form or because of a very prolonged absence of a qualified Church witness— the civil ceremony itself can serve as an extraordinary canonical form for the celebration of the sacrament of matrimony (cf. Canon 1098). For non-Christians and often even for non-Catholic Christians, this civil ceremony can have constitutive value both as legitimate marriage and as sacramental marriage.

4. INDISSOLUBILITY OF MARRIAGE

4.1. The Principle

The early Church's Tradition, based on the teaching of Christ and the apostles, affirms the indissolubility of marriage, even in cases of adultery. This principle applies despite certain texts that are hard to interpret and examples of indulgence—the extension and frequency of which are difficult to judge— toward persons in very difficult situations.

4.2. The Church's Doctrine

The Council of Trent declared that the Church has not erred when it has taught and teaches, in accordance with the doctrine of the Gospel and the apostles, that the marriage bond cannot be broken through adultery. Nevertheless, because of historical doubts (opinions of Ambrosiaster, Catharinus, and Cajetan) and for some more-or-less ecumenical reasons, the Council limited itself to pronouncing an anathema against those who deny the Church's authority on this issue.

It cannot be said, then, that the Council had the intention of solemnly defining marriage's indissolubility as a truth of faith. Still, account must be taken of what Pius XI said in *Casti Connubii*, referring to this canon: "If therefore the Church has not erred and does not err in teaching this, and consequently it is certain that the bond of marriage cannot be loosed even on account of the sin of adultery, it is evident that all the weaker excuses that can be, and are usually brought forward, are of no value whatsoever. And the objections brought against the marriage bond are easily answered" (cf. *DS*, 1807).

4.3. *Intrinsic Indissolubility*

Intrinsic indissolubility of matrimony can be considered under various aspects and grounded in various ways:

—*From the point of view of the spouses.* Their intimate conjugal union as a mutual donation of two persons, just as their very marital love itself and the welfare of the offspring, demands that indissoluble unity. From this is derived the spouses' moral duty to protect, maintain, and develop the marital covenant.

—*From God's vantage point.* From the human act by which the spouses give and accept each other rises a bond, based on the will of God and written in nature as created, independent of human authority and removed from the sphere of power of the spouses, and thus intrinsically indissoluble.

—*From a Christological perspective.* The final and deepest basis for the indissolubility of Christian matrimony lies in the fact that it is the image, sacrament, and witness of the indissoluble union between Christ and the Church that has been called the *bonum sacramenti*. In this sense indissolubility becomes a moment of grace.

—*From the social perspective.* Indissolubility is demanded by the institution of marriage itself. The spouses' personal decision comes to be accepted, protected, and reinforced by society itself, especially by the ecclesial community. This is for the good of the offspring and for the common good. This is the juridico-ecclesial dimension of matrimony.

These various aspects are intimately tied together. The fidelity to which the spouses are held and which ought to be protected by society, especially by the ecclesial community, is demanded by God the Creator and by Christ who makes it possible through his grace.

4.4. *Extrinsic Indissolubility and the Power of the Church over Marriages*

Hand in hand with the practice, the Church has elaborated a doctrine concerning its powers over marriages, clearly indicating its scope and limits. The Church acknowledges that it does not have any power to invalidate a sacramental marriage that is concluded and consummated (*ratum et consummatum*).

For very serious reasons and with concern for the good of the Faith and the salvation of souls, all other marriages can be invalidated by competent Church authority or—according to another interpretation—can be declared self-invalidating. This doctrine is nothing more than an individual example of the theory, today more or less generally accepted by Catholic theologians, on the evolution of Christian doctrine in the Church.

Neither is it to be excluded that the Church can further define the concepts of sacramentality and consummation by explaining them even better, so that the whole doctrine on the indissolubility of marriage can be put forward in a deeper and more precise presentation.

5. THE DIVORCED WHO HAVE REMARRIED

5.1. *Gospel Radicalism*

Faithful to the radicalism of the Gospel, the Church cannot refrain from stating with St. Paul the apostle: "To those now married, however, I give this command (though it is not mine; it is the Lord's): a wife must not separate from her husband. If she does separate, she must either remain single or become reconciled to him again. Similarly, a husband must not divorce his wife" (1 Cor 7:10–11). It follows from this that new unions following divorce under civil law cannot be considered regular or legitimate.

5.2. *Prophetic Witness*

This severity does not derive from a purely disciplinary law or from a type of legalism. It is rather a judgment pronounced by Jésus himself (Mk 10: 6ff.). Understood in this way, this harsh norm is a prophetic witness to the irreversible fidelity of love that binds Christ to his Church. It shows also that the spouses' love is incorporated into the very love of Christ (Eph 5:23–32).

5.3. *"Nonsacramentalization"*

The incompatibility of the state of remarried divorced persons with the precept and mystery of the Paschal love of the Lord makes it impossible for these people to receive, in the Eucharist, the sign of unity with Christ. Access to eucharistic Communion can only be had through penitence, which implies detestation of the sin committed and the firm purpose of not sinning again (cf. *DS*, 1676).

Let all Christians, therefore, remember the words of the apostle: "Whoever eats the bread or drinks the cup of the Lord unworthily, sins against the body and blood of the Lord. A man should examine himself first; only then should he eat of the bread and drink of the cup. He who eats and drinks without recognizing the body eats and drinks a judgment on himself" (1 Cor 11:27–29).

5.4. *Pastoral Care of the Divorced Who Have Remarried*

While this illegitimate situation does not permit a life of full communion with the Church, still Christians who find themselves in this state are not excluded from the action of divine grace and from a link with the Church. They must not, therefore, be deprived of pastoral assistance (cf. Address of Pope Paul VI, Nov. 4, 1977).

They are not dispensed from the numerous obligations stemming from baptism. They ought to be concerned about the Christian education of their offspring. The paths of Christian prayer, both public and private, penitence, and certain apostolic activities remain open to them. They must not be ignored but rather helped, like all other Christians who are trying, with the help of Christ's grace, to free themselves from sin.

5.5. *Combating the Causes of Divorce*

The need for a pastoral action to avoid the multiplication of divorces and of new civil marriages of the divorced seems ever more urgent. It is recommended that future spouses be given a living awareness of all their responsibilities as spouses and parents. The real meaning of matrimony must be ever more adequately presented as a covenant contracted "in the Lord" (1 Cor 7:39). In such a way Christians will be better disposed to observe the command of God and to witness to the union of Christ and the Church. And that will redound to the greater personal advantage of the spouses, their children, and society itself.

8B

CHRISTOLOGICAL THESES ON THE SACRAMENT OF MARRIAGE

1. SACRAMENTALITY OF MARRIAGE AND THE MYSTERY OF THE CHURCH

The sacramentality of Christian marriage appears much more clearly if one does not separate it from the mystery of the Church. "Sign and means of intimate union with God and of the unity of the whole human race", as the Council said (*LG,* 1), the Church rests upon the indefectible relationship that Christ reestablished with her to make her his Body. The identity of the Church does not then depend just on the power of men but on the love of Christ that the apostolic preaching increasingly announces and to which we adhere through the outpouring of the Spirit. Witness of this love that makes her live, the Church is then the sacrament of Christ in the world because it is the visible Body and the community that proclaims the presence of Christ in the history of men. Certainly, the Church—sacrament whose greatness Paul declared (Eph 5:32)—is inseparable from the mystery of the Incarnation because it is the mystery of a body; it is inseparable also from the economy of the Covenant because it rests upon the personal promise that the risen Christ made to remain "with" her "all days, even to the end of the world" (Mt 28). But the Church sacrament depends further on a mystery that one can describe as conjugal. Christ is bound to her in virtue of a love that makes the Church the Spouse of Christ in the energy of only one Spirit and the unity of one Body.

2. UNION OF CHRIST AND THE CHURCH

The marital union of Christ and the Church does not destroy but, on the contrary, accomplishes what the conjugal love of man and woman announces

This document was approved by the Commission "*in forma generica*".

Sixteen theses on the sacrament of marriage are presented in this paper which was approved in substance by the members of the Commission.

in its own way, what it implies or already realizes, as regards communion and fidelity. In effect, the Christ of the Cross accomplishes the perfect oblation of himself that the spouses desire to accomplish in the flesh without, however, ever coming to realize perfectly. He accomplishes in regard to the Church he loves as his own body what husbands should do for their spouses, as St. Paul said. On his part, the Resurrection of Jesus in the power of the Spirit reveals that the oblation he made on the Cross bears fruit in this same flesh in which it is accomplished, and that the Church loved by him so much he would die for it can initiate the world into this total communion between God and men from which it benefits as the Spouse of Jesus Christ.

3. CONJUGAL SYMBOLISM IN SCRIPTURE

Thus the Old Testament rightly used a conjugal symbolism to express the inexhaustible love that God feels toward his people and which he intends, through the people, to reveal to all mankind. In the prophet Hosea notably, God is presented to us as the Spouse whose tenderness and fidelity without measure will finally win over Israel, who is, from the start, unfaithful to the measureless love with which it is graced. The Old Testament in this way opens us to an uninhibited understanding of the New Testament in which Jesus is many times called the Spouse par excellence. He is called that by the Baptist in John 3:29; Jesus calls himself that in Matthew 9:15; Paul calls him Spouse in the same way in two places, 2 Corinthians 11:2 and Ephesians 5; Revelation does it also in 22:17–20, not to mention the many explicit allusions to this title that one finds in the eschatological parables of the Kingdom in Matthew 22:1–10 and 25:1–12.

4. JESUS THE SPOUSE PAR EXCELLENCE

Ordinarily neglected by Christology, this title should once again find all its meaning for us. Just as he is the Way, the Truth, the Life, the Light, the Gate, the Shepherd, the Lamb, the Vine, the Man himself, because he receives from the Father "the primacy in everything" (Col 1:18), Jesus is also truly and rightfully the Spouse par excellence, that is, the "Master and Lord", when one thinks of someone who loves the other, who is different from himself, as he loves his own flesh. It is then from this title of Spouse and from the mystery it evokes that a Christology of marriage should begin. In this domain, as in every other, "no one can lay any foundation except the one that has been laid namely, Jesus Christ" (1 Cor 3:10). However, the fact that Christ is also the Spouse par excellence is not to be separated from the fact that he is "the second" (1 Cor 15:47) and "the final Adam" (1 Cor 15:45).

5. ADAM, FIGURE OF HIM WHO IS TO COME

The Adam of Genesis, who is inseparable from Eve and to whom Jesus refers in Matthew 19 when he treats the question of divorce, is not fully identified unless one sees in him "the figure of him who is to come" (Rom 5:14). The personality of Adam insofar as it is the initial symbol of all humanity is not, then, a narrow personality closed upon itself. It is, like that of Eve, of a typological order. Adam is related to him to whom he owes his final meaning and to us also: Adam cannot be thought of without Christ, but Christ in his turn cannot be thought of without Adam, that is, without all mankind, without all the human also, whose appearance Genesis salutes as willed by God in a very singular way. This is because the conjugality that constitutes Adam in his nature as man is attributed also to Christ, who fulfilled it by restoring it. Ruined by a lack of love before which Moses himself had to bow, it finds again in Christ the truth that belongs to it. With Jesus there appears in the world the Spouse par excellence who can as the "second" and "last Adam" save and reestablish the true conjugality that God does not cease to wish for the benefit of the "first Adam".

6. JESUS, RENEWER OF THE PRIMORDIAL AUTHENTICITY OF THE COUPLE

Discerning the Mosaic law on divorce as the historical result of "the hardness of their hearts", Jesus dares to present himself as the renewer who is resolved to restore the primordial authenticity of the couple. In the power that he has to love without limit and to realize by his life, death, and Resurrection, unparalleled union with all mankind, Jesus reestablishes the true meaning of the thought of Genesis, saying "man should not separate what God has united". In his eyes, man and woman can love each other from now on as God, from all time, desires that they should love, because in Jesus is manifested the source of that love, which establishes the Kingdom. Also, Christ leads all the couples of the world to the initial purity of promised love; he abolishes the prescription in which duty contributed to their misery, lacking the power to suppress its cause. In Jesus' view, the original couple become what they should always have been in the eyes of God: the prophetic couple beginning with whom God reveals the conjugal love to which mankind aspires, for whom it is made but which it can only attain in him who teaches divinely to men what it is to love. From then on, faithful, lasting love, the conjugality that the "hardness of heart" transforms into an impossible dream, finds again in Jesus the status of a reality that he alone, as the last Adam and as Spouse par excellence, is capable of giving to it once again.

7. THE SACRAMENTALITY OF CHRISTIAN MARRIAGE, APPARENT IN FAITH

The sacramentality of Christian marriage becomes apparent in faith. Christ draws into his energy the conjugal love of the baptized, visibly part of the Body of Christ that is the Church, in order to communicate to it the authenticity that outside of him this love would lack. He does it in the Spirit, in virtue of the power that he has, as second and final Adam, of appropriating and of making the conjugality of the first Adam succeed. He does it also in accord with the visibility of the Church in which conjugal love, consecrated to the Lord, becomes a sacrament. The spouses attest within the Church that they are committed to a conjugal life and expect from Christ the force to accomplish this form of love that without him would perish. For this reason, the mystery proper to Christ, as Spouse of the Church, radiates and can be radiated within the couples that are consecrated to him. Their conjugal love is deepened and not disfigured because it refers back to the love of Christ who sustains and establishes them. The special outpouring of the Spirit, as the grace proper to the sacrament, makes it possible that the love of the couples becomes the very image of the love of Christ for the Church. However, this constant outpouring of the Spirit never dispenses the Christian couple from the human conditions of fidelity, because the mystery of the second Adam has never supplanted or suppressed in anyone the reality of the first Adam.

8. CIVIL MARRIAGE

As a consequence, then, entrance into Christian marriage could not be accomplished by the sole recognition of a purely "natural" right to marriage, whatever may be the religious value that one recognizes in this right or that it possesses in fact. No natural right can ever, in fact, define by itself the content of a Christian sacrament. If one claims that in the case of marriage, one would falsify the meaning of the sacrament, which has as its end to consecrate to Christ the love of the baptized spouses so that Christ may realize the transforming effects of his own mystery in them. In this light, then, there is a basic difference between the secular states, which see in civil marriage an act that is sufficient to establish the conjugal community from the social point of view, and the Church, which, while not denying value to such marriage for the nonbaptized, questions whether it can ever suffice for the baptized. Only the sacrament of marriage is appropriate for them, and this supposes on the part of the future spouses the will to consecrate to Christ a love whose human value depends finally on the love that Christ himself bears us and that he communicates to us. It follows, then, that the identity of the sacrament and of the "contract", on which the apostolic Magisterium formally pronounced in the nineteenth century, must be understood in a manner that truly respects the mystery of Christ and the life of Christians.

9. CONTRACT AND SACRAMENT

The act of conjugal union, often called a contract, which acquires the reality of sacrament in the case of baptized spouses, does not become so by the simple juridical effect of baptism. The fact that the conjugal promise of a Christian husband and wife is a true sacrament flows from their Christian identity, renewed by them on the level of the love that they vow to each other in Christ. Their conjugal pact, in free giving to each other, consecrates them also to him who is the Spouse par excellence and who will teach them to become, themselves, perfect spouses. The personal mystery of Christ penetrates, then, from the interior, the natural human pact or "contract". This becomes sacrament only if the future spouses freely consent to enter into the conjugal life, pronouncing their vows in Christ, into whom they were incorporated by baptism. Their free integration into the mystery of Christ is so essential to the nature of the sacrament that the Church intends to be assured, by the ministry of the priest, of the Christian authenticity of this commitment. The human conjugal alliance does not become sacrament by reason of a juridical statute that is efficacious by itself, independent of one's having freely consented to baptism. It becomes this in virtue of the publicly Christian character that fundamentally affects the mutual commitment and that makes it possible, moreover, to specify in which sense the spouses are themselves ministers of such a sacrament.

10. THE SPOUSES, MINISTERS OF THE SACRAMENT
IN AND THROUGH THE CHURCH

Since the sacrament of marriage is the free consecration to Christ of a
beginning conjugal love, the couple are evidently the ministers of a sacrament
that concerns them in the highest way. However, they are not ministers in
virtue of a power that one can call "absolute" and in the exercise of which the
Church, strictly speaking, has no right to intervene. They are ministers as
living members of the Body of Christ in which they exchange their vows
without ever making of their decision, which is irreplaceable, just the pure
emanation of their love. The sacrament as such flows entirely from the
mystery of the Church in which their conjugal love makes them share in a
privileged way. No couple, then, can bestow the sacrament on themselves
without the consent of the Church, nor can they do this in a form different
from that which the Church has established as the most expressive of the
mystery into which the sacrament introduces the couple. It belongs, then,
to the Church to examine the dispositions of the future couple to see if
they really correspond to the baptism that they have received. It is her
duty, moreover, to dissuade them, if there is need, from performing an
action that would be derisory in relation to him to whom it witnesses. In their
exchange of consent that makes the sacrament, the Church remains the sign
and the guarantee of the gift of the Spirit that the spouses receive in committing themselves to each other as Christians. The baptized couple are never
ministers of the sacrament of the marriage *without* the Church, or even
less, beyond the Church; they are ministers *in* the Church and *by* the
Church, without ever leaving in the background the Church whose mystery
governs their love. A sound theology of the minister of the sacrament
of marriage has not only great importance for the spiritual authenticity of the
couples, but also important repercussions for our relationship with the
Orthodox.

11. INDISSOLUBILITY OF MARRIAGE

In this context the indissolubility of marriage also appears in fresh light. Since
Christ is the true Spouse of the Church, Christian marriage cannot become
and remain an authentic image of the love of Christ for the Church without
entering in its way into the fidelity that defines Christ as the Spouse of the
Church. Whatever may be the suffering and the psychological difficulties that
can result from fidelity, it is impossible to consecrate to Christ—in order to

make it a sign or sacrament of his own mystery—a conjugal love that involves the divorce of one or of both the parties whose first marriage was truly valid, though in some cases this is not clear. But if the divorce, as is its intent, declares a legitimate union is already destroyed and permits, on that account, a person to contract another, how can we claim that Christ would make of this other "marriage" a real image of his personal relationship with the Church? Even if it can claim some consideration under some aspects, above all when we deal with a case of the party who is unjustly abandoned, the new marriage of the divorced cannot be a sacrament, and it creates an objective incapacity to receive the Eucharist.

12. DIVORCE AND THE EUCHARIST

Without refusing to examine the attenuating circumstances and even some-times the quality of a second civil marriage after divorce, the approach of the divorced and remarried to the Eucharist is plainly incompatible with the mystery of which the Church is the servant and witness. In receiving the divorced and remarried to the Eucharist, the Church would let such parties believe that they can, on the level of signs, communicate with him whose conjugal mystery they disavow on the level of reality. To do so would be, moreover, on the part of the Church to declare herself in accord with the baptized at the moment when they enter or remain in a clearly objective contradiction with the life, the thought, and the being itself of the Lord as Spouse of the Church. If the Church could give the sacrament of unity to those who have broken with her on an essential point of the mystery of Christ, she would no longer be the sign of the witness of Christ but rather a countersign and a counterwitness. Nevertheless, this refusal does not in any way justify any procedure that inflicts infamy and that contradicts in its own way the mercy of Christ toward us sinners.

13. WHY THE CHURCH CANNOT DISSOLVE A MARRIAGE THAT IS "RATUM ET CONSUMMATUM"

This Christological vision of Christian marriage allows one to understand why the Church cannot claim for herself the right to dissolve a marriage *ratum et consummatum*, e.g., a marriage that is sacramentally contracted in the Church and ratified by the spouses through the marriage act. In effect, the entire communion of life, which humanly speaking defines the marriage, evokes in its own way the realism of the Incarnation in which the Son of God becomes one with mankind in the flesh. In committing themselves to each other without reserve, the couple signifies by this act their effective transition to the conjugal life in which love becomes a sharing as absolute as possible of each other. They thus enter into the human behavior whose irrevocable character was recalled by Christ and which he made an image that reveals his own mystery. The Church cannot have any power, then, over the reality of a conjugal union that has passed into the power of him whose mystery she must announce and not hinder.

14. PAULINE PRIVILEGE

What we call Pauline privilege does not in any way contradict what we have just stated. In the light of what Paul explains in 1 Corinthians 7:12–17, the Church recognizes the right to annul a human marriage that is revealed Christianly unlivable for a party who is baptized, on account of the opposition that the one who is not baptized makes to the baptized party. In this case, the "privilege", if it truly exists, plays a role in favor of the life of Christ, whose importance can prevail in a legitimate way in the eyes of the Church over a conjugal life that cannot and could not be effectively consecrated to Christ by such a couple.

15. CHRISTIAN MARRIAGE CANNOT BE ISOLATED FROM THE MYSTERY OF CHRIST

Whether we treat, then, of the scriptural or dogmatic, moral, human, or canonical aspects of marriage, Christian marriage can never appear isolated from the mystery of Christ. This is because the sacrament of marriage to which the Church testifies and to which she educates, and which she permits couples to receive, is not really livable except in a constant conversion of the spouses to the very Person of Christ. This conversion to Christ is, then, an intrinsic part of the nature of the sacrament, and it directly governs the meaning and scope of such a sacrament in the life of a couple.

16. A VISION THAT IS NOT TOTALLY INACCESSIBLE TO NONBELIEVERS

However, this Christological vision is not in itself totally inaccessible to nonbelievers themselves. Not only does it have its own coherence, which points to Christ as the sole foundation of what we believe, but it also reveals the greatness of the human couple who can speak to a conscience, even to one that is a stranger to the mystery of Christ. Moreover, the human point of view as such can be explicitly integrated into the mystery of Christ under the heading of the first Adam, from whom the second and last Adam is never separable. To show this clearly in the case of marriage would open the present reflection to other horizons that cannot be treated here. We have wished to recall above all how Christ is the true foundation, often ignored by Christians themselves, of their own marriage insofar as it is a sacrament.

9

SELECT QUESTIONS ON CHRISTOLOGY

In our time, the question of Jesus Christ has come to be raised with new sharpness at the levels of both piety and theology. Many new elements are being contributed by biblical studies and by historical research on the great Christological councils. With fresh insistence, men and women in our time pose the questions raised long ago: "Who is this man?" (cf. Lk 7:49) "Where did he get all this? What kind of wisdom is he endowed with? How is it that such miraculous deeds are accomplished by his hands?" (Mk 6:2). Obviously, no answers to these questions will do if merely confined to the domain of the history of religions. In the course of these recent inquiries, valuable avenues have been opened up. But tensions have developed as well, not only among experts in theology but also between some of these and the teaching office of the Church.

This situation has induced the International Theological Commission to take part in this extensive exchange of ideas in the hope that it will be able to contribute some appropriate clarifications. As it will soon appear, the International Theological Commission has not undertaken the ambitious project of presenting a complete Christology. It has deemed it wiser to bring its attention to bear on some points of particular importance, or on points whose difficulty has been brought to light by contemporary discussions.

I. HOW TO GAIN ACCESS TO THE KNOWLEDGE OF THE PERSON AND WORK OF JESUS CHRIST

A. *Historical Inquiries*

1. Jesus Christ, the object referent of the Church's Faith, is neither a myth nor any sort of abstract notion. He is a man who lived in a concrete milieu and who died after having lived his own life within the unfolding of a historical

Reprinted from the *Australasian Catholic Record*.
This document was approved by the Commission "*in forma specifica*".

process. It follows that historical research concerning Jesus Christ is demanded by the Christian Faith itself. That such research is fraught with difficulties is a fact we know full well from the twists and turns it has taken in the course of time.

1.1. The New Testament does not intend to convey mere historical information concerning Jesus. It seeks above all to hand down the witness that ecclesial faith bears concerning Jesus and to present him in the fullness of his significance as "Christ" (Messiah) and as "Lord" (*Kyrios,* God). This witness is an expression of faith and seeks to elicit faith. A "biography" of Jesus in the modern sense of this word cannot be produced, if it were taken to entail a precise and detailed account. However, the same applies to various personages in antiquity and in the Middle Ages. Besides, we should not draw from this fact excessively pessimistic conclusions as to the possibility of coming to know the historical life of Jesus. Today's biblical scholarship shows well why we should not.

1.2. More often than not in the last few centuries, historical research on Jesus has been directed against the Christological dogma. And yet this antidogmatic sentiment is not a necessary precondition for the appropriate application of the historical-critical method.

Within the boundaries proper to exegetical research, it is certainly legitimate to reconstruct a purely historical image of Jesus, or to put it more realistically, to bring to light and test the historicity of certain facts relative to the historical existence of Jesus.

However, some have undertaken to reconstruct images of Jesus by discarding the witness of the early communities. These scholars believed that, by following this course, they would attain to a historical view both complete and precise. Implicitly and explicitly, however, these researchers are ruled by philosophical prejudices of greater or lesser scope, prejudices that stipulate what modernity expects the ideal man to be. Others are controlled by psychological suspicions concerning the consciousness of Jesus.

1.3. Today's Christologies must be careful not to lapse into these errors. The danger is particularly great for the so-called Christologies from below according to the extent to which they aim to depend on a purely historical kind of research. There is no doubt as to anyone's right to take into account the most recent exegetical inquiries, but we also need to be cautious, lest we should in turn fall victim to the prejudices mentioned above.

B. *Unity of the Earthly Jesus and the Glorified Christ*

2. The great value of scholarly inquiries on the Jesus of history is beyond doubt. Inquiries of this sort are particularly important for fundamental theol-

ogy and in exchanges with nonbelievers. All the same, a truly Christian knowledge of Jesus cannot rest content with these limited perspectives. Our knowledge of the Person and work of Jesus Christ is inadequate as long as we dissociate the Jesus of history from the Christ as proclaimed. We cannot secure a full knowledge of Jesus unless we take into account the living Faith of the Christian community, which sustains this vision of the facts. This applies whether we seek historical knowledge of Jesus, or inquire into the origins of the New Testament, or engage in Christological reflection.

2.1. The New Testament texts are themselves intent upon fostering an ever deeper knowledge and acceptance of faith. Hence, they do not envisage Jesus Christ in keeping with the perspective proper to the literary genre of pure history or biography—retrospectively, as it were. The universal and eschatological significance credited to the message and Person of Jesus Christ requires that a mere historical evocation should be transcended just as much as purely functional interpretations. Besides, the modern notion of history, advocated by some in opposition to the Faith and according to which history is the bare and objective presentation of a reality now past, differs from history as antiquity understood it to be.

2.2. The substantive and radical unity between the Jesus of history and the glorified Christ pertains to the very essence of the Gospel message. Should Christological inquiry limit itself to the Jesus "of history", it would be incompatible with the essence and structure of the New Testament, even before being disavowed from without by a religious authority.

2.3. Theology can grasp the meaning and import of the Resurrection of Jesus only in the light of the event of his death. Likewise, theology cannot understand the meaning of Jesus' death except in the light of his life, deeds, and message. The totality and coherence of the saving event that is Jesus Christ imply his life, death, and Resurrection.

2.4. The original and primitive synthesis of the earthly Jesus with the risen Christ surfaces in various "confessional formulas" and "homologies", which mention at the same time and with the same particular insistence, both the death and the Resurrection of Jesus. Together with Romans 1:3ff., we can quote, among other texts, 1 Corinthians 15:3–4: "I handed on to you first of all what I myself received: that Christ died for our sins in accordance with the Scriptures." These texts posit an authentic connection between the story of a man and the significance of Jesus Christ, which endures forever. In a nutshell, they set forth "the history of the essence" of Jesus Christ. This synthesis continues to be an example and a model for any genuine Christology to follow.

2.5. This Christological synthesis does not only presuppose the confession of faith of the Christian community in its dimension as historical fact; it also shows that, by her presence in the various periods of history, the Church continues to be the place where the true knowledge of the Person and work of Jesus Christ is to be found. Apart from the assistance provided by the mediation of ecclesial faith, the knowledge of Jesus Christ is no more possible today than in New Testament times. Outside the ecclesial context, there is no Archimedean lever, even though, ontologically, our Lord always preserves vis-à-vis the Church the priority of his position and his primacy.

2.6. Within this broader framework, a return to the earthly Jesus is beneficial and indispensable today in the field of dogmatic theology. The untold riches of Jesus' humanity need be brought to light more effectively than was done by the Christologies of the past. As Pope John Paul II has said in his encyclical *Redemptor hominis,* 8–10, Jesus Christ illustrates and illuminates to the highest possible degree the ultimate measure and the concrete essence of man. Looked upon from this perspective, Jesus' brotherhood and solidarity with us by no means detract from his divinity. It will appear in what follows that the Christological dogma, authentically understood, precludes all pseudo-opposition between the humanity and divinity of Jesus.

2.7. The Holy Spirit, who disclosed Jesus as the Christ, imparts to the faithful the very life of the triune God. He evokes and quickens the faith in Jesus as Son of God, raised to glory and present within human history.

This is what the Catholic Faith affirms. This is also the faith of all Christians to the extent to which these, in going beyond the New Testament, faithfully preserve the Christological dogmas of the Fathers of the Church, proclaiming them, teaching them, and bearing witness to them in the depth of their lives.

II. THE CHRISTOLOGICAL FAITH OF THE FIRST COUNCILS

A. *From the New Testament to the Council of Nicaea*

1. The theologians who in our time raise doubts about the divinity of Christ often argue that this dogma cannot have emerged from genuine biblical revelation; its origins are traceable to Hellenism. Deeper historical inquiries show, on the contrary, that the thought pattern of the Greeks was totally alien to this dogma and that they rejected it with the utmost vigor. To the faith of Christians who proclaimed the divinity of Christ, Hellenism opposed its own dogma of the divine transcendence, which it regarded as irreconcilable with the contingency inherent to the human history of Jesus of Nazareth. Greek philosophers experienced the particular difficulty entailed in accepting the notion of a divine incarnation. In the name of their teaching on the godhead, Platonist philosophers regarded this notion as unthinkable. The Stoics, in

turn, could not manage to reconcile the Christological dogma with their cosmological doctrine.

2. It was in order to respond to these difficulties that, more or less openly, many Christian theologians borrowed from Hellenism the notion of a secondary god (*deuteros theos*), or of an intermediate god, or even of a demiurge. Obviously, this was tantamount to clearing the way to the threat of subordinationism. This subordinationism was already latent in some of the Apologists and in Origen. Arius made a formal heresy of it. He maintained that the Son occupies an intermediate position between the Father and the creatures. The Arian heresy offers a good illustration of how the dogma of Christ's divinity would have looked had it truly emerged from the philosophy of Hellenism and not from God's own revelation. At the Council of Nicaea in 325 A.D., the Church defined that the Son is consubstantial (*homoousios*) with the Father. In so doing, the Church both repudiated the Arian compromise with Hellenism and deeply altered the shape of Greek, especially Platonist and neo-Platonist, metaphysics. In a manner of speaking, it demythicized Hellenism and effected a Christian purification of it. In the act of dismissing the notion of an intermediate being, the Church recognized only two modes of being: uncreated (nonmade) and created.

To be sure, *"homoousios"*, the term used by the Council of Nicaea, is a philosophical and nonbiblical term. It is evident all the same that, ultimately, the Fathers of the Council only intended to express the authentic meaning of the New Testament assertions concerning Christ, and to do this in a way that would be univocal and free from all ambiguity.

In issuing this definition of Christ's divinity, the Church found support also in the experience of salvation and in man's divinization in Christ. In turn, the dogmatic definition impressed its own determination and mark on the experience of salvation. There was, then, an in-depth interaction between lived experience and the process whereby theological clarification was achieved.

3. The theological reflections of the Fathers of the Church did not ignore the special problem connected with the divine preexistence of Christ. Note in particular Hippolytus of Rome, Marcellus of Ancyra, and Photinus. Their attempts are bent on presenting the preexistence of Christ not at the level of ontological reality but at that of intentionality: Christ had preexisted in the sense of having been foreseen (*kata prognosin*).

These presentations of the preexistence of Christ were judged inadequate by the Catholic Church and condemned. Thus the Church gave expression to her own belief in an ontological preexistence of Christ, for which it found support in the Father's eternal generation of the Word. The Church also referred to the clear-cut New Testament affirmations concerning the active role played by the Word of God in the creation of the world. Obviously, someone who does not yet exist, or is only intended to exist, cannot play any such role.

B. *The Council of Chalcedon*

4. The whole Christological theology of the Church Fathers is concerned with the metaphysical and salvific identity of Christ. It undertakes to answer these questions: "What is Jesus?" "Who is Jesus?" "How does Jesus save us?" We can, therefore, look upon the theology as an understanding on the move, and as a theological and dynamic articulation of the mystery of God's perfect transcendence and immanence in Christ. For this quest for meaning is conditioned by the convergence of two sets of data: on the one hand, the Old Testament Faith proclaims that God is wholly transcendent; on the other, there is the Christ event, which is thought of as God's own personal and eschatological intervention in the world. The immanence here in question is a superior one, qualitatively different from the indwelling of God's Spirit in the prophets. The affirmation of transcendence is nonnegotiable. It is postulated by the affirmation of the full and authentic divinity of the Christ. It is likewise indispensable if we are to go beyond so-called reductive Christologies: Ebionism, Adoptionism, Arianism. It also makes it possible to refute the thesis, monophysite in inspiration, that posits an admixture of God and man in Jesus, the result being that the immutability and impassibility of God are undone. On the other hand, the idea of immanence, bound up as it is with the belief in the Incarnation of the Word, makes it possible to affirm against the docetism of the Gnostics the real and authentic humanity of Christ.

5. During the controversies between the schools of Antioch and Alexandria, it was difficult to perceive how transcendence, that is, the distinction between the two natures, could be reconciled with immanence, that is, the hypostatic union. In 451 A.D. the Council of Chalcedon (*DS,* 301–2) undertook to show how the two viewpoints could be reconciled by having recourse to two expressions at the same time: "without confusion" (*asygchytôs*) and "without division" (*adiairetôs*). We can see there the apophatic equivalent of the formula that affirms "the two natures and the one hypostasis" of Christ. "Without confusion" obviously refers to the two natures and asserts that the humanity of Jesus is an authentic one. In keeping with the wishes of the anti-Arians, this formula bears witness at the same time to God's transcendence, for God is said to remain God, while man remains man. It excludes any intermediate state between divinity and humanity. "Without division" proclaims the very deep and irreversible union of God and man in the person of the world. God's full immanence in the world is asserted as well. It is on this immanence that Christian salvation and man's divinization are grounded.

In these assertions the conciliar Fathers attained a new level in their perception of transcendence, for the transcendence they asserted is not only "theological" but "Christological". No longer are we told only that God infinitely transcends man but that the Christ, both God and man, infinitely transcends the whole human kind and all history. According to the Council's Fathers, the absolute and universal character of the Christian Faith resides in this second mode of transcendence, which is both eschatological and ontological.

6. What, then, does the Council of Chalcedon represent in the history of Christology? The dogmatic definition of Chalcedon does not pretend to offer an exhaustive answer to the question "How can God and man coexist in Christ?" It is precisely in this coexistence that the mystery of the Incarnation resides. No definition can exhaust the richness of this mystery by means of affirmative utterances. It behoves rather to proceed by way of negation and mark off a place from which we may not depart. Within this place of truth, the Council locates the "one" and the "other", which seemingly exclude each other: transcendence and immanence, God and man. Both these aspects must be asserted unrestrictedly, while excluding anything that would smack of juxtaposition or admixture. In Christ, then, transcendence and immanence are perfectly conjoined.

In view of the cognitional categories and methods employed, one can take the view that the New Testament has undergone a measure of Hellenization. Yet, on the other hand, the definition of Chalcedon radically transcends Greek thought, for it lets coexist two viewpoints that Greek philosophy had always regarded as irreconcilable: divine transcendence, the very soul of the Platonic system, and divine immanence, which is the spirit of the Stoic theory.

C. *The Third Council of Constantinople*

7. In order to establish a correct Christological doctrine, we must not limit ourselves to taking into account the development of ideas that resulted in the Council of Chalcedon. In addition, we must pay attention to the last Christological councils, and especially to the Third Council of Constantinople in 681 A.D. (*DS*, 556ff.).

In the definition of this council, the church demonstrated her ability to clarify the Christological problem better than she had already done at the Council of Chalcedon. By the same token, she showed her readiness to reexamine the Christological questions because of the new difficulties that had surfaced in the meantime. She wanted to deepen still further a knowledge she had acquired by pondering what Sacred Scripture had to say concerning Jesus Christ.

The Lateran Council in 649 A.D. (*DS*, 502ff.) had condemned monothelism and thereby paved the way for the Third Ecumenical Council of Constantinople. In the year 649 A.D., thanks largely to St. Maximus the Confessor, the Church set forth more clearly the essential role that the human will of Christ had played in the work of our salvation. By the same token, she had also underlined the relation between this free human will and the hypostasis of the Word. For in this Council the Church declares that our salvation had been willed by a Divine Person through a human will. So interpreted in the light of the Lateran Council, the definition of the Third Council of Constantinople is rooted in the doctrine of the Fathers of the Church and of the Council of Chalcedon. But, on the other hand, it also helps us in a very special way to respond to the exigencies of our time in the matter of Christology. These exigencies tend to afford a better perception of the place occupied in the salvation of mankind by the humanity of Christ and by the various "mysteries" of his life on earth, such as his baptism, his temptations, and the "agony" of Gethsemane.

III. THE MEANING OF THE CHRISTOLOGICAL DOGMA TODAY

A. *Christology and Anthropology in the Perspectives of Modern Culture*

1. In a sense, Christology must take on and integrate the vision that contemporary man acquires of himself and of his own history through the reinterpretation that the Church makes available to the believer. In this fashion, we can remedy the imperfections that Christology derives from an excessively narrow use of what is referred to as "nature". We can also link to Christ, who brings all things under his headship (Eph 1:10), what contemporary culture legitimately contributes to a more precise perception of the human condition.

2. The confrontation of Christology with contemporary culture contributes to the new and deeper knowledge that man acquires today about himself. On the other hand, Christology probes into the truth of that knowledge; when necessary, it submits it to a criterion of its own, as is the case, for instance, in the spheres of politics and religion. This applies particularly to the latter. Religion is either negated and totally repudiated by atheism, or it is interpreted as a means of attaining to the ultimate depths of all things, without reference to a transcendent and personal God. As a result, religion risks assuming the appearance of pure "alienation" from humanness, while Christ loses his identity and uniqueness. In both cases, the result, logically, is this: the human condition loses its dignity, and Christ sheds his primacy and greatness. There is no remedy for this situation unless anthropology be renewed in the light of the mystery of Christ.

3. Paul's doctrine of the two Adams (cf. 1 Cor 15:21; Rom 5:12–19) is the

Christological principle in terms of which the confrontation with human culture is to go forward and gain clarity, as well as the criterion in terms of which the merits of contemporary inquiries in the field of anthropology are to be assessed. Given the parallelism between the two Adams, Christ, who is the second and last Adam, cannot be understood without taking into account the first Adam, that is, our human condition. The first Adam, on the other hand, is perceived in the truth and wholeness of his humanity only if he makes himself accessible to Christ who saves and divinizes us by his life, death, and Resurrection.

B. *The Genuine Meaning of Today's Difficulties*

4. Many of our contemporaries experience difficulties when the dogma of the Council of Chalcedon is presented to them. Terms such as "nature" and "person", which the Fathers of the Council use, undoubtedly retain the same meaning in today's parlance, but the realities they denote are referred to in the various philosophical terminologies by different concepts. For many, the phrase "human nature" no longer denotes a shared and immutable essence; it evokes only a pattern or a summary of the phenomena that, in most cases, we happen to observe in people. Very often, the concept of person is defined in psychological terms to the detriment of the ontological aspect of personhood.

Today many voice even severer difficulties with regard to the soteriological aspects of the Christological dogmas. They recoil from any notion of salvation that would inject heteronomy into existence as project. They take exception to what they regard as the purely individualistic character of Christian salvation. The promise of a blessedness to come seems to them a utopia that distracts people away from their genuine obligations, which, in their view, are all confined to this world. They want to know what it is that mankind had to be redeemed from and to whom the ransom had to be paid. They grow indignant at the contention that God could have exacted the blood of an innocent person, a notion in which they sense a streak of sadism. They argue against what is known as "vicarious satisfaction" (that is, through a mediator) by saying that this mode of satisfaction is ethically impossible. If it is true that every conscience is autonomous, they argue, no conscience can be freed by another. Finally, some of our contemporaries lament the fact that they cannot find in the life of the Church and of the faithful the lived expression of the mystery of liberation that is proclaimed.

C. *Permanent Significance of the Christological Faith as to Intent and Content*

5. In spite of all these difficulties, the Christological doctrine of the Church and the dogma defined at the Council of Chalcedon most especially retain a definitive value. It is no doubt permissible, and it may indeed be opportune, to seek a deeper understanding of that dogma, but it can never be allowable to reject it. Historically speaking, it is a mistake to say that, at Chalcedon, the Fathers of the Council bent the Christian dogma to suit Hellenistic ideas. On the other hand, the contemporary difficulties mentioned above show that some of our contemporaries are profoundly ignorant as to the authentic meaning of the Christological dogma. Nor do they entertain a correct view of the truth of the God who creates the visible and invisible world.

In order to attain to faith in Christ and in the salvation that he brings, we need to accept a number of truths that account for the Christ and his salvation. The living God is love (1 Jn 4:8), and through love he created all things. At the dawn of time, this living God—Father, Son, and sanctifying Spirit—created man in his own image and conferred upon him the dignity of a person endowed with reason in the middle of the world. In the fullness of time, the triune God crowned his own work in Christ Jesus. He made Christ the mediator of the peace and Covenant he was offering to the whole world for the benefit of all human beings and for all time to come. Jesus Christ is the perfect human being: he lives entirely from and for God the Father. At the same time, he lives entirely with human beings, and for their salvation, that is, for their fulfillment. He is, therefore, the example and the sacrament of the new humanity.

The life of Christ affords us a fresh understanding of God and of man as well. Just as "the God of Christians" is new and specific, so too "the man of Christians" is new and original, when compared with all the other conceptions of man. God's condescension (Titus 3:4) and, if the word be allowed, his "humanity", establish a solidarity between God and humans through the Incarnation, which is a deed of love. They also make possible a new man who finds his glory in service, not in domination.

Christ's existence is for the benefit of people (*pro-existentia*). For their sakes, he takes on the form of a servant (cf. Phil 2:7); for them he dies and rises to a true life (cf. Rom 4:24). This life of Christ, lived as it is for the sake of others, helps us to perceive that, for man, genuine autonomy consists neither in superiority nor in opposition. A man animated by a spirit of superiority (*supra-existentia*) seeks to stand out in front and dominate others. When controlled by a spirit of opposition (*contra-existentia*), man treats others unjustly and seeks to manipulate them.

A conception of human life derived from the life of Christ comes at first as a shock. This is indeed the reason why it demands conversion of everyone, and not only once at the beginning but continuously and through perseverance until the end. Such conversion as this can emerge only from a freedom renewed by love.

D. *The Need to Actualize Christological Doctrine and Preaching*

6. As history takes its course, and cultural changes occur, the teachings of the Council of Chalcedon and Constantinople III must always be actualized in the consciousness and preaching of the Church, under the guidance of the Holy Spirit. This indispensable actualization is an obligation binding both upon the theologians and upon the apostolic solicitude of shepherds and faithful.

6.1. The task of theologians is, first of all, to construct a synthesis in which are underlined all the aspects and all the values of the mystery of Christ. Into their synthesis theologians need draw the authentic findings of biblical exegesis, and of the research on the history of salvation. Moreover, they will have to give appropriate consideration to the manner in which the religions of the various peoples manifest a concern for salvation, and to the way in which people generally attempt to secure authentic liberation. Just as much must they be mindful of the teachings of saints and doctors.

A synthesis of this kind cannot but enrich the formula of Chalcedon through more soteriological perspectives. It will thus convey its full meaning to the phrase "Christ died for us."

Theologians must also devote their full attention to perenially difficult questions; for example, the questions relative to the consciousness and knowledge of Christ and to the manner of conceiving the absolute and universal value of the redemption effected by Christ for all and once for all.

6.2. Let us now turn to the whole Church, God's messianic people. This Church is entrusted with the task of letting all human beings, and all nations, share in the mystery of Christ. To be sure, this mystery is the same for all, and yet it must be set forth so that all should be able to assimilate it and celebrate it in their own lives and cultures. This task is all the more imperative in view of the fact that, in our time, the Church is increasingly conscious of the originality and value of the various cultures. It is through their cultures that people express, through symbols, gestures, notions, and specific languages, the meaning they credit to life. This brings with it certain consequences. The mystery has been revealed to the holy people whom God chose; Christians have believed it, professed it, celebrated it. This is a fact that cannot be duplicated in history. And yet, to an extent, this mystery opens itself up to new ways of expressing it, ways yet to be discovered. Thus, in every nation and age, disciples will give their faith to Christ the Lord and become one Body with him.

The Mystical Body of Christ comprises a large diversity of members. To all it gives the same peace in unity but without overlooking the traits that make them distinctive. The Spirit "maintains everything in unity, and knows every tongue" (Introit of the ancient Roman Liturgy for Pentecost; cf. Wis 1). From this Spirit all nations and all human beings have received their own particular riches and charisms. Because of these, God's universal family grows richer, since with the same voice and heart, and yet also in their own different tongues, God's children call upon their heavenly Father through Jesus the Christ.

IV. CHRISTOLOGY AND SOTERIOLOGY

A. *"For the Sake of Our Salvation"*

1. God the Father "did not spare his own Son but handed him over for the sake of us all" (Rom 8:32). Our Lord became man "for our sake and for the sake of our salvation." "God so loved the world that he gave his only Son, that whoever believes in him may not die but may have eternal life" (Jn 3:16). If so, the Person of Jesus Christ cannot be separated from the deed of redemption. The benefits of salvation are inseparable from the divinity of Jesus Christ. The Son of God is the only one who can authentically rescue us from the sin of the world, from eternal death, and from the enslavement to the law, in keeping with the Father's will and with the cooperation of the Holy Spirit.

Some theological speculations have failed adequately to preserve this intimate connection between Christology and soteriology. Today, it is always imperative to seek ways better to express the reciprocity of these two aspects of the saving event, which is itself undivided.

In this study, we want to limit ourselves to the consideration of two problems. Our first inquiry is historical in nature and is located within the time when Jesus lived on earth. It revolves around the question "What did Jesus think concerning his own death?" Precisely because of the value we intend to attach to the answer, the question must be envisaged in terms of historical research, and of all the critical exigencies binding upon such research (cf. below, no. 2). Needless to say, this research must be complemented by taking into account the Paschal understanding of redemption (cf. below, no. 3). To repeat, the International Theological Commission does not intend to expound and explicate a complete Christology. Among other things, it overlooks the problem of Jesus' human consciousness. Here it seeks only to set forth the foundation of the mystery of the Christ, in keeping with both the earthly life of Jesus and his Resurrection.

Our second inquiry unfolds at a different level (cf. below, no. 4). It will show how rich in soteriological teachings is the diversity of terminology by which the New Testament refers to the deed of redemption. We will attempt to systematize these teachings and set forth their whole theological meaning. Needless to say, this inquiry must be conducted in confrontation with the texts of Holy Scripture themselves.

B. *During His Earthly Life Jesus Is Oriented toward the Salvation of Mankind*

2.1. Jesus was perfectly aware that, in his words and actions, in his existence and Person, the Kingdom and the reign of God were at once a present realization, an expectation, and a coming (cf. Lk 10:23ff.; 11:20). Accordingly, he presented himself as the eschatological Savior and gave a direct, albeit implicit, explanation of his own mission. He was ushering in the eschatological salvation, since he was coming after the last of the prophets, John the Baptist. He was bringing God and his reign to presence, and the time of promise to fulfillment (Lk 16:16; Mk 1:15a).

2.2. If, for Jesus, the Passion was a failure and a shipwreck, if he felt abandoned by God and lost hope in his own mission, his death could not be construed then, and cannot be construed now, as the definitive act in the economy of salvation. A death undergone in a purely passive manner could not be a "Christological" saving event. It must be the consequence, the willed consequence, of the obedience and love of Jesus making a gift of himself. It must be taken up in a complex act, at once active and passive (Gal 1:4; 2:20). The moral ideal of his life and, in a general way, the manner of his conduct show that Jesus was oriented in the direction of his own death and prepared to undergo the same. He was thus actualizing the exigencies he himself had set forth for the benefit of his disciples (cf. Lk 14:27; Mk 8:34–35; Mt 10:28, 29, 31).

2.3. At the moment of his death, Jesus expresses his will to serve and give his life (cf. Mk 10:45). This is the result and prolongation of the attitude that marks his whole life (Lk 22:27). Both his life and his death grow out of a fundamental attitude that is the will to live and die for God and for others. This is what has been called an existence-for-others, or a proexistence. Because of this orientation on his part, Jesus was by his very "essence" ordained to be the eschatological Savior who effects "our" salvation (cf. 1 Cor 15:3; Lk 22:19–20b), the salvation of "Israel" (Jn 11:30) as well as of the Gentiles (Jn

11:51ff.). This salvation is meant for the multitude (Mk 14:24; 10:45), for all people (2 Cor 5:14ff.; 1 Tim 2:6), for the "world" (Jn 6:51c).

2.4. How are we to interpret this fundamental disposition, as it becomes manifest in Jesus during his life, to exist, namely, for others, to offer and give himself totally to the point of undergoing death? In essence, this disposition is a lucid readiness on his part to conform to God's will. Obviously, the unfolding of the events through which he lived would inevitably add more vitality and concreteness to this orientation. And so, it was with hope and confidence that Jesus, as eschatological mediator of salvation and as the envoy of God's Kingdom, waited for the reign that affirms itself and becomes established with finality (cf. Mk 14:25 and parallels).

Although Jesus was entirely open to God's will, he had the capacity to perceive questions that emerged. Would God bestow full and total success to the proclamation of the Kingdom? Would Israel prove incapable of clinging to the eschatological salvation? Was it necessary for him to be baptized with the baptism of death (cf. Mk 10:38ff.; Lk 12:50) and to drink the cup of suffering (cf. Mk 14:36)? Would the Father want to establish his reign, if Jesus should meet with failure, with death, nay, with the cruel death of martyrdom? Would the Father, in the end, ensure the saving efficacy of what Jesus would have suffered by "dying for others"?

Jesus gathered affirmative answers to these questions from his awareness of being the eschatological mediator of salvation, the reign of God come to presence. Hence, he was able to arrive in all confidence at the solution to the problems that arose. This confidence on his part may be asserted and understood in terms of what Jesus says and does at the Last Supper (Lk 22:19ff. and parallels). He is prepared to go to his death, and yet he awaits and announces his Resurrection and exaltation (Mk 14:25); he reasserts the promise and presence of the eschatological salvation.

2.5. How did Jesus understand and express his own fundamental disposition to exist for others, his own readiness to serve and abide by a dedication to others that presided over his conduct and even his death? It was not necessary for Jesus to do this in keeping with the mental categories and patterns provided by Israel's tradition of sacrificial cult. Had he done this, we would have, as it were, a personalizing internalization on his part of "the vicarious and expiatory death of the martyr for the sake of others". Specifically, we would have the Passion of the "Servant of Yahweh" (cf. Is 53).

In fact, it was possible for Jesus to interpret and live (cf. below, no. 3.4) these concepts by impressing upon them a deeper meaning and transforming them. There would thus have been in his soul an expression of the "disposition to exist for others". Be that as it may, Jesus' orientation toward the salvation of mankind can in no way be interpreted so as to entail equivocation and ambiguity. That orientation is meaningless unless it includes personal knowledge and awareness and a resolute disposition on the part of the subject who offers himself (cf. below, no. 3.3).

C. *The Eschatological Redeemer*

3.1. God raised Jesus from the dead and exalted him, and thereby confirmed that Jesus is the Savior of the believers once for all and definitively. He thus certified him as "Lord and Christ" (Acts 2:36), the Son of Man who comes to judge the world (cf. Mk 14:62). He showed Jesus to be "Son of God in power" (Rom 1:4). Believers discovered a new enlightenment in Jesus' Resurrection and exaltation. These showed them that in Jesus' death salvation had become a reality. Before Easter, it would not yet have been possible to express these truths in this fashion and in perfectly unambiguous words.

3.2. In the foregoing remarks two elements deserve very special consideration.

a. Jesus was aware that he was the definitive Savior of the Last Times (cf. above, no. 2.1) and that he was announcing and bringing to presence the reign of God (cf. above, nos. 2.2 and 2.3).

b. Jesus' Resurrection and exaltation (above, no. 3.1) showed that his death was a constitutive element of the salvation being brought in by the reign and the power of God (cf. Lk 22:20 and parallels). In 1 Corinthians 11:24, the death of Jesus is set forth as a constitutive element of the New Covenant about to be realized in a definitive and eschatological manner.

These two elements entitle us to conclude that the death of Jesus is endowed with salvific efficacy.

3.3. If we speak in a strict sense and just at a purely notional level, it is not easy to describe as "expiatory substitution" or as "vicarious expiation" the action by which God irrevocably effects salvation through the life and death of the eschatological Savior, as well as through the Resurrection that makes him Savior in a definitive and irreversible manner. We can, however, so interpret God's action if the death and deeds of Jesus stand connected to an existential and fundamental disposition on his part, which includes personal knowledge (cf. above, no. 2.5) and the will to take on himself as a proxy the sufferings (cf. Gal 3:13) and the sin of the human kind (cf. Jn 1:29; 2 Cor 5:21).

3.4. If Jesus could realize, thanks to a gratuitous gift, the effects of this vicarious expiation, this was only because he accepted to be "given by the Father", and he himself gave his own self to the Father who accepted him at the Resurrection. What we have here is a ministry of "existence-for-others" in the death of the preexistent Son (Gal 1:4; 2:20).

This is certainly the reason why, when the mystery of salvation is envisaged in this fashion, and we speak of a "vicarious expiation", we must bear in mind a twofold analogy.

The voluntary "oblation" of the martyr, and especially the oblation of the Servant of Yahweh (Is 53), differs totally from the immolation of animals, as "images from shadows" (cf. Heb 10:1).

There is even greater need to emphasize the "oblation" of the eternal Son and to insist even more decisively on the analogy between the two situations. For as the eternal Son "enters the world", he comes to do "God's will" (cf. Jn 10:7). It was "through the eternal Spirit" that he "offered himself up unblemished to God" (Heb 9:14). (This situation is appropriately called a sacrifice by the Council of Trent, for example [DS, 1753], but there the term must be restored to its original meaning.)

3.5. The death of Jesus has been a "vicarious expiation" with definitive efficacy because the gesture of the Father surrendering and giving his Son (cf. Rom 4:25; 8:32; cf. Jn 3:16; 1 Jn 4:9) is taken up in exemplary fashion and in reality, as the Christ gives himself with perfect love in self-surrender and dedication to others (cf. also Eph 5:2, 25; cf. 1 Tim 2:6; Titus 2:14).

What was traditionally called "vicarious expiation" must be understood, transformed, and raised to the height of a "trinitarian event".

D. *Unity and Diversity of Soteriological Reflection in the Church*

4. The origins and the core of the whole soteriology are to be found already in the early Church before Paul. This soteriology rests on the words and consciousness of Jesus himself. Jesus knows that he is to die for all, for our sins; in this perspective he lives out his entire earthly life, he suffers, and he rises from the dead.

We can list five main elements: (1) the Christ gives himself; (2) he takes our place in the mystery of salvation; (3) he frees us "from the wrath to come" and from all evil powers; (4) in so doing, he fulfills the salvific will of the Father; and (5) he wants to insert us into the life of the Trinity through participation in the grace of the Holy Spirit.

It is the task of later theology to show how these elements fit together.

Thomas Aquinas underlines five ways in which the work of redemption takes effect: merit, satisfaction, redemption, sacrifice, and efficient cause. Other ways can no doubt be added.

Both in the New Testament and in the different periods of the history of theology, some facets of soteriology are underlined more sharply than others. However, all the aspects must be regarded as approaches to the paschal mystery; as much as possible, they must be elaborated into synthetic views.

5. During the patristic age both in the East and in the West, "exchange" is

the dominant aspect in soteriological reflection. In the Incarnation and Passion, an exchange takes place between the divine and the human nature in general. More precisely, the state of sin is exchanged for the state of divine sonship. The Fathers did, however, refine and circumscribe the notion of exchange, as they took into account the eminent dignity of Christ. Christ took on the characteristic affections (*pathê*) of sinful human nature only in an external way (*schetikos*). He did not himself become "sin" (2 Cor 5:21) except in the sense of becoming a "sacrificial oblation for sin".

6. Anselm proposed another theory, the theory that has prevailed until very recent times. The Redeemer does not take the sinner's place in the strict sense but performs a unique deed that, in God's eyes, makes compensation for the debt mankind has incurred because of their sins. He accepts a death to which he was not subject, and because of the hypostatic union that death has infinite value.

This death of the Son realizes the design of salvation of the whole Trinity. In this "satisfaction theory" the expression "died for us" means above all that Christ accepted death "for our sakes", not "in our stead".

Thomas Aquinas retains the substance of this conception of the mystery of salvation and blends with it elements derived from patristic theology. He stresses that Christ is the head of the Church, and that the grace that he possesses as head is passed on to all the members of the Church because of the organic conjunction that obtains within the Mystical Body.

7. Some recent authors seek to reinstate the notion of "exchange" (*commercium*) on which Anselm's theology had laid no stress. Two lines of inquiry have been opened up by them.

a. Some put forward the concept of solidarity, a concept that is open to several interpretations. Interpreted strictly, solidarity sets forth the manner in which the suffering Christ, in his own way, takes on the experience of the estrangement from God that sinners live through. Speaking in broader terms, these theologians refer only to the sole determination of the Son to disclose, both through his life and through his death, the Father's unconditional forgiveness.

b. Through the concept of substitution, the stress falls on the fact that Christ truly takes on the condition of sinners. This is not to say that God punished or condemned Christ in our stead, a theory erroneously advanced by many authors, Reformed theologians in particular. Other theologians recoil from these views and emphasize only that the Christ was subjected to "the curse of the law" (cf. Gal 3:13), that is, to God's aversion to sin, or to "the wrath of God", as it is called, this being but an aspect of God's love and "jealousy" for his covenanted people, whenever it fails to be loyal.

8. The interpretation of redemption as substitution may be grounded exegetically and dogmatically. Contrary to the claim heard here and there, this interpretation is not fraught with internal contradiction.

The freedom of creatures is not wholly autonomous: it is always in need of an assistance from God. Once freedom has turned away from God, it cannot make its way back to him by its own resources alone. On the other hand, man was created in order to be integrated into the Christ and thereby share in the life of the Trinity. No matter how great be the sinner's estrangement from God, it is not as deep as the sense of distance that the Son experiences vis-à-vis the Father in the kenotic emptying of himself (Phil 2:7), and in the anguish of "abandonment" (Mt 27:46). We are dealing here with that aspect of the distinction among the Persons of the Blessed Trinity that relates specifically to the economy of the redemption. It goes without saying that, within the Trinity, the three Persons are perfectly united in the identity of the same nature, and in an infinite love.

9. Both the objective expiation of sin and the participation in the divine life of grace must be regarded as inseparable aspects of the deed of salvation. Needless to say, man's acceptance of grace must be an act of freedom, an authentically recovered freedom. The whole Tradition of the Church, grounded on Sacred Scripture, teaches that, if the deed of salvation is to be realized and explained, it must be linked to two mysteries. Jesus is truly God, and yet he is in total solidarity with us, for he has taken on man's nature integrally.

10. As we consider redemption in its totality, we may not ignore "the spiritual participation" of the Virgin Mary in the sacrifice of Christ. From the moment she acquiesced to the Incarnation, her consent persisted without change. As *Lumen Gentium,* 61 (Abbott, 91), shows so well, Mary's consent represents faith in the eternal Covenant as it attains to the level of supreme perfection.

Nor should we overlook the intimate connection between the Cross and the Eucharist, two complementary aspects of the same deed of salvation. On the one hand, Jesus takes man's sin onto his own flesh; on the other, he gives his own flesh to man. The eucharistic celebration establishes a necessary connection between the sacrifice of Christ and the oblation that the Church makes of herself. Thus the Church comes to be embodied in the eternal oblation in which the Son offers his own self to the Father and is brought to its perfection in the Holy Spirit.

V. CHRISTOLOGICAL DIMENSIONS IN
NEED OF RENEWED EMPHASIS

1. Biblical and classic Christology includes extremely important perspectives that, for some reason or other, are not being shown today the attention they deserve. We would like to underline here two of these aspects by way of a

corollary to the presentation of the International Theological Commission. The first concerns the pneumatological dimension of Christology; the second, the cosmic dimension. Our presentation will be a limited one. Within the framework of a conclusive report, a systematic presentation would be out of place.

As far as pneumatology is concerned, we will limit ourselves to a biblical inquiry, which, needless to say, paves the way to further inquiries and already discloses the richness of the theme.

The cosmic influence of Christ draws attention to the ultimate dimension of Christology. Here we are dealing not only with Christ's action on all creatures "in the heavens, on the earth, and under the earth" (cf. Phil 2:10) but also with his governance with regard to the cosmos as a whole and to the whole of history.

A. *The Anointing of Christ by the Holy Spirit*

2. The Holy Spirit cooperates uninterruptedly in the redemptive deed of Christ. "He covers the Virgin Mary with his shadow, which is why her offspring is holy and will be called the Son of God" (Lk 1:35). When Jesus is baptized at the Jordan (Lk 3:22), he receives "the anointing" in order to carry out his mission as Messiah (Acts 10:38; Lk 4:18), while a voice from heaven declares him to be the Son on whom the Father's favor rests (Mk 1:10 and parallels). From that moment on, Christ is in a special way "guided by the Holy Spirit" (Lk 4:1) to commence and bring to fruition his ministry as "servant". By the finger of God (Lk 11:20), he casts out devils; he announces that "the reign of God is at hand" (Mk 1:15) and that it is to be brought to consummation by the Holy Spirit (Roman Missal; cf. Heb 2:14). Finally, through his Spirit, God the Father raises Jesus from the dead and fills mankind with him. Mankind thus puts on the form of humanity proper to the glorified Son of God (cf. Rom 1:3–4; Acts 13:32–33), after having known the form of humanity proper to the servant. The glorified humanity of Christ was also empowered to bestow the Holy Spirit on all human beings (Acts 2:22). The new and eschatological Adam can thus be called "a life-giving spirit" (1 Cor 15:45; cf. 2 Cor 3:17). And so, in a very real sense, the Mystical Body of Christ is animated by the Spirit of Christ forever.

B. *The Lordship of Christ over the Cosmos*

3.1. In St. Paul and in the body of Pauline literature, the risen Christ is often referred to as the one "under whose feet [the Father] placed all things". This expression occurs in a variety of applications. It appears in these very terms in 1 Corinthians 15:27, Ephesians 1:22, and Hebrews 2:8; in equivalent terms in Ephesians 3:10, Colossians 1:18, and Philippians 3:21.

3.2. Regardless of its provenance (perhaps Gen 1:26 through Ps 8:7), this expression refers first of all to the glorified humanity of the Christ and not to his divinity alone. For it is to the incarnate Son that it pertains to "have all things placed under his feet", since it is he who has destroyed the power to enslave held by sin and death. Since, through his Resurrection, Christ has gained control over the corruptibility immanent in the first Adam and has thus become in his own flesh "a spiritual body" par excellence, he inaugurates the rule of incorruptibility. This is why he is "the second and last Adam" (1 Cor 15:46–49), to whom "everything has been made subject" (1 Cor 15:27) and who can "subject everything to himself" (Phil 3:21).

3.3. The fact that the power of death has been abolished by Christ implies not only for mankind but also for the cosmos a renewal that is one and the same, and which at the end of time will yield its manifest effects. Matthew speaks of this as a "new creation" (palin-genesis; Mt 19:28), and Paul discerns there that which every creature is awaiting (Rom 8:19), while the book of Revelation (21:1), using the terminology of the Old Testament (Is 65:17; 66:22) does not hesitate to speak of "new heavens" and of a "new earth".

3.4. An unduly narrow anthropology that disdains, or at least overlooks, that essential aspect that is man's relation to the world can induce us to underestimate the value of the New Testament affirmation of Christ's lordship over the cosmos. And yet affirmations such as this have a considerable importance for our time. Because the natural sciences have made such progress, it seems as if we now perceive more clearly than at any time in the past how important the world is, what impact it makes on man's existence, and what questions it raises within that existence itself.

3.5. More often than not, the major objection against the cosmic aspect of Christ's lordship in his Resurrection and Second Coming is bound up with a certain conception of what Christology is. For, if it is true that the humanity of Christ should never be confused with his divinity, it is equally true that we should not separate the one from the other. In fact, these two errors have one and the same result. Whether the humanity of Christ be absorbed into his divinity or isolated from it, in either case the acknowledgment of the cosmic lordship that the Son of God receives in his glorified humanity is slighted just as much. The divinity of the Word is alone credited with what now pertains (as the New Testament texts quoted above testify) to his humanity, insofar as it is the humanity of Jesus Christ who was made Lord, and as Lord was given "the name above every other name" (Phil 2:9).

3.6. Besides, since the cosmic lordship of Christ pertains to the one who is "the firstborn of many brothers" (Rom 8:29), it pertains to his lordship that it should become ours as well in him. In fact, some of this spiritual "identity" that Christ gives us already exists (cf. 1 Cor 3:21–23). True, it will become fully manifest only at the Second Coming, and yet already now it truly confers on us the capacity to be free vis-à-vis all the powers of this world (Col 2:15), so much so that we can love Christ through all the changes in the world, our own death included (cf. Rom 8:38–39; 1 Jn 3:2; Rom 14:8–9).

3.7. This cosmic lordship of Christ should not, however, conceal from us a lordship of another kind that he does and must exercise with regard to human history and society, especially by means of justice, the signs of which are practically indispensable, if the Kingdom of God is to be proclaimed at all. Yet this lordship of Christ himself over man's history cannot achieve its summit except within the lordship he exercises over the cosmic world as such. For history remains practically captive to the play of the world and death, as long as, before the final Coming, the amazing primacy of Christ cannot yet attain an unrestricted actualization of itself for the good of all mankind.

10

THEOLOGY, CHRISTOLOGY, ANTHROPOLOGY

INTRODUCTION

At its plenary session in 1979 the International Theological Commission chose Christology as its theme for consideration; in 1980 it published its conclusions (cf. the Latin text "Quaestiones selectae de Christologia", in the periodical *Gregorianum* 61 [1980]: 609–32, and also several translations into modern languages).

Upon completion of the second five-year period of its work (1974–79), the Commission itself was reconstituted. The majority of the members, especially of those present for the first time, wished to continue the study of the theme of Christology. Although the new Commission had complete liberty to discuss all Christological questions, nevertheless for reasons of prudence and to save energy and time, reexamination of areas covered in the document that had already been published was to be avoided.

The program for the plenary session of 1981 required amplifications and supplementary considerations. In the first place, it was to expound the relationship of Christology to the other ways of talking about God and to faith in the triune God. Having laid this foundation, it would be necessary to determine the complex relationship between Christology and anthropology. In the second place, two questions intimately linked to the foundations of Christology needed particular attention: the preexistence of Jesus Christ and today's disputed question about the suffering of God. Both themes exemplify how contemporary problems and classical solutions can clarify and enrich each other in productive dialogue.

From this point of view both Christology documents from the two sessions can be seen as complementing each other so as to form a unity; this judgment, however, is left to the well-disposed reader.

Reprinted from *The Irish Quarterly*. This document was approved by the Commission "*in forma specifica*".

I. THE FOUNDATION AND CONTEXT OF CHRISTOLOGY

The context of Christology includes the human desire for and the knowledge man has of God, the revelation of the Triune God, and the image of man in contemporary anthropology and in the Incarnation of Jesus Christ. If these basic elements are not first treated adequately, Christology itself is placed in danger. Even the effort to elaborate a doctrine of man will as a consequence be rendered obscure. These are the reasons why thought must be given to a new clarification of the setting of all Christology.

A. *The Economy of Jesus Christ and the Revelation of God*

1. What is the relationship between Christology and the problem of the revelation of God? To avoid all *confusion* and all *separation* of the two aspects of this question, the complementary character of the two approaches to it must be maintained. The first descends from God to Jesus: the other returns from Jesus to God.

1.1. *Confusion* between Christology and Theology results if one supposes that the name of God is totally unknown outside of Jesus Christ, and that there exists no other Theology than that which arises from the Christian revelation. This does not respect the mystery of man the creature in whom there wells up a fundamental desire for God, intimated in religious and in philosophical teachings all throughout history. It also neglects the importance of the traces of God in creation (cf. Rom 1:20). In addition, it denies the economy of the revelation of the unique character God in the Old Testament, which the Church recognized from the very beginning, as well as the theocentric attitude of Jesus, who asserted that the God of the Old Law was his own Father. Furthermore, one creates a serious ambiguity in the understanding of the confession "Jesus is the Son of God"—an ambiguity that, in the last analysis, can result in an atheistic Christology.

1.2. A *separation* between Christology and Theology supposes the idea that in any part of the body of Theology, the notion of God elaborated by philosophical wisdom can take the place of reflection upon revealed faith. It also misunderstands the originality of the revelation given to the people of Israel—revelation embodied in the Christian Faith with radical newness—while diminishing the importance of the event of Jesus Christ. Paradoxically, this separation can lead to the opinion that Christological investigation is sufficient of itself and is turned in on itself, with no reference to God.

2. It seems that we can apply here—with the appropriate adaptations—the

criterion of the Chalcedonian definition: distinction without confusion or separation must be maintained between Christology and the problem of God. Such a distinction exists between the two periods of revelation, which correspond to each other. The first is the universal manifestation of himself that God gave in the primordial creation; the second is the personal revelation that developed throughout the history of salvation, from the time of the Old Covenant until the coming of Jesus Christ.

3. Thus there exists a complementary interaction between understanding Jesus in light of the idea of God and finding God in Jesus.

3.1. In the first place, the believer cannot recognize in Jesus the full manifestation of God, except in the light of the notion of and the desire of God that lives in the heart of man. Even though it admitted certain errors, this light has had an effect upon the religions of many peoples and upon philosophical studies; it was already visible in the revelation of the one God in the Old Testament; it is always present in men's consciences today, notwithstanding the bitterness of atheism. One finds it in the search for absolute values such as justice or fraternity. This light is fundamentally presupposed in the confession of faith, "Jesus Christ is the Son of God."

3.2. A second observation must be made with humility—not just because Christians' faith and behavior do not live up to the standards of the totally gratuitous revelation that reached its fulfillment in Jesus Christ, but also because the revealed mystery surpasses all theological formulations: the mystery of God, insofar as it was definitively revealed in Jesus Christ, contains "unfathomable riches" (cf. Eph 3:8) surpassing and indeed transcending the thoughts and desires of the philosophical and religious mind. By opening a free and ever-widening road to God—who always lies beyond—this mystery guards, confirms, and leads to its proper fullness whatever is true in these thoughts and desires. No matter their errors and deviations, it guides them, as they themselves wish, into paths more correct and ample. And from these sources the mystery of faith, which is always open to being understood more profoundly, accepts the intuitions and religious experiences of mankind for integration into itself, so that the catholicity of Christian faith may be more fully realized.

3.3. For Jesus Christ, bringing to completion the revelation made in the whole history of salvation shows the mystery of God, whose triune life is the source of a most loving communication in himself and to us. This God, already revealed in the Old Testament and definitively announced by Jesus Christ, made himself near to man (cf. Dt 4:7; Clement of Alexandria, *Stromata*, 11, 5.4). In many of the non-Christian religions it is rather that man seeks God. But in this revelation it is God who first and from the beginning seeks out man and loves him from the depths of his heart. This discovery, surpassing all previous conceptions of God, and satisfying them beyond all desire, is immanent in the confession of faith, "Jesus Christ is the Son of God."

B. *The Relationship between Theocentrism and Christocentrism*

1. In the recent history of Western Theology (and so leaving medieval Theology out of consideration) the question treated so far can be discussed from different perspectives, namely, "Theocentrism" and "Christocentrism". The question these terms pose is whether the proper object of Christology is immediately God or Jesus Christ. We consider this problem by addressing, formally and logically, the relationship between Theocentrism and Christocentrism.

1.1. In fact the question rests on a false foundation if the Theocentrism that one opposes to Christocentrism is not a Christian Theism (that is, revealed and Trinitarian) but is in some sense a "natural" Theism, which places in doubt either the possibility or the fact of revelation. The question immediately vanishes because, in the first place, there is lacking in Theism a purely "natural" reason that could contradict Christocentrism; in the second place, Christian Theocentrism and Christocentrism are in fact one and the same.

1.2. Christian Theism consists properly in the Triune God, and he is known uniquely in the revelation to us in Jesus Christ. Thus, on the one hand, knowledge of Jesus Christ leads to a knowledge of the Trinity and attains its plenitude in the knowledge of the Trinity; on the other hand, there is no knowledge of the Triune God except in knowledge of Jesus Christ himself. It follows that there is no distinction between Theocentrism and Christocentrism: the two terms denote the same reality.

1.3. Leaving aside less suitable interpretations, Christocentrism properly connotes the Christology of Jesus of Nazareth, which, taken in its own more profound sense, expresses the "singularity" of Jesus Christ. But this singularity of Jesus Christ properly accords with the revelation of the Trinity when it is defined on the one hand by the singular relationship of Jesus himself with the Father and the Holy Spirit, that is, with God; and, in consequence, on the other hand, by the singular condition according to which Jesus exists with and for men.

2. Christian Theism does not exclude natural Theism, but on the contrary presupposes it in its own way. For Christian Theism takes its origin from God revealing himself according to a most free intention of his will; while natural Theism pertains intrinsically to human reason, as the First Vatican Council teaches (cf. *DS*, 3004, 3026).

3. *Natural Theism* is not the same as, and therefore is not to be confused with, either the Theism/monotheism of the Old Testament or historical Theism, that is, the Theism that non-Christians have professed in various ways

in their religions. The monotheism of the Old Testament has it origins in a supernatural revelation and therefore retains an intrinsic relation to—indeed, demands—the Trinitarian revelation. Historical Theisms do not arise from a "pure nature" but from a nature subject to sin, objectively redeemed by Jesus Christ and elevated to a supernatural destiny.

C. *Christology and the Relevation of the Trinity*

1. The economy of Jesus Christ reveals the triune God. Jesus Christ, however, is recognized in his mission only if the unique presence of God in him is properly understood. For this reason Theocentrism and Christocentrism illustrate and need each other. Still, there remains the question of the relationship of Christology to the relevation of the Triune God.

1.1. Detect from the New Testament that in the witness of the primitive Church, it was always held with certainty that through the event of Jesus Christ and the event of the gift of the Holy Spirit God had revealed himself to us as he is. In himself he is such as appeared to us: "Philip, he who sees me sees the Father" (Jn 14:9).

1.2. This therefore is the role that the three divine names play in the eternal life of God, according to the economy of salvation, and according to the Greek Fathers' understanding of the matter. This is for us the only definitive source of all knowledge of the mystery of the Trinity. The elaboration of the doctrine of the Trinity had its beginnings in the economy of salvation. Again, an eternal and immanent Trinity is of necessity presupposed by an economic Trinity. Theology and catechetics must both take into account this datum of the primitive Faith.

2. Therefore a fundamental axiom of modern Theology is best put in the following terms: the Trinity that manifests itself in the economy of salvation is an immanent Trinity, and it is this Trinity that gives itself freely and graciously in the economy of salvation.

2.1. Any kind of distinction, then, between Christology and the Trinity is to be avoided in Theology and catechetics. The mystery of Jesus Christ belongs to the structure of the Trinity. The mystery of the Trinity is Christological. Such a distinction can take on either a neoscholastic form or a modern form. It was the practice of neoscholasticism to segregate the consideration of the Trinity from the whole Christian mystery; nor did it take sufficient account of the Trinity in its understanding of the Incarnation and the deification of man. The Trinity's importance for both the body of the truths of faith and Christian life was repeatedly neglected.

The modern distinction places a veil between men and the eternal Trinity, as if Christian revelation was already inviting man to know the triune God and participate in his life. As far as the eternal Trinity is concerned, this leads to a certain "agnosticism", which can in no way be accepted. For if God is greater than anything we can think about him, Christian revelation asserts that that "extra" greatness is always of a trinitarian nature.

2.2. In the same way, anything leading to confusion between the event of Jesus Christ and the Trinity must be avoided. The Trinity was not simply brought about in the history of salvation by means of the Cross and Resurrection of Jesus Christ, as though a historical process were necessary for God to emerge as Trinitarian. Therefore, the distinction must be maintained between the immanent Trinity, where liberty and necessity are the same thing in the eternal essence of God, and the Trinity of the economy of salvation, where God exercises his liberty absolutely, with no suggestion of his being forced to it.

3. This distinction between the "immanent" Trinity and the "economic" Trinity is intrinsic to their real identity. It is not to be used as justifying new modes of separation but is to be understood according to the way of affirmation, negation, and eminence. God is beyond all divisions one might attribute to him. In the economy of salvation we see the Eternal Son take on in his own life the "kenotic" event of birth, of human life, and of the death on the Cross. This event, in which God reveals himself absolutely and definitively, affects in some way the being proper to God the Father, insofar as he is the kind of God who accomplishes these mysteries and really shares them as belonging to himself, together with the Son and the Holy Spirit. For not alone in the mystery of Jesus Christ does God the Father reveal and communicate himself to us freely and graciously through the Son and in the Holy Spirit; but also, the Father leads a Trinitarian life with the Son and the Holy Spirit in a manner most profound and almost new, according to our way of speaking, insofar as the Father's relationship to the incarnate Son, in the communication of the gift of the Spirit, is the very relationship that constitutes the Trinity. In the intimate life of the Triune God the very potential exists for the realization of these events, which, through the inexplicable freedom of God, take place for us in the history of salvation brought by Our Lord Jesus Christ.

These great events in the life of Jesus clearly make applicable to us, and make efficacious in a new way, the eternal word of generation, in which the Father says to the Son: "You are my Son: this day have I begotten you" (Ps 2:7; cf. Acts 13:33; Heb 1:5; 5:5; and also Lk 3:22).

D. *The Relationship between Christology and Anthropology*

1. Modern Christology often is based more upon, and developed from, an anthropology, as a new principle of understanding, than upon the Theology of the Triune God. This methodology has its greatest impact on the field of

soteriology. The purpose of the redemption is conceived more as a hominization than as the deification of man. In this process, the crisis in metaphysics, already evident in the field of philosophy, has had great consequences at the very heart of Theology. The disjunctive antithesis between "ontological" considerations and merely "functional" considerations (which some hold are closer to the Biblical mind) has serious consequences, which are well known in modern Theology. Granted that the relationship between anthropology and Christology has to be worked out anew in terms of their mutual analogies; over and above this, the problem of the deification of man must be treated separately by way of a small excursus (cf. E).

The announcement of Jesus Christ the Son of God is made under the Biblical sign "for us" ("*pro nobis*"). Thus it is necessary to treat the whole Christology under the aspect of soteriology. For this reason, and more-or-less correctly and laudably, some modern attempts have been made to work out a "functional" Christology. But, conversely, it is likewise true that "existence for others" means Jesus Christ cannot be separated from his relationship and intimate communion with the Father and must for that very reason be rooted in his eternal sonship. The proexistence of Jesus Christ, in which God communicates himself to man, presupposes preexistence. Otherwise the proclamation of Jesus Christ as Savior would be merely a fiction and an illusion, incapable of defending against the modern accusation that it is an ideology. To ask whether Christology should be functional or ontological is to pose false alternatives.

2. The anthropological element in Christology can be considered under three aspects in accord with the Biblical typology of Adam-Christ (Rom 5:12–21; 1 Cor 15:45–49).

2.1. Just as faith presupposes man to be a subject whom God created free, with the capacity of being open to and responding to God, so Christology needs anthropology. It is for this reason that Theology, following the teaching of the Second Vatican Council, acknowledges that a relative autonomy — that is, an autonomy of secondary causation based in a relationship to God the Creator — should be assigned to man and to the world; a just liberty should be conceded to the sciences (cf. *GS,* 36, 41, 56; *LG,* 36; *AA,* 7), and in a positive way Theology should make use of the anthropological orientation of modern times. Christian faith ought to demonstrate its proper character by cultivating and guarding the transcendence of the human person (cf. *GS,* 76).

2.2. The Gospel of Jesus Christ not only presupposes man's essence and existence but also brings him to full perfection. This perfection, at least implicitly sought, desired, and hoped for by all men, is transcendent and infinite and can be found only in God. Man's true hominization therefore attains its apex in his divinization, in his friendship and communion with God, by which man is made the temple of God, enjoying the presence of the

Father, Son, and Holy Spirit. The adoration and worship of God, especially Eucharistic worship, makes man fully human. Therefore, Jesus Christ, at once God and man, is found to be the eschatological fullness of man, and in him alone is found the "measure of the stature of the fullness of man" (cf. Eph 4:13). Only in Jesus Christ is man's limitless openness concretely found. It is especially in Jesus Christ that the mystery of man and his exalted vocation are truly shown to us (cf. GS, 22).

The saving history of the people of the Old Testament serves as a type that justifies man's hope that God does not deceive, and that in new ways this hope will be fulfilled abundantly in the Person and work of Christ.

2.3. The identity and perfection of man as they are found in Christ challenge any human absolutism that the sinner chooses for himself. For this reason the preaching of the Gospel cannot be separated from a warning of judgment and a call to conversion. The following of the Cross and communion with the crucified Jesus Christ do not destroy man but signify and can even bring about the end of many forms of alienation, which result ultimately from the power of sin and the slavery of the law and death. This signifies and confers the freedom to which we have been called through Jesus Christ (cf. Gal 5:1–13). For this reason it is the Pasch of the Lord, namely, participation in the Cross and Resurrection of Jesus Christ, which show the true way by which man is brought to perfection.

3. In this triple view of man, which Christology gives, the mystery of God and man is shown to the world as the mystery of love. Under the guidance of the Christian Faith one can elaborate a vision that embraces all things. Furthermore, even if this vision critically examines the yearnings of modern men, it also affirms, purges, and improves them.

In ancient philosophy substance in general was at the center of things, but here the center is a "metaphysic of charity", namely, the person, whose most perfect act is the act of charity.

Such an interpretation of prophetic and Christological reality is also of fundamental importance in applying the precepts of morality, both personal and social. In these matters the Faith ought to presuppose a relatively autonomous ethical standard (cf. Rom 2:14ff.), while at the same time judging it critically by the standard of Jesus Christ, so that man's dignity is advanced with justice in human society, while justice is surpassed by Christian love, which ought to be the soul of justice. In this way, the human ethical standard, which is of itself open to very many interpretations, is rendered Christian. Therefore from the Gospel of Jesus Christ one correctly derives the duty to participate in building a "civilization of love" in human history.

E. *The Image of God in Man,*
or the Christian Meaning of the "Deification" of Man

1. "The Word of God is made man, that man may become God" (Athanasius, *De Inc.,* 54:3). This axiom of the soteriology of the Fathers, above all of the Greeks, is denied in our own times for various reasons. Some assert that "deification" is a typically Hellenistic notion of salvation and is conducive to a mentality of flight from the world, together with a denial of human values. In their view deification removes the difference between God and man and leads to a fusion without distinction. They oppose to this patristic axiom another that they maintain is more adapted to our age: "God is made man, so that man may be made more human." Certainly the words "deification", *"theôsis"*, *"theopoiêsis"*, *"homoiôsis theo"*, etc., of themselves are ambiguous. Therefore the genuine or Christian sense of "deification" in its major aspects must be explained.

2. Certainly Greek philosophy and religion acknowledged some "natural" kinship between the human and the divine mind. The biblical revelation, however, clearly treats man as a creature, who by contemplation and love moves toward God. It is not man's intellectual capacity but conversion of heart, a new obedience, and moral action that bring man closest to God. This is impossible without God's grace. Man can become what God is only by grace.

3. Stronger arguments arise from Christian preaching. Created in the image and likeness of God, man is called to a sharing of life with God, who alone can fulfill the deepest desires of the human heart. The idea of deification reaches its summit by virtue of the Incarnation of Jesus Christ. The Word assumes our mortal nature so that we can be freed from death and sin and can share in the divine life. Through Jesus Christ we are partakers in the divine nature (2 Pet 1:4). Deification consists in the very grace that frees us from the death of sin and communicates to us the divine life itself. We are sons in the Son.

4. The Christian meaning of our proposition is made much more profound through the mystery of Jesus Christ. Just as the Incarnation of the Word does not change the divine nature, in the same way the divinity of Jesus Christ does not change or dissolve human nature but rather makes it more itself and perfects it in its original condition of creaturehood. Redemption does not, in a general way, simply convert human nature into something divine but renews human nature along the lines of the human nature of Jesus Christ.

According to Maximus the Confessor, this idea is further determined through the final experiences of Jesus Christ, namely, his Passion and his abandonment by God. The more deeply Jesus Christ participates in human mystery, the more man participates in the divine life.

In this sense deification properly understood can make man perfectly human: deification is the truest and ultimate hominization of man.

5. This process whereby man is deified does not take place without the grace of Jesus Christ, which comes especially through the sacraments in the Church. The sacraments join us in a most efficacious and visible fashion, and under the symbols of our own fragile life they join us to the divine grace of the Savior (cf. *LG*, 7). More than that, this deification is not communicated to the individual as such but as a member of the Communion of Saints. Moreover, the invitation given by divine grace to the human race takes place in the Holy Spirit. Christians therefore should realize the holiness they have achieved in their way of life (*LG*, 39–42). The fullness of deification belongs to the beatific vision of the Triune God, which takes the soul into the Communion of Saints.

II. SOME LEADING THEMES IN MODERN CHRISTOLOGY

So far the basis and dimensions of trinitarian and anthropological Christology have been presented. Some other problems of a less general nature should also be examined in the concrete. Among these we have selected two. The first concerns the preexistence of Jesus Christ, which holds a middle position between Christology and Trinitarian Theology. A second question concerns the "changelessness" versus the "suffering" of God. Both questions have prominent places in modern Christological discussion. (A third and further theme concerns the human knowledge and consciousness of Christ; we have not been able to bring this to a satisfactory conclusion yet. We hope that in the future this theme will be the subject of further studies.)

A. *The Problem of the Preexistence of Jesus Christ*

1. Since classical Christology could always presuppose Trinitarian Theology, the preexistence of Jesus Christ did not present a great problem. But in modern Christological research, where the earthly life of Jesus has been subjected to considerable scrutiny (cf. *Quaest. Select.*, 1.A and B), preexistence has often been presented as something alien to biblical faith and religion and made to seem rather as something Greek; a form of speculation simply, in fact, a myth that betrays the true human nature of Jesus. It is therefore said that the

preexistence of Jesus Christ is to be understood today not literally but in purely symbolic terms. It is simply a way of speaking of his uniqueness, his irreducible originality, and of the way in which Jesus transcends the world and history. Jesus Christ had a more-than-worldly origin. In these modern interpretations the idea of preexistence seems to have exhausted its purpose and been surpassed.

2. Attempts to claim that the biblical statements about the preexistence of Jesus Christ arose from mythical, Hellenistic, and gnostic sources do not hold water: today, in fact, relationships are detected with the intertestamental literature (cf. Eth. Enoch 48:3.6; 4 Ezra 13) and above all with Old Testament sources, especially in the Wisdom Theology (Prov 8:22ff., Sir 24). In addition, much more is made of elements within biblical Christology itself: the unique relationship of Jesus on earth with God the Father ("Abba" on the lips of Jesus); the unique mission of the Son and his glorious Resurrection. In the light of this exaltation the origin of Jesus Christ is openly and definitively understood: sitting at the right hand of God in his postexistence (i.e., after his earthly life) implies his preexistence with God from the beginning before he came into the world. In other words, his eschatological state can be no different from his pre-Incarnation state and vice versa. The unique mission of the Son (cf. Mk 12:1–12) is inseparable from the Person of Jesus Christ, who not only had a prophetic role, which was temporal and limited, to play on earth but also has a coeternal origin from the Father. The Son of God received everything in eternity from God the Father. In the light of this eschatological-soteriological perspective we must say that Jesus Christ cannot open the way to eternal life for us if he is not himself "eternal". The eschatological message and the eschatological doctrine presuppose a divine preexistence of Jesus Christ.

Jesus Christ's origin from the Father is not a conclusion of subsequent reflection but is made clear by his words and the facts about him, namely, that Jesus took it for certain that he had been sent by the Father. Therefore, at least in an indirect fashion, one finds manifested the consciousness of Jesus with regard to his eternal existence as Son of the Father, whose task it is to reconcile the whole world to God. (One can see as primary fundamental elements the "I" of Jesus Christ in the Synoptic Gospels, the words "I am" (*ego eimi*) in the fourth Gospel, and the "mission" of Jesus in many New Testament writings.)

3. Biblical studies have shown how the original datum has evolved through various stages and in different aspects within the limits of the New Testament as the full meaning of the preexistence of Jesus becomes clear:

The eternal election and predestination of Jesus Christ (cf. Eph 1:3–7, 10ff.; 1 Pet 1:20).

The sending of the Son of God into the world and into the flesh (cf. Gal 4:4; Rom 8:38; 1 Tim 3:16; Jn 3:16ff.):

"Kenosis", Incarnation, death, and glorious Resurrection of Jesus Christ on the Cross, as steps on the way from the Father, all of which show the soteriological and salvific meaning of the event of Jesus Christ (cf. insup. Phil 2:6–11).

Jesus Christ was already present and active in the history of the people of Israel in a hidden way (cf. 1 Cor 10:1–4; Jn 1:30, 8, 14:58).

Jesus Christ, as the intermediary in the creation of the world, now also keeps the world in being. He is Head of the Body of the Church and the reconciler of all things (cf. 1 Cor 8:6; Col 1:15ff.; Jn 1:1–3, 17; Heb 1:2 ff.). All mediators, or acts of mediation that seemed to have significance for salvation, are taken away or must be understood in a subordinate fashion. Jesus Christ himself has absolute preeminence over against all other acts of mediation, and in his work and in his Person are God's final action and event.

Jesus Christ obtains the lordship of the universe and gives redemption to all, a process that is understood as a new creation (cf. Col 1, 15ff.; 1 Cor 8:6; Heb 1:2ff.; Jn 1:2).

In the exaltation of Jesus Christ, the process of vanquishing evil powers has begun (cf. Phil 2:10; Col 1:16–20).

4. The postbiblical word "preexistence" includes many Christological elements. Even if this conception is in fact based on Scripture, at the same time preexistence is not invoked there in an isolated fashion and does not constitute the only reason for the statements of the New Testament. We are speaking of a systematic concept that synthesizes many theological meanings. In many statements it rather furnishes a background (*l'arrière-plan, Hintergrund*) or a presupposition of the reason for the other aims. Therefore, just as we cannot be satisfied with a purely formal use of the term, neither must we use it in a univocal fashion but rather analogically, carefully, and according to the context and the richness of the various doctrinal elements already mentioned. Although it is subject to multiple interpretations, the concept of preexistence does not signify only an "interpretation" that would in the end be purely subjective but in fact the real ontological origin of Jesus Christ, his origin outside of time, of which he is also consciously aware, as we have already said. Understood in the biblical sense, preexistence does not signify only that Christ is coeternal with God. This expression connotes the whole movement and Christological mystery, beginning from existence with the Father, including the "kenosis" and the Incarnation, the infamous death on the Cross, and the glorious exaltation. In the end it attests to the redemption of all men, to the primacy of Christ in the Church, and to universal and cosmic reconciliation.

All this is presented in terms of redemptive suffering. Almost all of these formulations of the preexistence of Jesus Christ are found in hymnic contexts. For this reason they take the form of testimony and praise, born of the Church's experience of the presence of the Lord. This soteriological and doxological character does not exclude a Christological meaning, but it does impose clear limits on those forms of speculation about preexistence that do not respect the specific character of the term.

5. The concept of the preexistence of Jesus Christ has acquired greater clarity as Christological reflection has evolved. In certain places the prefix "pre" (e.g., "before all things", "before Abraham") has and keeps a temporal meaning, granted the historical character of Christian salvation; but in the last analysis it signifies absolute and extraterrestrial primacy over the whole of creation. In the Christological field, in the Nicaean-Constantinopolitan Creed (cf. *DS*, 125), such a preexistence acquires after the Arian crisis, a definite stamp. The Son of God generated from the Father is not created, but consubstantial with the Father.

In that way the idea of the preexistence of Jesus Christ is par excellence, as was said above, the point at which Christology and Trinitarian Theology meet and come together (I, C and D). Between the Son in the eternal life of God, and the Son in the earthly life of Jesus Christ, there is a most strict correspondence or, better still, a real identity, nourished by the unity and the filial union of Jesus Christ with God the Father. The preexistence of Jesus Christ should also be understood from the point of view of the history of Jesus Christ and above all from his completion in the event of Easter. From the beginning of Christological reflection, the preexistence of Jesus Christ, coeternal with the Father—that is, if we consider it as a descending movement and, as it were, from above—was equally understood in relation to the gift of Jesus Christ for the life of the world. Such relationships are rooted in the eternal sonship through which Jesus Christ is generated by the Father. This relationship is expressed by the biblical concept of "mission". The gift of salvation will be valid for us and for all mankind only if it is born in God, namely, in the preexisting Son of the Father. This shows anew the soteriological character of preexistence.

B. *The Trinitarian Aspect of the Cross of Jesus Christ, or the "Suffering of God"*

For historical or systematic reasons God's immutability or impassibility is often called into question in today's Theology, above all in the context of a Theology of the Cross. In that way different theological conceptions of the suffering of God have arisen. It is necessary to know how to separate false ideas from elements in accord with the biblical revelation. Since discussion of this problem continues, we limit ourselves to a first approach, which nevertheless seeks to point to a solution to the question.

1. The supporters of this Theology assert that their ideas can be found in the Old and New Testaments and in some of the Fathers. But the influence of modern philosophy has certainly had a greater weight, at least in the systematic presentation of this Theology.

1.1. Hegel was the first to postulate that for the idea of God to be comprehensive, it has to include "the suffering of the negative", that is, the "hardship of abandonment" (*"die Härte der Gottlosigkeit"*). In him there is a fundamental ambiguity: Does God have or not a real need of the world? After Hegel some Protestants and certain Anglicans developed so-called kenotic theologies, which are "Cross-centered". According to these the Passion of the Son touches the whole of the Trinity in different fashions and manifests above all the suffering of the Father who abandons his Son: "Since he has spared not his own Son but has consigned him for all of us" (Rom 8:32; cf. Jn 3:16). It also shows the suffering of the Holy Spirit, who in the Passion takes upon himself the "distance" between the Father and the Son.

1.2. According to many of our contemporaries, this Trinitarian suffering is rooted in the very divine essence itself; according to others, it is based on a certain emptying of himself on the part of God the Creator, who in some sense binds himself to human freedom or, in virtue of a pact, freely forces himself to hand over his Son—a fact that they say makes the suffering of the Father more deep than all the suffering of creation.

In recent years a few Catholic authors have made similar suggestions, maintaining that the principal role of the Crucified consisted in manifesting the suffering of the Father.

2. One could often suppose from the Old Testament, the divine transcendence notwithstanding (cf. Jer 7:16–19), that God suffers because of the sins of men. Perhaps not all the expressions can be explained as simple anthropomorphisms (see, for example, Gen 6:6: "Yahweh repents that he had made man on earth and he sorrows about it in his heart"; Dt 4:25; Ps 78:41; Is 7:13; 63:10; Jer 12:7; 31:20; Hos 4:6; 6:4; 11:8ff.). Rabbinic theology is even stronger in this respect and speaks, for example, of a God who abandons himself to lamentation because of the Covenant, which he has made and which constrains him, or because of the destruction of the Temple; and at the same time affirms the weakness of God when faced with the powers of evil (cf. P. Kuhn, *Gottes Trauer und Klage in der rabbinischen Überlieferung* [Leiden, 1978], pp. 170ff., 275ff.).

In the New Testament, the tears of Jesus (cf. Lk 19:41), his anger (cf. Mk 3:5), and the sadness he feels are themselves also manifestations of a certain way of behavior on God's part. In other places it is stated explicitly that God gets angry (cf. Rom 1:18; 3:5; 9:22; Jn 3:36; Rev 15:1).

3. Without doubt the Fathers underline (against the pagan mythologies) the *"apatheia"* of God, without denying in this way his compassion for the suffering of the world. For them the term *"apatheia"* indicates the opposite of *"pathos"*, a word that means involuntary suffering imposed from the outside or as a consequence of fallen nature. When they admit natural and innocent suffering (like hunger or sleep), they attribute these to Jesus Christ or to God inasmuch as he feels compassion for human suffering (Origen, *Hom. in Ez,* VI, 6; *Comm. in Math.,* XVII, 20; *Sel. in Ez,* 16; *Comm. in Rom,* VIII, 9; *De Prin.,* IV, 4:4). From time to time they use a dialectical form of expression: God has suffered in Jesus Christ in an impassible fashion because he has done it in virtue of a free choice (*Greg. Thaum. Ad Theopompum,* IV–VIII).

According to the Council of Ephesus (cf. the letter of St. Cyril to Nestorius: *COD,* 3:42), the Son makes his own the sufferings inflicted on his human nature (*oikeiôsis*). Attempts to reduce this proposition (and others like it in the Tradition) to a simple "manner of speaking" do not sufficiently recognize its profound meaning. But the Christology of the Church does not allow us to affirm formally that Jesus Christ could suffer according to his divine nature (cf. *DS,* 16, 166, 196f., 284, 293f., 300, 318, 358, 504, 635, 801, 852).

Despite what has just been said, the Fathers cited above clearly affirm the immutability and impassibility of God (e.g., Origen, *Contra Celsum,* IV, 4). Thus they absolutely exclude from the divine essence that mutability and that passivity that would permit a movement from potency to act (cf. Thomas Aquinas, *S.Th.,* I, q. 9, a. 1c). Finally, the following considerations have been taken into account in the Tradition of the Faith of the Church to clear up this problem.

4.1. With regard to the immutability of God it must be said that the divine life is inexhaustible and without limit, so much so that God has no need whatever for creatures (cf. *DS,* 3002). No human event could gain for him anything new or actuate in him any potentiality whatsoever. God, therefore, could not be subject to any change either by way of diminution or by way of progress. "Therefore, since God is not susceptible to change in any of these different ways, it is proper to him to be absolutely immutable" (Thomas Aquinas; *S.Th.,* I, q. 9, a. 2c). The same affirmation is found in Sacred Scripture with regard to God the Father, "in whom there is no variation or shadow due to change" (James 1:17). But this immutability of the living God is not opposed to his supreme liberty, something that the event of the Incarnation clearly demonstrates.

4.2. The affirmation of the impassibility of God supposes and implies this way of understanding his immutability, but this is not to be understood as though God remained indifferent to human events. God loves us with the love of friendship, and he wishes to be loved by us in return. When this love is offended, Sacred Scripture speaks of suffering on the part of God. On the other hand, it speaks of his joy when the sinner is converted (Lk 15:7). "To suffer is a more sane reaction and closer to immortality than complete insensibility" (Augustine; *En. in Ps,* 55:6). The two aspects need each other. If one or the other is neglected, the concept of God as he reveals himself is not respected.

5. Modern and medieval theology have underlined more the first of these aspects (cf. 4.1). In reality, the Catholic Faith today defends the essence and the liberty of God and opposes exaggerated theories (cf. above, B, 1). But the other aspect (cf. above, 4.2) merits further attention.

5.1. Today man desires and searches for a Divinity that will be omnipotent and certain but that does not appear indifferent; one, moreover, that is full of compassion for the miseries of man and in that sense "suffers with them". Christian piety has always rejected the idea of a Divinity indifferent to the vicissitudes of creatures. It is even inclined to admit that, just as "compassion" is among the most noble human perfections, it can be said of God that he has a similar compassion without any imperfection and in an eminent degree, namely, the "inclination of commiseration . . . and not the absence of power" (Leo I, *DS,* 293). It is maintained that this compassion can coexist with the eternal happiness itself. The Fathers called this total mercy toward human pain and suffering "the passion of love", a love that in the Passion of Jesus Christ has vanquished these sufferings and made them perfect (cf. *Greg. Thaum. Ad Theopompum;* John Paul II, *Dives in Misericordia,* 7; *AAS,* 72, 1980, 1199ff.).

5.2. As far as the question of the "suffering of God" is concerned, there is undoubtedly something worth retaining in the expressions of Holy Scripture and the Fathers, as well as in some recent theologies, even though they require clarification as shown above. This should perhaps also be said with regard to the Trinitarian aspect of the Cross of Jesus Christ. The eternal generation of the Son and his role as the immaculate Lamb who would pour out his precious blood are equally eternal and precede the free creation of the world (cf. 1 Pet 1:19ff.; Eph 1:7). In this sense, there is a very close correspondence between the gift of divinity that the Father gives to the Son and the gift by which the Father consigns his Son to the abandonment of the Cross. Since, however, the Resurrection is also present in the eternal plan of God, the suffering of "separation" (see above, B, 1.1) is always overcome by the joy of union; the compassion of the Trinitarian God for the suffering of the Word is properly understood as the work of most perfect love, which is normally a source of joy. As for the Hegelian concept of "negativity", this is radically excluded from our idea of God.

We have learned that in attempting to reflect on these matters human and theological reasoning encounter some of the greatest of all difficulties (such as "anthropomorphism"). But in a remarkable fashion they also encounter the ineffable mystery of the living God and realize the limits of thought itself.

CONCLUSION

We neither can nor wish to deny that the picture we have presented of our researches is indebted to modern scientific Theology. All the same, the reality we have studied, i.e., the living Faith of the whole Church in the Person of our Lord Jesus Christ, tends—beyond the frontiers of particular cultures—to achieve an ever-greater universality in the knowledge and love of the mystery of Jesus Christ. As the Apostle Paul made himself "all things to all" (1 Cor 1:22), we in our turn must insert the evangelical message concerning Jesus Christ more deeply into all the languages and cultural models of different peoples. A task of the greatest difficulty! We can accomplish it only if we can remain in continuous dialogue with the Holy Scripture, with the Faith, and with the Magisterium of the Church, but also with the riches of the Traditions of all the particular Churches and of human experience lived in every culture in which the action and effects of the Holy Spirit can be present (cf. GS, 44; AG, 15, 22; Paul VI, EN, 64; AAS, 68, 1976, 54f.: John Paul II, FC, 10; AAS, 74, 1982, 90f.). We are encouraged to press on toward this goal by recalling the words spoken to the Apostles: "You shall be witnesses to me in Jerusalem and in all Judaea and in Samaria, and unto the ends of the earth" (Acts 1:8).

11

PENANCE AND RECONCILIATION

In the preaching of Jesus the call to conversion is connected immediately with the good news of the coming of the Kingdom of God (cf. Mt 1:14f.). Thus, when the Church, following Jesus and by virtue of the mission that it has received, calls to conversion and announces the reconciliation that God has worked through the death and Resurrection of Jesus Christ (cf. 2 Cor 5:18–20), it preaches a God who is rich in pity (Eph 2:4) and who is not ashamed to be called the God of men (cf. Heb 11:16).

This is why the message that proclaims God as the true God and announces the coming of his Kingdom is at the same time the message of salvation for man and of the reconciliation of the world. By contrast, sin, which does not acknowledge God as God and which refuses the community with God that God offers man since the beginning of creation, signifies at the same time the alienation of man from the meaning and goal of his human nature as well as the alienation of men from each other. Even when we are not faithful, God nevertheless remains faithful. This is the reason why he concluded a Covenant, first with the people he had chosen; and then, in the fullness of time he renewed this alliance by making Jesus Christ the unique mediator between God and man (1 Tim 2:5). He concluded this New and eternal Covenant through the blood Jesus Christ has shed for the many for the forgiveness of sins (Mt 26:28).

If this is the center of the Christian message, then the theme of penance and reconciliation concerns the Church, which is, for the world, the sacrament of reconciliation in its entire existence, in its doctrine as well as in its life. On the other hand, one may say also that the loss of the sense of sin, which we see occurring nowadays in many parts of the world, has its roots in the loss of the sense of God and leads subsequently to a loss of the sense of man. For this reason, in preaching conversion and reconciliation, the Church remains faithful both to God and to man; as a steward entrusted with the divine mysteries (cf. 1 Cor 4:1) it serves at the same time the salvation of man.

In this context, which is both theological and anthropological, "without separation and confusion", the International Theological Commission submits

Reprinted from *Origins*, Jan. 2, 1984. This document was approved by the Commission "*in forma specifica*".

its paper, which it was asked to prepare for the Synod of Bishops, 1983. It is not its intention to say everything on the subject, and it does not want to dwell on what is generally known and acknowledged. It is nevertheless of the opinion that it would not meet the expectations that are with reason placed on it, if it would immediately or even exclusively deal with the theological and pastoral problems that are more immediately pressing. It is convinced that penance and reconciliation are of great importance in the encounter with the various cultures in which men live. On the other hand, it also believes that there is an inseparable link between the doctrine and the living praxis of the Church. For this reason it proposes to submit its reflections in three stages:

1. an analysis of the contemporary anthropological situation of (the sacrament of) penance in relation to the present crisis of man
2. the biblical, historical, and dogmatic foundations of the doctrine of (the sacrament of) penance
3. reflections on some important questions of the doctrine and the praxis of (the sacrament of) penance

A. ANTHROPOLOGICAL CONTEXT OF PENANCE

I. *The Essence of Penance from an Anthropological Point of View*

1. Guilt and sin, penance and conversion, are found everywhere among men. They are to be found in all religions and cultures, even if they have taken different forms in the course of history. The call to penance and the message of the Old and New Testaments concerning reconciliation given by God presuppose these universal human phenomena and purify and transcend them.

In the understanding of the Bible, conversion and penance are man's answer to God's offer of a reconciliation, rendered possible and conveyed by God's grace. Penance is, therefore, at the same time a gift of God and a free, *morally responsible* act of man (*actus humanus*), in which man as the responsible subject avows his evil acts but at the same time changes his life by a personal decision and gives it a new direction to God. It follows from this union of the divine and human in the act of penance that pastoral efforts in favor of a renewal of the penitential attitude and of the sacrament of penance must take, necessarily, the anthropological element into account, i.e., the economic, sociological, psychological, and spiritual presuppositions of penance.

2. The contemporary crisis in the understanding and praxis of penance is concerned neither exclusively nor always primarily with dogmatic, disciplinary, and pastoral questions of detail. In large areas of the present world a loss of the

sense of sin, and hence of penance, has occurred. This situation has many causes. We should, in the first case, draw attention to causes that are internal to the Church. Because of the way in which it was practiced in the Church until the recent past, many Christians felt that it was void of meaning and efficacy from the human point of view. The practice of penance as it is has, in many cases, hardly anything to do with the life of man and the dramatic situation of the present day.

To this a more extraecclesial aspect must be added. The present crisis of penance is, in the last analysis, rooted in a crisis of modern man, in particular of man influenced by the ideas of Western civilization, and by the way in which he understands himself to the exclusion of any realization of sin and guilt in his life. Nowadays guilt and sin are very often no longer understood as an original element of man's personal responsibility but as secondary phenomena, derived from nature, culture, society, history, circumstances, the unconscious, etc. They are therefore to be explained as an ideology or as an illusion. In this way personal conscience has been weakened, and the often unconscious influences of the social norms of a largely de-Christianized world have become stronger.

3. The renewal of the anthropological presuppositions of penance must therefore begin with the renewal of the understanding of man as a morally and religiously responsible person. The personal dignity of man consists in his human liberty, which entails the possibility of becoming guilty, a truth that must be restressed. The task of realizing oneself is part of being human. Basic to the notion of the primacy of the person over things is the idea that man is not only an object of anonymous physiological, economic, social, and cultural forces but is also a free, responsible subject, who is himself the cause of tensions, disruptions, and alienations in the world. It follows that where sin and guilt are no longer basically acknowledged, something essentially human is endangered in man.

4. The unconditional dignity of man as a person is based, in the last analysis, on his relation to God, on his likeness to God, and on his being called by grace to enter into communion with God. For this reason man himself remains an unsolved problem to which only God can give the full and completely certain answer; yes, God and communion with God are the answers to the problem that man not only has but also is in his innermost self (GS, 21). Therefore, the renewal of man and of the awareness of his personal dignity must begin with conversion to God and the renewal of community with him. Conversely, when the Church calls man a convert to God it is a "sign and protection of the transcendence of the human person" (GS, 76).

II. *Anthropological Dimensions of Penance*

1. The human person is essentially linked to a body. This implies dependence on physiological, economic, sociological, cultural, and psychological conditions. In addition, man's guilt and sins express themselves in the organizations and structures created by man and by society. In their turn these organizations and structures exercise a profound influence on people living in them, render the exercise of liberty more difficult, and may even be an invitation to sin. Structures that come from sin and are marked by it may have an alienating and destructive influence on man. Nevertheless, despite the weight of their influence on the personal conduct of individuals we can, at the most, speak of "sinful structures" and "structural sin" only in an analogous sense. In the proper sense of the term only man is capable of sin. However, because these structures are the product of sin and can again become an occasion of sin, and even invite to sin, penance and conversion, whenever possible, must work for a change in these structures. Such changes presuppose personal conversion and must be brought about by means that agree with and that lead to reconciliation.

The question of how this can be brought about depends on the position and the possibilities of the individual in a given society. Large sections of mankind nowadays are forced to accept a whole world of suffering and penance because of evil structures in the economic, social, and political fields. The attempt to escape from these structures entails for many a renouncing of possessions or positions; this can also be a penitential experience. The attempt to palliate or remove evil structures may even lead to great sacrifices and persecution, which must then be borne in a spirit of penance.

In these different ways it becomes clear to us that confession and penance must, of necessity, have a bodily and worldly dimension and lead to bodily fruits of penance. By such a conversion of the entire person to God, the return and homecoming of all reality to God take place.

2. Corporeal and social dimensions must be borne in mind equally in the human person. Hence, conversion to God is irrevocably connected with conversion to one's brother. For God is the Father of all men. Through him and under him all men make up one family. Conversion is, for that reason, only authentic when it includes the implementation of the exigencies of justice and the struggle for a just order, for peace and justice. Reconciliation with God must lead to reconciliation with our brethren and must contribute to the establishment of a communion of love for which the Church is the sacrament, that is, a sign and instrument. Conversion to God, however, has not only social consequences but also social presuppositions. Only those who experience love can open themselves in love for God and for their neighbors. Therefore, penance should not be understood as a mere private and innermost attitude. Because (not "although") it is a personal act, it also has a social

dimension. This point of view is also of importance for the justification of the ecclesial and sacramental aspects of penance.

3. Man is a being who lives in time and history. He can only find his own identity when he avows his sinful past and opens himself to a new future. Sin may indeed be understood as an *incurvatio hominis* or as *amor curvus*. Conversion consists in man giving up this egotistical, stifling concentration on himself and opening up to God and his fellowmen. Both things take place in the confession of guilt. Here man confesses his sinful past as his own, by opening himself up before God and before man, saying what he has on his mind, so that he may reach a fresh future in the community with God and with his brethren. From the anthropological point of view such an avowal is already an essential element of penance, and already at the level of psychical and social life it has a liberating and reconciling effect. The renewal of the sacrament of penance can take this anthropological insight as its starting point and in this way render personal confession of sins understandable again. It may, and should, learn also from these anthropological insights and conceive the sacrament of penance more clearly as a sacrament with a dialogue structure and realize it as such in practice.

4. Wherever men convert themselves in this way, do penance and confess their guilt, they touch upon the deepest secret of the person, which in its turn refers to the secret of God. Wherever this happens, by way of anticipation, man's hope is fulfilled in the ultimate meaning and in the eschatological reconciliation of the world, which in its plenitude has been given and revealed to us only through Jesus Christ. Because penance in its general human and religious form anticipates in a fragmentary way what is given by Jesus Christ to those who believe, it may be designated as a *sacramentum legis naturae* (cf. St. Thomas Aquinas, *In IV Sent.*, 22, q. 2, a. 3).

B. THEOLOGICAL FOUNDATIONS OF PENANCE

I. *The Theological Foundations*

1. The message of the Old and New Testaments, which surpasses by far all human expectations, is intrinsically theocentric. Its object is that the divine being of God and his glory are revealed, that his Kingdom comes, that his will be done, and his name be hallowed (Mt 6:9; Lk 11:2). Correspondingly, the Decalogue begins with these words: "I am the Lord your God" (Ex 20:2; Dt 5:6). The demand that man give himself wholly to God and to his fellowmen acquires with Jesus a new height and depth of content and also an intensity that surpass those of the Old Testament (cf. Mt 12:29–31 par.).

By contrast, sin is the attitude and act of a man who does not acknowledge God and his Kingdom. For this reason it is described in holy Scripture as disobedience, as idolatry, and as the willful autonomy of man carried to an extreme. Because of such an aversion from God and an inordinate conversion to created things and values, man ultimately misses the truth that he is a creature; he is alienated from himself (cf. Rom 1:21ff.). By returning again to God in conversion, he also finds again the meaning of his own existence.

2. The Old Testament idea of God is determined by the idea of Covenant. God is described as a loving bridegroom, a bountiful father; he is *dives in misericordia,* always intent on forgiveness and reconciliation, always ready to renew his Covenant. It is also true that God's wrath is a reality. It shows that in his love God allows himself to be affected because of the evil in the world and that he reacts against injustice and lies. In this perspective sin is described as breaking the Covenant, and it is compared to adultery.

But finally, already in the prophets, hope in the grace and faithfulness of God is the first and last word. Radical demands and a call to conversion are wholly and definitively embedded in Jesus' message of salvation (Lk 6:35). With him the Gospel has an absolute priority over the law. This does not mean that there are no longer any moral demands. Rather, the moral demands and call to conversion that Jesus makes can be understood and realized only in the framework of his joyous message. Man's conversion and total surrender are only made possible by the promise of God's love and his prevenient will to forgive, which make man free and encourage him. Conversion and penance, therefore, are no mere human efforts but a gift of grace. For in his own attempts at conversion man is always conditioned by sin and injustice and by a lack of peace, freedom, and reconciliation. Only God can heal man in his innermost self and grant him a qualitatively new start by giving him a new heart (Jer 31:33; Ezek 36:26). It is not that we reconcile ourselves with God; it is God who through Christ reconciles us to him (2 Cor 5:8).

3. Neither sin nor the conversion of man is understood in an individualistic way in the Old and New Testaments. On the contrary, and especially with the prophets, sins against social justice are condemned by God in the name of the Covenant. The Old and New Testaments consider man in solidarity with his people and with the whole of mankind (cf. Gen 3; Rom 5), that is, in solidarity with the new people of God. On the other hand, the prophets of the seventh and sixth centuries before Christ had already discovered man's personal responsibility as an individual.

Conversion to Jesus Christ calls the individual away from his attachment to his own people in order to insert him into the new people of God, which embraces all peoples. More particularly, the grace of conversion requires a triple answer from man: in the first place, a real change of heart, a new spirit and intention, are necessary. Conversion and penance are a fundamental option (cf. on this point C, III, 3f) of the person directed toward God, as well as a complete renunciation of sin.

In the second place, Jeremiah expected the sinner to confess his guilt publicly and to promise to correct his conduct "before Yahweh" (Jer 36:5–7). According to Jesus, well-intentioned, confident faith (cf. Mk 1:15), contrite confession, and prayer for pardon are likewise the beginning of conversion and the starting point of a change of life (cf. Lk 11:4; cf. 18:10–14).

Finally, penance should express itself in a radical revolution of one's entire life and in all its areas. The fulfillment of justice and readiness to forgive one's neighbor belong above all to this (cf. Mt 18:21–35; Lk 17:4).

II. *Christological Foundations*

1. The Old Testament already looks forward to the New Covenant in which God gives man a new heart and a new spirit (Jer 31:31–33; Ezek 36:26f.). Isaiah expects the "servant of God" (Is 53), Malachi the "angel of the Covenant" (Malachi 3:1). Jesus knows that the salvation of the coming Kingdom of God is already present in his own existence (Lk 10:23f.). Hence, according to him the center of the demand for conversion consists in accepting, in faith and as a child, salvation that is already promised (Mk 10:15), in converting oneself to him in belief (Lk 12:8ff.), in the hearing and keeping of his word (Lk 10:38–42; 11:27f.), and in following him (cf. Mt 8:19f., 21f.).

Conversion, therefore, now also consists in decision for Jesus, in which the coming Kingdom of God is at the same time decided on. But Jesus must have realized from the very start that in his demand he was asking too much from his disciples and hearers, and that, from a human point of view, he would fail, just like the prophets and the Baptist. But in his confidence in God his Father he could nevertheless carry on with his message and connect it, probably from the very beginning, with the thought of his suffering (cf. Mk 12:1–12). In baptism we die as Jesus died on the Cross, and this is the fundamental basis of all Christian penance.

2. The New Testament denotes the Cross of Jesus Christ with concepts such as vicarious representation, sacrifice, atonement. All these concepts are nowadays poorly understood by a great number of people and hence must be carefully deciphered and interpreted. In an introductory and preparatory way this can be done by pointing to the solidarity itself of human life: the being, deeds, and omissions of the other and the others affect the individual in his own being and doing. In this way, a new understanding can be reached of the fact that by his obedience and his self-surrender "for the many", Jesus Christ's work of redemption becomes fully understandable only if one adds to this that in Jesus Christ God himself has entered into the *conditio humana*. In this

way, through the Person of the God-Man Jesus Christ, God has reconciled the world to himself (cf. 2 Cor 5:14, 17). Redemption from sin, otherwise known as the forgiveness of sin, takes place therefore by means of the *admirabile commercium.* God has made "the sinless one into sin so that in him we might become the justice of God" (2 Cor 5:21; cf. Rom 8:3f.; Gal 3:13; 1 Pet 2:24). "In the human nature united to himself the Son of God, by overcoming death through his own death and Resurrection, redeemed man and changed him into a new creation" (*LG,* 7). "By the very fact that human nature was assumed, not absorbed in him, it has been raised in us also to a dignity beyond comparison. For by his Incarnation, he, the Son of God, has in a certain way united himself with each man" (*GS,* 22; cf. International Theological Commission, *Select Questions on Christology* [1979], see Chapter 9 above.

3. Christian penance is a participation in the suffering and death of Christ. This comes about *per fidem et caritatem et per fidei sacramenta* (St. Thomas Aquinas, *S.Th.,* III, q. 49, a. 3, ad 6). Christian penance has its foundation in baptism, which is the sacrament of conversion for the forgiveness of sins (Acts 2:38) and the sacrament of faith. Therefore, it should have a determining influence on the entire Christian life (cf. Rom 6:3ff.).

Christian penance must therefore not be understood in the first place as an ethical and ascetic event but as basically sacramental, viz., the gift of a new existence, granted by God, which also urges ethical and ascetical practice. It should not only take place in individual acts, but it should also characterize the entire Christian life. In this statement the justified concern of Luther's first thesis on indulgences, October 31, 1517, is also intimated. As a matter of fact, penance should not be reduced by being considered in a personal isolation. Following Jesus as it does, it must be understood both as obedience to the Father and as a vicarious service for the others and for the world.

III. *The Ecclesial Foundations*

1. The work of reconciliation with God through Jesus Christ remains a living reality present to us through the action of the Holy Spirit and acquires its encompassing fulfillment in the community of the faithful. This does not mean that through the action of the Holy Spirit reconciliation may not also take place outside of the boundaries of the Church.

Nevertheless, the Church is, in Jesus Christ, the sacramental sign of forgiveness and reconciliation for the entire world. It is this in a threefold way: (a) it is the Church of the poor, of the suffering, and of those deprived of their rights. It strives to alleviate their needs and to serve Jesus Christ in them; (b) it is the Church of sinners, which is at the same time holy and has to go the road of conversion and renewal; (c) it is the persecuted Church, which "presses

forward amid the persecutions of the world and the consolations of God"
(*LG,* 8).

Thus the Church lives a life based on the pardon of God in Jesus Christ. It
is not only the sign of this reconciliation but also its efficacious instrument in
the world (cf. *LG,* 1:11f.). It is this also by preaching and mediating the
reconciliation that God has granted us in Jesus Christ. It does so by the word
of penance and reconciliation, by the sacrament of penance, and by its entire
ministry of reconciliation.

2. The Church can only be the sacramental sign of reconciliation for the
world when and if the word and the ministry of reconciliation are alive in it.
According to the example of the God who reconciles, the fraternal community of the faithful also implies willingness to forgive (cf. Eph 4:32; Col 3:13;
Lk 17:3f.; Mt 18:21f.).

The reconciliation received from God aims at fraternal forgiveness (cf. Mt
5:23f.; 6:12, 14f.; Mk 11:25f.). When the community forgives, the reconciling
love of Jesus Christ addresses itself to the sinful brother. Admonition and
blame (cf. Mt 18:15f.) are meant to save the brother whose salvation is
endangered. This care for the erring brother must be untiring and the readiness to forgive unlimited (cf. Mt 18:21).

The seriousness of God's offer of salvation requires that another aspect be
considered. By sin the Church itself is wounded, precisely as the sign of the
reconciliation between God and men, and between men among themselves.
For this reason faults against the worship of God and offenses against fraternal
love are intimately connected. The judgment comprises both aspects, as is
shown by the way Jesus identifies himself with the humblest of his brothers
(cf. Mt 25:40–45). Hence the Church itself must time and time again be
purified from evil and take the road of conversion and renewal (*LG,* 8). Thus
conversion to God is at the same time a movement toward our brothers and
reconciliation with the ecclesial community. He who converts himself must
go over the road along which reconciliation first came to him. *Ecclesiae caritas
quae per Spiritum Sanctum diffunditur in cordibus vestris, participum suorum peccata
dimittit* (St. Augustine, *In Evang. Ioan.,* 121, 4). Thus there is no forgiveness
of faults without the Church. Reconciliation with the Church and reconciliation with God cannot be separated from one another.

3. Despite its admonitions to forgive without limit, the New Testament
does not discount the possibility of serious offenses against Christian love
toward God and one's neighbors. Here a praxis of reconciliation in stages
becomes visible: obtaining the favor of the brother, admonition, correction,
strong language, exclusion (cf. Mt 18:15–20; also 1 Cor 5:1–13; 2 Cor 2:5–11;
7:10–13). Here stubbornness and persistence in a particular wrong attitude are
very important criteria for the seriousness of the fault. A measure of exclusion
can become unavoidable for the sake of the health of the community.

4. The power to forgive sins, which Jesus possesses (cf. Mk 2:1–12), is also given "to men" (Mt 9:8). In certain passages of the New Testament it is the Church as a whole which in this regard stands in the limelight, although it is indicated that it has ministries and that there are different offices. Even if in a few texts the group of persons to which a task is assigned cannot be fully ascertained (cf. Mt 18:15–20; Jn 20:22f.), the general duty to reconciliation (cf. Mt 5:23f.) is nevertheless distinguished from the general ministerial power to forgive or to retain sins.

The word and the ministry of reconciliation are indeed committed in a special way to the apostolic ministry in the Church. This ministry stands in the place of Christ, and through it we hear God (2 Cor 5:20; cf. 1 Cor 5:1–13; 2 Cor 2:5–11; 7:10–13). Here the relation with the encompassing power to teach and to direct, granted to Peter, is important (cf. Mt 16:18f.). Precisely with regard to sins that exclude from the Kingdom of God (1 Cor 6:9f.; Gal 5:20f.; Eph 5:5; Rev 21:8, 22:15; cf. Heb 6:4–6; 10:26f.; 1 Jn 5:16; Mt 12:31f.), the full power to forgive or to retain sins cannot but be granted to him to whom the keys of the Kingdom of heaven have been given.

A fundamental transgression against God and the Church can only be overcome by an unmistakable, authentic word of forgiveness in the name of Jesus Christ and on his authority (*auctoritas*). The specific power required for this was given by Jesus to the ministry, which presides with authority over the Church and to which the ministry of unity has also been committed.

Through this authorized ministry instituted by Jesus Christ, God himself accomplishes the forgiveness of sins (cf. Mt 16:19; 18:18; Jn 20:23). In accordance with what Christ established, God forgives through the Holy Spirit when the Church absolves from sins by her official ministers. This structure of the sacrament of penance became ever clearer to the Church when in the course of its history it kept reflecting on the meaning of holy Scripture (cf. the importance of Mt 16:19 and 18:18 in Tertullian, *De Pudicitia*, XXI, 9f.; Origen, *De Oratione*, 28, on Jn 20:23), and it was declared final and binding by the Council of Trent (cf. the reference to Jn 20:23 in *DS*, 1670, 1679, 1684, 1692, 1703). The Second Vatican Council moved the ecclesial aspect of penance once more to the foreground (*LG*, 11; cf. also the revised *Ordo Paenitentiae*).

Summing up we must therefore say: The exclusion (*excommunicatio* = to bind) from the community of the Church, the *universale salutis sacramentum*, is valid in heaven (before God), and means the exclusion from the sacraments of salvation, in particular from the Eucharist. Readmission (*reconciliatio* = to absolve) to the full communion with the Church (= the Communion of the Eucharist) is at the same time reconciliation with God (forgiveness of sins). Thus in sacramental penance the readmission to full sacramental Communion with the Church is the sacramental sign (*res et sacramentum*) of the renewed communion with God (*res sacramenti*). This idea the early Church had of the sacrament of penance should again be urged more clearly on the mind of the Church by preaching and catechesis.

5. Penance must be seen in an organic relationship with the other sacraments. In the first place it is present in all as the word of reconciliation in the comprehensive teaching of the Church. A central witness to this is the Article in the Creed: "I believe . . . in the forgiveness of sins."

Forgiveness shows itself in the conversion, by which the believer turns away from his previous sinful life, converts himself with all his heart to God, who by the remission of his sins liberates him from his situation without grace and opens a new life for him in the Spirit. This conversion basically takes place by faith and baptism. In baptism the gift of the Spirit is sealed; the believer becomes a member of the Body of Christ, the Church.

Therefore baptism also remains the basis for the forgiveness of later sins. The penance of the baptized, which for those born from water and the Spirit often appeared to be wholly impossible and in the early Church was felt to be possible only once, requires not only—as in baptism—sincere contrition as a disposition to forgiveness but also the firm will to mend one's life. Expiation is also involved, as well as confession before the Church represented by its official ministers. Although it ‑refers back to baptism, penance is a sacrament of its own with a sacramental sign of its own and a special effect. According to its innermost nature it is a complement of baptism (cf. the classical expressions *paenitentia secunda:* Tertullian, *De Paenitentia,* VII, 10; *secunda planca salutis, De Paenitentia,* IV, 2; XII, 9; quoted in *DS,* 1542; *laboriosus quidam baptismus,* Gregory Nazianzen, *Oratio,* 39, 17, quoted in *DS,* 1672).

As a second baptism the sacrament of penance is at the same time presupposed for receiving the other sacraments (cf. Richard of St. Victor, *De Potestate Ligandi et Solvendi,* 21). This applies in particular to the Eucharist, which is the culminating point of the spiritual life of the Church and of the individual faithful (*LG,* 11). The "anointing of the sick" has already from the beginning of the Church a relationship with the forgiveness of sins (cf. James 5:15; furthermore *DS,* 1695f., 1699, 1716). "*Hoc sacramentum praebet etiam, si necesse est, veniam peccatorum et consummationen paenitentiae christianae*" (*Ordo unctionis infirmorum, Praenotandam,* no. 6, with a reference to *DS,* 1694, 1696).

At the approach of the end of man's pilgrimage, or at least in the case of a serious physical threat to his life, the anointing of the sick is a particular form of the renewal of baptism. All this shows the close connection between baptism, penance and anointing of the sick and their relationship with the Eucharist, which is the center of the sacramental life of the Church.

IV. *Foundations in the Light of the History of Dogma and of Theology*

a. Nonvariables in the Historical Development

1. The essential structure of the sacrament of penance is already attested in the apostolic and postapostolic Church. A particular, although not exclusive, importance attaches to the expression "binding and loosing" of Matthew 16:19 and 18:18, as well as to its variant in John 20:23 (cf. above, B, III, 4). The essence of this sacrament, therefore, consists in the fact that the reconciliation of the sinner with God takes place by the reconciliation with the Church.

Correspondingly, the sign of the sacrament of penance consists in a dual process: on the one hand, in the human acts of a conversion inspired by love (*contritio* and *conversio*), external confession, satisfaction (*satisfactio*). This is the anthropological dimension. On the other hand, it consists in the fact that the ecclesial community, under the direction of the bishop and the priest, offers forgiveness of sins in the name of Jesus Christ, establishing the necessary forms of satisfaction, prays for the sinner, and does penance with him vicariously, so as to absolve him finally and to pronounce his full belonging to the ecclesial community. This is the ecclesial dimension.

2. In the historical development of the sacrament of penance the decisive process consists in that the personal character of this sacrament was ever better acknowledged and expressed. In this process of personalization, the living Tradition of the Church has carried on and brought to completion the evolution that had already established itself in the Old Testament and in the passage from the Old to the New Testament, and made it in a profound way her very own (cf. above, B, I, 3). Since this basic orientation of the biblical testimony has found expression in the universal consensus of the Church, it is now irreversible. This also had the effect, it is true, of pushing the ecclesial dimension of the sacrament of penance into the background of consciousness for a long time. In our century this community aspect of penance has been rediscovered. The Second Vatican Council and the new *Ordo Paenitentiae* have taken up this insight. Yet it should have still deeper roots in the awareness of the faithful so that we may reach again an objective balance of both aspects of penance.

To carry out this pastoral task correctly in our own time, a more through-going knowledge of the history of the sacrament of penance is required. This will show, in addition to the permanence of the essential elements, a variation that cannot be ignored. And in this way it also points to the freedom the Church today has—*"salva eorum substantia"* (*DS*, 1728; cf. 3857)—in the renewal of the sacrament of penance.

b. Variables in the Historical Development

1. Reconciliation in the Church has always been related to two different situations of Christian life: on the one hand, the realization that we live a life based on and given in baptism imposes on us a continuous struggle against daily sins. On the other hand, the praxis of penance should bring back to a life of grace and return the rights of baptism to those who violated the seal of baptism by sins that lead to death and that are irreconcilable with Christian existence.

In the early Church everyday sins were forgiven by liturgical prayers in which the entire community participated, in particular during the celebration of the Eucharist on Sunday; in addition, many other forms of penance had their importance (cf. below, C, I, 3). In the proper sense of the term, the discipline of penance in the early Church was concerned with the second situation. In the transition from public to private penance, the sacrament, which was now administered repeatedly, was more and more extended from mortal to venial sins. One single form of the sacrament now related to the two different situations of the Christian life mentioned above.

2. That form of the confession of sins, which is tied to spiritual direction, is a very ancient treasure of the Church. On the one hand, it belongs to the very structure of the sacrament instituted by Jesus Christ. On the other hand, as can be seen in the monastic and spiritual traditions, it also has a place outside the sacrament. Both these data are factors in the development that is guided by the spiritual experience of the Church. At the end of the period of the primitive Church, in the early and high Middle Ages, this led to a growing desire for private confessions of one's sins; spiritual direction and sacramental confession became increasingly connected with each other.

3. The Church has shown that it enjoys a wide margin of freedom with regard to the discipline and the pastoral aspects of reconciliation, in that it attempted to shape the discipline of its sacraments—the basic structure of which is unchangeable—in accordance with the needs of the Christian people and for the benefit of the ministry to the faithful. The most conspicuous change has been the passing from the predominance of public penance to the prevalence of private penance.

Because of the difficulties and the disaffection attaching to the more ancient practice, the Church, at a time of change in the area of secular living, arrived at a renewed discipline, which was not possible without drawbacks and conflicts. This made the sacrament more attractive and gave it a form that proved more fruitful. This new form of the sacrament also led to a change in the order of the acts of penance: originally reconciliation was granted only after the imposed satisfaction had been carried out; now the absolution was given immediately after the confession of sins.

4. Moreover, the Church passed from a discipline that knew certain cases of unforgivable sins, that is, of lifelong penance, to a discipline under which all sins are forgiven. Furthermore, there was a transition from the practice of administering penance once only to a penance that could be repeated; from the imposition of very severe penances that extended over a long spell of time to lighter penance; from a penance that was originally mainly public, which corresponded to public sins, to private penance; from reconciliation reserved to the bishop to absolution granted by the priest; from the deprecatory to the indicative formula of absolution.

5. The form of the acts of the penitent was also subject to a noteworthy change. It often happened that one of these was emphasized so much that others were relegated to the background. Public penance in the primitive Church stood under the sign of public satisfaction, which lasted for a set period of time; private penance in the Middle Ages and in the modern period, on the other hand, underlined the importance of contrition; in our own time the accent is more on confession. Since this confession often concerns less serious sins, the sacrament of penance in many cases took the form of a "cheap sacrament". "Confession", "contrition", and satisfaction must be considered once more, therefore, in their intrinsic relationship.

c. The Doctrine of the Council of Trent

1. The doctrinal statement of the Council of Trent on the sacrament of penance (*DS*, 1667–93, 1701–15) must be understood as an answer to certain precise questions that were actual in those days in the controversy with the Protestants. This context and this intention are of great importance for the interpretation of the decree of Trent on the sacrament of penance.

In the sixteenth century the questions relating to reconciliation and the sacrament of penance, which were the subject of controversy between Catholics and Protestants, were mainly concerned with the following points:

a. the institution by Jesus Christ of penance as a sacrament different from baptism

b. the relation of justifying faith to contrition, to confession, to satisfaction, and to sacramental absolution

c. the obligation to confess all mortal sins, and furthermore the question whether such a confession is possible, whether it is required by God or by the Church, whether it contradicts justification by faith, whether it leads to peace or to a troubled conscience

d. the function of the confessor, in particular whether he is correctly described as the one who announces the unconditional promise of the pardon of sins by God for the sake of Christ, or whether he must also be designated as a physician, guide of souls, one who established the order of creation, which was disturbed by sin, and a judge

2. In answer to these questions the Council of Trent taught the following points about sacramental confession:

a. It serves the spiritual good and salvation of man, and this without necessarily leading to the disturbance of conscience: on the contrary, the fruit of this sacrament is frequently peace of joy of conscience, and comfort of the soul (*DS,* 1674, 1682).

b. Confession is a necessary part of the sacrament of penance, and it is not right to reduce the sacrament simply to announcing an unconditional promise of God's forgiveness through the merits of Christ (*DS,* 1679, 1706, 1709).

c. Confession must be clear and unambiguous where there is question of mortal sins; this obligation does not exist in the case where it is impossible to remember one's sins (*DS,* 1682, 1707).

d. The integral confession of mortal sins is required by God's saving will (*iure divino*), in order that the Church can exercise through the sacred ministry the task of a judge, a physician, a director of souls, and that of reestablishing the order of creation disrupted by sin (*DS,* 1679, 1680, 1685, 1692, 1707).

3. Despite the differences concerning the necessity of the confession of all mortal sins, there is a noteworthy consensus between the Council of Trent (*DS,* 1680, 1682) and the basic writings of the Lutheran confession with regard to the spiritual fruits of the confession of sins and of absolution. This is important in the ecumenical dialogue and can be a point of departure for discussions on differences that still remain.

4. Despite contemporary cultural pluralism, there are lasting real needs common to all men and to which the manifold aid coming to man by God's pity from the sacrament of penance provides even today the best answer:

a. healing of spiritual diseases
b. growth in one's personal spiritual life
c. being an occasion for the reestablishment of the order disturbed by sin, and for promoting justice, as this is demanded by the social nature of both sin and forgiveness
d. the effective attribution of the forgiveness of sins by God and by the Church in a time in which there often is enmity between men and among nations
e. placing one's sins and state of mind before the judgment of the Church, which by its pastoral ministry watches over the authenticity of conversion to God and to the Church

5. Since these human and spiritual needs are real and in the sacrament of penance means of salvation answering to them have been given by God, the confession of grave sins, which, after a careful examination of his conscience, the sinner remembers, must have in virtue of God's saving will (*iure divino*) an indispensable place in obtaining the absolution. If not, the Church cannot accomplish the tasks assigned to it by Jesus Christ in the Holy Spirit (*iure divino*), viz., the service of a physician, direction of souls, the advocacy of justice and love in private as well as in public life, heralding the divine promises of forgiveness and peace in a world often dominated by sin and animosity, a judgment of the authenticity of the conversion to God and to the Church.

6. The integral confession of mortal sins, therefore, necessarily belongs to the sacrament of penance (*iure divino*), and thus it is not left to the judgment of the individual or to the decision of the Church. However, the Council of Trent does acknowledge the concept of a sacramental confession *in voto* (*DS*, 1543). For this reason, in extraordinary emergency situations in which such an integral confession is not possible, the Church can allow the postponement of the confession and grant the absolution individually or in a group (general absolution), without previous confession. In such a situation the Church acts with the spiritual possibilities of the moment, but must see to it that mortal sins are confessed subsequently and must instruct the faithful about this obligation by appropriate means. The Council of Trent does not itself pronounce on the nature and extent of these emergency situations.

To solve difficult pastoral problems the extension, recommended by many, of the situations mentioned in the *Normae Pastorales* of 1972 and in the *Ordo Paenitentiae* is not the only possible solution. For situations in which there is no *copia confessorum* (*DS*, 1661) the Council rather points to the efficacy of contrition for reconciliation, made perfect by love (*contritio*), which grants reconciliation with God when it includes the *votum sacramenti* and hence the *votum confessionis* (*DS*, 1677). How the Church should proceed in this matter concretely on the basis of the doctrine of the Council of Trent is a question of pastoral prudence and love (cf. on this below, C, II, 4).

C. REFLECTIONS ON SOME QUESTIONS
THAT ARE OF IMPORTANCE FOR THE
PRACTICE OF THE SACRAMENT

I. *Unity and Diversity of the Forms of Penance*

1. There are certain forms of penance in pre- and extrabiblical religion. They attest the presence in humanity of a primitive knowledge about guilt and the need of redemption. The Christian message of penance and reconciliation presupposes that once and for all penance and satisfaction have been made by Jesus Christ in the obedient ministry of his life and death on the Cross. Christian penance, therefore, is chiefly distinguished from the practice of penance in other religions by the fact that it lets itself be determined by the Spirit of Jesus Christ and brings it to expression under the signs of the personal attitude of penance and in bodily works of penance.

For this reason the Christian forms of penance must be animated at least inchoately and *in nucleo* by faith, hope, and love. Faith above all is the ground, the permanent center, and the principle of life for Christian penance. Hope gives the converted the firm confidence that he may proceed with God's help on the road of conversion and so attain eschatological salvation. Connected with this is the so-called gradualism of the character of penance: it may start with "lower" motivations: fear of punishment, fear of God's judgment, etc. (cf. *DS*, 1526, 1678), and from these ascend to the "higher" motivations.

Love of God and of one's neighbor is the deepest motive for repentance for the baptized, for his conversion, and for his passage to a new life (*DS*, 1526, 1676). From this comes a new way of living in community with God and with one's fellowmen (cf. above all A, II, 2f; B, III, 2, 4).

2. Although the forms of Christian penance and of forgiveness of sins are many, there is, despite this pluriformity, a structural unity of the entire process: insight into one's personal guilt or into that of the community, repentance for what has been done or omitted, confession of one's guilt, willingness to change one's life, (including, where possible, a basically necessary reparation for inflicted damage), prayer for forgiveness, reception of the gift of reconciliation (absolution). The praxis of confession, therefore, is, in the several forms of penance, a dynamic process with a coherent structure. The pastoral education for and the catechesis of reconciliation must consequently keep in mind the whole as well as the balance of individual elements.

3. Penance, although one, unfolds itself in a variety of ways. Holy Scripture and the Fathers stress the three basic forms that go together: fasting, praying, and charity (Tob 12:8, referred to in *DS*, 1543). Origen (*Hom. in*

Lev., II, 4) and Cassian (*Coll. patrum,* XX, 8) present more detailed lists of forms of the forgiving of sins. Besides the effects of the grace of baptism and the suffering of martyrdom, which are fundamental, they mention among others, reconciliation with one's brother, the tears of penance, care for the salvation of one's neighbor, the intercession of the saints, and love.

In the living Tradition of the Church, the reading of holy Scripture and the recital of the Our Father are added to this. We should, however, also mention the factual conversion in one's daily life, inspired by faith, for instance, the change of attitude and mentality, speaking with others in a community on guilt and sin, gestures of reconciliation, *correctio fraterna,* a confession in view of reconciliation; certain forms of spiritual direction are of the nature to redeem sins, as, for instance the *révision de vie,* the *capitulum culpae,* a talk with one's spiritual director, confession to *staretz* in connection with monastic practice. The ethical consequences of a new direction of life should not be forgotten: a change in one's living style, asceticism and manifold renouncement, acts of charity, works of mercy, expiation, and vicarious suffering.

The liturgical forms of the forgiveness of sins consist not only in penitential celebrations but also in meditation and prayer, the intercession of the Church, and the Liturgy of the Hours, in reading the meditation of holy Scripture, and in the celebration of the Eucharist (cf. *DS,* 1743 and below, C, IV, 1). In addition to the specifically sacramental forms of forgiveness of sins (cf. the three celebrations in the *Ordo Paenitentiae*), the three ways of carrying out remission in the present discipline of penance should also be recalled (cf the *absolutio a censuris* and the *dispensatio ab irregularitae* in the *Ordo Paenitentiae,* appendix 1). The times and days of penance in the course of the liturgical year are more particular occasions on which the Church performs the ministry of penance.

II. *Individual Confessions, Reconciliation Services, General Absolution*

1. Awareness of the wealth and multiplicity of the forms of penance has often grown dim. It must therefore be made stronger and receive attention both in preaching and in the pastoral practice of penance. Isolating the sacrament of penance from the context of the entire Christian life, which is inspired by the spirit of reconciliation, leads to an atrophy of the sacrament itself. Narrowing down the ministry of reconciliation to only a few forms can make one coresponsible for the crisis in the sacrament of penance and the well-known dangers of ritualism, and of a reduction to the state of a private exercise of piety.

The various means of reconciliation should, therefore, not be placed in competition with each other. Rather, the intrinsic unity and dynamic relationship between the individual forms of penance should be explained and made visible. The forms mentioned above (cf. C, I, 3) are shown above all to be useful for "venial sins". Forgiveness of sins can indeed be granted in many ways: forgiveness of the sins of everyday life is always given when contrition informed by love is present (*contritio*) (cf. *DS*, 1677).

2. To the extent that the forms of penance mentioned above and the dimensions of reconciliation are practiced more clearly and in a more convincing way in the daily life of the Christian, the desire for sacramental private confession is also bound to increase. Above all grave sins must be expressed in the most individual and comprehensive way possible before the Church and its official representatives. A general confession of sins is not sufficient, because the sinner must, inasmuch as possible, give concrete expression to the truth of his guilt and the nature of his sins, and also because such an individual, personal confession of guilt strengthens and deepens true contrition. Both anthropological (A, II, 3) and theological (B, III, 4; B, IV, c, 2.5f) considerations favor this thesis.

Sacramental power is needed to forgive such sins. It is true that today the authentic form of private confession needs to be profoundly renewed in its spiritual aspects, and this in connection with the revised *Ordo Paenitentiae*. Without such a renewal the Church will not be able to cope with the crisis of the sacrament of penance. For this a better spiritual and theological formation of priests is required, in order that they may be able to deal with what is now demanded from confession, viz., the latter should contain more elements of spiritual direction and of fraternal exchange. Under this aspect the so-called confession of devotion retains its importance.

3. The term *celebrationes paenitentiales* is often understood in different ways. Among such penitential celebrations one thinks principally of the liturgical celebrations of a congregation in which the call to penance and the promise of reconciliation are given expression, and a general confession of sins takes place without individual confession or an individual or general absolution. This type of penitential celebration can help place the community aspects of sin and forgiveness more to the foreground. They can awaken and deepen the spirit of penance and reconciliation. However, they must not be placed on the same level as the sacrament of penance, much less replace it.

In their orientation these penitential celebrations are certainly directed toward sacramental private confession, but they do not merely have the function of inviting to conversion and creating the dispositions required for the sacrament: with regard to daily sins, they can become a true occasion of pardon, provided there is a real spirit of conversion and sufficient contrition (*contritio*). In this way the *celebrationes paenitentiales* may acquire an efficacious significance for salvation, even if they are not a sacramental form of penance.

4. The *Ordo Paenitentiae* also mentions a common celebration of reconciliation with a general confession and general absolution. This presupposes ethically and juridically unambiguous norms that must be observed in pastoral work (cf. the *Normae pastorales circa absolutionem sacramentalem generali modo impertiendam* of 1972, and the *Ordo Paenitentiae,* Pastoral Introduction, 35).

It follows from this that this form of sacramental reconciliation applies to extraordinary situations of emergency. As current praxis has occasionally shown, the granting of general absolution outside such extraordinary emergency situations easily leads to basic misunderstandings of a fundamental nature about the essence of the sacrament of penance, and in particular about the basic necessity of personal confession of sins, the efficacy of sacramental absolution, which presupposes contrition, and at least the *votum confessionis.* This type of misunderstanding and the ensuing abuses damage the spirit of the sacrament of reconciliation.

The difficult and even somewhat dramatic pastoral situations in many parts of the Church today mean that many faithful hardly have the possibility of receiving the sacrament of penance. In these critical situations it is indispensable to show the faithful concerned ways that will enable them to have access to the forgiveness of sins and to receiving the Eucharist. In these cases the Tradition of the Church, confirmed by the Council of Trent, acknowledges the possibility of a Christian obtaining the forgiveness of grave sin by perfect contrition. According to the same Tradition perfect contrition also always implies the desire (*votum*) of receiving the sacrament of penance as soon as possible (*DS,* 1677).

Where there is no *copia confessorum,* such a perfect contrition is probably a sufficient disposition for receiving the Eucharist, according to the doctrine of the Council of Trent (*DS,* 1661; cf. above, B, IV, c, 6). In most situations of such pastoral emergency this possibility is more suitable than general absolution, because in this way the obligation to the later personal confession can be made psychologically more understandable to most of the faithful. The ecclesial dimension of such a perfect act of contrition can be expressed by the penitential celebrations we mentioned above.

5. The contemporary crisis of penance and of the sacrament of penance cannot be solved by stressing only one form of penance, but only by means of a view that takes into account the complex relationships between the different forms of penance and how they mutually complement each other. In this matter it will also be important to integrate in a better way the individual forms of penance into the administration of the sacrament of penance, in order to bring sacramental penance more forcefully into the consciousness of the faithful.

III. *Sin, Grave Sin, Venial Sins*

1. Conversion, as a turning away from sin and a turning to God, presupposes an awareness that sin is outside of and contrary to salvation. The contemporary crisis of the sacrament of penance is intimately connected with a crisis in the sense of and understanding of sin, as can be seen in many parts of the world. The fact that the pastoral efforts of the Church (in sermons, catechesis, personal talks, for example) in many ways have not been as good as they ought also plays a role in this contemporary crisis for a good number of Christians (cf. above, A, I, 2). Therefore it is necessary to express again the authentic, Christian understanding of sin.

It is true that holy Scripture does not provide a proper definition of sin, but it nevertheless brings a rich variety of individual statements, which, in many ways, and with regard to different aspects, contain an interpretation of sin. Thus in holy Scripture, among other things, sin is called:

a. being outside of salvation (*hamartia*): atheism, refusal to acknowledge God (Rom 1:18ff.), a breaking of the alliance with God.
b. opposition to the revealed will of God (*anomia*): contradiction of the law of God and his Commandments.
c. injustice (*adikia*): the refusal to live in the justice that God has given.
d. falsehood and darkness (*pseudos, skotos*): opposition to the truth of God, to Jesus Christ, who is the way, the truth, and the life (Jn 14:6), to one's fellowmen, and to the truth of being man. He who sins does not come into the truth of being man. He who sins does not come into the light but remains in darkness (cf. also above, B, I, 1–3).

Against this background it becomes clear that every sin stands in a relationship with God: it is an aversion from God and his will, and it makes created things absolute. The sense and the understanding of sin can only be developed with the conjunction of preaching about God and his message of salvation. For this it is necessary that the sense of God is renewed and deepened. One can understand how it is that only God can forgive sins only if it is made clear that sin stands in a relation to God.

2. Already in the parenesis and the practice of penance of the early Christian communities distinctions concerning the nature of sins were made:

a. sins that exclude from the Kingdom of God, such as leading an immoral life, idolatry, adultery, pederasty, avarice, and so on (cf. 1 Cor 6:9f.), and that also lead to exclusion from the community (cf. 1 Cor 5:1–13) (cf. above, B, III, 4)
b. the so-called daily sins (*peccata quotidiana*)

The fundamental difference between grave and nongrave sins is taught by the entire Tradition of the Church, even if important differences in terminology and in the appraisal of individual sins occur.

Attempts are often made to replace this division into grave sins and nongrave sins, or to complete it by the threefold distinction between *crimina* (*peccata capitalia*), *peccata gravia*, and *peccata venialia*. This tripartite division has its justification on the phenomenological and descriptive levels. On the theological level, however, we may not obscure the fundamental distinction between the "Yes" and "No" to God, between the state of grace, life, and communion and friendship with God on the one hand, and the state of sin, aversion from God, on the other hand, which leads to the loss of eternal life. For from the nature of both types of sins it follows that there cannot be a third between them. In this way the traditional dual distinction gives expression to the serious character of man's moral decision.

3. With these distinctions and divisions of the earlier centuries, the Church has already taken into account—each time in the ways of thinking and the forms of expression of a particular period—that which today is of importance in the contemporary insights and circumstances in doctrinal proclamations of the Magisterium and in theological reflection.

a. From the subjective side, the freedom of the human person must be seen from the point of view of its relation to God. Thus at the very center of his being as a person, man has the possibility of saying "No" to God as a basic decision. This then becomes a fundamental decision concerning the meaning of his existence. This fundamental decision takes place in man's heart, in the midst of his personal being. But on the level of man's existence in time and space, it is mediated by concrete acts in which this fundamental decision expresses itself in a more or less complete way. To this must be added that on account of his fractured existence, which was made so by original sin. Even while maintaining his fundamental "Yes" to God, man can live with "a divided heart", i.e., he can live and act without engaging himself fully.

b. From the objective side, there are on the one hand the Commandments that are of grave obligation, with the obligation to an act in which one gives himself entirely, and on the other hand the Commandments that only impose a light obligation. Transgressions of these latter Commandments can ordinarily be called sin in an analogous sense only, but they may nevertheless not be considered insignificant. For even such acts are part of a free decision and can become the expression of a fundamental decision.

4. The Church teaches this theological understanding of grave sin when it speaks about it as a revolt against God, a refusal of God, and a turning of oneself toward created things. It does so when it considers a grave sin that contradicts Christian love or the order of creation willed by God in an important matter, above all in the violation of the dignity of the human person.

The Sacred Congregation for the Doctrine of the Faith stresses this second aspect in referring to the answer Jesus gave to the young man who asked him: "Master, what must I do to possess eternal life?" Jesus said to him: "If you wish to enter eternal life, keep the Commandments." He said: "Which?" Jesus replied: "You must not kill. You must not commit adultery. You must not steal. You must not bear false witness. Honor your father and your mother and love your neighbor as yourself" (Mt 19:16–19) (cf. the Declaration on Some Questions of Sexual Ethics, 1975, 10).

In conformity with this doctrine of the Church, the fundamental option determines in the last analysis the moral condition of man. But the concept of fundamental option is not a criterion that allows one to distinguish concretely between grave and venial sins. The concept, rather, is a help to make the nature of grave sin theologically clear. Although basically man can express his option or change it in a single act, viz., in those cases in which this act is done with full awareness and complete freedom, it is not necessary that this fundamental option in its entirely enter into each individual act, so that each sin does not have to be, *eo ipso,* a revision of an (explicit or implicit) fundamental option.

According to the ecclesiastical and theological Tradition, a grave sin is not so readily possible, and is not what is normal for a Christian who lives in the state of grace and who earnestly takes part in the sacramental life of the Church. The reason for this is the "gravity pull" of grace (cf. St. Thomas Aquinas, *De Veritate,* q. 27, 1 ad 9).

IV. *Penance and the Eucharist*

1. The question of the relationship between penance and the Eucharist places before us two facts in the Tradition of the Church that seem to contradict each other but that in reality are enriched owing to this tension.

a. On the one hand the Eucharist is the sacrament of unity and of love for Christians who live in grace. The early Church only admitted to holy Communion Christians who, when they had committed sins that lead to death, had been reconciled after their public penance. For the same reason the Council of Trent demands that he who is aware of having committed a grave sin should not receive holy Communion or celebrate the Mass before having received the sacrament of penance (*DS,* 1647, 1661). However, the Council does not say that this is *iure divino;* rather it transposes the obligation to examine oneself to the level of discipline—so as to eat this bread and drink this cup only after having done this (1 Cor 11:28). Therefore, this obligation can admit of an exception, for instance, when there is no *copia confessorum;* in this case, however, contributors must include the *votum sacramenti* (cf. above, B, IV, c, 6; II, 4). Nevertheless, the Council does not accept the broader interpretation of Cajetan (*DS*, 1661). Therefore the Eucharist is no alternative to penance in the Church.

b. On the other hand, the Eucharist does forgive sins. The early Church was convinced that the Eucharist forgives daily sins (cf. the testimony of the ancient liturgies). The Council of Trent also speaks of the Eucharist as a "counterpoison by which we are freed from venial faults and are preserved from grave sins" (*DS,* 1638; cf. 1740). The Eucharist grants the forgiveness of grave sins by means of the grace and the gift of penance (*DS,* 1743), which according to the doctrine of the Council includes sacramental confession at least *in voto* (cf. above, B, IV, c, 6).

This power of the Eucharist to forgive venial sins has its basis in the fact that it is the *memoria,* i.e., the sacramental representation (*repraesentatio*) of the sacrifice of Jesus Christ, which was once and for all, whose blood was to be poured out in forgiveness of sins (Mt 26:28) (cf. *DS,* 1743).

2. Confession and Communion of children. The education of the conscience of children to the understanding of sin and penance must take into account their age and their experience. The conscience and experience of adults cannot be simply transplanted. Correspondingly, the confession of children as the sacrament of conversion (*metanoia*) cannot be considered the end of religious instruction. The child will grow in the living understanding of penance precisely by the practice of the sacraments.

CONCLUSION

The renewal of the attitude and of the sacrament of conversion and of reconciliation is connected with the message about God, who is rich in pity (Eph 2:4), and above all with the message of reconciliation that God has given once and for all through the death and Resurrection of Jesus Christ. This message he keeps permanently present in the Church in the Holy Spirit. The renewal that is conversion and reconciliation only becomes possible, therefore, when we succeed in awakening again the sense of God and in deepening in the Church the spirit of the imitation of Jesus as well as the attitude of faith, hope, and love. The renewal of the sacrament of penance is only possible within the whole made up by the organic structure of all sacraments and forms of penance.

This all-embracing spiritual renewal, which springs up from the heart of the Christian message, includes a renewal of the sense of the personal dignity of man, who by grace is called to community and friendship with God. Only when man converts himself and acknowledges that God is God, and when he lives out of a communion with God, will he discover the true meaning of his own existence. For this reason it is important that in the attempts at a renewal of this sacrament its anthropological dimensions be taken into account, and the inseparable connection between reconciliation with God and reconciliation with the Church and with one's fellowmen is brought about. In this way, in creative faithfulness to the Tradition of the Church, and along the lines of the new *Ordo Paenitentiae,* we can give the sacrament of penance a form that answers to the spiritual needs of man.

Finally, but by no means least in importance, the Church must be by her confession, liturgy, and *diakonia* the sacrament, that is, the sign and instrument of reconciliation for the world. Through all that which it is and which it believes, it must witness in the Holy Spirit to, and render present, the message of reconciliation that God has given through Jesus Christ.

12

PROPOSITIONS ON THE DIGNITY AND RIGHTS OF THE HUMAN PERSON

1. INTRODUCTION

1.1. *The Importance of This Study*

The Church's mission is to announce the *kerygma* of salvation for all mankind, which was achieved by the death and Resurrection of Christ. This salvation has its origin in the Father, who sent the Son, and it is given to individual human beings as a participation in the divine life, through the infusion of the Spirit. The acceptance of the Christian *kerygma* demands faith; and the new life that results from grace implies a change of life, a conversion, with many consequences in all phases of the life of the believer. It is not possible for the Church to omit preaching the dignity and rights of the human person. Every Christian must strive to realize these values for every human being. This duty and right of God's people to proclaim and defend actively the dignity of the human person is particularly urgent today because of the simultaneous appearance of two compelling factors: on one hand, there is a deep crisis as to the nature of human and Christian values; on the other, the modern conscience is profoundly sensitive to injustices perpetrated against human beings. The new Code of Canon Law (747 § 2) speaks clearly about this obligation and right: "It is in the Church's competence to proclaim the moral principles of the social order in all times and places and to make judgments on all human matters, when this is demanded by the fundamental rights of human beings or the salvation of souls." Today in the preaching and action of the Church, this proclamation has happily an outstanding place.

The ITC wishes to cooperate in this thrust to the best of its ability. When certain possible misunderstandings (1.2–3) have been excluded, some propositions of a theological nature will be presented (2.1–2.2.3) in this regard, first from the teachings of Holy Scripture (2.1.1) and from the present teaching of

This document was approved by the Commission *"in forma specifica"*.

the Roman Magisterium (2.1.2). The movement of thought will be twofold. The "natural law of nations" (*GS*, 79) and the theology of salvation history will be both scrutinized. Special attention will be paid to these, especially in today's situation, so that it will appear how human dignity, both actively and passively, should be viewed in man as created (2.2.1), in man as sinner (2.2.2), and in man as redeemed (2.2.3). Finally, in the last part certain comparisons will be made and certain points of a philosophical and juridical nature will be proposed.

1.2. *The Hierarchy of Human Rights*

Certain human rights are so "fundamental" (Decl. 1948) that they can never be gainsaid without belittling the dignity of human persons. In this regard the International Pact of 1966 (art. 412) presents certain rights that can never be put aside, e.g., every person's inherent right to life (art. 6), recognition of the dignity of the physical person and the fundamental equality of persons (art. 16), freedom of conscience and religion (art. 17). Religious liberty may in some respects (the Supreme Pontiff, John Paul II, speaking to participants in the Fifth Colloquium Juridicum: *L'Osservatore Romano,* March 11, 1984, p. 6) be regarded as the basis of all other rights. Some, however, would claim this primacy for equality.

There are other rights of a lesser nature (International Convention, 1966, art. 5.2) but also basically essential. Among these are civil, political, economic, social, and cultural rights concerned with more particular situations. Indeed, in some sense these rights will appear at times as contingent consequences of fundamental rights, as conditions involved in practical application, and also as closely bound to actual circumstances of times and places. Consequently, provided there is no denial of the fundamental rights themselves, these lesser rights may present themselves as less immune, especially in difficult circumstances.

Finally, there are other human rights that are not requisites of the rights of nations or strictly obligatory norms but postulates of an ideal of progress toward a universal "humanization". What is at stake here is the achievement of the highest human ideal, and this is the obligation—since this is the desire of all citizens—of all those charged with the care of the common good and political life. International assistance may be necessary here in particular cases (Decl. 1948, end of Prologue).

When it comes to a judgment about the practical implementation of these lesser rights, the demands of the common good must be borne in mind or, in other words, the totality "of social conditions that make possible, for groups and for individuals, the full and timely attainment of their own perfection" (*GS*, 26).

1.3. *Variation in the Meaning of "the Dignity of Human Persons"*

The notion of human dignity is not presented univocally today. Some define it in terms of man's absolute autonomy without any relationship to a transcendent God, denying moreover the very existence of a God who creates and cares (*GS,* 20; cf. 3.1.3). Others, while certainly taking due account of man's intrinsic worth and honoring his personal freedoms, in a word his relative autonomy, see all this as ultimately grounded in the supreme transcendency of God, even if this is presented in differing versions (*GS,* 12, 14–16, 36; cf. 2.1.2, 2.2.1, 2.2.3). Finally, others find the source and meaning of man's status, at any rate since the fall (2.2.2), above all in man's union with Jesus Christ, Our Lord, who is God and man in a perfect way (*GS,* 22, 32, 38, 45; cf. 2.2.3).

2. THE THEOLOGY OF THE DIGNITY AND RIGHTS OF MEN

2.1. *In Some Theological Sources*

2.1.1. The Biblical Perspective

It is true that the Bible does not use a twentieth-century vocabulary, but it does supply premises from which a developed doctrine about the dignity and rights of human beings may be deduced.

The basis of the moral and social life of Israel is the Covenant between God and man. In this merciful attitude toward man's deprivation, God manifests his intimate character, his justice (*sedaqua Yahweh*), and demands in turn man's obedience to the divine ordinances. Such obedience includes reverence for the rights of others with respect to life, honor, truth, the dignity of marriage, and the use of possessions. In a most special way the *anawim Yahweh,* the poor and oppressed, are deserving of respect. In return for his gifts God asks of man a life spirit of mercy and loyalty (*hesed weemeth*). The rights of people involve obligations and duties on the part of others, a fact that the apostle Paul will demonstrate later by showing in depth the implications of charity in the second part of the Decalogue (Rom 13:8–10).

In the Old Testament the prophets hammered home the need for utter sincerity in observing the demands of the Covenant (Jer 31:31–39; Ezek 36); they protested with passion against individual and corporate injustice. They fanned the hope of the people in a future Savior.

This new and final Kingdom of God was preached by Jesus and in fact set in motion in his Person and in his activity. He demands a complete change of heart, *metanoia,* in his disciples and announces to them a new way of living, a new justice, in which they will imitate the ways of the heavenly Father (cf. Mt 5:48; Lk 6:36) and, as a result, hold and treat all men as brothers. Jesus favored the poor and miserable and opposed the arrogance of those made self-sufficient by power and wealth. In his death and Resurrection, by words and example, he championed *existence for others,* that is, the supreme gift of his own life in sacrifice. He "did not count . . . a thing to be grasped" (Phil 2:6) and so "emptied himself" (Phil 2:7). "He was made obedient unto death" (Phil 2:8), and for the good of all he poured out and offered his blood in a New Covenant (Lk 22:20).

The apostolic writings show the Church of Christ's disciples to be a new creation brought about by the Holy Spirit. By his operation human beings are given the dignity of being God's adopted children. Where relations with others are concerned, the harvest of the Holy Spirit is love, peace, patience, kindness, goodness, restraint, gentleness. On the other hand, excluded are quarrels, contentiousness, envy, rage, selfish ambitions, dissensions, murder, etc. (cf. Gal 5:19–23).

2.1.2. The Roman Magisterium Today

The Roman Magisterium, which is supreme in the Catholic Church, is in our time a staunch protagonist in many documents of the doctrine of the dignity of the human person and of human rights. The constant preaching and action of the following Popes should be brought to mind: John XXIII (*Pacem in Terris*), Paul VI (*Populorum Progressio*), John Paul II (*Redemptor Hominis, Dives in Misericordia, Laborem Exercens,* and his addresses during his worldwide pastoral visits). More attention too should be paid to the teaching of Vatican II, especially in the pastoral constitution *Gaudium et Spes,* 12ff., on human dignity, 41, on human rights, etc. The new Code of Canon Law (1983), which is, as it were, the last act of Vatican II,[1] gives special treatment to "the obligation and rights of all the faithful" (208–23) in the life of the Church.

In today's apostolic preaching two main and complementary lines appear. The first, which may be called a line of ascent, belongs to the natural law of peoples, buttressed by reasoning and debate but confirmed and raised to a

---

[1] The Holy Father, John Paul II, has often spoken in this vein, e.g., addresses "To the Introductory Courses to the New Code", "To Bishops", 2: *L'Osservatore Romano,* Nov. 21–22, 1983, p. 4; "To Canon Lawyers", 3: *L'Osservatore Romano,* Dec. 9–10, 1983, p. 7; address "To Sacred Roman Rota": *AAS* 76 (1984): 644; the apostolic exhortation *Redemptionis Donum,* 2: *AAS* 76 (1984):514.

higher level by Divine Revelation, thanks to the Gospel. Here man appears not as an object and instrument to be used but as an intermediate end in himself, whose welfare both personal and ultimately as a being for God must be our aim. Man enjoys a spiritual soul, reason, freedom, conscience, responsibility, an active role in society. All interpersonal relationships between people must be conducted in such a way that this fundamental human dignity be given full honor, that justice and kindness be fully observed, and the needs of all be fulfilled to the best of our ability.

The second line of today's apostolic preaching on man's rights may be called a line of descent. It shows the basis and demands of human rights in the light of the Word of God coming down to share the human condition and in the paschal sacrifice, so that all men should be endowed with the dignity of God's adopted sons and both benefit from and contribute to a deeper justice and charity. In the course of propositions still to come, this Christological foundation for human rights will get very special attention when considered in the light and grace of the theology of salvation history. At this point all that needs to be noted is that the principle of reciprocity, affirmed by so many religions and philosophies as the foundation of human rights, should find a Christological meaning in the preaching of Christ: "Therefore be merciful as your heavenly Father is merciful.... Do to men as you would wish them to do to you" (Lk 6:36, 31).

2.2. The Dignity and Rights of Human Persons in the Light of "the Theology of Salvation History"

2.2.1. Man as a Created Being

According to the doctrine of the Second Vatican Council, special attention should be paid to the theology of salvation history by seeking out the links between this theology and our human dignity. This link is especially obvious in the light of Christ as Creator (Jn 1:3), as incarnate (Jn 1:14), as "given up to death because of our sins, and raised to life to justify us" (cf. Rom 4:25).

In the first place let man be looked at as a created being. Therein the wisdom, power, and goodness of God appear, a fact that Scripture often recalls (especially Gen 1–3). And even human reason is at home here (Rom 1:20). Indeed, the theological doctrine that sees man under certain aspects as God's creation converges with metaphysics and moral philosophy.

The biblical model of the creation of man reveals three very important considerations.

Man in his fullness is historically spirit, soul, body (1 Th 5:23). He is not simply the product of a general evolution of matter but the result of specialized divine action and made in God's likeness (Gen 1:27). Man is not simply body; he is endowed too with intelligence, seeking for truth, with a conscience and a sense of responsibility that he is to follow in the pursuit of the good in freedom. It is in these attributes that the foundation of man's dignity is to be found, a most prized gift always and in everyone.

Indeed—and this is the second biblical datum—human beings are created as social beings, differing in sex (Gen 1:27; 2:24). Sex is the source of marriage, in which the spouses are united in mutual love and respect for each other, as also for the children born of this love considered in all its fullness. Families go on to form larger units, communities and societies, where the same respect for persons must flourish. All human beings, since they are God's creation and endowed with the same fundamental characteristics, deserve the highest consideration. Granted man's social nature, personal growth, and social progress go hand in hand. Indeed, since human beings absolutely need society, the origin, the subject, and the goal of all social institutions is and should be the human person (GS, 25 § 1).

The third aspect of man considered in his state of "created nature" is in his God-given mission to "preside" (Gen 1:26) over all created things as a terrestrial viceroy. Herein he develops his dignity in various ways, in the creation of art, in scientific discovery and invention, in philosophy and culture in general, etc. Nor can a preoccupation with human rights be omitted here, since all human activities must be governed by just distribution among all of common responsibilities, efforts at production, and distribution of the fruits of labor. "As man's potential grows, so do his personal and social responsibilities" (GS, 34 § 3).

2.2.2. Man as a Sinner

The second stage of the history of salvation is marked by the reality of sin. As Paul the apostle wrote to the Romans (1:21): "Knowing God, they have refused to honor him as God, or to give him thanks. Hence all their thinking has ended in futility, and their misguided minds are plunged in darkness." Abandoning justice toward God and their brothers, they gave priority to selfishness, a spirit of domination, wealth unjustly acquired, the jettisoning of responsibilities, and false pleasures of all kinds. This conduct led to blindness and hardening of heart, which the Magisterium constantly denounces in these times as the loss of *a sense of sin,* a phenomenon that is very widespread. Because of this most serious moral vacuum, there is a danger that the preaching and practice of human rights will often be rendered simply sterile. At times, in effect, all efforts are directed at changing *sinful structures,* with no allusion whatever to the need for a radical change of heart. We must not forget that such *structures* are the result of personal sins, which in turn are rooted in original sin, and, when viewed cumulatively, are at times referred to as the *sin of the world.* What is worse, granted man's permanent selfish bent since the fall, the more technical and economic capabilities he enjoys, the more subject he becomes to the temptation to see himself as an absolute lord (rather than as a viceroy under God) and go on to create for others even more oppressive structures.

Since the Church puts forth her doctrine of sin in the fullest terms possible, she urges men to *metanoia,* so that they will abandon injustice and embrace justice in all its scope. This justice must recognize God's rights and those of man, our brother. In that way the preaching of the doctrine of sin is a valid contribution toward promoting the rights of persons. By means of this doctrine Christians have an original contribution to make in the universal effort to promote the quest for these rights. In the forceful preaching of the Church, sin and its influence in creating sinful structures are highlighted not as an exercise in pessimism but so that men may look to that way of recovery and rebuilding to be found in the grace Christ offers to all. Historically speaking, *fallen nature* is an expectation of the redemption. Besides, fallen nature—even in the case of the most depraved—is not to be regarded as stripped of every right and dignity and incapable of anything positive in the social field (cf. Rom 2:14). It is God's image deformed but to be remade by grace, and which, even prior to this reformation, has its rights and should be urged both personally and as far as the world is concerned to move toward better things. This exhortation should not be made in such a way as to lead men to think this earth is the sum of their hope. A Christian's theological hope is focused on the ultimate, and not on anything less. The effort to make this earth better must always go on, even if, as in the case of Christ himself, the only earthly results are the Cross and human failure. Even in this likeness to the crucified Christ, the man who strives for justice is preparing God's final Kingdom.

2.2.3. Man Redeemed by Christ

The importance of the *theology of salvation history* taught by Vatican II also comes to the fore if the effects of the redemption won for us by Christ, Our Lord, are considered. By his Cross and Resurrection Christ, the Redeemer, offers to men salvation, grace, and an active charity and opens in a most ample way access to participation in the life of God. At the same time, "by the same token [he] animates, purifies, and strengthens those generous aspirations that urge on humanity to make human life better and to subject the whole earth to that enterprise" (GS, 38 § 1).

Christ gives these gifts, tasks, and rights to *redeemed nature,* and he calls all men to become one with him in his paschal mystery, "by that faith that is active in love" (Gal 5:6). It is by this that we know what love is: that Christ laid down his life for us. And we in our turn are bound to lay down our lives for our brothers (1 Jn 3:16), indulging no more in selfishness, envy, greed, wicked desires, the boast of wealth, concupiscence of the eyes, and the pride of life (1 Jn 2:16). For his own part Paul the apostle describes this death to sin and new life *in Christ* in such a way that, as a result, Christ's disciples will not be conceited or think too highly of themselves (cf. Rom 12:3) but will as members of the Christian fellowship honor the different vocations and "gifts" allotted by God to different people (Rom 12:4–8), "let fraternal love breed warmth of mutual affection and give pride of place to one another in esteem" (Rom 12:10), "care as much about each other as about yourselves. Do not be haughty, but go about with humble folk. Do not keep thinking how wise you are. Never pay back evil for evil. Let your aims be such as all men count honorable" (Rom 12:16–17; cf. Rom 6:1–14; 12:3–8).

The teaching, example, and paschal mystery of Jesus are a confirmation that men's efforts to build a world more in keeping with human dignity are just and reasonable. And they also act as the index of crisis whenever these efforts become misdirected, either by aiming at a purely earthly utopia or by using means opposed to the Gospel. And they surpass these efforts when the latter take on a merely human cast inasmuch as the Gospel opens up a new and specifically Christian religious foundation for human rights and dignity and gives men new and wider perspectives as God's adopted sons and brothers in Christ—who suffered and rose again.

Christ was present and is present to all human history. "In the beginning was the Word. . . . All things came to be through him" (Jn 1:1–3). "He is the image of the invisible God; his is the primacy over all created things. In him everything in heaven and on earth was created" (Col 1:15–16; cf. 1 Cor 8:6; Heb 1:1–4). In his Incarnation he conferred maximum dignity on human nature. For that reason the Son of God is united in some way to every man (GS, 22 § 2; RH, 8). He shared the human condition in all its aspects, except sin, in his life on earth. In the spiritual and bodily sufferings he underwent, notably in his Passion, he took his part with us in our common nature. His passage from death to Resurrection is a new gift to be communicated to all men. In Christ, who died and rose again, are to be found the firstfruits of the new man, transformed and transformable to a higher state.

In that way in heart and action, every follower of Christ must shape himself in terms of the demands of the new life and act according to *Christian dignity.* He will be particularly sensitive to honoring the rights of all (Rom

13:8–10). Following the law of Christ (Gal 6:2) and the new Commandment of charity (cf. Jn 13:34), he will not be selfish or insistent on what is his (cf. 1 Cor 13:5).

In his use of terrestrial realities, the Christian should cooperate with the revelation of the glory of creation and so free it from the shackles of servitude to sin (cf. Rom 8:19–25), so that it will serve to give justice to all on the lines of "the values of human dignity, fraternal union, and freedom" (*GS*, 39 § 3). In that way we who bore the likeness of the terrestrial Adam in our mortal lives because of sin must now through a new life bear the likeness of the heavenly Adam (cf. 1 Cor 15:49), who is always the one *who exists for* the good of all men.

3. COMPARISONS AND SUGGESTIONS

3.1. *Comparisons*

3.1.1. The Variety of Human Conditions

Having explained the specific Christian teaching on the dignity and rights of human persons as it is presented in current Christian theology, the International Theological Commission regards it as opportune to look at the same topic in terms of its relationship with other disciplines, various cultures, and the present-day social, economic, and political milieus in the so-called First, Second, and Third Worlds.

The concept of the dignity of the human person and of the rights of man, which in a very special way was worked out under the influence of the Christian doctrine on man, has also been buttressed by all the statements of this century. Today, however, whether through misinterpretation or direct violation, it is too often seriously obstructed and even disfigured!

Looking back over the last thirty years we find good reasons for rejoicing at the significant progress made in this field. We cannot at the same time pass over in silence the fact that the world in which we live has more than its share of instances of injustice and oppression. One is easily inclined to observe that there is a growing divergence between the genuinely significant statements of the United Nations and the at times massive increase in violations of human rights at all levels of society and worldwide.[2]

Faced with this state of affairs, today's Christian wishes to distinguish good from evil not, indeed, to condemn, but to ensure that all become more aware and effective in pursuing the welfare of all by observing and esteeming the rights and dignity of human persons. As a Christian he urges not alone the acceptance of the Kingdom of Christ, a Kingdom of justice, love, and peace, but also seeks to create human and reasonable conditions among human beings. He is aware of his own specific Christian identity, which involves obedience, even on earth, to the "paradoxical laws" of God's Kingdom,[3] and of the intimate ties that link him to all men of goodwill. In this spirit the International Theological Commission was of the opinion that two suggestions in particular could be proposed even to non-Catholics.

The first belongs to general philosophical inspiration, whether traditional or contemporary. The second is more concrete and aims at securing better international collaboration and a better juridical approach even by powers and governments that in certain cases may care little for people's liberties.

3.1.2. The First World

In the so-called First World[4] the dignity and rights of man are loudly proclaimed and care is taken toward their practical implementation. This is a considerable value. But, if the rights of men are understood merely in a formal way with stress on the factor of autonomy, such a view may bring on a view of liberty that runs the strong risk of not producing genuine human dignity. Paradoxically, genuine liberty and dignity can be corrupted in such a situation, as the following examples indicate. Many countries in the First World are very rich, and the citizens enjoy great personal liberty, and both are strongly fostered. However, in these societies

---

[2] John Paul II, *Letter to K. Waldheim*, United Nations Secretary-General, 30th anniversary of the "Universal Declaration of the Rights of Man": *AAS* 71 (1979): 122. On this matter the Holy Father added further: "If the truths and principles in this document [i.e., the "Universal Declaration of the Rights of Man" by U.N.] were to be forgotten or ignored and were thus to lose the genuine self-evidence that distinguished them at the time they were brought painfully to birth, then the noble purpose of the United Nations Organization could be faced with the threat of a new destruction", *Address to U.N.*, 9: *AAS* 71 (1979): 1149.

[3] *Epistle to Diognetus* 5: Funk 1, 396–400.

[4] The expression *First World* is little used, and then only among politicians and sociologists. It derives from the use of the term *Third World*, a term that arose in India after World War II. *GS*, 9, contrasts "developing nations . . . with other richer nations developing more rapidly".

the incentive to "consumerism" often bears in itself the seeds of selfishness.[5] In these First World societies the sense of higher values is often lost (naturalism); everyone looks only to his own interests (individualism); and the willingness to accept moral norms vanishes (autonomism;[6] practical laxism; the right, so-called, to be different). What happens then is that limits imposed on one's liberty with a view to the common good or for the maintenance of the rights and liberties of other people are resented, and an exaggerated libertarianism becomes the principle of social and moral life.[7] Further, in one and the same country extreme social differences exist, and not enough is done to avoid this or oppose it. While this is not exclusively true of the *First World,* it must be said that the prevailing mentality leads to the exploitation of the weak by those who are more powerful. And this is a sure way to a crisis in the matter of rights.

What has been said so far reveals that the legal norms that are promulgated in such societies with skill and much fanfare for the protection of the dignity and rights of man are insufficient—for that matter, they are never sufficient anywhere—unless men, having changed their hearts, and being renewed in the charity of Christ, do their very best to live according to the demands of social justice and in the spirit of their religious conversion.

3.1.3. The Second World

If we move from the First to the Second World, that is, to the world that has for its common characteristic what is called *real Marxism,* we meet various difficulties, the principal ones possibly being the evolution of Marxism itself and the differing complexions of post-Marxist theorizing. Here we shall consider only the kind of Marxism that is in vogue in some particular regime or other today, where the constitutions and laws have one way of looking at man and another way of acting, so much so that while the rights of man are

---

[5] "The blind love of one's own interest and the preoccupation with domination constantly allures the soul." Paul VI, apostolic Letter *Octogesima Adveniens* to Card. Roy, 15: *AAS* 63 (1971): 412.

[6] Those who defend this self-autonomy absolutely do not see that "in the divine disposition of things itself the just autonomy of the creature is by no means removed; rather it is given its true dignity and stability" (*GS,* 41). On the contrary, in any false conception of autonomy, "the dignity of the human person is by no means saved but perishes rather" (ibid).

[7] John XXIII gives a good description as to how the elements of social life should be balanced in the best way possible: "Since men are by nature gregarious, it is right that they should live side by side and seek each other's good. For that reason a proper way of living together demands that they should be unanimous as to mutual rights and obligations in principle and practice." Encyclical Letter *Pacem in Terris: AAS* 55 (1963): 264f.; cf. Paul VI, apostolic Letter *Octogesima Adveniens* to Card. Roy, 23: *AAS* 63 (1971): 417f.

verbally recognized, the meaning is quite different. This problem is presented not merely as a piece of information but for the sake of the Christians who must coexist in such places and who are required to cooperate. They are more-or-less tolerated as citizens but, in fact, tainted with suspicion.

According to *historical materialism* man is not created by God (a myth distorting reality) but is simply a result of the evolution of matter. Genuine human progress will be attained when the conditions of production and the human labor entailed are changed for the collective good by changing the economic structures on which the whole so-called *superstructure* is built and sustained. To attain this end each and every citizen must collectivize himself to the utmost.

As far as the rights and liberties of the citizen are concerned, three points are given maximum consideration.

All must embrace the law of the necessary evolution of matter realizing itself in the life of the collectivity; any concessions made to the individual are never to be regarded as a strictly private possession, but as an interim moment on the way to definitive common possession in the collectivity—and this in the light of the theory of a future final and perfect collective society.

Good and evil are defined solely in terms of historical evolution favoring the collectivity.

Therefore, the individual conscience does not exist but only the collective conscience as mirrored in the individual.

It is clear that the Marxist vocabulary on human dignity, rights, liberty, the person, conscience, religion, etc., differs altogether not only from the Christian teaching but also from the concepts of international law as expressed in many charters. Marxism sieves all these through its own mind.

In spite of these difficulties a wise and efficacious dialogue should be entered into and kept going.

3.1.4. The Third World

Other problems concerning the rights of man arise in the context of the so-called Third World. Here, obviously, conditions differ, where the *new peoples* may wish to make a large issue of retaining their native culture, to increase their political independence, and to promote technical and economic progress. It is therefore the social aspects of the rights of man that are paramount in these cases. The postcolonial period is not without an ambiguous inheritance; the colonial period was guilty of many injustices, and, consequently, these peoples properly expect a greater justice in political and economic relationships.

The new peoples frequently voice the objection that the full rights of international justice are not sufficiently acknowledged in their case. Their public power and political weight seem to them to be weaker than what prevails in the countries of the First and Second Worlds. A poorer nation can rarely vindicate its sovereignty fully unless it makes a pact with a richer or more powerful nation, which will wish to dominate.

The economy and international trade are often laden with injustices, for example, in the sale of what the country produces or in the wages of those who labor for the foreign and multinational concerns. Assistance from the rich nations is often minimal. Often again, rich nations show to poor nations that hardness of heart that was castigated by the prophets and by Our Lord Jesus himself. Rarely are the indigenous cultures prized as having value for the peoples themselves or for others. It is clear that in the Third World regions, also, there are deficiencies that must be removed if we are to make real progress. In these circumstances there is serious need for the witness of the Catholic Church in favor of those who are so sorely weighed down.

3.2. *Suggestions*

3.2.1. The Insights of Personalistic Philosophy

We have seen that there are many difficulties in the First, Second, and Third Worlds when it comes to the real definition and application of human rights. The Christian response to such difficulties is, we remember (3.1.1), the vitality "of a faith, believed and applied in the moral order" (*LG,* 25 § 1), as well as theology and Christian philosophy. Nor should other aids be forgotten, both practical (as far as international law is concerned, 3.2.2) and doctrinal (cf. 2.1 and 2.2). Especially in the field of philosophy, the International Theological Commission wishes to draw attention to helps of an introductory and explanatory kind that the present insights of personalism offer, particularly when they are rooted in a "permanently valid philosophical patrimony" (*OT,* 15), and in that way strengthened by traditional teaching.

As against materialistic naturalism (3.1.3) and atheistic existentialism, modern communitarian personalism teaches that man by his very nature, or at a more eminent level of being, has a finality that surpasses the physical *processus* of this world. This personalism is radically different from individualism; its primary approach is to see man in his relationship to others, and only in a secondary way does it see him as related to things. A person exists as such, and is able to attain fulfillment, only when he is united to and communicating with others. Understood like this, a personalist community is altogether different from purely political and social societies, which make little of spiritual reality and real autonomy.

In this perspective we should do well to seek out the basis of this personalism in traditional Christian philosophy, and St. Thomas Aquinas in particular. To grasp this more readily, it will help to recall that for Aquinas natural substances exist for action. Actions constitute the perfection of things. Among natural things, however, man has a singular status since he has intellect and liberty. Man, as a rational substance, has control of his own action, and this fact is honored by a special name. Man is a person. Some actions he shares with the animal kingdom, but certain actions belong to him alone: actions of reason (intellect) and will. Inasmuch as he is a free person, he must follow the vocation his reason will have shown him. This does not tie him to a single course. He is free to choose his own type of life and follow his own path. Every person, therefore, is defined also in terms of a vocation to be realized and a final destiny.

The exigencies that spring from his intimate personal being are so many tasks for his will. This duty (or necessity), which he may accept or reject, demands in the first place that man be conscious of who he really is and live in accordance with his own level of being. This duty can be understood in a more special way under the influence of religion. God's design is the source of what a man is as a human being and what it implies. To seek one's own perfection is to obey God's will.

Before all else he must inquire into the nature of that perfection, which should be regarded as the proper end and final destiny of the human being. This involves two questions: In what reality will man find this perfection (*finis qui*)? Through what action will he attain that thing that will make him happy (*finis quo*)?

According to personalism, the reality is another person, and the action is love. Love unites. However much a person is one and the same (ego) and consequently remains subjectively his own center in life, at the same time, if he is to be a full person, that *ego center* must journey somehow in love to another person, who then becomes the objective center of his life (other ego, other self, thou). In mutual love *I* and *thou* remain two, and still they become one (*us* in personalist usage). It is obvious that we have here a *gospel tracer* leading toward the New Testament doctrines of the union of the Divine Persons in the Most Holy Trinity as well as the union of people between themselves and with Christ, the Head, in the Mystical Body.

In human society justice guards and protects *the otherness* of the person, which can never be denied a free man. This virtue is founded on the respect every man owes to another. A person is not a means to be used but an end in himself and must be honored as such. Love involves this respect and justice inasmuch as it invites men to work in full freedom to ensure the good of others.

The rights of the human person depend on justice. Man has a right in justice to all the means necessary to develop himself and attain to fulfillment, subject indeed to the common good. What is specifically due him is the right to life. Then, since a man cannot develop himself without the enjoyment of material goods, he ought to have disposition of them. On the other hand, as master of himself, he should have the right to appropriate freedom and to coresponsibility.

In this perspective, which touches on faith, theology, and philosophy, certain hopes are now put forward, as a practical conclusion, toward a common and universal respect for human rights.

3.2.2. Proposal for a Common and Universal Observance of Human Rights

We have seen that in today's world there is a reasonably general consensus on the normative moral value of the rights of man. It is also clear that there is considerable disagreement when the discussion is centered on philosophical justification, juridical interpretation, or political possibilities, where the rights of man are concerned. As a result there is much ambiguity in this field. In practice we frequently meet injustices and violations of the freedoms of the person.

This granted, today in the matter of the realization of the rights of men, we should note what follows: since the value of human dignity makes it the highest good to be pursued in the moral order and the basis of juridical obligation, human rights must be clearly defined and given juridical expression.

The possibility of applying these fundamental rights in this way will depend on achieving a consensus that transcends differing philosophical and sociological conceptions of man. Should such a consensus be arrived at, it will serve as a basis for a common interpretation of the rights of man, at least in the political and social fields.

Such a basis is to be found in that triad of fundamental principles, namely, liberty, equality, and participation. This triad underlies the rights attached to personal liberty, juridical equality, and the exercise of the activities belonging to social, economic, cultural, and political life. The links that exist between the elements of this triad exclude a one-sided interpretation, e.g., liberalistic, functionalistic, or collectivistic.

All nations, then, in putting these fundamental rights into practice, should see to it that the elementary conditions for a dignified and free life exist. In such a matter it will of course be necessary to keep in mind the special conditions of each nation from the point of view of culture and social and political life.

Once the fundamental rights have been defined, they should be written into the Constitution and everywhere given juridical sanction. But it will be impossible to have the rights of man fully and universally acknowledged and reduced to practice unless all states, especially in the case of conflicts, recognize the jurisdiction of some international institution and refrain from using absolute power in the matter. To reach indeed this international juridical consensus, it will be necessary in a methodical way to set aside old ideological conflicts and also the narrower conception of ways of living that distinguish certain communities.

In the same way, in the family of nations each and every citizen should treasure these fundamental rights and cultivate the values that sustain them.

13

SELECT THEMES OF ECCLESIOLOGY ON THE OCCASION OF THE EIGHTH ANNIVERSARY OF THE CLOSING OF THE SECOND VATICAN COUNCIL

PREFACE

In this document the International Theological Commission will examine some of the great themes of the Dogmatic Constitution on the Church *Lumen Gentium.*

On the twentieth anniversary of the closing of the Second Vatican Council, the right approach seemed to be *both* by way of a direct study of the texts of the Constitution *and* via an analysis of the ecclesiological questions posed so sharply since its writing. First and foremost, it is Chapters I, II, III, and VII of *Lumen Gentium* that form the object of the studies presented in our report. We felt it important to go back over some of the Constitution's key positions. These have proved particularly fruitful in the life and theology of the Church, in the service of that *aggiornamento* desired by John XXIII and Paul VI. But they have also at times been so neglected and distorted as to have almost lost their original meaning. In addition, we found it necessary to examine certain other questions, whose presence in the Constitution is not so obvious. Examples would be the inculturation of Gospel and Church or the foundation of the Church by Christ. These themes have achieved considerable celebrity in later discussion.

Finally, without in any way regarding the Code of Canon Law of 1983 as a document of the same nature, and with the same bearing, as a conciliar Constitution, we have nevertheless made frequent appeal to it, in order to bring out more clearly the differences, convergence, and reciprocal illumination that relate these two great ecclesiological measures to each other. It has not escaped our attention that, writing some few months before the Extraordinary Synod of November 1985, our work may constitute a contribution to the task which that gathering will carry out.

This document was approved by the Commission *"in forma specifica".*

I. THE FOUNDATION OF THE CHURCH BY JESUS CHRIST

I.1. *The State of the Question*

The Church has consistently held to the assertion not only that Jesus Christ is the Church's foundation (*DS*, 774) but also that he himself willed to found a Church and did effectively so found one. The Church is born from the free decision of Jesus (*DS*, 3302ff.). The Church owes her existence to the gift Jesus made of his life on the Cross (*DS*, 539, 575). For all these reasons, the Second Vatican Council calls Jesus Christ the founder of the Church (e.g., *LG*, 5).

On the other hand, certain representatives of modern historical criticism of the Gospels have sometimes sustained the thesis that Jesus did not in fact found a Church and that, moreover, in virtue of the priority he gave to the announcing of the Kingdom of God, he did not have in mind to found one. The effect of this way of seeing things was to disassociate the foundation of the Church from the historical Jesus. Scholars even renounced the terms "foundation" and "institution" in this connection and deny their application to the acts they referred to. The birth of the Church, as many prefer to call it, is henceforth to be considered as a postpaschal event. And that event itself was increasingly interpreted in purely historical and/or sociological terms.

The disaccord between the Faith of the Church, recalled above, and certain conceptions tendentiously attributed to modern historical criticism has given rise to a number of problems. To tackle these problems, and find a solution to them, it will be necessary to remain on the territory of historical criticism and use its methods, while at the same time seeking out a new way of justifying and confirming the Church' Faith.

I.2. *The Different Senses of the Word "Ekklêsia"*

"Church" (*ekklêsia*) is a theological term carrying a rich charge of meaning, bestowed upon it from the very beginning of the history of revelation as the New Testament discloses that to us. *Ekklêsia* (*qahal*) certainly derives from the Old Testament idea of the "gathering of the people of God", both through the mediation of the Septuagint and via Jewish apocalyptic. Despite Israel's rejection of him, Jesus did not found a distinct synagogue or create a separate community in the sense of a "holy remnant" or a secessionist sect. On the contrary, he wished that Israel might be converted, addressing to her a message of salvation ultimately to be transmitted in a universal way (cf. Mt 8:5–13; Mk 7:24–30). Yet the Church, in the full theological sense of the word, did not exist until after Easter, taking then the form of a community composed, in the Holy Spirit, of both Jews and Gentiles (Rom 9:24).

The term *ekklêsia,* absent from the Gospels save for three appearances in Matthew (16:18; 18:17), carries in the New Testament as a whole three possible meanings, which are apt to overlap: (1) the gathering of the community, (2) each of the local communities, and (3) the universal Church.

I.3. *The Notion, and Starting Point, of the Foundation of the Church*

In the Gospels, two events in particular express the conviction that the Church was founded by Jesus of Nazareth. The first is the renaming of Peter (Mk 3:16) following his profession of messianic faith, a renaming that has reference to the founding of the Church (cf. Mt 16:16ff.). The second is the institution of the Eucharist (cf. Mk 14:22ff.; Mt 26:26ff.; Jn 22:14ff.; 1 Cor 11:23ff.). Jesus' *logia* about Peter and the entire narrative about the Last Supper play a role of paramount importance in the debate about the founding of the Church. And yet, in present circumstances it seems better not to tie the question of the founding of the Church by Jesus Christ simply and solely to a saying of Jesus or to a particular event of his life. In a certain sense, the whole of Jesus' activity and destiny constitutes the root and foundation of the Church. The Church is, as it were, the fruit of the life of Jesus. The foundation of the Church presupposes the totality of the saving action of Jesus in his death and Resurrection as well as in the sending of the Spirit. This is why it is possible to identify, within the total activity of Jesus, certain elements that prepare the way for, take steps toward, or constitute the crucial stages of the founding of the Church.

This is already true of the prepaschal deportment of Jesus. Many of the fundamental aspects of the Church, which will only appear in a plenary fashion after Easter, can already be glimpsed in the earthly life of Jesus and find their grounding there.

I.4. *Steps and Stages in the Process of Founding the Church*

The steps and stages we have just mentioned possess, even when taken separately, some value as testimony to a dynamism in Jesus' ministry leading to the foundation of the Church. This is more clearly so when they are seized in their cumulative orientation. In them the Christian recognizes the saving design of the Father and the redemptive action of the Son, both communicated to mankind by the Holy Spirit (cf. *LG,* 2–5). The preparatory elements, steps, and stages may be identified and described in their detail as follows:

—the Old Testament promises about the people of God, promises presupposed by the preaching of Jesus and continuing to maintain their validity for human salvation

—Jesus' generous appeal to all his hearers, an appeal aimed at their conversion and carrying an invitation to believe in him

—the call and institution of the Twelve as a sign of the future reconstitution of all Israel

—the renaming of Simon Peter and his privileged place in the circle of the disciples and his mission

—the rejection of Jesus by Israel and the schism between the Jewish people and his disciples

—the fact that Jesus, in instituting the Supper, persists in preaching the universal Reign of God, which consists in the gift of his life for the benefit of all

—the rebuilding, thanks to the Lord's Resurrection, of the ruptured communion between Jesus and his disciples, and the postpaschal initiation into ecclesial life, strictly so called

—the sending of the Holy Spirit, which makes the Church a divine creation (the "Pentecost" of the Lucan conception)

—the mission to the Gentiles and the Church of the Gentiles

—the definitive break between the "true Israel" and Judaism

No single step, taken in and by itself, could constitute the total reality, but the entire series, taken as a unity, shows clearly that the Church's foundation must be understood as a historic process, that is, as the becoming of the Church within the history of revelation. The Father

> determined to call together in a holy Church those who should believe in Christ. Already present in figure at the beginning of the world, this Church was prepared in marvelous fashion in the history of the people of Israel and in the old alliance. Established in this last age of the world, and made manifest in the outpouring of the Spirit, it will be brought to glorious completion at the end of time (*LG,* 2).

At the same time, as this process unfolds, the permanent and definitive fundamental structure of the Church comes into being. The earthly Church is herself already the place of reunion for the eschatological people of God. This earthly Church continues the mission confided by Jesus to his disciples. In this perspective, one may call the Church "the seed and beginning on earth of the Kingdom of God and of his Christ" (cf. *LG,* 5, and Section X below).

I.5. *The Permanent Origin of the Church in Jesus Christ*

Founded by Christ, the Church does not simply depend on him for her external—historical or social—provenance. She comes forth from her Lord in a much deeper sense, since he it is who constantly nourishes her and builds her up in the Spirit. According to Scripture, as understood in Tradition, the Church takes her birth from the riven side of Jesus Christ (cf. Jn 19:34; *LG*, 3). She is "obtained by the blood of" the Son (Acts 20:28; cf. Titus 2:14).

This fundamental structure is expressed in different ways through a variety of biblical images: Bride of Christ, flock of Christ, God's building, temple, people, house, plantation, field (cf. *LG*, 6), and above all, Body of Christ (*LG*, 7), the image that Paul develops in the eleventh chapter of his First Letter to the Corinthians, alluding doubtless to the Eucharist, which furnished him with the profound basis of his interpretation (cf. 1 Cor 10:16ff.). This formulation is given even more generous expression in the Letter to the Colossians and the Letter to the Ephesians (cf. Col 1:18; Eph 1:22; 5:23): Christ is the Head of his Body, the Church. The Savior "fills the Church, who is his Body and his fullness, with his divine gifts (cf. Eph 1:22–23) so that she may increase and attain to all the fullness of God (cf. Eph 3:19)" (*LG*, 7).

II. THE CHURCH AS THE "NEW PEOPLE OF GOD"

II.1. *The Multiplicity of Designations of the Church*

The Church, radiant with the glory of Christ (cf. *LG*, 1), manifests to all men "the utterly gratuitous and mysterious design of the wisdom and goodness" of the eternal Father, who elects to save all men by the Son and in the Spirit (cf. *LG*, 2). In order to underline at one and the same time the presence in the Church of this transcendent divine reality and the historically expressive character of its manifestation, the Council designated the Church by the word "mystery".

Because the proper name that would express the whole reality of the Church is known only to God, human language experiences its own radical insuffiency to express fully the "mystery" of the Church. It has to have recourse to a multiplicity of images, representations, and analogies, which, moreover, will never be able to designate more than partial aspects of the reality. The use of these formulations should suggest the transcendence of the "mystery" over against every reductionism, whether conceptual or symbolic. Furthermore, the use of a multiplicity of such formulations here will permit one to avoid these excesses that concentration on one single formula would inevitably cause. This is already suggested by *Lumen Gentium* in its sixth paragraph: "In the Old Testament the revelation of the Kingdom is often made under the forms of symbols. In similar fashion the inner nature of the Church is now made known to us in various images." Within the New Testament corpus, up to eighty comparisons for the Church have been counted. The plurality of images to which the Council draws our attention is intentional. It is meant to bring out the inexhaustible character of the "mystery" of the Church. For she shows herself to those who contemplate her as "a reality impregnated with God's presence and, thus, so constituted that she admits of ever new and more profound explorations of herself" (Paul VI, speech opening the second session of the Council, September 29, 1963 [*AAS*, 55 (1963): 848]). And so the New Testament presents us with images "taken either from the life of the shepherd or from cultivation of the land, from the art of building or from family life and marriage. These images have their preparation in the books of the prophets" (*LG*, 6).

It is true that these images do not all possess the same evocative power. Some, such as that of "the body", have an importance of the first order. One will readily agree that without use of the "Body of Christ" comparison, applied to the community of Jesus' disciples, the reality of the Church would scarcely be accessible to us at all. The Pauline Letters develop this comparison in various directions, as *Lumen Gentium* mentions in its seventh paragraph. And yet, though the Council gives the image of the Church as Body of Christ its proper place, it gives pride of place to another image, that of the "people of God"—if only because this latter image gives the second chapter of the Constitution its very title. One can say, indeed, that the expression "people of God" has come to stand for the ecclesiology of the Council. It is not too much to say that this image was deliberately preferred by the Council to "Body of Christ" or "temple of the Holy Spirit", even though these last are certainly not ignored by it. This choice was made for reasons at once theological and pastoral. In the minds of the Council fathers, these two types of consideration reinforced each other. The expression "people of God" had an advantage over other designations in that it could render better that sacramental reality that all the baptized share in common, both as a dignity in the Church and as a responsibility in the world. At the same time, it could undermine the communitarian nature and historical dimension of the Church—as many of the fathers wanted.

II.2. *"People of God"*

But in itself, the expression "people of God" has a significance that does not appear on a cursory examination. As with every theological expression, it requires reflection, deepening, and clarification if falsifying interpretations are to be avoided. Even on the linguistic level, the Latin term *populus* does not seem to provide a direct translation of the Greek *laos* of the Septuagint. *Laos,* as used in the Septuagint, is a term with a characteristic and quite specific meaning. It is not just religious but is quite definitely soteriological and, as such, destined to find its own fulfillment in the New Testament. *Lumen Gentium* presupposes the biblical meaning of the term "people". The Constitution takes up that term with all the connotations that Old and New Testaments have bestowed upon it. In the expression "people of God" it is, moreover, the genitive "of God" that provides the phrase with its own specific, determinate significance, by situating it in that biblical context where it appeared and developed. Consequently, any interpretation of the term "people" of an exclusively biological, racial, cultural, political, or ideological kind must be radically excluded. The "people of God" derives "from above", from the divine plan, that is, from election, Covenant, and mission. This is supremely true if we turn our attention to the fact that *Lumen Gentium* does confine itself to the Old Testament concept of the "people of God" but goes beyond it by speaking of the "new people of God" (*LG,* 9). This new people of God is made up of those who believe in Jesus Christ and are "reborn" through Baptism in water and the Holy Spirit (Jn 3:3–6). It is, then, the Holy Spirit who "by the power of the Gospel permits the Church to keep the freshness of her youth [and] constantly renews her" (*LG,* 4). And so the expression "people of God" receives its proper meaning from a constitutive reference to the trinitarian mystery revealed by Jesus Christ in the Holy Spirit (*LG,* 4; *UR,* 2).

The new people of God presents herself as a "community of faith, hope, and charity" (*LG,* 8), whose source is the Eucharist (*LG,* 3, 7); the intimate union of each believer with his Savior, something inseparable from the unity of the faithful with each other, is the fruit of active belonging to the Church and transforms the total existence of Christians into a "spiritual worship". The communitarian dimension is essential to the Church, if faith, hope, and charity are to be exercised and communicated within her. That dimension is also necessary insofar as such communion, once it takes root in the "heart" of every believer, must also be deployed and realized on a communal, objective, and institutional level. On this societal level too the Church is summoned to live in the remembrance and expectation of Jesus Christ and to announce his Good News to all men.

III. THE CHURCH AS "MYSTERY" AND AS "HISTORIC SUBJECT"

III.1. *The Church as Simultaneously "Mystery" and "Historic Subject"*

The deep intention of the conciliar Constitution *Lumen Gentium*—an intention by no means contradicted in postconciliar reflection—was that the expression "people of God", used conjointly with other ecclesiological terms, should underline the character of the Church as "mystery" and as "historic subject", for at all levels of her action the Church effectively brings both of these characteristics into play, and that in such a way that one cannot separate the one from the other. "Mystery" here refers to the Church as deriving from the Trinity, while "historic subject" has to do with the Church as a historical agent, contributing to history's overall direction.

Avoiding the dangers of seeing these aspects in a dualistic fashion or as opposed terms, we must reach a more profound view of that correlation in "the Church as people of God", which gives the relationship between "mystery" and "historic subject" its basis. In fact, it is the Church's mystery character that determines her nature as a historic subject. But also, and correlatively, the historic subject angle serves in turn to express the nature of this mystery. In other words, the people of God is simultaneously mystery and historic subject, in such a fashion that the mystery constitutes the historic subject and the historic subject discloses the mystery. It would be sheer nominalism to separate out, in "the Church as people of God", these two aspects.

"Mystery" when applied to the Church refers to the free choice of the Father's wisdom and goodness to communicate himself, something that he does in the missions of the Son and the Holy Spirit, "for us men and for our salvation". Creation and human history take their rise from this divine act, whose "principle", in the most pregnant sense of the word (Jn 1:1), lies in Jesus Christ, the Word made flesh. Now exalted at the Father's right hand, Christ pours out the Holy Spirit to become the "principle" of the Church, constituting her as Christ's Body and Spouse. Thus the Church has a particular, unique, and exclusive reference to Christ, and so her meaning is not indefinitely open.

It follows, then, that the trinitarian mystery is made present and operative within the Church. From one point of view, the mystery of Christ as Head, the wholly universal, inclusive, and recapitulating principle of the *Christus totus*, encompasses and involves the mystery of the Church. Yet from another point of view, Christ's mystery does not purely and simply subsume that of the Church within itself. Thus we must recognize that the Church possesses an eschatological character. The continuity between Jesus Christ and the Church is therefore not direct but "mediate". It is assured by the Holy Spirit, who, being the Spirit of Jesus, acts in order to bring about in the Church the

Lordship of Jesus Christ, itself realized through obedience to the will of the Father.

III.2. *The Church as "Historic Subject"*

The Church's "mystery", as her creation by the Holy Spirit as the fulfillment and fullness of the mystery of Jesus Christ her Head, and so the revelation of the Trinity, is truly a historic subject.

The Council's desire to underline this aspect of the Church comes through clearly in its recourse to the category of "people of God", on which we have already reported. In its Old Testament antecedents, that expression carries the exact connotation of a historic subject in relation to the Covenant with God. Furthermore, this characteristic is confirmed in the New Testament fullness of time. Taking her stand on Christ, by the Spirit, the "new" people of God broadens her horizons, giving them a universal bearing. It is precisely by reference to Jesus Christ and the Spirit that the new people of God is constituted in her identity as a historic subject.

The fundamental property of this people, a property that distinguishes her from all others, lies in a corporate life lived in remembrance and expectation of Jesus Christ and so in commitment to mission. Certainly, this new people of God actualizes this fundamental property through the free and responsible choice of each of her members. Yet this is only possible because of the support provided by an institutional structure ordered to this end (the Word of God, the New Law, the Eucharist, and the other sacraments, charisms, and ministries). At every level, remembrance and expectation provide the people of God with her exact specificity, giving her a historic identity that of its nature preserves her in every situation from the perils of disintegration and loss of corporate selfhood. Remembrance and expectation cannot be severed from the mission for whose sake the people of God is permanently assembled. In fact, one can say that the mission derives essentially from the remembrance and expectation of Jesus Christ in the sense that the latter dispositions are the foundation of the former. For the people of God knows by faith, and from her remembrance and expectation of Jesus, what other peoples do not know and will never be able to know about the meaning of existence and human history. This knowledge, this Good News, the people of God must announce to all men by virtue of the mission laid upon her by Jesus himself (Mt 28:19). Should she fail, then despite human wisdom, that "wisdom of the Greeks" to which Paul refers, and notwithstanding scientific and technological progress, men will remain in slavery and darkness. Seen in this light, the mission that constitutes the historic goal of the people of God generates a kind of activity that no other human activity can replace. This special activity is at one and the same time negatively critical and positively stimulating. It realizes that human life way through which the salvation of each man can be worked out. To underestimate the proper function of mission and so to reduce it to something less than itself can only aggravate the sum total of the problems and evils that this world has to suffer.

III.3. *Fullness and Relativity of the Historic Subject*

But approached from another angle, a stress on the people of God as historic subject and on that people's constitutive reference to the remembrance and expectation of Jesus Christ enables one to take in the relative and incomplete quality of the Church's life. "Remembrance" and "expectation" speak in the same breath of "identity" and "difference".

"Remembrance" and "expectation" express "identity" in the sense that the reference of the new people of God to Christ through the Spirit renders this people not a "different", independent, and diverse reality but a reality filled with that "remembrance" and "expectation" that attach her to Jesus Christ. In this perspective, the purely relative character of the new people of God stands out strikingly: that people cannot become an autonomous body since she is totally dependent on Jesus Christ. It follows that the new people of God is not concerned with the validation of her own genius or with proposing or imposing such a genius on the world at large. Rather, the Church can do nothing more than proclaim and communicate in the remembrance and expectation of Jesus Christ, her own life-giving source: "It is no longer I who live, but Christ who lives in me" (Gal 2:20a).

Correspondingly, if "remembrance" and "expectation" bestow the presence of an Other, and through that express a "relativity" in relation to that Other, then they also imply incompleteness. For this reason, the new people of God, whether in the case of her individual members or of the totality that those members compose, remains always "on the way" (*in via*), in a situation that here below will never be finished. The destination of God's people is simply to make herself ever more faithful and obedient in her remembrance and expectation. Her true position is incompatible, therefore, with any kind of arrogance or feeling of superiority. Her situation vis-à-vis Christ must, on the contrary, arouse her to a humble effort of conversion. The new people of God does not ask of others more that she requires of herself. What she offers, indeed, is not what belongs to her in her own right but what she has received from God irrespective of previous merit.

III.4. *The New People of God in Her Historical Existence*

It is from the Holy Spirit that the new people of God receives her "consistency" as a people. If one may refer to the words of the apostle Peter, that which "was no people" can only become a "people" (cf. 1 Pet 2:10) through him who unites her from above and from within so as to realize her union in God. The Holy Spirit brings the new people of God to life in the remembrance and expectation of Jesus Christ and gives her the task of proclaiming the Good News of this remembrance and expectation to all mankind. It is not a question in this remembrance, expectation, and mission of a reality that is imposed on top of or laid side by side with a preexisting existence and activity. In this respect, the members of the people of God do not form a particular group differentiated from other human groups at the level of their daily activities and occupations. The activity of Christians is no different from that by which all men, whoever they may be, "humanize" the world. For the members of God's people as for everyone else, there are only the ordinary, common conditions of human living, which all are called to share in solidarity, though also in the diversity of their various callings.

And yet being members of the people of God *does* give Christians a special responsibility in regard to this world. "What the soul is in the body, let Christians be in the world!" (*LG*, 38, cf. *Letter to Diognetus, 6*). Since the Holy Spirit is himself termed the Soul of the Church (*LG*, 7), Christians receive in this selfsame Spirit the mission to realize in the world something as vital as that which the Spirit realizes in the Church. This is not a matter of an additional action over and above the preexisting technological, artistic, and social action of mankind but rather the confronting of human activity in all its forms with the Christian hope, or, to keep the preferred vocabulary of this document, with the demands of the remembrance and expectation of Jesus Christ. It is from "within" human projects that Christians, and especially the laity, are so called that

> being led by the spirit of the Gospel, they may contribute to the sanctification of the world, as from within like leaven, by fulfilling their own particular duties. Thus, especially by the witness of their life, resplendent in faith, hope, and charity, they must manifest Christ to others (*LG*, 31).

And so the new people of God is not marked by a mode of existence or mission that can substitute for what is already given in human existence and its many projects. Rather, the remembrance and expectation of Jesus Christ should serve to convert or transform from within that human mode of existing and acting already lived out in a given group of men. One might say here that the remembrance and expectation of Jesus Christ whence the new people of God draws her life constitutes the "formal" element (in the Scholastic sense of that term), giving structure to the concrete existence of human beings. That concrete existence may then be called the "matter" (once more, in the Scholastic sense): a material element that, while of course endowed with responsibility and freedom, can receive one of a variety of further determinations in order to fashion a way of life that is "according to the Holy Spirit". Such ways of life enjoy no a priori existence. They cannot be determined in advance. They come in a rich diversity and cannot be foreseen even though they can all be referred to the constant action of a single Holy Spirit. But what these diverse ways of life have in common as a recurring constant in their makeup is that all express "in the ordinary circumstances of family and social life, which, as it were, constitute their very existence" (cf. *LG*, 31), the demands and the joy of the Gospel of Christ.

IV. THE PEOPLE OF GOD AND INCULTURATION

IV.1. *The Necessity of Inculturation*

Both as "mystery" and as "historic subject" the new people of God

> is a community composed of men . . . who, united in Christ and guided by the Holy Spirit, press onward toward the Kingdom of the Father and are bearers of a message of salvation intended for all men. That is why Christians cherish a feeling of deep solidarity with the human race and its history (*GS*, 1).

Since the mission of the Church among men is to "lend embodiment to the Kingdom of God", the new people of God

> does not take away anything from the temporal welfare of any people. Rather she fosters and takes to herself, insofar as they are good, the abilities, resources, and customs of peoples. In so taking them to herself she purifies, strengthens, and elevates them (*LG*, 13).

As *Gaudium et Spes* suggests, the general term "culture" seems able to gather together the totality of personal and social traits that characterize man, allowing him to take up and become master of his condition and destiny (*GS*, II.53–62).

Thus the Church in its evangelizing mission must "bring the power of the Gospel into the very heart of culture—and cultures" (John Paul II, *CT*, 53). For without this, the Church's message of salvation would not truly reach those to whom she communicates it. Reflection on what is involved in the process of evangelization makes one aware of this in an ever more lively way to the degree that humanity grows in the knowledge that it has of itself. Evangelization only hits its mark when man, both as unique person and as member of a community (and one profoundly touched by that membership) receives the Word of God and makes it bear fruit in his life. So much is this so that Paul VI was able to write in *Evangelii Nuntiandi* of:

> sectors of the human race that must be transformed, for the purpose of the Church is not confined to preaching the Gospel in ever-extending territories and proclaiming it to ever-increasing multitudes of men. She seeks by virtue of the Gospel to affect and, as it were, recast the criteria of judgment, the standard of values, the incentives and life standards of the human race that are inconsistent with the Word of God and the plan of salvation (*EN,* 19).

And indeed, as the Pope remarks in the same document: "The rift between the Gospel and culture is undoubtedly an unhappy circumstance of our times" (*EN,* 20).

To designate this perspective and action whereby the Gospel can be inserted into the very heart of human culture, it has become usual nowadays to invoke the word "inculturation". Pope John Paul II wrote: "The term 'acculturation' or 'inculturation' may be a neologism, but it expresses very well one factor of the great mystery of the Incarnation" (*CT,* 53; cf. speech to the Pontifical Biblical Commission, June 26, 1979; speech to the bishops of Zaire, June 3, 1980; allocution to Korean intellectuals and artists, May 3, 1984). And while in Korea the Pope underlined the dynamic nature of this inculturation:

> The Church must take to herself everything in the peoples. We have before us a long and important process of inculturation, ordered to the Gospel's penetration to the very heart of living cultures. To encourage this process is to respond to the profound aspirations of the peoples and to help them enter the sphere of faith itself.

While not at all claiming to offer here a complete theology of inculturation, we simply wish to recall its foundation in the mystery of God and Christ in order to seek out its significance for the present mission of the Church. No doubt the need for inculturation is felt by all Christian communities. Yet we today should be particularly attentive to the situations experienced by the churches of Asia, Africa, Oceania, and North and South America—whether these churches are young churches or, on the contrary, already long established.

IV.2. *The Foundation of Inculturation*

The doctrinal basis of inculturation is found firstly in the diversity and multiplicity of created beings, an expression of God the Creator's own intention, desirous as he was that this diversified multitude should illustrate the more richly the innumerable aspects of his goodness (cf. St. Thomas, *S. Th.,* Ia, q. 47, a. 1). But that foundation is situated more deeply still in the mystery of Christ himself: in his Incarnation, life, death, and Resurrection.

Just as God the Word assumed a concrete humanity in his own Person and lived out all the particularities of the human condition in a given place and time, and in the midst of a single people, so the Church, following Christ's example and through the gift of his Spirit, has to become incarnate in every place, every time, and every people (cf. Acts 2:5–11).

In the same way that Christ proclaimed the Gospel making use of all those familiar realities that made up the culture of his people, so the Church cannot dispense herself from borrowing elements drawn from human cultures for the construction of the Kingdom.

Jesus said, "Repent and believe in the Gospel" (Mk 1:15). He confronted a sinful world right up until his death on the Cross, so as to make men capable of this conversion and this believing. It is the same with cultures as with persons: there is no achieved inculturation unless there is also denunciation of the limitations, errors, and sin that indwell them. Every culture must accept the judgment of the Cross upon its life and its language.

Christ has risen. He reveals man fully to himself, bestowing upon him the fruits of his perfect redemption. Just so a culture that turns to the Gospel finds there its own liberation and brings to light new riches that are at once the gifts of the Resurrection and its promises.

In the evangelization of cultures and the inculturation of the Gospel, a wondrous exchange is brought about: on the one hand, the Gospel reveals to each culture and sets free within it the final truth of the values which that culture carries. On the other hand, each and every culture expresses the Gospel in an original fashion and manifests new aspects of it. Thus inculturation is an aspect of the recapitulation of all things in Christ (Eph 1:10) and of the catholicity of the Church (*LG,* 16, 17).

IV.3. *Various Aspects of Inculturation*

Inculturation has profound repercussions on all aspects of a church's existence. And so here we can usefully remind ourselves of how this affects a given church's life and language.

So far as ecclesial *life* is concerned, inculturation consists of a better correspondence between the church institution's concrete forms of expression and organization and those positive values that make up a culture's own identity. Inculturation also involves the positive presence and active commitment of a church in those areas of a culture where its deepest human problems dwell. It is not simply the appropriation of cultural traditions. It is also a service of man, of all men. It penetrates every relationship in a transforming way. Attentive to the values of the past, it looks toward the future as well.

In the domain of *language,* here taken in its cultural-anthropological sense, inculturation is primarily an act of appropriation of the content of faith in the words, concepts, symbols, and ritual behavior of a given culture. Accordingly, it requires the elaboration of a doctrinal response, simultaneously fresh yet faithful, open yet critical in its approach to new problems, both intellectual and ethical, attached to the aspirations and refusals, the values and the deficiencies of that culture.

But if cultures are various, the human condition is one and the same. This explains why intercultural communication is not only possible but actually necessary. Thus the Gospel, addressing itself as it does to what is deepest in man, has a transcultural value. Its specificity must, therefore, be recognizable from one culture to another. And this means the openness of each culture to the rest. We can recall here that the Gospel "has always been transmitted by means of an apostolic dialogue that is itself inevitably part of a certain dialogue of cultures" (*CT,* 53).

By presence and coresponsibility in human history, the new people of God is always encountering new situations. She must constantly recommence her task of bringing the power of the Gospel to bear on the heart of human culture and of individual cultures. Yet some situations and periods demand a special effort in this regard. This is particularly true today of the evangelization of the peoples of Asia, Africa, Oceania, and North and South America. Whether these churches are newly founded or already have a certain antiquity, they find themselves in a special situation where inculturation is concerned. The missionaries who brought the Gospel to these "non-European" churches could not avoid bringing with that Gospel elements of their own culture. By definition they could not do what could only be achieved by Christians belonging to those newly evangelized cultures. As Pope John Paul II remarked to the bishops of Zaire: "Evangelization has its own stages, and moments of deepening." When such non-European churches became aware for the first time of their own originality and the tasks which that involves, they naturally seek to create new forms of expression for the single Gospel in ecclesial life and language. Their efforts in this direction, carried out in communion with the Holy See and with the aid of the rest of the Church, will surely be decisive for the future of evangelization, despite the difficulties that these communities are encountering and the delays that are part and parcel of such an enterprise.

In this total task, the promotion of justice is not just one element among many, but a most important and urgent one. The proclamation of the Gospel must take up the gauntlet of local and worldwide injustice. It is true that in this area certain deviations of a combined political and religious nature have appeared. But such deviations should not lead one to neglect or suppress the necessary task of promoting justice. On the contrary, they point up the urgency of theological discernment, founded on as scientific an analysis as is possible and ever subject to the light of faith (cf. *Jesus Christus, vis liberationis, Instruction on Certain Aspects of the Theology of Liberation,* Congregation for the Doctrine of the Faith, 1984). Nor should it be forgotten that local injustice is often enough part of that worldwide nexus of injustice of which Pope Paul VI spoke so strikingly in *Populorum Progressio.* The promotion of justice concerns the Catholic Church spread throughout the world: it needs the mutual assistance of all particular churches and the strong backing of the apostolic Roman See.

V. PARTICULAR CHURCHES AND THE CHURCH UNIVERSAL

V.1. *Some Necessary Distinctions*

Following the dominant use at the Second Vatican Council, a use reflected in the new Code of Canon Law, in what follows we propose to distinguish between "particular church" and "local church". The "peculiar" or "particular church" is in the first place the diocese (cf. canon 368), "loyal to its pastor and formed by him . . . in the Holy Spirit through the Gospel and the Eucharist" (*CD,* 11). Here the criterion invoked is essentially *theological.* The expression "local church" (*ecclesia localis*), on the other hand, represents a usage dropped by the Code. The "local church" can refer to a more-or-less homogeneous grouping of particular churches, whose formation results in most cases from the givens of geography, history, language, or culture. Under the guidance of Providence, these churches have developed (in the past, as, for example, with the "ancient patriarchal churches") or are developing (in our own day) a patrimony of their own at once theological, juridical, liturgical, and spiritual. Here the criterion invoked is principally of a *sociocultural* kind.

We also wish to distinguish between the essential structure of the Church and its concrete, changing form (or organization). The "essential structure" comprises everything in the Church that derives from divine institution (*jure divino*), by means of its foundation through Christ and the gift of the Holy Spirit. This structure can only be a single structure, and it is destined to endure throughout time. However, this essential, permanent structure is always clothed in a concrete expression and organization (*jure ecclesiastico*), the result of contingent and changing factors, historical, cultural, geographic, and political. Indeed, the Church's concrete form is normally subject to evolution. It is the locus where legitimate and even necessary differences are manifest. The diversity of organization does not contradict, however, the unity of structure.

This distinction between essential structure and concrete form or organization should not be taken to imply a separation. The essential structure is always implicated in a concrete form, and without this form it cannot truly exist. This is why the concrete form is not just neutral in terms of the essential structure: it has the power to express that structure faithfully and efficaciously in a given situation. In certain respects to identify what is proper to the structure and what to the form or organization may require a delicate act of discernment.

The particular church, bound as it is to its bishop and shepherd, belongs by its very nature to the Church's essential structure. And yet in the course of the centuries, this same structure has been figured forth in various ways. The mode of functioning embraced by a particular church as well as different kinds of grouping of a number of particular churches together belong to the side of concrete form and organization. And this is of course the case with "local churches", localized as they are by their origins and traditions.

V.2. *Unity and Diversity*

These distinctions being clear, we must nevertheless underline the fact that for Catholic theology the unity and diversity of the Church share a common originating reference: both refer to the Triune God where the differentiated Triad of Persons exists in the unity of a single Godhead. The real distinction of Persons in no way divides the single nature. Trinitarian theology shows us that true differences can only exist in unity. What has no unity cannot support difference, as J. A. Moehler pointed out. We can apply these reflections analogically to the theology of the Church.

The Church of the Trinity (cf. *LG,* 4), whose diversity is manifold, receives her unity from the gift of the Holy Spirit who is himself the unity of the Father and the Son.

Catholic universalism must therefore be distinguished from those falsifying accounts of universality that one finds in totalitarian doctrines, in materialistic systems, in the false ideologies of scientism and the cult of technology, and indeed in imperialistic strategies of every kind. No more should Catholic universalism be confused with a uniformity that would destroy legitimate particularities. Again, one ought not try to assimilate that universalism to a systematic postulation of the uniquely singular, subversive as that would be of essential unity.

The Code of Canon Law (canon 368) has adopted a formula of *Lumen Gentium* (23), which states that "it is in these (particular churches) and formed out of them that the one and unique Catholic Church exists". Between the particular churches and the universal Church there exists a mutual interiority, a kind of osmosis. The universal Church finds its concrete existence in each church where it is present. Reciprocally, each particular church is "formed after the model of the universal Church" (*LG,* 23) and lives in intense communion with that Church.

V.3. *The Service of Unity*

At the heart of the universal network of particular churches of which the single Church of God is made up, there is a unique center and reference point: the particular Church of Rome. That Church, with which, as St. Irenaeus wrote, "every other church must be in accord", presides in charity over the universal communion (cf. St. Ignatius of Antioch, *Ad Rom., Proem.*). Indeed, Christ Jesus, the eternal Shepherd,

> in order that the episcopate itself . . . might be one and undivided . . . put Peter at the head of the other apostles, and in him he set up a lasting and visible source and foundation of the unity both of faith and of communion (*LG,* 18).

Successor of the apostle Peter, the Roman Pontiff is Christ's Vicar and the visible head of the whole Church over which he exercises "full, supreme, and universal power" (*LG,* 22).

Lumen Gentium wished to associate its reiteration of the doctrines of the primacy and teaching authority of the Roman Pontiff with its "doctrine concerning bishops, successors of the apostles" (4. *LG,* 18). The college of bishops, which stands in succession to the college of the apostles, shows forth at one and the same time the diversity, universality, and unity of the people of God. For the "bishops, successors of the apostles . . . together with Peter's successor, the Vicar of Christ and the visible head of the whole Church, direct the house of the living God" (*LG,* 18). And that house is the Church. It follows that the episcopal college, "together with their head, the Supreme Pontiff, and never apart from him . . . have supreme and full authority over the universal Church" (*LG,* 22). Each bishop, in his particular church, "enjoys a solidarity with the entire episcopal body to whom has been entrusted, in succession to the apostolic college, the task of watching over the Church's credal purity and unity" (Paul VI, apostolic letter *Quinque jam anni,* December 8, 1970). Thus he is "bound to have such care and solicitude for the whole Church, which, though it be not exercised by any act of jurisdiction, does for all that redound in an eminent degree to the advantage of the universal Church" (*LG*, 23). In the same way, the bishop will govern his diocese bearing in mind that it is "constituted after the model of the universal Church" (*LG*, 23; cf. *CD*, 11).

The "collegial feeling" (*affectus collegialis*) that the Council has aroused among the bishops has, since its meeting, found concrete expression in the important role played by *episcopal conferences* (cf. *LG*, 23). Through this means, the bishops of a given nation or territory exercise "together" or "jointly" certain of their apostolic and pastoral responsibilities (cf. *CD*, 38; *Code Iuris Canonici*, 447).

It may also be noted here that these episcopal conferences not infrequently develop mutual relations of good neighborliness, collaboration, and solidarity, especially on a continental level. Continental episcopal assemblies gather together delegates of various conferences on the basis of earth's great geographic units. Thus one finds, for instance, the Latin American Episcopal Conference (CELAM), the Symposium of Episcopal Conferences of Africa and Madagascar (SECAM), the Federation of Asian Bishops' Conferences (FABC), and the Council of European Bishops' Conferences (CCEE). To our age of massive geopolitical unification and organization, such assemblies offer a concrete expression of the Church's unity in the diversity of human cultures and situations.

It is impossible to deny the usefulness, and even the pastoral necessity, of both episcopal conferences and their continental federations. But does this mean that one should see in them, as is sometimes done on account of the cooperative character of their work, specifically "collegial" institutions, understood in the strict sense of *Lumen Gentium* (22, 23) and *Christus Dominus* (4, 5, 6)? These texts do not allow of any rigorous ascription to episcopal conferences or their continental federations of the adjective "collegial". (We refer here to the adjective "collegial" since the noun "collegiality" nowhere exists in the documents of the Second Vatican Council.) That episcopal collegiality that stands in succession to apostolic collegiality is *universal* and can only be understood, by reference to the *whole* Church, in terms of the *totality* of the episcopal body in union with the Pope. These conditions are realized in the case of the ecumenical Council, and may be realized in the united action of the bishops dispersed around the world, for the reasons set forth in *Christus Dominus,* 4. In a certain sense, they may also be realized in the Synod of Bishops, which may give a true, if partial, expression to universal collegiality, because, "as it will be representative of the whole Catholic episcopate", it will "be as testimony to the participation of all the bishops in hierarchical communion in the care of the universal Church" (*CD*, 5; cf. *LG*, 23). By contrast, institutions like episcopal conferences (and their continental federations) have to do with the concrete organization or form of the Church (*jure ecclesiastico*). To describe them by such terms as "college", "collegiality", and "collegial" is to use language in an analogical and theologically "improper" way.

But to say this in no way lessens the importance of the practical role that episcopal conferences and their continental federations must play in the future, notably in what concerns the relations between particular churches, "local" churches, and the universal Church. The results already attained allow one to feel in this regard a well-founded confidence.

It is nonetheless true that in that condition of wayfarers that is ours difficulties may well emerge in the relations between particular churches as well as in their own relationship with the See of Rome, charged as that is with the ministry of universal unity and communion. The sinful tendency of man makes him turn differences into oppositions. This is why we must never abandon the search for the best means of expressing Catholic universality, which will also be the best means of enabling the most diverse human elements to compenetrate one another in the unity of the Faith. All this must be done in communion with the See of Rome and under her authority.

VI. THE NEW PEOPLE OF GOD
AS A HIERARCHICALLY ORDERED SOCIETY

VI.1. *Communion, Structure, and Organization*

From the moment of her emergence in history, the new people of God is structured around the pastors chosen by Jesus Christ himself in his appointment of the apostles (Mt 10:1–42) with Peter at their head (Jn 21:15–17).

> That divine mission, which was committed by Christ to the apostles, is destined to last until the end of the world (cf. Mt 28:20), since the Gospel, which they were charged to hand on, is, for the Church, the principle of all its life for all time. For that very reason the apostles were careful to appoint successors in this hierarchically constituted society (*LG*, 20).

Thus the people of God, the Church, cannot be disassociated from the ministries that give her her structure, and especially the episcopate. For with the death of the apostles, the episcopate became that veritable "ministry of the community" that bishops carry out with the help of presbyters and deacons (ibid.). Henceforth, if the Church presents herself as a single people and communion of faith, hope, and charity, within which Christ's faithful "are ... endowed with true Christian dignity" (*LG,* 18), this people and communion are provided with ministries and means of growth that will assure the common good of the whole body. One cannot then separate out structural from vital aspects in the Church, since these aspects are coinvolved at the deepest level.

> The one Mediator, Christ, established and ever sustains here on earth his holy Church, the community of faith, hope, and charity, as a visible organization through which he communicates truth and grace to all men. But the society structured with hierarchical organs and the mystical Body of Christ, the visible society and the spiritual community, the earthly Church and the Church endowed with heavenly riches, are not to be thought of as two realities. On the contrary, they form one complex reality that comes together from a human and a divine element (*LG,* 8).

The communion that gives definition to the new people of God is therefore a social communion of a hierachically ordered sort. As the *nota praevia explicativa* of November 16, 1964, makes clear:

> Communion is a concept held in high honor in the ancient Church (as also today, notably in the East). By it is meant not some vague sentiment but an organic reality that calls for juridical expression and yet at the same time is ensouled by love.

It is here that one may reasonably raise the question of the presence and significance of juridical organization in the Church. While the ontological, sacramental function of the Church may be distinguished from its canonical-juridical aspect (cf. the *nota praevia explicativa* of November 16, 1964), it is nonetheless true that in differing degrees both aspects are absolutely necessary for the Church's life. Bearing in mind the partial or relative analogy (*non mediocrem analogiam*) (*LG,* 8) of the Church with the Word incarnate as the text of *Lumen Gentium* (8) portrays it, we will not forget that

> as the assumed nature, inseparably united to him, serves the divine Word as a living organ of salvation, so, in a somewhat similar way, does the social structure of the Church serve the Spirit of Christ, who vivifies it in the building up of the Body.

The analogy drawn here with the Word incarnate enables us to affirm that the Church as "organ of salvation" must be understood in such a way as not to fall foul of either of those two heretical excesses in Christology known to antiquity. Thus we shall avoid, on the one hand, an ecclesial "Nestorianism" that would recognize no subsistent relationship between the divine and the human elements in the Church's life. On the other hand, we must be equally vigilant against an ecclesial "Monophysitism", for which everything in the Church is "divinized", leaving no space for the defects and faults of the Church's organization, the sad harvest of the sins and ignorance of men. The Church is, of course, a sacrament, but she is not sacramental to the same intensity or with parity of perfection in everything she undertakes. Since we shall be returning to the theme of the Church as sacrament, it will suffice to note here that the domain where the Church's sacramentality takes on its most potent form is that of the Liturgy (cf. SC, 7, 10). Next comes the ministry of the Word in its highest expressions (cf. LG, 21, 25). Then lastly we have the functioning of the pastoral office with its canonical authority or power of government (LG, 23). It follows that ecclesiastical legislation, even if it takes its rise from an authority whose origin is divine, cannot avoid being influenced in some measure by ignorance and sin. In other words, ecclesiastical legislation is not and cannot be infallible. But this by no means signifies that it is without importance in the mystery of salvation. To deny the Church's law all positive, salvific value would be, in the last analysis, to restrict the Church's sacramentality to the sacraments alone and so to enfeeble the Church's visibility in everyday life.

VI.2. *The Action of the Hierarchically Ordered Society*

In the fundamental structure of the Church one can identify principles that throw light on her organization and canonical-juridical practice:

1. As a visible community and social organism, the Church needs norms that express her fundamental structure and give greater definition to certain conditions of communal life in virtue of judgments of a prudential kind. These conditions may change, and indeed faithfulness to the Holy Spirit may *require* that they change.

2. The goal of ecclesiastical legislation can be nothing other than the common good of the Church. This common good includes in an unbreakable union both the safeguarding of the deposit of faith received from Christ and the spiritual progress of the sons of God, the members of Christ's Body.

3. If the Church has need of norms and law, then we must recognize that she enjoys legislative authority (LG, 27; cf. *Codex Iuris Canonici*, 135, 333, 336, 391, 392, 445, 455, etc.). Such a legislative authority will scrupulously respect the general rule recalled by the conciliar *Declaration on Religious Liberty.* According to this principle, "man's freedom should be given the fullest possible recognition and should not be curtailed except when and insofar as is necessary" (DH, 7). Such a power also implies that legitimate legal measures must be accepted and executed by the faithful with a religious obedience. However, the exercise of this authority demands from pastors a special attention to the formidable responsibility that legislative power carries with it. Connected

with this is the grave moral duty to make appropriate prior consultation, and also the obligation to proceed when necessary to subsequent rectification.

The presence of juridical elements in the Church's dispositions for the ordering of her own life suggests some further considerations. Christian liberty is one of the features characteristic of the New Covenant or the "new people of God" and constitutes an innovation when compared with the Old Law. And yet the advent of this freedom, already connected as it was in the witness of Israel's prophets with the internalization of the Law (cf. Jer 31:31), does not involve the total disappearance of external law from the Church's life, at least so long as she is still "on pilgrimage" in this world. The New Testament itself presents us with fragments of ecclesial law (Mt 18:15–18; Acts 15:28ff.; 1 Tim 3:1–13; 4:17–22; Titus 1:5–9; etc.). The earliest of the Church Fathers concerned themselves with developing rules for the establishment and maintenance of good order in the community. We see this happening in Clement of Rome, Ignatius of Antioch, Polycarp of Smyrna, Tertullian, Hippolytus, and others. Councils, both ecumenical and regional, made disciplinary decisions, which they promulgated alongside their doctrinal definitions properly so called. Law was thus already important in the ancient Church. But it did not always take written form. There was also a customary law, which was no less mandatory and often constituted the source of the "holy canons" that were later set down in writing.

VII. THE COMMON PRIESTHOOD OF THE FAITHFUL IN ITS RELATION TO THE MINISTERIAL PRIESTHOOD

VII.1. *Two Forms of Participation in the Priesthood of Christ*

The Second Vatican Council gave renewed attention to the common priesthood of the faithful. The expression "common priesthood" and the reality that it covers have deep biblical roots (cf., for instance, Ex 19:6; Is 61:6; 1 Pet 2:5, 9; Rom 12:1; Rev 1:6; 5:9–10) and received abundant commentary from such Church Fathers as Origen, St. John Chrysostom, and St. Augustine. And yet this phrase had very nearly vanished from the vocabulary of Catholic theology because of the antihierarchical use made of it by the Reformers. Still, it is appropriate to remember here that the Roman Catechism mentioned it quite explicitly. *Lumen Gentium* gives a remarkable role to the theme of the "common priesthood of the faithful". It affects both the individual persons of the baptized and the Church community, which is called "priestly" in its *ensemble* (*LG,* 11).

Elsewhere the Council has recourse to the expression "the ministerial or hierarchical priesthood" (*LG,* 10) to designate "the sacred ministry . . . exercised (in the Church by bishops and priests) for the good of their brethren" (*LG,* 13). Although this phrase does not appear directly or explicitly in the New Testament, it has been used constantly in Tradition since the third century. The Second Vatican Council went back to it regularly, while the Synod of Bishops of 1971 devoted to it a document all its own.

The Council links the common priesthood of the faithful to the sacrament of baptism. It also says that for Christians this priesthood has as its goal and content the offering of "spiritual sacrifices . . . through all (their) . . . works", or again, in St. Paul's exact phrase, Christians are "to present your bodies as a living sacrifice, holy and acceptable to God" (Rom 12:1). The Christian life is seen, therefore, as a praise offering to God, the worship of God carried out by each person and by the whole Church. This priesthood finds its expression in the holy Liturgy (*SC,* 7), and in witnessing to faith and proclaiming the Gospel (*LG,* 10) on the basis of that supernatural sense of faith that all the faithful share (cf. *LG,* 12). It is actualized concretely in the daily life of the baptized, in which the very stuff of existence becomes a self-offering incorporated into Christ's paschal mystery. The common priesthood of the faithful (or of the baptized) brings into sharp focus the profound unity that links liturgical worship to the spiritual yet down-to-earth worship of everyday life. We should stress here that such a priesthood can only be understood as sharing in the priesthood of Christ. No praise arises from earth to the Father except through Christ's agency as the only Mediator. This implies that Christ is sacramentally active here. And this is so. In the Christian economy, the offering of one's life is only fully realized thanks to the sacraments and most especially thanks to the Eucharist. For are not sacraments at once sources of grace and the cultic expression of self-offering?

VII.2. *Relation between the Two Priesthoods*

The Second Vatican Council restored its plenary meaning to the expression "the common priesthood of the faithful". But it then had to put the question of how this common priesthood was related to the ministerial or hierarchical priesthood. Clearly, both have their basis and source in the unique priesthood of Christ: "The priesthood of Christ is shared in various ways, by both his ministers and the faithful" (*LG,* 62; cf. 10). In the Church both carry a sacramental reference to the sanctifying Person, life, and activity of Christ. For the full blossoming of life in the Church, which is Christ's Body, the common priesthood of the faithful and the ministerial or hierarchical priesthood can only be complementary or "ordered to each other". There is, however, this nuance, that from the viewpoint of the finality and full maturation of the Christian life the common priesthood must be primary, even if from the viewpoint of the visible, organic pattern of the Church and its sacramental functioning priority lies with the ministerial priesthood. *Lumen Gentium* is clear and definite about these relationships in its tenth paragraph:

> Though they differ essentially and not only in degree, the common priesthood of the faithful and the ministerial or hierarchical priesthood are nonetheless ordered one to another; each in its proper way shares in the one priesthood of Christ. The ministerial priest, by the sacred power that he has, forms and rules the priestly people; in the person of Christ he effects the eucharistic sacrifice and offers it to God in the name of all the people. The faithful, indeed, by virtue of their royal priesthood, participate in the offering of the Eucharist. They exercise that priesthood, too, by the reception of the sacraments, prayer and thanksgiving, the witness of a holy life, abnegation, and active charity.

VII.3. *Sacramental Foundation of the Two Priesthoods*

As these words demonstrate, a theological account of the interrelation of these two priesthoods and their articulation must be in terms of the sacramental, and above all eucharistic, reality present in the Church's life. We have already underlined the fact that the sacraments are at once sources of grace and expressions of the spiritual offering of all one's life. Now the liturgical worship of the Church in which such self-offering reaches its fullness can only be realized when the community is presided over by someone who can act *in persona Christi*. This is the absolutely necessary condition if the "spiritual worship" is to receive its plenitude by being included in the sacrificial self-offering of the Son himself.

> Through the ministry of priests the spiritual sacrifice of the faithful is completed in union with the sacrifice of Christ, the only Mediator, which in the Eucharist is offered through the priests' hands in the name of the whole Church in an unbloody and sacramental manner until the Lord himself comes. The ministry of priests is directed to this and finds its consummation in it. For their ministration, which begins with the announcement of the Gospel, draws its force and power from the sacrifice of Christ and tends to this, that "the whole redeemed city, that is, the whole assembly and community of the saints should be offered as a universal sacrifice to God through the High Priest who offered himself in his Passion for us that we might be the Body of so great a Head" (St. Augustine) (*PO*, 2).

The common priesthood of the faithful and the ministerial priesthood of bishops and priests are strictly correlative because they derive from a single source, Christ's priesthood, and aim at a single, definitive end: the offering of the whole of Christ's Body. This is so true that St. Ignatius of Antioch was able to affirm that without bishops, presbyters, and deacons one cannot speak of the Church at all (cf. *Ad Trall.*, 3, 1). The Church only exists as the structured Church, and this is equally true if one uses the "people of God" idea, an idea that it would be quite wrong to identify with the laity alone, with bishops and priests left to one side.

Similarly, the "supernatural appreciation of the Faith" concerns "the whole people, when, 'from the bishops to the last of the faithful', they manifest a universal consent in matters of faith and morals" (*LG*, 2). It is utterly implausible to set over against each other the sense of faith of the people of God and the hierarchical Magisterium of the Church. The appreciation of faith to which the Council testifies is one that, "aroused and sustained by the Spirit of truth", only truly receives the Word of God when guided by the sacred teaching authority (cf. *LG*, 12).

Within the single new people of God, common priesthood and the ministerial priesthood of bishops and priests are inseparable. The common priesthood embraces the fullness of its own ecclesial possibilities, thanks to the ministerial priesthood, while the ministerial priesthood itself only exists for the sake of the exercise of the common priesthood. Bishops and priests are indispensable for the life of the Church and the life of the baptized. Yet bishops and priests are also called to live out fully this same common priesthood, and, in this sense, they too need the ministerial priesthood. "I am a bishop for you; I am a Christian with you", remarked St. Augustine (*Sermo*, 340, 1).

Because of their different orientations, the common priesthood of all the faithful and the ministerial priesthood of priests and bishops are distinguished by one essential difference (which is not simply a difference of degree). Acting in the "role" of Christ, bishop and priest make him present vis-à-vis the people. At the same time, they also represent the whole people before the Father.

Of course, there are some sacramental acts whose validity depends on the fact that their celebrant has, in virtue of ordination, the power to act *in persona Christi*, "in the role of Christ", or *in munere Christi*, "in Christ's office". However, one should not rest content with this statement in arguing for the legitimacy of the place of the ordained ministry in the Church. That ministry belongs to the essential structure of the Church and thus to her "face", her visibility. The essential structure of the Church and her self-presentation include a "vertical" dimension, the sign and instrument of the initiative and priority of the divine action in the Christian economy.

VII.4. *The Vocation of the Laity*

The above reflection is helpful in explaining certain statements of the new Code of Canon Law about the common priesthood of the faithful. Following the thirty-first paragraph of *Lumen Gentium,* canon 204, 1, links baptism to the way Christians share in the priestly, prophetic, and royal functions of Christ.

> Christ's faithful are those who, since they are incorporated into Christ through baptism, are constituted the people of God. For this reason they participate in their own way in the priestly, prophetic, and kingly office of Christ. They are called, each according to his or her particular condition, to exercise the mission that God entrusted to the Church to fulfill in the world.

In the spirit of that mission of the whole of God's people, which laymen exercise in both Church and world, canons 228, 1, and 230, 1 and 3, envisage the admission of laymen to ecclesiastical office and charge: for example, to the ministries of lector, acolyte, and others (cf. *CIC* 861, 2; 910, 2; 1112). But it would be a woeful misreading of these authorizations to see them as licensing a suppression of the difference between the respective roles of bishops, priests, and deacons and those of laymen. The role of the layman in ecclesiastical office and charge, as seen in the canons cited above, is certainly fully legitimate. Indeed, it is absolutely necessary in certain situations. But it cannot possess the fullness of that ecclesial sign quality that belongs to the ordained minister in his proper capacity as the sacramental representative of Christ. The extension of ecclesiastical office and charge to the laity should not lead to any obscuring of the visible sign of the Church, the people of God as hierarchically ordered, and that by Christ its Head.

Nor should the eligibility of laymen for these offices betray one into forgetting that, just as bishops, priests, and deacons or—at a different level—religious men and women have their own proper vocation within the totality of the Church's common mission, so do the laity. As the thirty-first paragraph of *Lumen Gentium* puts it:

> By reason of their special vocation it belongs to the laity to seek the Kingdom of God by engaging in temporal affairs and directing them according to God's will. They live in the world, that is, they are engaged in each and every work and business of the earth and in the ordinary circumstances of social and family life, which, as it were, constitute their very existence. There they are called by God that, being led by the Spirit to the Gospel, they may contribute to the sanctification of the world, as from within like leaven, by fulfilling their own particular duties. Thus, especially by the witness of their life, resplendent in faith, hope, and charity, they must manifest Christ to others.

VIII. THE CHURCH AS SACRAMENT OF CHRIST

VIII.1. *Sacrament and Mystery*

The Church of Christ, "God's new people", presents herself as inseparably mystery and historic subject. To express the simultaneous divine and human reality of the Church, *Lumen Gentium* has recourse, as we have seen, to the term "sacrament". The importance of this word is seen from the crucial place it occupies in the opening paragraph of that text: "Since the Church, in Christ, is in the nature of a sacrament—a sign and instrument, that is, of communion with God and of unity among all men". As *Lumen Gentium* unfolds, we find two more applications of "sacrament" to the Church (9, 48), neither further explained. Apparently the principle laid down in the first paragraph is meant to suffice. As applied to the Church, "sacrament" has become a somewhat popular term, though not as much so as "people of God". In any case, some clarifications of its bearing will not be amiss.

The application of the word "sacrament" to the Church allows one to underline the Church's origination in and absolute dependence on God and Christ (cf. *SC*, 5). It also makes clear the Church's orientation toward the manifestation to men, and presence among them, of God's universal love— something that comes about through the intimate union or communion of all men with Father, Son, and Holy Spirit, as well as by the communion of men with each other. "Sacrament" brings into sharp relief the deep structure of Christ's "mystery" and, in relation to that, the authentic nature of the true Church.

> The Church is essentially both human and divine, visible but endowed with invisible realities, zealous in action and dedicated to contemplation, present in the world, but as a pilgrim, so constituted that in her the human is directed toward and subordinated to the divine, the visible to the invisible, action to contemplation, and this present world to the city yet to come, the object of her quest (*SC*, 2; cf. *LG*, 8).

It is worth remembering that when, half a century ago, Catholic theologians restored to a honored place the Church's title as sacrament, they wanted to give back to Christianity its ample communitarian and social, rather than individualistic or even institutional, character. Christianity is in its very essence a mystery of union and unity: intimate union with God, unity of men among themselves.

The ecclesiological use of the term "sacrament", translating as that does the *sacramentum* of Latin, sends us back to the Greek *mystêrion*, whose meaning it fundamentally shares. As we have already stressed, the "mystery" is the divine decree whereby the Father effects his saving will in Christ, while revealing that will through the created consistency of temporal reality.

VIII.2. *Christ and the Church*

Certainly we must not lose sight of the fact that the expression "sacrament" can no more serve as a rigorous definition or exhaustive description of the Church than can any other word, metaphor, image, analogy, or comparison. Still, calling the Church "sacrament" strikingly highlights the Church's link with Christ. And so the biblical images of the Church as Christ's Body and Bride can be brought into connection with the Church as sacrament. The same is true of the "new people of God" formula, in the two distinct yet inseparable refractions to which that formula leads: mystery and historic subject. In fact, the term "sacrament" can serve as a formal transcript on all of the biblical images of the Church listed in the first chapter of *Lumen Gentium,* bringing home to us as these do the complementary notes of identity and difference by which Christ and the Church are related. The Church is truly indwelt by the presence of Christ in such a way that who finds her, finds him. Thus Christ is present in baptism and Eucharist, in the Word of God, in the Christian assembly (Mt 18:20), in the witness of the apostolic ministry (Lk 10:16; Jn 13:20), in the service of the poor (Mt 25:40), in the apostolate.... Yet at the same time, the Church, as made up of men, and sinful men at that, needs conversion and purification. She must ask from her Lord the spiritual gifts that are needful for her mission in the world. It is true that the Church is the efficacious sacrament of union with God and of unity for the human race. But at the same time, she must ceaselessly implore God's mercy, praying first of all for her own members, that they may not lose the unity of God's sons and daughters. In other words, the Lord is present *in* the Church (Rev 21:3, 22), but he never ceases to stand *before* her, drawing her on in the Holy Spirit to greater things still (cf. Jn 5:20), toward the definitive presence of God as "all in all" (1 Cor 15:28; Col 3:11).

In expectation of Christ's Coming at the end of time, the Church experiences the ravages of sin in her members and undergoes the trial of their divisions. The men and women who compose the Church can sometimes present obstacles to the action of the Holy Spirit. Just because pastors enjoy legitimate authority does not mean that they will automatically be safeguarded from malpractice and error. More structurally, because the sacrament is "sign and instrument", the symbolic and social reality that constitutes it at one level (*res et sacramentum*) initiates us into a greater and more fundamental reality, a reality that is divine (*res tantum*). And this is true in the case of the Church.

She depends wholly on Christ her goal, without ever becoming confused with the One who is her Lord.

VIII.3. *The Church, Sacrament of Christ*

It should be clear by now that when "sacrament" is applied ecclesiologically, some further explanation is required. Manifestly, the Church cannot be an eighth sacrament, if only because when we use that word for the Church we use it analogically. In fact, the meaning at stake here is more basic than with the seven sacraments, yet also more diffuse. As already pointed out, not everything in the Church has the same efficaciously saving quality as in the seven sacraments. Let us note too that if the Church is a sacrament, Christ himself is the "primordial" sacrament on which the Church depends: "He is before all things, and in him all things hold together. He is the head of the Body, the Church" (Col 1:18). Through the category of sacrament, something quite essential about the Church's reality finds expression. The meaning of this term as applied to the Church is not a fiction. The reason why, long before the Council, Catholic theologians were turning again to this word bequeathed them by the Church Fathers was precisely so that they could help the Church come to a better grasp of herself. So the sense here is that of "the Church, sacrament of God", or "sacrament of Christ". More precisely, since Christ himself may be called "the sacrament of God", the Church, in an analogous way, may be called "the sacrament of Christ". It is because she is his Bride and Body that the Church has bestowed upon her this name, "sacrament". And yet it is self-evident that the Church can only be a sacrament by way of total dependence on Christ, who is intrinsically the "primordial sacrament". And as for the seven sacraments, they have neither reality nor meaning except in the total context of the Church.

Finally, let us note that, as applied to the Church, "sacrament" connotes the salvation that, realized through union with God in Christ, leads men to common unity. One might indeed link "sacrament" and "world", stressing that the Church is the sacrament of the world's salvation, inasmuch as the world needs salvation, and the Church has received a mission to offer that salvation to those who need it. In this perspective we can say that the Church is the sacrament of Christ for the salvation of the world.

A theology of the Church as sacraments allows us to be more attentive to the concrete responsibilities of the Christian community. It is through the life, witness, and daily action of Christ's disciples that men will be led toward their Savior. Certain men, through a knowledge of the "sign" that the Church is and through the grace of conversion, will discover for themselves the greatness of God's love and the truth of the Gospel, so that for them the Church will be quite explicitly the "sign and instrument" of salvation. Others, more mysteriously and in a fashion known only to God, will be associated by the Holy Spirit with Christ's paschal mystery and so with the Church (*LG,* 14, 16; *AG,* 7; *GS,* 22, 5).

IX. THE SINGLE CHURCH OF CHRIST

IX.1. *Unity of the Church and Diversity of Christian Elements*

[There is one] sole Church of Christ, which in the Creed we profess to be one, holy, catholic, and apostolic, which our Savior, after his Resurrection, entrusted to Peter's pastoral care (Jn 21:17), commissioning him and the other apostles to extend and rule it (cf. Mt 28:18ff.), and which he raised up for all ages as "the pillar and mainstay of the truth" (1 Tim 3:15). This Church, constituted and organized as a society in the present world, subsists in the Catholic Church, which is governed by the successors of Peter and by the bishops in communion with him. Nevertheless, many elements of sanctification and of truth are found outside its visible confines. Since these are gifts belonging to the Church of Christ, they are forces impelling toward Catholic unity (*LG,* 8).

In point of fact, one can hardly overlook either the Church's theological unity or the de facto pluralism of history:

Many Christian communions present themselves to men as the true inheritors of Jesus Christ; all indeed profess to be followers of the Lord, but they differ in mind and go their different ways as if Christ himself were divided (*UR,* 1).

Such divisions are a cause of scandal and a hindrance to the evangelization of the world. And so the Council proposed to establish at one and the same time the presence of the Church of Christ in the Catholic Church and the existence, outside the visible limits of that Church, of spiritual elements or blessings by which Christ's Church is built up and lives (cf. *UR,* 3).

IX.2. *The Unicity of the Catholic Church*

First of all we should call to mind the "fullness of grace and truth entrusted to the Catholic Church" (*UR,* 3). In this the Church is a beneficiary of the fact that

it was to the apostolic college alone, of which Peter is the head, that we believe that our Lord entrusted all the blessings of the New Covenant, in order to establish on earth the one Body of Christ into which all those should be fully incorporated who belong in any way to the people of God (*UR,* 3).

The spiritual dimension of the Church cannot be sundered from the visible. The one Church, unique and universal, Jesus Christ's Church can be recognized historically in the visible Church constituted around the college of bishops and its head, the Pope (cf. *LG,* 8). The Church is found wherever the successors of the apostle Peter, and of the other apostles, realize in a visible way continuity with the source. And such apostolic continuity comes accompanied by other essential elements: Holy Scripture, doctrinal faith and Magisterium, sacraments, and ministries. Such elements assist the rise and development of existence in Christ. Like the orthodox Faith itself, they are the essential instrument and the specific means by which the growth of the divine life among men is nurtured. In fact, it is out of these elements that the true Church is constructed. We can quite legitimately see the entire saving work of God in the world in reference to the Church, since it is in her that the means of increase in the Christ life have reached their summit and perfection.

The *Decree on Ecumenism* speaks rightly of the "sacred mystery of the unity of the Church" and lists its essential components:

> It is through the faithful preaching of the Gospel by the apostles and their successors—the bishops with Peter's successor at their head—through their administering the sacraments, and through their governing in love, that Jesus Christ wishes his people to increase, under the action of the Holy Spirit, and he perfects its fellowship in unity: in the confession of one Faith, in the common celebration of divine worship, and in the fraternal harmony of the family of God (*UR,* 2).

If the Church is the setting forth of the total life of the risen Lord, then the name "Church" may be applied in its fullness wherever this sacramental life and apostolic faith exist in their integrity and continuity. Such elements we believe to exist in fullness and par excellence in the Catholic Church. This is what *Lumen Gentium* (8) wishes to underline when it says: "This Church, constituted and organized as a society in the present world, subsists in the Catholic Church, which is governed by the successor of Peter and by the bishops in communion with him." The Church is found wherever the successors of the apostle Peter and of the other apostles realize in a visible way continuity with the source. To this Church there has been made the gift of unity, and we believe that this unity "subsists in the Catholic Church as something she can never lose" (*UR,* 4). The Church is realized in fullness, then, in the society directed by Peter's successor and the bishops in communion with him.

IX.3. *Elements of Sanctification*

However, the full and perfect presence of the Church of Christ in the Catholic Church does not rule out the presence of Christ's Church in

> many elements of sanctification and of truth . . . found outside [the] visible confines [of the Catholic Church]. Since these are gifts belonging to the Church of Christ, they are forces impelling toward Catholic unity (*LG,* 8).

Numerous elements of sanctification and truth, therefore, exist by God's own gift for the Church, outside the visible organism of the Catholic Church yet truly belonging to the order of salvation. The Council affirms two characteristics of these "many elements", one factual and the other theological. As a matter of fact, one can observe elements of sanctification and truth in development outside the visible, social organism of the Catholic Church. Theologically speaking, such elements "are forces impelling toward Catholic unity".

Thus there are outside the Catholic Church not only numerous real Christians but also numerous truly Christian principles of life and faith. And so the Catholic Church can speak in *Unitatis Redintegratio* of the "Eastern churches", and in relation to the West of "separated churches and ecclesial communities" (14, 19). Authentic ecclesial values are present in the other Christian churches and communities. This presence summons everyone, whether Catholic or non-Catholic, to "examine their own faithfulness to Christ's will for the Church and, wherever necessary, undertake with vigor the task of renewal and reform" (*UR,* 4; cf. 6, 7). The conciliar decree on ecumenism has given a precise description of Catholic ecumenical principles and Catholic ecumenism in action in relation to both the Eastern churches and the separated Western churches and ecclesial communities. These statements taken in their entirety constitute a development of the doctrine found in *Lumen Gentium,* and notably in its eighth paragraph:

> It is through Christ's Catholic Church alone, which is the universal help toward salvation, that the fullness of the means of salvation can be obtained. . . . [Yet] the separated churches and communities as such, though we believe they suffer from . . . defects . . . have been by no means deprived of significance and importance in the mystery of salvation.

Our examination leads to the conclusion that the "true Church" cannot be understood as some utopia that all the divided, fragmented Christian communities of today are seeking to attain. The "true Church" and its unity are not to be sought exclusively "ahead". They are already given to us in the Catholic Church, in which Christ's Church is really present.

The followers of Christ are therefore not permitted to imagine that Christ's Church is nothing more than a collection (divided, but still possessing a certain unity) of churches and ecclesial communities. Nor are they free to hold that Christ's Church nowhere really exists today and that it is to be considered only as an end that all churches and ecclesial communities must strive to reach (Declaration *Mysterium Ecclesiae* of the Congregation for the Doctrine of the Faith, June 24, 1973).

But this only adds greater urgency to Jesus' prayer: "That they may all be one; even as thou, Father, art in me, and I in thee, that they also may be in us, so that the world may believe that thou hast sent me" (Jn 17:21). Correlatively, there is an all the greater obligation on Christians and on all Christian communities to tend henceforth and with all their strength toward this unity that is the object of our hope.

X. THE ESCHATOLOGICAL CHARACTER OF THE CHURCH: KINGDOM AND CHURCH

X.1. *The Church as Simultaneously Earthly and Heavenly*

Chapter VII of *Lumen Gentium,* entitled "The Eschatological Character of the Church *in via* and Its Union with the Church in Heaven",[1] has not proved of much interest to those commenting on the Second Vatican Council. Yet it is in a certain sense the key to a reading of Chapter II, since it defines the goal toward which the people of God is moving. That goal is already outlined in *Lumen Gentium,* 9. The messianic people has for her destiny "the Kingdom of God, which has been begun by God himself on earth and which must be further extended until it is brought to perfection by him at the end of time". This goal is reaffirmed at the start of paragraph 48 of the same conciliar Constitution:

> The Church, to whom we are all called in Christ Jesus and in whom by the grace of God we acquire holiness, will receive her perfection only in the glory of heaven, when will come the time of the renewal of all things.

Moreover, the pastoral Constitution *Gaudium et Spes* offers the same teaching:

> Proceeding from the love of the eternal Father, the Church was founded by Christ in time and gathered into one by the Holy Spirit. She has a saving and eschatological purpose that can only be fully attained in the next life (*GS,* 40).

[1] In Flannery, *The Pilgrim Church* (New York, 1975).

In addition, Chapter VII of *Lumen Gentium* broadens the perspective on the Church by reminding us that the people of God, in her present condition as a historic subject, is already eschatological and that the pilgrim Church is one with the Church of heaven.

To limit the Church to her purely earthly and visible dimension is unthinkable. While she journeys on this earth, the invisible founts from which she lives and by which she is ceaselessly refreshed are located "where Christ is seated at the right hand of God, where the life of the Church is hidden with Christ in God until she appears in glory with her Spouse (cf. Col 3:1–4)" (*LG*, 6). Such is the work that the Holy Spirit accomplishes "by the power of the Gospel [permitting] the Church to keep the freshness of youth. Constantly he renews her and leads her to perfect union with her Spouse" (*LG*, 4). This goal toward which the Holy Spirit impels the Church is what determines at the deepest level the life of the pilgrim Church. It is for this reason that believers from now on have their citizenship (*politeuma*) "in heaven" (Phil 3:20; *LG*, 13, 48). Even now, "the Jerusalem above . . . is our mother" (Gal 4:26; cf. *LG*, 6). It is part of the Church's mystery that this goal is already secretly present in the pilgrim Church. This eschatological character of the Church does not lead to any downplaying of temporal responsibility. On the contrary, it guides the Church into the way of imitating Christ, the Poor Man and Servant. It is from her intimate union with Christ and from the gifts of his Spirit that the Church receives the strength to offer herself up in the service of all men and of the whole man. As she "presses onward toward the Kingdom of the Father" (cf. *GS*, 1), the Church weighs, nevertheless, the distance still to be traversed before her final fulfillment. She recognizes, therefore, that she counts sinners among her children and that she stands in continuous need of repentance (cf. *LG*, 8). Yet this distance, often painful to experience as it is, cannot suppress the fact that in all her different stages of life the Church is essentially one: this is true whether we think of the Church's prefiguration in creation, her preparation in the Old Testament, her constitution in "these, the last, times", her manifestation by the Holy Spirit, or, lastly, her fulfillment in glory at the end of the ages (cf. *LG*, 2). Moreover, if the Church is one at different stages of the divine economy, she is also one in her three dimensions: wayfaring, undergoing purgation, and glorification: "All . . . who are of Christ and who have his Spirit form one Church and in Christ cleave together (cf. Eph 4:16)" (*LG*, 49).

X.2. *Church and Kingdom*

It is this perspective of unity that we must bear in mind as we tackle the difficult question of the relation between the Church and the Kingdom.

Although many Church Fathers, medieval theologians, and sixteenth-century Reformers were generally happy to identify Church and Kingdom, we have come since then, and especially in the last two hundred years, to put a greater or lesser distance between them, accentuating somewhat unilaterally the eschatological aspect of the Kingdom and the historical aspect of the Church. The Council did not treat this question explicitly, but the interrelation of its various texts enables us to discern the effective teaching of *Lumen Gentium* in this matter.

Examining the texts that deal with the final consummation, one finds no difference between Church and Kingdom. On the one hand, we read that "while she slowly grows to maturity, the Church longs for the completed Kingdom" (*LG*, 5). On the other, the final fulfillment will be realized "when Christ presents to his Father an eternal and universal Kingdom" (*GS*, 39; cf. 1 Cor 15:24; *PO*, 2). Yet again, the Council affirms that the Church "will be brought to glorious completion at the end of time": "At that moment, as the Fathers put it, all the just from the time of Adam, 'from Abel, the just one, to the last of the elect', will be gathered together with the Father in the universal Church" (*LG*, 2). It is the Holy Spirit who leads the Church to "perfect union with her Spouse" (*LG*, 4). The same Church "with all her strength hopes and desires to be united in glory with her King" (*LG*, 5). Moreover, the Council can say of the people of God that "her destiny is the Kingdom of God", adding that she will be "brought to perfection by him at the end of time" (*LG*, 9). It is clear that in the Council's teaching there is no difference so far as eschatological reality is concerned between the final realization of the Church (as *consummata*) and of the Kingdom (as *consummatum*).

What, then, is their relation at the present time? The most explicit text on this subject (*LG*, 5) offers a glimpse of how subtle the relation between the ideas of Kingdom and Church really is. In their beginnings, the destinies of the Church and the Kingdom seem inseparable: "For the Lord Jesus inaugurated his Church by preaching the Good News, that is, the coming of the Kingdom of God" (*LG*, 5). The origins of the Church and the advent of the Kingdom of God are presented here in perfect synchronicity. The same is true of the growth of each. Those who receive the word of Christ in faith and "are numbered among the little flock of Christ (cf. Lk 12:32) have truly received the Kingdom" (*LG*, 5). We find the same thing, once again, where belonging to the Church is concerned: "He determined to call together in a holy Church those who should believe in Christ" (*LG*, 2). And so one can use the same terms for describing the growth both of Kingdom and of Church. It is, in fact, in the growth of the Church that the Council discerns the growth of the Kingdom: "To carry out the will of the Father, Christ inaugurated the Kingdom of heaven on earth. . . . The Church—that is, the Kingdom of Christ already present in mystery—grows visibly through the power of God in the world" (*LG*, 3; cf. *DV*, 17; *LG*, 13). The pilgrim Church is therefore "the Kingdom of God already mysteriously present", and in growing she moves toward the final Kingdom. Yet her growth is nothing other than the accomplishing of her mission: "The Church... receives the mission of proclaiming and establishing among all peoples the Kingdom of Christ and of God, and she is, on earth, the seed and the beginning of that Kingdom" (*LG*, 5, 9). This evocation of the Church as "seed" and "beginning" of the Kingdom expresses their simultaneous unity and difference.

So Church and Kingdom converge in their own mode of growth, a growth only realized in and through confirmation to the Christ who gave his life for the life of the world. The Kingdom suffers violence (cf. Mt 11:12), and in this, the Church has no different destiny. She "presses forward amid the persecutions of the world and the consolations of God" (St. Augustine, cited in *LG*, 8). The Church is the holy Church, though including sinners among her own (*LG*, 8). The Kingdom itself, "mysteriously present" (*in mysterio*), is hidden in the world and history, and so not yet purified of elements that are a stranger to it (cf. Mt 13:24–30, 47–49). As a divine-human mystery, the Church transcends the *socialis compago* or sociological configuration of the Catholic Church (*LG*, 8, 13–17). Belonging to the Kingdom cannot *not be* belonging — at least implicitly — to the Church.

X.3. *Is the Church the Sacrament of the Kingdom?*

To complete the previous chapter devoted to the Church as sacrament, it may be of use to ask here whether one can call the Church the sacrament of the Kingdom. This is not just a question of terminology. It is a truly theological question to which our work in its entirety enables us to offer a circumstantial answer.

We note first of all that the Council has nowhere used this expression, even if the word "sacrament" is, as we have seen, utilized in a variety of contexts. However, the expression "the Church, sacrament of the Kingdom", appears to be valid when understood in the following perspective:

1. In its ecclesiological application, the term "sacrament" is used analogically, as the first paragraph of *Lumen Gentium* stresses: *"Veluti sacramentum..."*.
2. The expression's aim is to relate, on the one hand, the Kingdom, understood in the plenary sense of its final realization, with, on the other hand, the Church in its "wayfaring" aspect.
3. The term "sacrament" here is understood in its full sense of *jam praesens in*

mysterio (cf. *LG*, 3), where the reality present in the sacrament (the pilgrim Church) is the Kingdom itself.

3. The Church is not a mere sign (*sacramentum tantum*) but a sign in which the reality signified is present (*res et sacramentum*) as the reality of the Kingdom.

5. The notion of the Church cannot be limited to its temporal and earthly aspect alone. Conversely, the notion of the Kingdom includes a presence "already" *in mysterio*.

X.4. *Mary: The Realized Church*

One could not offer a true reading of the Constitution *Lumen Gentium* without integrating somehow the bearing of its eighth chapter into our understanding of the mystery of the Church. Church and Kingdom find their highest realization in Mary. The Church's identity as the proleptic presence *in mysterio* of the Kingdom is illuminated in an unsurpassable way when we look at Mary, the dwelling of the Holy Spirit, model of faith, the *Realsymbol* of the Church. This is why the Council affirms of her that "in the most Blessed Virgin the Church has already reached that perfection whereby she exists without spot or wrinkle (cf. Eph 5:27)" (*LG*, 65). The often painful distance between the pilgrim Church and the final Kingdom is already transcended in Mary. As the *assumpta,* she "became like her Son who himself rose from the dead, anticipating thereby the destiny of the just" (Paul VI, *Profession of Faith,* 15). Because of this, the Mother of Jesus "is the image and beginning of the Church as she is to be perfected in the world to come" (*LG*, 68; cf. *SC*, 103).

14

THE CONSCIOUSNESS OF CHRIST
CONCERNING HIMSELF AND HIS MISSION

INTRODUCTION

The International Theological Commission has treated the subject of Christology twice already.[1] In the report published in 1980 some members spoke of the need for a synthesis, to be worked out by theologians, that would frame the Chalcedonian doctrine on the Person and nature of Christ in a soteriological perspective. In the same context reference was made to the very difficult question of Christ's knowledge and consciousness.[2] Three years later the questions of the preexistence of Jesus Christ and the Trinitarian aspect of his Passion were treated. Without prejudice to the future, the Commission noted that the investigation of the consciousness and human knowledge of Jesus still awaited completion.[3]

As in past years, the Commission still wishes "to highlight even better the role in man's salvation performed by the humanity of Christ and by the different 'mysteries' of his early life, such as the baptism, the temptations, and the 'agony' in Gethsemane".[4] For that reason the decision was made to undertake new research into the cognitive and affective life of him who knows the Father and who willed to reveal him to others. It is not the intention of the Commission to do this in all its aspects, granted that all are important. The spirit of the times demands, however, that some answers at least be given to questions about Jesus Christ that trouble human minds and hearts.

No person of sense would place his hope in an individual void of human

---

Translated by Michael Ledwith. This document was approved by the Commission "*in forma specifica*".

[1] International Theological Commission, *"Questiones Selectae de Christologia"*: *Gregorianum* 61 (1980): 609–32; *"Theologia-Christologia-Anthropologia"*: *Questiones Selectae: Altera Series: Gregorianum* 64 (1983): 5–24; transl. Michael Ledwith, "Theology-Christology-Anthropology", in *The Irish Theological Quarterly*, vol. 49, no. 4, pp. 285–300.

[2] *"Questiones Selectae"*, III, D.6.1, p. 622.

[3] *"Theologia-Christologia-Anthropologia"*, II, n. 1, p. 16.

[4] *"Questiones Selectae"*, II, C.7, p. 619.

mind and intelligence. This problem is not something confined to the fourth century. It is still a live question, even if the context is different.[5]

The use of the historical-critical method in Gospel study gives rise to questions about Jesus Christ, his consciousness of his own divinity, of his life and redemptive death, of his mission, of his teaching, and above all of his project of founding the Church. The scholars in the field have given various answers, at times one contradicting the other. These controversies show no signs of going away. Debate appears not only in scholarly journals but also at least occasionally in daily and weekly newspapers, in popular literature, and in the media in general.

These are obviously questions of importance for many different kinds of people, and particularly for Christians. The latter indeed often find it difficult to answer those who ask them the reasons for their hope (1 Pet 3:15). In fact, who would trust a Savior who may not have known who he was or was unwilling to be what he was?

It is clear, then, that the Church attaches maximum importance to the problem of the awareness (consciousness) and human knowledge of Jesus. We are not dealing with mere theological speculations but with the very foundation of the method and mission of the Church in all its intimacy. The Church, indeed, in announcing the Kingdom of God, calls men to repentance: she evangelizes; she proposes and makes available the means needed for reconciliation, freedom, and salvation; she wishes to communicate to all the revelation of the Father and the Son through the Spirit. She fearlessly presents herself to the world as the bearer of these tasks; she openly avows that such a mission and doctrine are committed to her by her Lord, Jesus. And to anyone who asks if this is the way things are, she is quick to answer in terms of her faith and conviction. Hence, the theological and pastoral importance today of the questions concerning the consciousness (awareness) and human knowledge of Jesus.

When these very important theological and pastoral questions are tackled, two complexes of arguments emerge in actual discussion. To begin with, attention must be directed to the relationship between ecclesiastical-dogmatic exegesis and historical-critical exegesis of Scripture, because these difficult hermeneutical questions are particularly acute in the field that concerns our inquiry. According to the teaching of the Second Vatican Council, scriptural exegesis "must seek out what the sacred writers really intended to say". In this search for the original meaning, account must also be taken of "the context and the unity of the whole of Scripture", which is to be interpreted "giving

---

[5] In that epoch the question concerned the full integrity of the humanity of Jesus Christ. St. Gregory of Nazianzen gave a valid reply when he called it madness to place one's hope in someone void of human intelligence (cf. *Epistola ad Cledonium: PG,* 37, 181, C.).

due weight to the living Tradition of the Church and to the analogy of faith".[6]

It is in this all-embracing way that the Commission will treat the matter, beginning with the biblical themes on the lines suggested by the Council. In fact, the study of Sacred Scripture should be "the soul of all theology".[7]

Another and equally difficult problem arises when it comes to studying the living Tradition of the Church. The Church and her theology live in history, and for that reason the explanation of the Faith once given for all time has to be made in the philosophical language of a given time, critically and to the point. The controversies surrounding the problem we have in mind arise precisely from differing philosophical conceptions. The exposition of the Commission rules out any a priori definitive philosophical terminology. We shall instead follow a common precomprehension in virtue of which we, as human beings, are present to ourselves in our "heart" in all our actions. At the same time we know that the consciousness of Jesus shares in the uniqueness and mysterious character of his Person, and that, for this reason, it evades any purely rational scrutiny. There is no other way of treating our problem except in the light of our faith that Jesus, the Christ, is the Son of the Living God (Mt 16:16).

FOUR PROPOSITIONS

Our study will limit itself, therefore, to some statements of what Jesus was conscious of with regard to his own personal mission. The four propositions that follow are placed at the level of what the Faith has always believed about Christ. They expressly avoid theological elaborations calculated to give an account of this datum of faith. There is, then, no reference to attempts to give theological formulation as to how such a consciousness could have been articulated within the humanity of Christ.

The commentaries on the four propositions follow broadly a three-stage design. To begin, what the apostolic preaching has to say about Christ will be stated. An effort will then be made to examine what the Synoptic Gospels, through the convergence of their various strands, permit us to say about the consciousness of Jesus. Finally, the testimony of John's Gospel will be examined, a Gospel that often states more explicitly what the Synoptics contain somewhat more implicitly, although no contradictions exist between them.

---

[6] *DV,* 12; cf. 9 and 10.
[7] *OT,* 16; cf. *DV,* 24.

FIRST PROPOSITION

The life of Jesus testifies to his consciousness of a filial relationship with the Father. His behavior and his words, which are those of the perfect "servant", imply an authority that surpasses that of the ancient prophets and belongs to God alone. Jesus drew this incomparable authority from his unique relationship with God, whom he calls "my Father". He was conscious of being the only Son of God and in this sense of being God himself.

Commentary

1.1. The postpaschal apostolic preaching, which proclaims Jesus as Son of God, is not a late development in the primitive Church: it is already in evidence at the very heart of the most ancient formulations of the *kerygma,* of the Confessions of Faith, and of the hymns (Rom 1:3f.; Phil 2:6ff.). St. Paul reaches the point of summing up his entire preaching in the expression "the Gospel of God about his Son" (Rom 1:3, 9; cf. 2 Cor 1:19; Gal 1:16). The "mission formulas" are of particular significance in this respect: "God has sent his own Son" (Rom 8:3; Gal 4:4). The divine sonship, then, is at the center of the apostolic preaching. It can be understood as an explanation, in the light of the Cross and Resurrection, of the relationship of Jesus with his own "Abba".

1.2. Indeed, calling God "Father", which is the pure and simple Christian usage now, goes back to Jesus himself. This is one of the very best attested data in the historical-critical study of Jesus. Not only, however, does he call God "Father" or "my Father" in general: as he turns to him in prayer, he invokes him as "Abba" (Mk 14:36; Rom 8:15; Gal 4:6), and this marks a novel element. The way in which Jesus prays (Mt 11:25) and the way he teaches his disciples to pray (Lk 11:2), implies a distinction (explicit after Easter; see Jn 20:17) between "my Father" and "your Father" and also implies the singular and nontransferable character of the relationship uniting Jesus and God. Before the mystery of Jesus was revealed to men, there was already in the consciousness of Jesus a personal perception of a most sure and profound relationship with the Father. From the fact that he called God "Father", it follows by implication that Jesus was aware of his own divine authority and mission. There is good reason, then, for finding the term "to reveal" in this context (Mt 11:27, par.; cf. 16–17). Knowing himself to be the one who knows God perfectly, Jesus as a result knows that he is at the same time the bearer of God's definitive revelation to men. He knows and is conscious of being "the" Son (Mk 12:6; 13:22).

In the strength of such consciousness, Jesus speaks and acts with the kind of authority that belongs to God alone. And man's eternal salvation is decided on the basis of his attitude to Jesus (Lk 12:8; Mk 8:38; Mt 10:32). From now on Jesus can call on his followers (Mk 1:17). To follow him means loving him before one's own parents (Mt 10:37), putting him ahead of any earthly good whatsoever (Mk 10:29), being ready to die "for my cause" (Mk 8:35). He speaks as the sovereign lawgiver (Mt 5:22–28), surpassing prophets and kings (Mt 12:41–42). He alone is the Master (Mt 23:8). All will pass away except his word (Mk 13:31).

1.3. The Gospel of John states more explicitly the origin of such unheard-of authority: it is because "the Father is in me and I in the Father" (10:38). "The Father and I are one" (10:30). The "I" who speaks and acts as sovereign lawgiver is of the same standing as the "I" of Yahweh (Ex 3:14).

Even from a historical point of view we have every reason for stating that the earliest apostolic proclamation of Jesus as Son of God is based on the very consciousness that Jesus himself had of being the Son and emissary of the Father.

SECOND PROPOSITION

Jesus was aware of the purpose of his mission: to announce the Kingdom of God and make it present in his own Person, in his actions, and in his words, so that the world would become reconciled with God and renewed. He freely accepted the Father's will: to give his own life for the salvation of all mankind. He knew the Father had sent him to serve and to give his life "for many" (Mk 14:24).

Commentary

2.1. The apostolic preaching on the divine sonship involves equally and indissolubly a soteriological significance. In fact, the sending of Christ and his arrival in the flesh (Rom 8:3), under the law (Gal 4:4), his self-humiliation (Phil 2:7), are all aimed at lifting us up: to justify us (2 Cor 5:21), to make us rich (2 Cor 8:9), and to render us sons through the agency of the Spirit (Rom 8:15f.; Gal 4:5f.; Heb 2:10). Such a sharing in the divine sonship, which comes into being in faith and is especially expressed in the prayer of Christians to the Father, presupposes the consciousness Jesus himself had of his own Sonship.

The entire apostolic preaching is based on the conviction that Jesus knew he was the Son, the Father's emissary; and without such a consciousness Christology and soteriology as well would lack a foundation.

2.2. The consciousness Jesus has of his unique filial relationship is the foundation and presupposition of his mission. Inversely, we can argue from mission to consciousness. According to the Synoptic Gospels Jesus knows that he has been sent to announce the Good News of the Kingdom of God (Lk 4:43; cf. Mt 15:24); it is for this end that he "came forth" (Mk 1:38, Greek) and has come (Mk 2:17). Filtered through his mission to mankind we can at the same time discover him whose emissary he is (Lk 10:16). With gestures and words Jesus manifested the purpose of his "Coming": to call sinners (Mk 2:17), "to seek and save what was lost" (Lk 10:16), not to abolish but to complete the law (Mt 5:17), bring the sword of separation (Mt 10:34), cast fire on the earth (Lk 12:49). Jesus knows he has "come" not to be served but to serve "and to give his own life as a ransom for many" (Mk 10:45).[8]

2.3. This "Coming" of his can have no other origin than God. The Gospel of St. John makes explicit in its mission Christology (*Sendungschristologie*) the more implicit Synoptic witness to Jesus' consciousness of his incomparable mission. He knows he has "come" from the Father (Jn 5:43), "come forth" from him (8:12; 16:28). The mission he received from the Father is not something imposed by an outside source. It belongs to him so intimately as to coincide with his whole being. It is his whole life (6:7), his food (4:34), he seeks nothing else (5:30), his will is consumed entirely by God's will (6:38), his words are the words of his Father (3:34; 12:49), his works are the Father's (9:4), so much so that he can say of himself, "He who sees me sees the Father" (14:9). The consciousness Jesus has of himself coincides with the consciousness of, say, a prophet's mission, granted at a particular time, even if it were "from the womb" (like Jeremiah, Jer 1:5; the Baptist, Lk 1:15; Paul, Gal 1:15). Even more, this mission is rooted in a first time "emergence" from God, "because I came out from God" (8:42), all of which presupposes, to be at all possible, that he had been "from the beginning with God" (1:1, 18).

2.4. The consciousness Jesus has of his mission also involves, therefore, the consciousness of his "preexistence". His mission (in time), in fact, is not essentially separable from his (eternal) procession: it is a "prolongation" of it.[9] His human consciousness of his mission "translates", so to speak, the eternal relationship with the Father into the idiom of a human life.

This relationship of the incarnate Son with the Father presumes in the first place the mediation of the Holy Spirit, who must therefore be always included in the consciousness of Jesus as Son. Already his purely human existence is the result of the action of the Spirit: from his baptism on, all his work—whether actively or passively among men or his communion in prayer with the Father—is realized only in and through the Spirit (Lk 4:18; Acts 10:38; Mk 1:12; Mt 12:28). The Son knows that as he fulfills the Father's will the Spirit guides and sustains him all the way to the Cross. There his earthly mission ended, "he gave up" (*paredoken*) "his Spirit" (*pneuma*) (Jn 19:30), a particular

[8] Cf. "*Questiones Selectae*", IV, B–C, pp. 624–27.
[9] Cf. St. Thomas, *In Sententias*, I, d. 15, q. 4, a. 1, sol.; I, q. 43, a. 2, ad 2.

in which some discern the introduction of the gift of the Spirit. From his resurrection and ascension onward, he becomes, as glorified man, that which he had been as God from all eternity: "a life-giving Spirit" (1 Cor 15:45; 2 Cor 3:17), a Lord fully able to pour out the Holy Spirit on us so as to raise us in him to the dignity of sons.

But this relationship of the incarnate Son with the Father is all the same expressed in a "kenotic" fashion.[10] To realize a perfect obedience, Jesus freely renounces (Phil 2:6–9) all that might impede that attitude. He refuses, for example, to call on the legions of angels at his disposal (Mt 26:53), he wishes to grow as a man "in wisdom, age, and grace" (Lk 2:52), to learn and to obey (Heb 5:8), to face temptations (Mt 4:1–11, par.), to suffer. None of this is incompatible with the affirmations that Jesus "knows all" (Jn 16:30), that "the Father has shown him all his works" (Jn 5:20; 13:3; Mt 11:27), if these affirmations are taken to mean that Jesus receives from the Father all that enables him to accomplish his works of revelation and of universal redemption (Jn 3:11–32; 8:38–40; 15:15; 17:8).

THIRD PROPOSITION

To realize his salvific mission, Jesus wanted to unite men with the coming Kingdom and to gather them around himself. With this end before him, he did certain definite acts that, if taken altogether, can only be explained as a preparation for the Church, which will be definitively constituted at the time of the Easter and Pentecost events. It is therefore to be affirmed of necessity that Jesus willed the foundation of the Church.

Commentary

3.1. According to the apostolic testimony, Christ and the Church are inseparable. In a recurring phrase in St. Paul, the churches are "in Christ" (1 Th 1:1; 2:14; 2 Th 1:1; Gal 1:22); they are the churches of Christ (Rom 16:16). To be a Christian means "Christ is in you" (Rom 8:10; 2 Cor 13:5); it is "to live in Christ" (Rom 8:2): "You are all one in Christ" (Gal 3:18). This unity is most of all expressed in terms of analogy with the unity of the human body. The Holy Spirit is the unifying principle of this body: "The Body of Christ" (1 Cor 12:27), or "in Christ" (Rom 12:5) and also "Christ" (1 Cor 12:12). Christ in heaven is the source of life and growth of the Church (Col 2:19; Eph

---

[10] Cf. Pontifical Biblical Commission, *Bible et Christologie,* n. 2.2.1.3 (Paris: Cerf, 1984), pp. 93–95; cf. also p. 45; trans. Joseph A. Fitzmyer, *Scripture and Christology. A Statement of the Biblical Commission with a Commentary* (New York: Paulist Press, 1986).

4:11–16). He is "the Head of the Body" (Col 1:18; 3:15, etc.), the "fullness" (Eph 1:22f.) of the Church.

Now this unbreakable unity between Christ and his Church is rooted in the supreme act of his life: the giving of his own life on the Cross. Since he loved her, "he gave himself up for her" (Eph 5:25), because "he wanted to present the Church to himself all glorious" (Eph 5:27; Col 1:22). The Church, the Body of Christ, takes its origin from the Body consigned to the Cross, from "the precious blood" (1 Pet 1:19) of Christ, which is "the price of our redemption" (1 Cor 6:20). In the eyes of the apostolic preaching the Church is the very purpose of the work of salvation brought about by Christ in his life on earth.

3.2. When he preaches the Kingdom of God, Christ is not simply announcing the imminence of a great eschatological change; he is, first of all, calling mankind to enter the Kingdom. The germ and the beginning of the Kingdom is "the little flock" (Lk 12:32) made up of those Jesus came to call around himself, and of whom he himself is pastor (Mk 14:27, par.; Jn 10:1–29; Mt 10:16, par.), he who came to gather together and free his sheep (Mt 15:24; Lk 15:4–7). Jesus speaks of such an assembly in using the image of guests invited to a wedding banquet (Mk 2:19, par.), of a sowing by God (Mt 13:24; 15:13), of a fisherman's net (Mt 13:47; Mk 1:17). The disciples of Christ form a city on a mountain summit visible from afar (Mt 5:14); they constitute the new family of which God himself is Father and where all are brothers (Mt 23:9). The parables of Jesus and the images he uses in describing those he came to call as followers involve an "implicit ecclesiology".

It is not a question of stating that this intention on the part of Christ involves an outright will to establish and give firm shape to all the institutional aspects of the Church in the way these have developed in the course of the centuries.[11] Instead, it is necessary to state that Jesus did will to give the community, which he gathered around himself, a structure that will remain until the full realization of the Kingdom. At this point note must be taken of the choice, first of all, of the Twelve and Peter as their head (Mk 3:14ff.). Such a choice, and what is more a deliberate one, aims at the definitive eschatological foundation of the people of God, which will be open to all mankind (Mt 8:11f.). The Twelve (Mk 6:7) and the other disciples (Lk 10:1ff.) have a share in the mission of Christ, in his power, but also in his fate (Mt 10:25; Jn 15:20). In them Jesus himself comes, and in him the one is present who sent him (Mk 10:40).

The Church will also have a prayer of her own, that which Jesus has given

---

[11] International Theological Commission, *Themata selecta de Ecclesiologia*, 1.4 (Rome: Libreria Editrice Vaticana, 1985), pp. 11ff.

her (Lk 11:2–4). Above all, she inherits the act of remembrance of his Supper, the center of the "New Covenant" (Lk 22:20) and of the new community reunited in the breaking of bread (Lk 22:19). Jesus taught those he had called around himself "a way of acting" that was new and different from that of the ancients (Mt 5:21, etc.), of the pagans (Mt 5:47), and of the great of this earth (Lk 22:25ff.).

Did Jesus will the foundation of the Church? Yes, but this Church is the people of God that he brings together, beginning first of all with Israel, through whom he aims at the salvation of all peoples. In fact, it is to "the lost sheep of the house of Israel" (Mt 10:6; 15:24) that Jesus knows himself to have been sent first, and to these he sends his disciples. One of the most moving expressions of the consciousness of his own dignity and mission on the part of Jesus is this lament (the lament of the God of Israel!): "Jerusalem, Jerusalem . . . how often would I have gathered your children together as a hen gathers her brood under her wings and you would not" (Lk 13:34; 19:41–44). God (Yahweh), indeed, in the Old Testament seeks without pause to unite the people of Israel into a single people, *his* people. That very "and you would not" does not change, to be sure, the intention, but the path followed by the calling together of all mankind around Jesus. From now on it will be "the times of the Gentiles" (Lk 21:24; Rom 11:1–6), principally, which will indicate the *Church* of Christ.

Christ was conscious of his saving mission. This brought with it the foundation of his *Church*, that is, the calling together of all mankind into "God's family". In the last analysis the history of Christianity is founded on the intention and the will of Christ to found his Church.

3.3. In the light of the Spirit the Gospel of St. John sees the whole life of Christ as illuminated by the glory of the risen One. In that way the vision enjoyed by the circle of the disciples of Jesus is already open to all those who "will believe in me through their word" (17:20). Those who were with him in his life on earth, those whom the Father had given him (17:6), whom he had guarded, and for whom "he had consecrated himself" (17:19) by giving his life, already represent all those who will have loved him (1:12) and who will believe in him (3:36). By faith they are united to him as shoots are to the vine, without which they would become desiccated (15:6). This intimate union between Jesus and believers, "you in me and I in you" (14:20), has on one hand its origin in the Father's plan when he "gives" the disciples to Jesus (6:39, 44, 65), but it is realized definitively by means of freely giving his life (10:18) "for his friends" (15:13). The paschal mystery is the permanent source of the Church (19:34): "And I, when I am lifted up from the earth, will draw all men to myself" (12:32).

FOURTH PROPOSITION

The consciousness that Christ had of being the Father's emissary to save the world and to bring all mankind together in God's people involves, in a mysterious way, a love for all mankind so much so that we may all say: "The Son of God loved me and gave himself up for me" (Gal 2:20).

Commentary

4.1. From its earliest formulation the apostolic preaching involves the conviction that "Christ died for our sins according to the Scriptures" (1 Cor 15:3), that "he gave himself for our sins" (Gal 1:4), and this was according to the will of God the Father, who "delivered him to death for our sins" (Rom 4:25; Is 53:6), "for us all" (Rom 8:32), "to redeem us" (Gal 4:4). God, who "desires all men to be saved" (1 Tim 2:4), excludes no one from his plan of salvation, which Christ embraces with all his being. The entire life of Christ, from "his entrance into the world" (Heb 10:5) to the giving of his life, is a single and unique gift "for us". And that precisely is what the Church has preached from the very outset (Rom 5:8; 1 Th 5:10; 2 Cor 5:15; 1 Pet 2:21; 3:18, etc.).

He died for us, because he loved us: "Christ loved us and gave himself up for us, a fragrant offering and sacrifice to God" (Eph 5:2). That "us" means all the people whom he wishes to reunite in his Church. "Christ loved the Church and gave himself up for her" (Eph 5:25). Now, this love has not been understood by the Church as just a general attitude but as a concrete love expressed in terms of personal consideration for every individual. This is how the Church sees things as she hears St. Paul emphasize respect for the "weak": "Do not let what you eat cause the ruin of one for whom Christ died" (Rom 14:15; 1 Cor 8:11; 2 Cor 5:14f.). To the faction-riddled Christians of Corinth, the same Paul puts the questions: "Is Christ divided? Was Paul crucified for you?" (1 Cor 1:13). And concerning the matter in hand, Paul, who never knew Christ "in the days of his flesh" (Heb 5:7), will be able to say: "And the life I now live in the flesh I live by faith in the Son of God, who loved me and gave himself up for me" (Gal 2:20).

4.2. The apostolic witnesses mentioned above to the death that Jesus underwent for love, in a most personal way, "for us", "for me", and "for my brothers", hold together in a single glance the unbounded love of the preexisting "Son of God" (Gal 2:20), the One who at the same time was acknowledged as the glorified "Lord". That "for us", full of the love of Jesus, has its foundation in the preexistence, and endures in the love of the glorified One who — having loved us (Rom 8:37) in his Incarnation and his death — "intercedes for us" now (Rom 8:34). The "preexistent" love of Jesus is the continuing element that characterizes the Son in all these "stages"—preexistence, earthly life, glorified existence.

This abiding nature of his love we find expressed in the words of Jesus. According to Luke 22:27, Jesus expresses the sum of his life on earth and his behavior under the image of "one who serves at table". "To be the servant of all" (Mk 9:35, par.) is the basic rule in the circle of disciples. Love as service reaches its climax in the farewell Supper, during which Jesus sacrifices himself and offers himself as the one who must die (Lk 22:19f., par.). On the Cross his life of service is transmuted into a death of service "for many" (Mk 10:45; 14:22–24). The service Jesus gave in life and death was also after all a service of the "Kingdom of God" in words and acts, to the point that he can even go so far as to present his life and works in his future in glory as "a waiting at table" (Lk 12:37) and as an intercession (Rom 8:34). It was a service of love that links God's deepest love with the love, full of self-abnegation, of one's neighbor (Mk 12:28–34).

The love to which the whole life of Christ witnesses is first of all shown to be a universal love, in the sense that no one who approaches him is excluded. This love goes in search of "the one who was lost" (Lk 15:3–10, 11–32), publicans and sinners (cf. Mk 2:17; Lk 7:34, 36–50; Mt 9:1–8; Lk 15:15), the rich (Lk 19:1–10) and the poor (Lk 16:19–31), male and female (Lk 8:2–3, 7:11–17, 12:10–17), the sick (Mk 1:29–34, etc.), the possessed (Mk 1:21–28, etc.), the anguished (Lk 6:21), and the persecuted (Mt 11:28).

This deliberate opening of the heart of Jesus to all and sundry is meant to transcend the limits of its own generation, as is evident in the "universalization" of his mission and promises. The Beatitudes surpass his contemporary audience; they have in mind all the poor, all the hungry (cf. Lk 6:20). Whoever accepts one of these little ones accepts Jesus himself, and by the same token him by whom he was sent (Mk 9:37). Only at the Final Judgment will it be clearly seen how far this presently hidden identification was actually developed (Mt 25:31–46).

4.3. This mystery is at the heart of our Faith: the inclusion of all mankind within this eternal love with which God so loved the world as to give his own Son (Jn 3:16). "By this we know love, that he [Christ] laid down his life for us" (Jn 3:16). Indeed, "the good shepherd gives his life for his sheep" (Jn 10:11); he knows them (Jn 10:14) and calls them each by his own name (Jn 10:3).

4.4. Simply because they have known this love,[12] personal to each, multitudes of Christians have dedicated themselves to the poor in love, without distinctions, and they continue to give testimony to this love, which knows how to identify Jesus in every one of "these smallest brothers of mine" (Mt

---

[12] Cf. GS, 22.3.

25:40). "Each and every single person is in question, since each one was included in the mystery of the redemption and Christ has united himself to each, forever, by means of this mystery."[13]

---

[13] John Paul II, *RH,* 13; *GS,* 22.

APPENDICES

I

1. STATUTES OF THE INTERNATIONAL THEOLOGICAL COMMISSION

1.1 Provisory statute (July 12, 1969), (cf. AAS 61 (1969), 540–41).

1. A Theological Commission has been established as part of the Congregation for the Doctrine of the Faith, whose task is to offer its services to the Holy See and in an especial way to the same Sacred Congregation in examining doctrinal questions of major importance.

2. The office of President of the Theological Commission is assumed by the Cardinal Prefect of the Congregation for the Doctrine of the Faith, who for individual sessions may delegate one of the cardinal members of the same Sacred Congregation.

3. The Cardinal President designates a secretary for the technical works of the Commission.

4. The Theological Commission is comprised of theologians of various schools and nations who are outstanding in the science of theology and fidelity toward the Magisterium of the Church.

5. The members of the Theological Commission are appointed by the Supreme Pontiff for five years upon the suggestion of the Cardinal Prefect of the Congregation for the Doctrine of the Faith, with previous consultation with the episcopal conferences; at the end of the fifth year they may be reappointed. The members will not total more than thirty.

6. The plenary assembly of the Theological Commission is convoked at least once a year.

7. If the study of particular questions requires it, the Cardinal President may institute special commissions of members who are highly specialized in the matter; such commissions cease to exist as soon as their work is completed.

8. The members of the Theological Commission may also be consulted through writing.

9. Questions and topics to be submitted for study may also be proposed to the Congregation for the Doctrine of the Faith by the Theological Commission or one of its members; the Sacred Congregation will then select the theme most opportune to treat.

10. The conclusions, which the Theological Commission may have reached in the plenary assembly or in the special commissions, as well as the individual views of its members, will be submitted to the Supreme Pontiff and presented to the Congregation for the Doctrine of the Faith for examination.

11. The members of the Theological Commission, having taken into account the bonds of collaboration with the Congregation for the Doctrine of the Faith, will maintain the pontifical secret concerning the themes being treated on the part of the Commission, according to the norms of the regulations of the Roman Curia.

Pope Paul VI in the audience given to the undersigned prefect of the Congregation for the Doctrine of the Faith on April 11, 1969, as well as with the letter of the Secretary of State no. 134829 of April 24, 1969, has approved for experimentation the statute of the Theological Commission.

Francesco Cardinal Seper, Prefect
Rome, July 12, 1969.

1.2. Definitive statute: Motu Proprio *Tredecim Anni,* August 6, 1982 (cf. AAS 74 (1982), 1201–5).

Already thirteen years have passed since our predecessor Paul VI, of happy memory, following the voting of the Synod of Bishops (cf. Discourse in the Consistory of April 28, 1969, AAS 61 (1969), 431–32), instituted the International Theological Commission (ITC). During these thirteen years, the scholars of sacred theology who have been called to this office have worked with great diligence and prudence and have offered the excellent fruits of their work. Therefore the Supreme Pontiff Paul VI and also we ourselves have received them willingly in order to give to them our paternal exhortation and manifest to them our gratitude for their studies and their efforts, a great part of which have already been noted, having been published upon the wish of Paul VI.

In 1969 the statutes of the ITC were approved *ad experimentum* (cf. AAS 61 (1969), 540–41). Now the time has arrived to give to these statutes a stable and definitive form, taking into account the experience which has been acquired up until this date, so that the Commission may be able to carry on better the task which has been entrusted to it. This task was expressly described by Paul VI in the discourse which he held during the first plenary session, affirming that this new institution was established "in order to offer its help to the Holy See and especially to the Sacred Congregation for the Doctrine of the Faith" (cf. AAS 61 (1969), 713f).

In reality, Peter and the other apostles, as well as their successors in sacred Tradition—and that is the Roman Pontiff and with him all the bishops of the Church—have received, in an absolutely singular way, the duty and the responsibility of the authentic Magisterium, in conformity with the command of Jesus: "Go therefore and teach all nations, baptizing them in the name of the Father and of the Son and of the Holy Spirit, teaching them to observe all that which I have commanded you. Behold, I am with you all days, even until the end of the world" (Mt 28:19–20). The Second Vatican Council, especially in the Dogmatic Constitution *Lumen Gentium* (III), in the footsteps of the entire tradition of the Church, calls these tasks by the name of charisms, which confer to it strength, efficacy, and authenticity.

Still, this specific office has need of the study and of the efforts of theologians, from whom, according to the words of the same Paul VI, one expects "a sure help . . . in fulfilling the office which has been entrusted by Christ to his apostles with the words: 'Go and teach all nations' " (AAS 61 (1969), 715). It is our wish that this help be given by the members of the ITC in a distinct and almost "institutional" way. They in fact, coming from different nations and having to deal with the cultures of different peoples, know better the new problems, which are like ancient problems with a new face, and therefore they can also better appreciate the aspirations and the mentality of the men of today. Therefore, they can be a great help in giving to the urgent problems today a response that is more profound and more consonant according to the norm of the faith revealed by Christ and handed down through the Church.

Therefore, after having considered everything attentively, *motu proprio* and with our apostolic authority we establish new statutes for the ITC and we order the following:

1. It is the duty of the ITC to study doctrinal problems of great importance, especially those which present new points of view, and in this way to offer its help to the Magisterium of the Church, particularly to the Sacred Congregation for the Doctrine of the Faith to which it is attached.

2. The President of the ITC is the Cardinal Prefect of the Sacred Congregation for the Doctrine of the Faith, who, however, in case of necessity and for individual sessions may delegate another moderator.

3. The ITC is made up of scholars of the theological sciences of different schools and nations; they should be eminent for their science, prudence, and fidelity toward the Magisterium of the Church.

4. The members of the ITC are appointed by the Supreme Pontiff, to whose judgment the Cardinal Prefect of this Sacred Congregation for the Doctrine of the Faith will make proposals, after having listened to the episcopal conferences.

Such members are appointed for five years, after which they may be reappointed. They should not number more than thirty, except in particular cases.

5. The General Secretary of the ITC, upon the proposal of the Cardinal President of the same Commission, is nominated for five years by the Supreme Pontiff and is part of the advisors of the Sacred Congregation for the Doctrine of the Faith. At the end of the fifth year, he may be reappointed.

It is advisable that the Cardinal President, before suggesting to the Supreme Pontiff the names of those persons suited for this office, consult as much as possible the members of the Commission. It is the specific task of the General Secretary to coordinate the work and to spread the written works of the same Commission during the sessions, as well as before and after the sessions.

6. A vice secretary is nominated by the Cardinal President. He helps the General Secretary in his ordinary work and he has special care of the technical and financial aspects.

7. The plenary session of the ITC is called at least once a year, unless contrary circumstances impede it.

8. The members of the ITC may be consulted also in writing.

9. Questions and subjects to be submitted for study are established by the Supreme Pontiff or by the Cardinal President. They may also be proposed by the Sacred Congregation for the Doctrine of the Faith, by other departments of the Roman Curia, by the Synod of Bishops, by episcopal conferences. However, what is prescribed in no. 136 of the apostolic constitution *Regimini ecclesiae universae*[1] must be observed.

10. In order to prepare for the study of particular questions, the Cardinal President establishes special subcommissions comprised of members who are especially competent in the matter to be studied.

The work of these subcommissions is guided by a member chosen by the Cardinal President so that, with common agreement of the General Secretary, he may conduct the preparation of the work of the plenary session. These subcommissions ordinarily should be made up of at least ten members: and for a special and brief session they may meet outside of Rome.

Other experts may be consulted, even non-Catholics. But those who are called for this consultation do not become members of the ITC.

Having completed the study and at the end of the fifth year, the subcommissions cease from their task, but they may be nominated or renewed for another five years.

11. The conclusions which the ITC reaches, whether in the plenary session or in the special subcommissions, as also, if it be judged opportune, the views of individual members, should be submitted to the Supreme Pontiff and should be given to the Sacred Congregation for the Doctrine of the Faith.

12. Documents which have been approved by the majority of the members of the ITC may also be published on condition that there is not any difficulty on the part of the Apostolic See.

Texts which have been approved only generically may be published as personal works of the members of the ITC, but they do not in any way engage the responsibility of the ITC. This is all the more so in the case of preparatory

---

[1] At the number indicated it is said that "no grave and extraordinary matter must be dealt with, unless the Supreme Pontiff has first been informed by the respective moderators".

reports or views of external experts. These different levels of responsibility should be clearly evident in the presentation of the texts.

13. The members of the ITC, for as much as regards the subject matter that has been treated by the Commission and taking into account their nature and importance, shall maintain complete secrecy, conforming themselves to the existing norms concerning the so-called professional secret.

Matters which regard the collaboration with the Sacred Congregation for the Doctrine of the Faith, whether collectively or individually, according to the nature of the things are covered by the secrecy proper to this Congregation, that is to say pontifical, according to what is written in the instruction regarding this secrecy (cf. AAS 66 (1974), 89–92).

We decree that all that which is established by the present letter *motu proprio* shall take effect with force of law beginning from the first of October of the current year, notwithstanding anything contrary.

Given in Rome, at St. Peter's, August 6, 1982, feast of the Transfiguration of our Lord Jesus Christ, fourth year of our pontificate.

John Paul II

II

LIST OF PAPAL PRONOUNCEMENTS
CONCERNING THE INTERNATIONAL THEOLOGICAL COMMISSION

Though it is not possible to present in this volume a complete text of Papal pronouncements concerning the International Theological Commission, still it seems opportune to present a list of them here indicating sources and principal topics.

Paul VI

1. Institution and purpose of the International Theological Commission

Consistory address, April 28, 1969: AAS 61 (1969), 431–32.
Discourse to Italian Bishops, April 11, 1970: AAS 62 (1970), 280–81.
Allocution to the Sacred College, June 22, 1970: AAS 62 (1970), 517.

2. Papal addresses to the International Theological Commission

October 6, 1969: AAS 61 (1969), 713–16 (purpose and methods of the I.T.C.)
October 11, 1972: AAS 64 (1972), 682–83 (theological research).
October 11, 1973: AAS 65 (1973), 555–59 (Theological pluralism).
December 16, 1974: AAS 67 (1975), 39–44 (Moral theology).

John Paul II

Papal addresses to the International Theological Commission

October 26, 1979: AAS 71 (1979), 1428–33 (Christology; the relationship between the Magisterium and theologians).

October 6, 1981: AAS 73 (1981), 703–06 (Christology).

December 5, 1983: AAS 76 (1984), 462–66 (The rights and dignity of the human person).

October 5, 1985: *Insegnamenti di Giovanni Paolo II,* VIII, 2 (1985), 853–56 (Bilancio di quindici anni di lavoro della C.T.I.).

III

LIST OF MEMBERS OF THE
INTERNATIONAL THEOLOGICAL COMMISSION

The First Five Years
Appointments of May 1, 1969; cf. DC 66 (1969), 495.

Rev. Barnabas Ahern, C.P. (United States)
Rev. Hans Urs von Balthasar (Switzerland)
Rev. Louis Bouyer of the Oratory (France)
Rev. Walter Burghardt, S.J. (United States)
Msgr. Carlo Colombo (Italy)
Rev. Yves Congar, O.P. (France)
Msgr. Philippe Delhaye (Belgium)
Rev. Johannes Feiner (Switzerland)
Rev. André Feuillet, P.S.S. (France)
Rev. Lucio Gera (Argentina)
Rev. Olegario Gonzalez de Cardedal (Spain)
Rev. Ignace Abdo Khalifé, S.J. (Lebanon)
Rev. Franz Lakner, S.J. (Austria)
Rev. Marie-Joseph Le Guillou, O.P. (France)
Rev. Joseph Lescrauwaet, M.S.C. (Holland)
Rev. Bernard Lonergan, S.J. (Japan)
Rev. Henri de Lubac, S.J. (France)
Rev. Andreas H. Maltha, O.P. (Holland)
Msgr. Jorge Medina Estevez (Chile)
Rev. Peter Nemeshegyi, S.J. (Japan)
Msgr. Stanislaw Olejnik (Poland)
Msgr. Gérard Philips (Belgium)
Rev. Karl Rahner, S.J. (West Germany)
Rev. Joseph Ratzinger (West Germany)
Msgr. Roberto Mascarenhas Roxo (Brazil)
Rev. Tomislaw Sagi-Bunic, O.F.M. Cap. (Yugoslavia)
Msgr. Rudolf Schnackenburg (West Germany)
Rev. Heinz Schürmann (East Germany)
Msgr. Tharcisius Tshibangu (Zaire)
Rev. Cipriano Vagaggini, O.S.B. (Italy)

Second Five Years
Appointments of August 1, 1974; cf. AAS 66 (1974), 520–21; DC 71 (1974), 759.

Rev. Barnabas Ahern*
Rev. Juan Alfaro, S.J. (Spain)
Rev. Catalino G. Arevalo, S.J. (Philippines)
Rev. Hans Urs von Balthasar*
Rev. Louis Bouyer*[1]
Rev. Walter Burghardt*
Msgr. Carlo Caffarra (Italy)
Rev. Raniero Cantalamessa, O.F.M. Cap. (Italy)
Rev. Yves Congar*
Msgr. Philippe Delhaye*
Rev. Edouard Dhanis, S.J. (Belgium)
Rev. Wilhelm Ernst (East Germany)
Rev. Olegario Gonzalez de Cardedal*
Rev. Edouard Hamel, S.J. (Canada)
Rev. Boguslaw Inlender (Poland)
Rev. Boaventura Kloppenburg, O.F.M. (Brazil)
Rev. Marie-Joseph Le Guillou*
Rev. Karl Lehmann (West Germany)
Rev. Joseph Lescrauwaet*
Rev. John Mahoney, S.J. (Great Britain)
Rev. Gustave Martelet, S.J. (France)
Msgr. Jorge Medina Estevez*
Rev. Vincent Mulago (Zaire)
Msgr. Joseph Ratzinger*
Rev. Georges Saber, O.L.M. (Lebanon)
Rev. Heinz Schürmann*
Rev. Otto Semmelroth, S.J. (West Germany)
Rev. Anton Strlé (Yugoslavia)
Rev. Jean-Marie Tillard, O.P. (Canada)
Rev. Cipriano Vagaggini*
Rev. Jan Walgrave, O.P. (Belgium)

---

[1] Father Bouyer did not accept the appointment for personal reasons and was replaced by Fr. Dhanis (cf. AAS 67 (1975), 286).

* The asterisk refers to previous lists.

Third Five Years
Nominations of August 12, 1980; cf. AAS 72 (1980), 977–78; DC 77 (1980), 112.

Rev. Barnabas Ahern*
Rev. Juan Alfaro*
Rev. Catalino G. Arevalo*
Rev. Hans Urs von Balthasar*
Msgr. Carlo Caffarra*
Msgr. Giuseppe Colombo (Italy)
Rev. Yves Congar*
Msgr. Philippe Delhaye*
Msgr. Wilhelm Ernst*
Msgr. Pierre Eyt (France)
Rev. Ivan Fucek (Yugoslavia)
Rev. Ferenc Gal (Hungary)
Rev. Edouard Hamel*
Rev. Walter Kasper (West Germany)
Rev. Elie Khalifé Hachem, O.L.M. (Lebanon)
Msgr. Boaventura Kloppenburg*
Msgr. Michael Ledwith (Ireland)
Msgr. Karl Lehmann*
Msgr. Jorge Medina Estevez*
Msgr. John Onaiyekan (Nigeria)
Rev. Carl Peter (United States)
Rev. Candido Pozo, S.J. (Spain)
Rev. Walter Principe, C.S.B. (Canada)
Msgr. Ignacy Rózycki (Poland)
Rev. Christophe von Schonborn, O.P. (Switzerland)
Msgr. Heinz Schürmann*
Rev. Bernard Sesboüé, S.J. (France)
Rev. John Thornhill, S.M. (Australia)
Rev. Cipriano Vagaggini*
Rev. Jan Walgrave*

Presidents of the Commission

His Eminence Cardinal Franjo Seper (1969–1981)
His Eminence Cardinal Joseph Ratzinger (from 1981)

Secretary of the Commission

Secretary General: Msgr. Philippe Delhaye (from 1972)
Assistant Secretaries: Msgr. Jozef Tomko (1969–1971), Msgr. Jozef Zlantnansky (1971–1974), Msgr. Pierre Jarry (1974–1985), Rev. Adriano Garuti, O.F.M. (1985).

IV

INDEX OF OTHER ECCLESIASTICAL DOCUMENTS
INDEX OF COUNCILS

PONTIFICAL ENCYCLICALS, LETTERS AND APOSTOLIC EXHORTATIONS

PONTIFICAL ALLOCUTIONS

OTHER DOCUMENTS

V

INDEX OF CODE OF CANON LAW

VI

SCRIPTURE INDEX

5:43: 310
6:7: 310
6:38: 310
6:39: 313
6:41f.: 123
6:44: 313
6:45: 100
6:48–50: 123
6:51: 27, 123, 198
6:65: 313
6:71: 36
7:16: 81
7:18: 100
7:38: 109
8:12: 310
8:19: 100
8:38–40: 311
8:42: 310
9:4: 310
10: 81
10:1–29: 312
10:3: 315
10:4–16: 29
10:7: 200
10:11: 27, 31
10:12–18: 31
10:14: 315
10:15: 27
10:17: 28, 29, 51
10:18: 28, 29, 51, 53, 81, 313
10:30: 309
10:32: 81
10:36: 28, 29, 38, 51
10:37: 81
10:38: 309
11:30: 197
11:51f.: 197
12:28: 81
12:32: 313
12:49: 81, 310
13:1: 38, 123
13:2–11: 123

13:3: 311
13:12–20: 38, 40
13:14: 126
13:20: 295
13:34: 110, 259
13:36: 38
14:6: 245
14:7: 100
14:9: 211, 310
14:14: 81
14:20: 313
14:26: 97, 124
14:58: 218
15:6: 313
15:12: 126
15:13: 313
15:15: 311
15:16: 97
15:20: 312
15:26: 64
15:27: 64, 97
16:8–11: 112
16:13f.: 97, 100, 124
16:14–15: 97, 100
16:28: 310
16:30: 311
17: 83, 218
17:4: 123
17:6: 313
17:8: 311
17:17: 38
17:18: 38, 82
17:19: 27, 313
17:20: 313
17:21: 300
17:21–23: 58
18:37: 29
19:13–14: 48
19:28–30: 123
19:30: 310
19:34: 271, 313
19:36: 27

8:5: 30
8:6: 33, 35
8:8: 30
8:11: 100
9:7: 30
9:9: 30
9:12: 30, 31
9:14: 33, 200
9:15: 35
9:19–22: 30, 31
9:23: 30, 31
9:24–25: 31, 33
9:26: 30, 31
9:27: 30
9:28: 33, 34, 82
10:1: 200
10:5: 314
10:5–7: 26, 33, 108
10:10: 31
10:12: 31
10:14: 26
10:16: 30
10:19: 21
10:22: 21
10:24: 21
10:26f.: 234
11: 31
11:8: 113
11:10: 114
11:13: 32, 114
11:14: 32, 114
11:15–16: 32
11:16: 225
11:17: 31
11:19: 114
11:35: 32
11:39: 32, 114
12:2: 31, 35
13:4: 164
13:12: 21
13:15: 21

13:16: 21
13:17: 35
13:20: 31, 34, 81

1 Peter

1:9: 22, 47
1:18: 27
1:19f.: 222, 312
1:20: 217
2:5: 96, 289
2:6–8: 96
2:9: 21, 22, 96, 289
2:10: 277
2:20: 21
2:21: 314
2:24: 232
2:25: 81
3:1–7: 164
3:15: 306
3:18: 33, 314
5:1: 41
5:2–4: 22, 41, 48, 81
5:5: 22, 41, 48

2 Peter

1:1: 52
1:4: 215
1:20: 95

1 John

2:1: 83
2:7: 126
2:16: 258
3:2: 205
3:16: 358
3:17: 84
4:8: 194
4:9: 123, 200
5:1: 108
5:16: 234

VII

INDEX OF PROPER NAMES

VIII

INDEX OF SUBJECTS

ABBREVIATIONS

AA	*Apostolicam actuositatem*
AAS	*Acta Apostolicae Sedis*
AG	*Ad Gentes*
CD	*Christus Dominus*
CIC	*Codex Iuris Canonici*
CT	*Cathechesi Tradendae*
DC	*La Documentation Catholique*
DH	*Dignitatis Humanae*
DV	*Dei Verbum*
DS	*Denzinger Schonmetzer*
EN	*Evangelii Nuntiandi*
FC	*Familiaris Consortio*
GS	*Gaudium et Spes*
LG	*Lumen Gentium*
OT	*Optatam Totius*
PO	*Presbyterorum Ordinis*
PP	*Populorum Progressio*
RH	*Redemptor Hominis*
SC	*Sacrosanctum Concilium*
S.Th.	*Summa Theologiae*
UR	*Unitatis Redintegratio*

DATE DUE

HIGHSMITH   # 45220